The Stone of Heaven

The Stone of Heaven

Unearthing the Secret History of Imperial Green Jade

Adrian Levy

and

Cathy Scott-Clark

Little, Brown and Company
Boston   New York   London

First American edition

For information on Time Warner Trade Publishing's online publishing program, visit www.ipublish.com.

Library of Congress Cataloging-in-Publication Data
Levy, Adrian.
The stone of heaven : unearthing the secret history of Imperial Green Jade /
Adrian Levy and Cathy Scott-Clark – 1st American ed.
p.   cm.
Includes bibliographical references and index.
ISBN 0-316-52596-0
1. Jadeite (Petrology) – Burma. I. Scott-Clark, Cathy. II. Title.
QE475.J27 L48   2002
553.8'76'09591 – dc21   2001037742

10 9 8 7 6 5 4 3 2 1

Q-FF

Printed in the United States of America

To everyone trapped under the fence

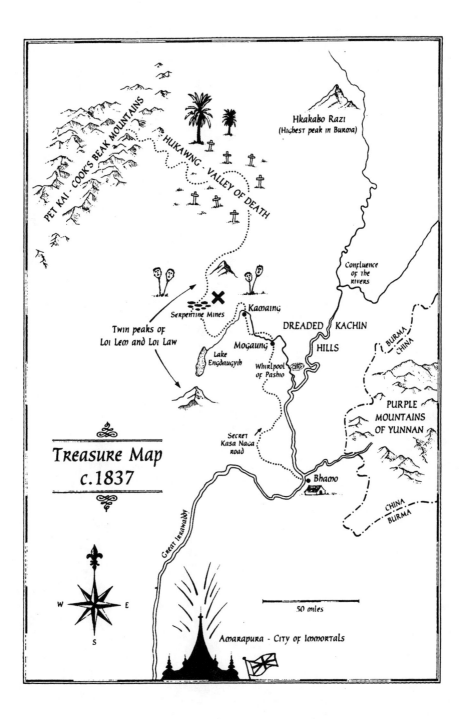

PET KAI - COOK'S BEAK MOUNTAINS

HUKAWNG - VALLEY OF DEATH

Hkakabo Razi
(Highest peak in Burma)

Confluence
of the
rivers

Twin peaks of
Loi Lem and Loi Law

Serpentine Mines

Kamaing

DREADED KACHIN

Mogaung

HILLS

Lake
Engdaugyih

Whirlpool
of Pashio

BURMA
CHINA

PURPLE
MOUNTAINS
OF YUNNAN

Treasure Map
c.1837

Secret
Kasa Naga
road

Bhamo

CHINA
BURMA

W   E

S

Great Irrawaddy

50 miles

Amarapura - City of Immortals

I step into the strange world of the digger. Picture a soil yellow and scarred with pits, honeycombed like a burrow, and at each pit's mouth, a rubbish heap. Overhead, intricate arrays of bamboo and in the background blue alpine mountains shimmering in the sun like steel. Set in this picture are the miners, people in blue clothes, and yellow parasol-like hats, people in loose trousers, showing legs tattooed with figures of tigers and dragons.

A silence as of death lies over the town where every human emotion is afoot. The miner suddenly grown rich, the gambler poised between the strokes of fate, the sorter dreaming of his England, the tired digger, the easy beauty – all of them lie buried here in the mist.

Remote as the place is, strange people drift here from far corners of the world. Beachcombers and other adventurers, Australians who have failed on Thursday Island, discharged soldiers who have fought over half the empire or say they have, voluble half-castes with restless eyes. They drift here drawn by the spell . . . undeterred by the company's typewritten warning on all the rest-houses on the way to the mines, that 'by going . . . they are undertaking a tiresome journey to no purpose'.

From *The Silken East* by V. C. Scott O'Connor, 1904

Contents

Illustrations

Sections of illustrations appear between pages 174 and 175; and 238 and 239. All pictures are from the authors' collection unless otherwise stated. In some instances it has not been possible to locate a copyright holder. The authors and publishers would be happy to make good any omissions in a subsequent edition.

Author Note

The book, wherever possible, uses Pinyin to transliterate Chinese into English, except where names and places are better known in their Wade-Giles format. However, some sources that we quote are reliant on the Wade-Giles system and we have not changed them.

To protect their identities we have changed the names of many of those we interviewed inside Burma.

Acknowledgments

A substantial part of this book was drawn from diaries, logs and files stored in India, China, Britain and America and we would like to thank the National Archives of India, in particular, for helping to point us in the right direction, as well as Lalit for driving us in the right direction. In London, the Oriental and India Office Library, the Royal Geographical Society and the National Arts Library were always patient. In Beijing, Professor Yang Boda helped us enormously, as did many in the Forbidden City. Thanks also to Terry Tong and friends, whose humour and hotpots prove that the world is, after all, a very small place.

Most of the story of jadeite has never been written down and without the help of Edmond Chin we would not have been able to unlock memories in Hong Kong, Taiwan or America. Rose Wong at Christie's, Peter Cheung and Quek Chin Yeow at Sotheby's, were also on hand with advice and suggestions. Samuel Kung was generous with his time, lunch and stories. Roger Keverne, in London, lent us his clients and friends. Chuang Ling and his family, in Taipei, helped us piece together the story of the transportation of the Imperial treasures from China to Taiwan. Michelle Ong Cheung and Avraham Nagar enthused us with their passion for stones. Frank and Charlotte Tieh were kind enough to spend time recalling the great Tieh Bao Ting. Mrs Tuyet Nguyet deserves thanks for many things but particularly her infectious enthusaism that could inspire anyone to love her collection of snuffboxes. Sammy Chow, in Kowloon, also talked a good tale and was admirably discreet. In the United States, Robert H. Ellsworth, curator of the Met Annex, thankfully wasn't and Lisa Hubbard of Sotheby's went out of her way to explain her history and the market. We would also like to thank James Watts at the Met.

Of course we cannot name any of those who have helped us inside Burma even though they are the people who made sure we achieved what many thought was impossible. We also thank the largely invisible activists in Chiang Mai: the dry Canadian, the sarcastic Americans (particularly the one who's never been to Chicago), the tireless Australians, the patient Thais (always helping with pictures and video footage), the Karen, Kachin, Shan and the many exiled Burmese whose futures depend on us keeping them out of this book. The same goes for all of the ethnic insurgent groups who have helped us over the years travel so safely along the Thai-Burma border. Many thanks also go to the nameless doctors inside and outside Burma, from France, Italy and the United States, who helped us place a context around our story (particularly the medic who was deported from Burma).

The Stone of Heaven would never have been written at all if it had not been for Toby Mundy who recognised a good story when he read it, even if he was in Staines at the time and it was buried in the pages of a colour supplement. Thanks to Richard Askwith and Kate Carr for placing it there. Thanks to Robert Kirby for steadying our hand and to Ion Trewin for his formidable eye that helped to polish the Stone of Heaven. Thanks also to all at Weidenfeld & Nicolson whose faith in the project was unflagging and who worked so hard in interpreting our ever-changing ideas.

Introduction

We could tell you that it was formed millions of years ago by a freak of nature at a point in South-east Asia where the earth's plates crashed into one another, forcing a river of magma, rich in aluminum, sodium and silicon, up through the crust, setting off a chain reaction that marbled the earth with veins of a unique substance. But we never intended to tell you a story about a stone.

It began with a newspaper cutting in November 1997. At a Christie's auction in Hong Kong, an anonymous collector paid almost £6 million for a necklace carved from a substance that the Chinese describe as *fei cui*, the colour of a kingfisher's neck-feathers. Glowing like a brilliant green jelly-baby, plump and cool to the touch, this stone became the most sought after in the world, fetching spectacular prices, eclipsing, carat for carat, rubies, sapphires, even diamonds.

Next we found the notebook. A British explorer had scratched down 'latitude 25'/26' north and 96'/97' east', the co-ordinates for a 'lost valley' in northern Burma from where he had fled on 5 April 1837, feverish and empty-handed. 'X' literally marked the spot on his hand-drawn map, an 'X' carefully inscribed onto a vast and hostile jungle concealed in the folds of the Himalayas, identifying a mine where, he had been told, lay one of the most remarkable treasures in the world, buried deep in the bedrock.

A few weeks later, we were in Thailand, researching a magazine article on the Burmese insurgency, sitting beside the Ping River in Chiang Mai, having lunch with a new friend on a quiet Sunday, when the stone cropped up unexpectedly. A French doctor on attachment in Asia, he had been examining refugees coming over the border and had picked up confusing stories about a mine, hidden, he said, in the hills of northern Burma, something about green stones and a gulag.

Six months later it found us again. This time in New Delhi. Trawling through mangled indexes in the National Archives, waiting for documents that never arrived, we stumbled across a reference to a journal that had been written by an East India Company man in 1795. Sent from Fort Williaim to 'a barbaric land', he was charged with investigating stories of a hidden valley of gems and a King who 'shone like the sun'. And soon we were unpicking faded pink ribbons that fastened packets marked 'Foreign & Secret', straining over barely legible extracts from a trove of forgotten Pali scripts that had once been painted onto lacquered bamboo boards.

An incredible story began to emerge from the pipe-tobacco-scented pages: a kingdom founded on legends, a jungle torn apart by warlords, a mine haunted by spirits, half-man, half-snake, and, in one trembling hand, a warning that it was encircled by wild tribes whose dead hung in cocoons from the trees. We found the journals of naive treasure hunters who trekked into the malarial jungle only to limp home with nothing but stolen glimpses of what lay beyond the heavy bamboo curtain – a smoking thicket that, they reported, 'rang with wild incantations'. Long-unread letters tumbled out of files, the private thoughts of British bureaucrats, a narrative of three bloody wars fought to wrestle control of a kingdom and a secret mine that refused to be pinned down in mineralogists' laboratories or by the cartographer's pen.

The manuscripts were delicate, mouldering in the humidity, a forgotten history that was falling apart before we had even pieced it together. But we couldn't stop reading, ordering box after box. Here were bombastic soldiers auditing the plunder from Burma, logging shipments of booty transported to London, secretly presenting the best to the British Royal Family. Then suddenly and inexplicably the entries stopped.

We returned to the indexes, frantically pulling up files, getting nowhere until we found the Chinese annals, fragments of Imperial chronicles looted from a palace in 1860. Spattered with the inky thumbprints of a long-dead translator, they told of a gem, foreign to China, that so bewitched an Emperor that he called it his 'Stone to Heaven', sacrificing hundreds of thousands of men in failed campaigns to seize its source, a mine in the jungles of northern Burma. But the annals were incomplete and on one freezing October morning, we pushed our bikes through the sweet-potato sellers and hawkers flogging Chairman Mao lighters, and into the archives of the Forbidden City in Beijing.

Sandwiched between silk, written in vermilion and black ink, we found a story about a small nugget of the stone that had survived a 3000-mile journey through the purple mountains of Yunnan to the Imperial Court. Carved into a priceless pendant on the orders of the Emperor, delicate tendrils twisting around a stem, its ripe surface was said to glisten as if sprayed with dew. Around the pendant revolved one of the Middle Kingdom's most poignant and tragic love stories.

The British had called it 'noble serpentine', comparing it to green magnesium crystals. The French likened it to the quartz-like 'chalcedony'. The Spanish claimed it as their *piedras hijades,* a 'stone of the flank' that cured all known kidney ailments. Even the Chinese seemed confused. So what was this lustrous, Burmese stone?

'China's just one long haul,' a friend had warned us, and inevitably the paper trail ran dry, scattered by wars and revolutions, documents salted away in caves and carried from the mainland on troop ships. Now we were left to bump along in the back of taxis, to weave on bicycles through the paddy, to race in search of private reminiscences that no one wanted to share.

Nothing is harder to find than a story that is reluctant to be told, and for months our phone calls were met with polite but firm rejections delivered in Cantonese, Mandarin, French and an Upper Eastside drawl, until we found ourselves in a greasy Kowloon office block.

'You're going about it the wrong way. It all starts with touch,' the dealer advised us before opening a handkerchief to reveal a handful of stones that looked like boiled sweets. 'You can dig up as much history as you like, but have you even seen or held the stone? You have to understand. You have to know,' he said conspiratorially, pressing pieces into our palms.

It was the first time we had ever seen jadeite up close and, like you, we had only ever thought of it as some foreign jewel, strewn across stalls in Chinatown street-markets, forgotten souvenirs brought back from Hong Kong and Beijing. But these stones gleamed with a syrupy hue, oozing colour as they warmed in our hands, drawing us in as we listened to how the dealer had once sold the finest pieces to First Ladies, drug tsars, warlords and movie stars. In only minutes we were hooked. Maybe it was the way the stones pulsed in the sunlight that pierced a broken blind. Maybe it was the way they acquired vivid new tones as they rolled around in our hands, encompassing a dozen shades on an artist's chart, one moment sap green, another, hooker's light. Maybe our judgement was skewed by the knowledge that we were holding stones worth millions of pounds.

Only then, in Hong Kong and Taiwan, London and New York, armed with the early stages of an addiction, did we open the doors to an intimate circle of collectors and dealers who led us through the pages of history that they had a hand in making. Our research switched to a tale of their times, Martini laughter and masked balls, greed, betrayal and conceit. Republicans and Communists who had turned to a stone to raise political parties and finance coups. Scholars and jewellers who had accompanied it on voyages from the Old World to the New. Electronics millionaires who had bought into its past, collecting pieces that had come back from the dead. Bright young heiresses who thought they shone like the stone they adored but whose friends were fickle and whose lovers were common thieves.

All of them asked if we had heard the story of a priceless pendant commissioned by an Emperor. Some said it had hung heavy around the neck of a forlorn concubine born smelling of the yellow jujube flower. Others claimed it had been hurriedly concealed by a Dragon Lady on her flight from British soldiers. One would tell us how it was rediscovered in the Palace of Established Happiness by the last Emperor of China, and followed him into exile to become the most sought-after jewel in the world.

For centuries it was Muslims who traded lapis from Afghanistan, turquoise from Persia, cat's eye from Ceylon and moonstone from Syria. Today, in Hong Kong's Canton Road, it is Muslims who pump the treadles of the grinders, lubricating the wheels with water and Carborundum, their eyelashes frosted by a fine spray of crystals. Dextrously they exploit colour and texture, transforming crude lumps of stone into exquisite treasures whose shapes shift in the light.

And those who find, buy or steal this 'Stone of Heaven' embellished, reset, buff and repackage it, grafting the Imperial onto the everyday, imposing old stories onto new gems, surgically altering history to create a new context for jewels that smothers any unsavoury realities.

Throughout our journey there was no one who wanted to discuss with us the rumours that were creeping out of the Burmese jungle. No one would talk about a callous regime that was said to have committed a calculating act of inhumanity that was almost beyond belief. Sitting down, once more, beside the Ping River, a year after our last visit to Chiang Mai, our friend told us how he had heard that the secret mine was now a valley of death, a place that incarcerated the debris of addiction and infection, sometimes loaded down and sunk in flooded shafts, sometimes gagged and executed in remote jungle clearings. It was a story that eclipsed the blood diamonds of Africa but no one knew more because no one could get through the battalions of soldiers who ringed the mines. 'It's impossible. Don't even try,' our friend warned us. But who likes to be told a story about a place that they are prevented from visiting?

Adrian Levy and Cathy Scott-Clark
November 2000

The Stone of Heaven

One

An Emperor's Obsession

Inside fusty chronicles penned in a forgotten, languid script that few can now understand, storytellers recorded how it all began. With precise brush-strokes they wrote in Manchurian of a bowl, an enormous black bowl that, they said, was stolen from a warrior's court and concealed somewhere in the Middle Kingdom. So vast was it and so cool to the touch that it reminded all those who had seen it of a giant turtle's upturned shell. And, they said, it was the wonder of the world, so rare that it exceeded 'the value of four great towns'.[1] But the treasure-hunts lapsed and the stories folded into folklore – until one icy dawn in October 1745, three centuries after the wondrous bowl had apparently vanished into thin air.

A whisper of torch-bearers slipped into the gloom but no one cheered them on as they drove their lamps into the snow, banked against the gabled pavilions of the great Meridian Gate. Several hundred lanterns emerged from behind the forbidding walls of the Imperial fortress, passing beneath the Five Towers of the Phoenix, but the good citizens were drawn around their braziers, wrapping themselves ever-tighter in cashmere and quilts, hiding their chapped faces from the freezing fog.

The grid of lanes and alleys that snaked around the fortress was lacquered in smoking sheets of ice that glazed the lakes and bridle-paths, that enveloped every tower and tree, that silenced the babble of the Imperial capital, transforming Peking into a petrified forest. It was too cold for stories.

But if anyone had poked a head out of a shuttered door on that bitter dawn they would have seen drummers and trumpeters, banner-men 'twelve in a row [carrying poles] eight feet long,

3

painted in red and decorated with gilded foliage' passing down the pale avenue of light.[2] A mounted Imperial guard, royal princes and military officers followed, 'weapons and harnesses on their horses and one sees nothing but silk fabrics, gold and silver embroidery and precious stones'.[3] Dressed in their ceremonial uniforms, rows of brass buttons sparkled in the lantern-light, helmet plumes crackled in the north-westerly that tore down from the Gobi Desert, where the sand dunes were already cloaked by snow.

A rumble of mandarins, civil and military, in canopied sedan chairs, hidden by thick velvet curtains to keep out the biting gale. Behind them, a clatter of Imperial yellow covered carts: bannermen, scribes, accountants, stewards, scholars, historians from the Hanlin Academy, skittering across the snow. With a thumping of drums and a rasping of horns the flotilla commissioned to undertake this most sensitive and confidential of missions wound its way out of the Forbidden City, the Emperor of China's secretive residence. An advance guard had scoured the route, slapping down shutters, slamming doors, removing unsightly obstructions, and now it returned to haul the Imperial procession across the city like a tug pulling a liner through ice-capped seas.

It finally glided to a halt outside the *Chen Wu Miao,* the Temple of the Celestial Emperor, a Daoist shrine built within sight of the Western Flowery Gate. The doors were thrown back, surprising temple servants who were busy preparing breakfast, sifting stones from rice and stirring pickled vegetables. Within minutes, a flurry of monks had gathered before the Imperial retinue. Shivering in their cotton robes, wiping the sleep from their eyes, they listened in disbelief as a herald announced that Emperor Qianlong wanted the bowl that their cabbage was steeping in. The Son of Heaven was offering to pay 1000 taels (50,000 grams) of silver, a fortune for a religious order. Who were they to argue? They drained out the brine, wrapped the 3500-kilogram bowl in silk and horse-hair mats and heaved it onto a wagon that slid, triumphantly, back to the Forbidden City.

The dawn raid appeared to all as an eccentric act by an Emperor who already possessed everything he could possibly need, but the kitchen bowl had a secret that Qianlong had stumbled across. Today the story is buried in the mouldering archives of China's Imperial dynasties, a vast library of 10 million documents that have preserved the minutiae of daily living in the Forbidden City. Among the decrees, orders, memorials, household accounts, menus, gift lists, inventories and genealogical records – the charts of Imperial hatch, match and dispatch, with the names of the living penned in vermilion and of the dead drawn in black – each volume bound in yellow silk, requiring the muscle of two curators to lift, is the story of what lay beneath the centuries of grime.

In his padded Imperial-yellow silk winter robes, embroidered with dragons and lined with white fox fur, his dangling cuffs shaped like horses' hooves protecting his hands from the cold, the six-foot Emperor would have loomed over his craftsmen as they peeled back the salt that caked the vessel. He would have stood transfixed as the pickle bowl began to glisten with dark-green and black veins, a mythical menagerie of dragons, giant fish, sea-pigs, frogs and a unicorn, all swimming in a turbulent sea emerging into the lamplight. The Emperor was triumphant. Here was one of the most celebrated pieces of carved jade in history, that many of his contemporaries believed was mythological.

It was legendary even in its own time, catching the eye of Marco Polo when he travelled across China between 1275 and 1292. The Venetian story-teller recorded in his journals how he spied the bowl in a banqueting hall in Khanbalik, Kublai Khan's 'city of treasures in gold and silver bullion, precious stones and pearls', from where he ruled one third of the globe.[4] A century later, a maudlin monk spotted the bowl in wondrous Khanbalik, and this time it was said to be brimming with wine. Odoric of Pordenone, an Italian friar touring China in the 1320s as assistant to Giovanni de Montecorvina, the Franciscan Archbishop of Peking, was awed by a vessel that was more than 'two paces in height'. Odoric, famed for 'wearing a vest of chain mail and subjecting himself frequently to flagellation', learned that it was carved from a mysterious stone that he called *merdacas*:

It is all hooped around with gold and in every corner thereof is a dragon represented as in act to strike most fiercely. And this jar has also fringes of a network of great pearls hanging therefrom and these fringes are a span in breadth. Into this vessel drink is conveyed by certain conduits from the court of the palace . . .[5]

When the Ming Dynasty vanquished the Yuan in 1368, Kublai Khan's Khanbalik was stripped by Chinese looters who left behind nothing but stories. How Qianlong rediscovered one of the only jades to survive the fall of the Great Khan's realm is not entirely clear.[6] But according to the annals of the Forbidden City, the 34-year-old Emperor of China now sat down before his trophy with paper and a brush to compose an extraordinary poem. When completed it would read like a serenade, an awkward attempt by the continent's most feared ruler to court a cold lump of jade. The 'Song of the Jade Bowl' that was inscribed on ten dark-green jade tablets, decorated with five-clawed dragons, was also carved inside the bowl itself in 1746. The poem begins with the Emperor being drawn into the currents of the carving:

> The measureless spirit of creation drives through infinite chaos. Terrifying waves seethe and surge through a waste of loud, contorted water, and the earth is borne up secure in the midst of a gulf of perils . . . All the monsters of the deep are here. Coral tortoiseshell and mermaids' pearl tears; a womb of precious things in unending abundance, destined to harmonise what is above and below, to ensure heaven's blessing.[7]

Qianlong worked himself up into an indignant fervour and if anyone at court had read this private verse they would surely have been concerned for his state of mind. The Emperor appeared to be pondering whether the great jade bowl had feelings:

> Alas, the pity that ancient treasure should turn to dust . . . Scrape off the moss, wash off the dirt, reveal the bright sparkle! If these things are to be abandoned to nature, what purpose is served by engraving words on them? . . . Men have affections and attachments – may not all matter have them also?[8]

Qianlong was still not content. He ordered a craftsman to re-carve large sections of the bowl, and with the skill of a plastic surgeon the oceans were embellished, made to boil and bubble, embedded with new swirling currents, and for the first time the bodies of the dragons and sea monsters were given life-like scales. Soon the vessel's links to the Yuan had been all but eradicated, transforming the bowl into a wonder of Qianlong's court.[9]

The Emperor ordered replicas to be placed throughout Peking so that he could look upon them wherever he went. The original was placed in a shrine, his craftsmen creating a marble plinth carved with rocks, clouds and auspicious swastikas in Beihai Park in Peking, where it still stands today. Qianlong must have chosen the site with the knowledge that this was where the pavilions, halls and temples of Khanbalik had also once stood. Then he sat down to eulogise it again and again, scarring and pitting the priceless artefact with a confusing array of Imperial thoughts.

The poems on the wine bowl would be among more than 800 that he would pen to jade, limping verses that mandarins privately worried were the sign of an unhealthy obsession, that Chinese scholars, in Peking's tea-houses, mocked as doggerel and that a British diplomat even damned as cant. 'They are less remarkable for invention than for philosophical and moral truths and resemble more the epics of Voltaire than those of Milton,' wrote George Staunton, secretary to a delegation that arrived in China in 1793.[10]

But what they all failed to appreciate was that through his jade poetry Qianlong hinted at something that was never set down in the empirical, cold annals of the Imperial court: how a tragedy turned his heart to a stone and how a stone came to represent love.

※

Qianlong's ancestors were nomads from Manchuria, a province 600 miles north-east of Peking, who overcame their Chinese neighbours in 1644. Qianlong's forefathers charged through the great Meridian Gate into a city that had been built by the Ming Dynasty Emperor Yongle in 1407. Its construction by an army of 200,000 builders commemorated the conquering of the Yuan, and Yongle had erected it slightly to the north of the legendary Khanbalik. But after the Qing Dynasty seized control they changed very little. The Meridian Gate remained the entrance to an impregnable city-within-a-city, one of four entrances on the cardinal points. They were still connected by 11,220 feet of ramparts, never lower than 32 feet, and protected more than 7,747,000 square feet of labyrinthine gardens and interlocking courtyards, halls and chambers. The citadel that rose above Peking was constructed to reflect the Ming's complex cosmology and their Qing conquerors simply adopted it wholesale.

The new rulers would demand to be revered, like Yongle, as Lords of 10,000 Years, celestial go-betweens, the sons of heaven who ruled the Middle Kingdom, a regal axis around which the world revolved. But in the eyes of their Chinese subjects, the Qing, who banned the Chinese ancient practice of footbinding, were secretly derided as impostors.

In 1711 a child was born inside the Forbidden City and named Hongli. He was raised on stories of how his ancestors had flown across the steppe. His Niuhuru clansmen, buffeted by the bitter gales that whipped their cheeks, wrapped themselves in fleece and hides, gripping the muscular flanks of their Mongolian ponies as they chased down their prey. And the boy embraced these martial skills, schooled in archery by the Manchu princes Yin Lu and Yin Hsi.[11] A parable in the Qing chronicles records how Hongli demonstrated his affinity with the lore of the steppe even before his teens. At the age of twelve he rode out to Mulan, a wooded region north of Jehôl, where the annual Rites of the Royal Hunting were about to be administered. A snarling bear blocked his path, but Hongli remained calm in his saddle while the animal was cornered and killed. Immediately he won the admiration of Emperor Kangxi, his grandfather, who suspected that here was a future ruler of China.[12]

Kangxi was aware of the difficulties facing a Manchurian dynasty that staked a claim to a Chinese kingdom, and reasoned that if Hongli was to command the Dragon Throne with authority, he would have to be steeped in Chinese traditions. The Qing archives reveal how an illustrious group of Han Chinese scholars including Fu Min, a Hanlin academic who was revered as one of the Middle Kingdom's greatest minds, was assembled to tutor the chosen child.[13] It was a difficult task. They complained of the boy's appalling handwriting and Hongli was evidently aware of his shortcomings. Writing to Chi Tseng-Yun, his tutor, he admitted: 'I am sorry to say that my calligraphy has not improved.'[14]

Kangxi praised his protégé in palace memorials for his 'remarkable martial and academic talents' and worried little about the boy's school reports. The Emperor surprised his Grand Councillors by inviting the child to witness the administration of national affairs at the Palace of Heavenly Clarity. Soon Hongli leapfrogged his brothers and was secretly designated heir-apparent. By the time the Emperor-to-be married at the age of sixteen, his head was filled with millenniums of Chinese philosophy and cosmology, all of which was founded on the folklore of a stone that defined an ancient civilisation.

The Emperor-to-be would not have known the word 'jade', as it was a European term coined by Nicholas Mondardes of Seville, a sixteenth-century doctor who used the substance to treat kidney complaints and named it his *piedras hijades*, 'stone of the flank'. Instead, Hongli struggled to perfect the character *Yü*, a pictograph that resembled three strings of pearls that dated to 2953 BC, when China was said to have been ruled by Fu Hsi, a mythical emperor born with the body of a serpent. The pearl-string pictograph literally meant 'virtue, beauty and rarity', and it would have dominated every aspect of the Emperor-to-be's curriculum that was woven around the writings of Confucius, for whom jade represented the essence of a gentleman.[15] The philosopher's commentaries on the Five Books – the Book of Rites, the Spring and Autumn Annals, the Book of History, the Book of Poetry and the Book of Changes – set texts that Hongli would have studied, were littered with references to the near-human qualities of jade.

Hongli learned that it was far more than just a silicate of calcium and magnesium that was found in distant wastelands ruled by Uighurs, Kazakhs and Mongols. 'It is a warm liquid and has a moist aspect like benevolence. It is solid, strong and firm like wisdom, pure and not easily injured like righteousness,' extolled Confucius. 'Like loyalty, its brilliancy lights all things near it like truth.' Jade was a 'gift to introduce persons to virtue' and 'in the whole world there is no one who does not welcome it like reason'.[16]

Stooped over his wooden lectern in a palace library, a wide-eyed Hongli would have learned how the stone of reason also possessed miraculous powers. Like the legendary ring of King Solomon that granted the wearer his heart's desire, those who mastered jade could raise the dead, strike down the faithless and protect a spirit on its journey to the afterlife. For thousands of years the Chinese had ground it into a powder that was drunk or eaten as an elixir of life. Combined with millet it made *fan yü*, an edible dough that bestowed immortality. Hongli's tutors would have taught him the apocryphal story of Wendi, the fourth Han Emperor, who in 164 BC drank from a jade cup inscribed 'master of mankind; may thy life be prolonged to the great delight of the world.'[17] In an obscure text stored in the Hanlin Academy written by Ko Hung, a Daoist scientist of the fourth century AD who dabbled in the occult, the boy would have read: 'if there be gold and jade in the nine apertures of the body, the corpse does not putrefy.' The annals from the fifth century AD were equally bewitching, telling the story of the courtier Lui Yu who stumbled across 100 pieces of jade in a field. He crushed the jade into a powder and ate it. 'When he died his body remained in its natural state despite the heat and humidity of summer,' a court historian wrote.[18]

Jade was 'the key to life everlasting' and the Chinese believed it came from the gods.[19] By the time Hongli was 22, when he was promoted to Prince of the First Degree, he would certainly have been familiar with the *Book of Changes* (I Ching). These 64 hexagrams, that were consulted as an oracle, forewarned that 'Heaven is Jade', a stone that had been hacked from a rainbow. It was a gift to be treasured by the Emperor of China, the Son of Heaven.

On 18 October 1735 the 24-year-old Hongli ascended to the Dragon Throne, discarding his white robes of mourning for ceremonial silks, trailed on his way to the Hall of Supreme Harmony by the Leopard Tail Troop, where he assumed the reign name Qianlong, the 'Untiring and Exalted' Emperor.

The new Son of Heaven was now surrounded by the most beautiful and eligible girls in China, hand-picked from noble families, dressed in shimmering silk and jade, their hair entwined with peonies and butterflies, their laughter filling the Western Palaces. But none of them could match Fucha, Qianlong's wife. The few passing references in Palace Memorials suggest that she was adored by the Emperor, who garlanded her in 'velvety and wild flowers'.[20] She appears on a painted scroll that he commissioned two years into his reign, taking pride of place beside her Son of Heaven, crowned in a winter head-dress, edged in fur, her collar trimmed with mink, her yellow robes signifying her status. To her left are portraits of Qianlong's eleven senior concubines, each woman's attributes noted beside her face: 'noble', 'joyful', 'sensitive', 'worthy of praise', 'excellent', 'pleasant', 'happy', 'distinguished', 'honest' and 'obedient'.[21] The Emperor locked the scroll away in a red lacquer box inscribed: 'in my heart there is the power to reign peaceably'. He was content and also possessive. Anyone who broke the seal on the box would be sentenced to death by a thousand cuts.[22]

Qianlong's happiness was to be short-lived. Fucha died unexpectedly of fever in 1748, aged only 36. What made her passing all the more unbearable was that she was in Dezhou, a city in the northern plains of Shantung Province, and he was miles away in Peking. When Fucha's body was returned to the capital, the Emperor posthumously crowned her his Empress Xiao Xian Chun, buried her in a lavish subterranean chamber in Qing Dong Ling, the Imperial necropolis north-east of Peking, surrounding her with jade lotuses, water lilies, encasing her body in a cinnabar box. And whenever he visited the tomb he would sit and write poems to the love of his life that would be inscribed on a lacquer plaque and placed in her Spirit Hall.

Nothing could shake Qianlong out of his grief. Every night concubines were sent to his Dragon Bed but all were barred entry. And every day, the Emperor's mother ordered kitchen staff to prepare delicacies. But the dishes of shredded Chinese cabbage garnished with peace fruits, served in bowls decorated with red waves, the swallows' nests smoked with duck slices and filled sausage, the fried wheat and rice-cakes presented on a silver platter, were all left untouched.[23] He spent days at a time shuttered away in his private apartments, surrounding himself with a Chinese birth-rite that he caressed and eulogised in verse, transferring his feelings into tiny rows of characters that were chipped onto cold, hard stone. Soon Qianlong would insist on sleeping on a jade bed and eating from a jade dinner service. The water he washed in would be cupped in a jade bowl, his hair combed with a jade brush. Everything from the tip of his riding-crop to the handle of his walking-stick, from the scabbards for his daggers to the grips of his pistols, would be inset with the stone. When Qianlong sat down to write his jade poetry, the ink would be mixed in a jade pot, and before he began he would relax his hands with a jade ball. His brush handle was made from carved jade and his arms rested on jade platforms that helped keep the ink from smudging. Qianlong played *mah-jong*, chess and draughts with counters carved from the stone, his eunuchs cooling him with fans whose delicate blades were intricately cut lozenges of jade. During the long and barren winters, eunuchs would attempt to lift their mourning master's black mood by planting evergreen flowers throughout his private apartments whose petals were scooped from boulders of green jade. Although the lives of Chinese emperors had, throughout history, been bound around jade, Qianlong's mother became increasingly disturbed by her son's obsessive behaviour.

Barely two years after he had buried Fucha, she arranged for Qianlong to marry Ula Nala, who donned the Phoenix Crown, with its tassels of pearls and tiers of gold filigree, to signify her rise to the position of Empress. Did Ula Nala realise what she was letting herself in for? Qianlong all but ignored his new wife, preferring to surround himself with a stone, pitching himself into an ambitious civil engineering project to construct a palace 'in the manner of the European barbarians'.[24] There he planned to wander among ornamental gardens filled with songbirds, to sit beside a lake where he would compose poems dedicated to Fucha and to his obsession.

Giuseppe Castiglione, a Milanese missionary who had arrived at court when Qianlong was a child, was now an influential figure in the Emperor's life, and had been honoured with a Chinese name, Lang Shih-ning. In happier days, Castiglione painted Qianlong hunting at Jehôl and resplendent in armour, mounted on a white charger, his saddle picked out with jade, the scabbard of his dagger fashioned from the stone, the flights of his arrows capped with it. Now, according to correspondence sent home to Italy and France by Castiglione's Jesuit assistants, the missionary was charged with creating a 'European fantasy', a 'palace where he [the Emperor] goes from time to time to take a stroll and to rest'. The grand folly would be a 'repository' for Qianlong's 'cabinet of European curiosities' – clocks and watches, glass and astronomical instruments, tapestries and globes, presents from foreign powers keen to trade with China.[25] More importantly, it would be a showroom for the Son of Heaven's burgeoning collection of jade.

From a parcel of land six miles north-west of Peking, beside Yüan-ming Yüan, Kangxi's favourite Summer Palace, there rose a Chinese Versailles decorated with Gobelin tapestries, presented by Louis XV. Its wooden pillars and glazed tiles were Oriental but the superfluous ornamentation, the emblems and niches, the fountains and the 'flower show' were Western. Here was the grand Palace of Delights of Harmony that resembled an Italian *casini*. Behind it there was an aviary and the Garden of Lanterns of Yellow Flowers, a labyrinth with a throne at its centre, along which 'on the fifteenth day of the eighth month' concubines would race, bearing 'water lily lanterns' like 'myriads of stars shining among a thousand green pine trees'.[26] To the right was a bamboo belvedere and opposite it were the domes of Fangwai Mosque. Father Michel Benoist, a Jesuit with a knowledge of hydraulics, was hired to construct an aquatic masterpiece, and before the Palace of Calm Sea he built a water clock. Twelve bronze animal heads, including an ox, a tiger and a monkey, were arranged in a crescent, each one spouting a jet of water for two hours every day. The European palaces were indeed a stately pleasure dome, and when completed they would come to represent the crowning achievement of *sheng-shih*, Qianlong's Prosperous Age.

❆

At the outset of his reign Qianlong had learned that many countries ringing his Empire were in default of *Pin-Li* or 'Ceremonial for Visitors Bringing Court Tribute'. Turkestan, Sungaria, Tibet, Laos, Korea, Vietnam, Siam and a distant and savage place referred to in the chronicles as Mien-Tien had all abandoned ancient pledges to present to the Dragon Throne 'products of the soil'.[27] As soon as Qianlong rose to power he announced that his empire was to be ruled like his palace, where he had placed 36 blades of grass in a *cloisonné* jar, instructing his eunuchs to count them every day in a ritual that was known as 'taking the grass as a standard'.[28] One by one, these lapsed tributary nations would be forced back into the Imperial fold, and it was jade that dictated the Emperor's military priorities.

In November 1999 we came across the story of a remarkable treasure box that was said to have been commissioned by Qianlong at the outset of these campaigns. According to palace memorials, in 1757 the Emperor ordered his carpenters to make a circular wooden container the size of a sunflower head. It was passed to the lacquer maker who repeatedly dipped it into a concoction of mercuric sulfide and the milky sap of the *rhus vernicflua* which when mixed, created a brilliant vermilion gel that set like fired porcelain. A master carver took the box and inscribed onto the cinnabar lacquer carp and cherry blossoms that swirled in the ripples of a pool. When it was returned to the Emperor he composed a poem that was incised in gilt characters beneath the lid: 'Jade is hard and unyielding. It is smooth, lustrous and exhibits the best of contemporary workmanship.'[29]

The box contained seven pegs on which would eventually sit seven jade archer's rings, smooth bands of stone that protected a hunter's thumbs, that would come to represent the Emperor's victories. And hidden beneath a wooden lining, he inscribed a secret verse:

> Fifty thousands steps are needed to scale the Kunlun mountains
> Jade is found in the streams there.
> The jade stones are carved into fine objects
>   and sent to the court as tributes
> Some are made into archer's rings to help draw the bow.
> With bows and arrows it is needless to be afraid of the enemies
>   as the Han Emperor Guangwu was . . .
> They also help conquering the barbarians outside the country.
> Their significance has always to be remembered.[30]

The word *xinsi* was picked out in gilt at the end of the poem, meaning it was completed in 1761, and it tells the story of the Emperor's first campaign against 'barbarians'. In 1755 his troops had set out to capture the Muslim-controlled snow-caps and sand-dunes of Sungaria and Eastern Turkestan. Led by the Western General Zhaohui, the soldiers had marched into this remotest of regions with 'bows and arrows', crossed hazardous and uncharted terrain, weathered ice-storms and sand-traps that had led them to resort to cannibalism, and still they managed to suppress a ferocious Muslim revolt. The Kunlun Mountains were once well beyond China's influence, but four years after Imperial archers had let loose a volley of arrows over the Land of the Blue Skies, Qianlong could boast that his soldiers knew how many steps it took to climb them. The victorious Western Campaign reincorporated the hostile and anarchic region of the Uighurs, Kazakhs and Mongols into a greater

China, doubling the nation's territory. General Zhaohui captured Kashgar, an outpost that separated the vast Taklamakan desert from the sheer peaks of the Karakorum range, winning for Qianlong the right to control and tax ancient trading routes. But more importantly, he seized Yarkand and Khotan, handing his Emperor complete control over the only source of Confucius's jade known to the Chinese. Such was Qianlong's joy that when General Zhaohui finally returned to Peking, a fair-skinned Uighur girl as a trophy of war at his side, he was welcomed outside the Forbidden City by the Son of Heaven himself in an unprecedented display of gratitude.

The immediate impact of the victory is revealed in the 10,000 records of tribute paid to the Emperor. These Palace Presentation Lists made of yellow satin, sandwiched between pieces of red and yellow paper that had to be folded six times before being placed into a yellow silk envelope, are stamped with a date, a serial number and the name of the nobleman who sent tribute. The Viceroy of Canton, for example, dispatched 33 items to court before 1760: imported enamel snuff-boxes, a goose-feather gauze, a zitan wood screen, writing desks and a carved throne, imported glass, a coral necklace and a gold statue. After the Western Campaign, the Viceroy presented to his Emperor jade sceptres, jade incense burners, a jade perfume bottle, jade screens, a jade tripod, a jade mountain carving, a jade tea bowl and even a jade toilet-box decorated with jade peonies.

Qianlong named the conquered region Sinkiang or the New Territories and extracted from it 8000 jin (more than 4000 kilograms) of raw jade every spring and autumn, brought to Peking on seemingly endless camel trains. To counter the 'adhesive fingers' of local chieftains, he dispatched his own bureaucrats to the region. Ch'i-shih-i, whose name means '71-year-old of the Cedar Garden', was one of the first officials to arrive in Sinkiang. The 'whole riverbed is covered with stones, large and small, mixed with which are the jade ones,' he reported. Some jades were 'as big as a bucket or small as one's fist or a chestnut'. Some were 'snow-white . . . some beeswax-yellow, cinnabar-red, or black as Chinese ink'. Scarcest were those that were 'mutton-fat white with red spots and spinach green streaked with bronze'.[31]

Qianlong's officials adopted an ancient practice. On either side of the banks two officials stood guard while 'experienced native, Muhammadans', 30 abreast, their arms interlinked, waded barefoot through the icy waters of the *Pai yu Ho* and the *Lu yu Ho,* the White and Green Jade Rivers. The moving cordons felt for jade with their toes, and it was believed that women were better suited to the task, as the female *yin* attracted the male *yang* that emanated from the stones.[32] When the jade anglers stooped down, a soldier struck a gong, Qing officials painted 'a red mark on the tally and the native delivers the jade'.[33]

Boulders and nuggets poured into Peking's Ruyi Guan, the Hall of Fulfilled Wishes, supervised by craftsmen Yao Renzong and Zhou Jingde, known as the Southern Masters. Qianlong would rise every morning at 4 a.m., never spending more than fifteen minutes on a breakfast of swallow's nest steeped in crystal sugar, complete his daily administrative tasks, and then dash to see what had arrived from Sinkiang overnight.[34] The stones that he lingered over were wrapped in horse-hair and immediately dispatched to one of eight factories spread throughout the Middle Kingdom.

The most respected carving centre was in Zhuanzhu Lane, a district in Soochow that lay in the coastal Jiangsu Province near Shanghai. Soochow not only produced the finest jades in China but was also an idyllic garden city of canals and parks that inspired a famous Chinese proverb: 'In heaven there is paradise; on earth Soochow.' The highly paid craftsmen, who all worshipped the jade spirit Qiu Chuji, were paid 5.6 grams of silver a day to transcribe Qianlong's verses, in the knowledge that a slip of the chisel could destroy a piece that might have taken a decade to complete. Their rituals of devotion and lapidary skills were passed from father to son, creating 'a long river of jade . . . thousand upon thousands of skilled artisans grinding away in silence, until they are hoary-haired and drained of blood and life itself; grinding until the rough stones were transformed into priceless artefacts of beguiling beauty.'[35]

The victory at Khotan kept the carvers busy, but their workload would only increase. Qianlong rounded up antique Chinese carvings that were remodelled according to his tastes. As he had done with Kublai Khan's bowl, he now did with thousands more ancient jade pieces, embossing them with his own seal and poetry, attributing his reign with the production of classic works of Chinese art. But sometimes this hybrid Emperor seemingly forgot the lessons of youth, drummed into his head by Fu Min. Palace memorials record how a 4700-year-old Chinese *cong*, an oblong-shaped tube once used in religious rituals to worship the earth, was turned into an Imperial flowerpot. An 8000-year-old disc-shaped *bi*, a Chinese instrument used by emperors in the annual Temple of Heaven ceremony, was transformed into a desktop screen and graffitied with Qianlong's verse.[36] Chinese scholars at the palace must have secretly trembled with rage.

What did the Emperor care? As Father Jean-Denis Attiret, one of Castiglione's deputies, noted in a letter sent back to France, Qianlong 'knows everything, or at least flattery tells him so, very loudly and perhaps he believes it; he always acts as though convinced of it.'[37]

When the Emperor ran out of antiques, he began to commission forgeries. The Southern Masters were ordered to study ancient catalogues and replicate the pieces within, staining or burning new jade stones to give them the appearance of antiquity. In one Palace Memorial, Qianlong gives precise instructions: 'bake the white jade Immortal and horse to create some stains so they look like Han jades and make an elegant stand for them.' In another, craftsmen were ordered to inscribe a new carving with the script 'Hsuan-ho yu wan', or 'for the pleasure of Hsuan-ho', a Song Dynasty Emperor.[38] Such was his haste to be fêted as the greatest collector in China that Qianlong even commissioned court artists to copy or doctor ancient paintings of legendary scholars, superimposing his head onto their bodies, as in the *Double Portrait*, a Five Dynasties painting by Chou Wen-chü that today hangs in the National Palace Museum in Taiwan.[39]

But there was one stone that was beyond his reach, a story as yet so incomplete in his mind that he could barely grasp a hold of it. Labouring in the library, Hongli had come across cryptic allusions to a kind of jade that was said by all to be the rarest gem in the world. As a boy he had read of the treasure of the Wei, a story from the time of the Eastern Zhou Dynasty, during which a warring state in north central China venerated a fantastical green stone, quite distinct from Confucius's waxy jade.[40] But the stone was not indigenous to the north.

He had lingered over the *Verse on the Western Capital* by the poet Bang Gu who, writing during the Han Dynasty, described a gem that appeared to 'glow as if lit by a hidden flame'.[41] Bang Gu called it *fei cui* after the iridescent green hue of the neck feathers of the kingfisher that nested in Guangxi Province, in southern China, the only thing on earth that was said to match its translucent colour. But the stone was not to be found in Guangxi.

The name cropped up again in the *Ku'ei T'ien Lu* or Small Collection of Incidents Relating to the Imperial Court, written by a Song statesman in 1067. The book recounted Ou-yang's confusion at seeing a bowl made from a glistening stone quite unlike any jades he had seen before. Perplexed, he had shown it to an old eunuch, Têng Pao-chi, who had told him: 'This is the precious jade, which is called *fei cui*. Among the precious things preserved in the palace of the Yi Sheng treasury there was a *fei cui* wine cup from which I first came to know of it.'[42] And here the paper trail ran out.

Qianlong scoured his history books for clues that could lead him to the source of this mysterious stone, as search parties he dispatched to the mines of Khotan repeatedly returned with empty hands. In the Chinese annals the Emperor would have read how Kublai Khan's hordes, returning to Khanbalik after invading a country to the far south-west that they called Mien, brought home soldiers' stories of a treasure valley studded with green gems. Within a century the King of Mien had founded a new capital at Ava, a glistening city on the East bank of a vast river, a place whose name in the ancient Buddhist language of Pali was Ratanapura, meaning 'the City of Gems'. The Ming's *Book of the Southern Barbarians* also talked of secret riches in the southern lands, revealing the existence of 'the treasure well', a place that was littered with green stones. And Qianlong would have read how repeated attempts by Ming soldiers and traders to locate it had all ended in disaster, as 'out of every ten, eight or nine persons died of malaria'.[43]

If the Emperor had consulted his geography book written by Sü Ki-yü, director of Peking Foreign University, he would have read that Mien was a 'torrid corner' 3150 miles to the south-west of Peking. It was a poisonous nation of 'ferocious free-booters' that was obscured by an impenetrable jungle inside which was a mine whose guardians were said to be brutal, cannibalistic savages. The kingdom in which the secret gem pit lay was legendarily wealthy, and the *Momein Annals,* stored in the Hanlin Academy, would have taunted Qianlong:

> In the King's dwellings the jars are made of gold, the treasury is covered with silver tiles, fragrant wood is used for cooking and the hall is ornamented with coloured jewels and pearls. There are two ponds, the sides of which are made of gold and the boats and oars are all ornamented with gold and jewels. When the King goes out on his Palankeen [*sic*] he reposes on a couch of golden cord but for long distances he rides on an elephant . . . The circular wall of his city is built of greenish glazed tiles and is 50 miles in circuit . . . Gold and silver are used for money . . . In trading with neighbouring states they use porpoise, cotton and green stones.[44]

But for hundreds of years, according to the *Pin-li,* this affluent land had been in flagrant contempt of the Dragon Throne. Mien or Mien-Tien, as the Qing called it, last sent 'products of the soil' to China when the Ming Emperor Longqing ruled in 1567. A reason had to be found for an expedition south.

In 1765, when Qianlong learned that a caravan of Chinese merchants attempting to cross the border between Yunnan and Mien-Tien had been ambushed and decapitated, he found the trigger for an invasion. These Southern Barbarians were 'a beastly, weevilly race that feeds on the foulest food', Qianlong raged in vermilion script that raced across the pages of palace memorials. His fury was captured by court librarian Jiang Liang Ji in the *Tung Hua Lu,* an Imperial history that is today stored in the Forbidden City's archives:

> I am not vainglorious and would willingly drop the whole business but I am not going to allow another man's spittle to dry on my face. Accordingly I ordered annual expeditions to make Mien-Tien as unhappy and uncertain as possible.[45]

It was war, and Wei Yüan, Qianlong's military historian, painstakingly recorded the raising of a Chinese invading party. 'Towards the end of August [1765] the flags were unfurled and the advance sounded.'[46] Among the first wave to be sent over the border, a force of 30,000 to 40,000 men, were 'skilled sorcerers from Sichuan', 'musketeers from Peking', 'grenadiers from Honan' and the most modern arsenal that the Emperor could deploy. His troops carried 'brass cannons', 'iron *cheveaux de frise* from Hunan' and a secret weapon – 'poisoned munitions' manufactured in Yunnan. It would be a campaign that would cost China 13 million taels or £3.25 million at a time when the treasury had a balance of only £30 million.[47] The Emperor was evidently determined to win at any cost.

From the Forbidden City Qianlong assumed a hands-on approach. Every day dozens of royal express messengers raced to Peking bearing battle reports, before returning to the border carrying his Imperial orders. But the jungle and the superior tactics of the barbarian armies decimated Chinese ranks. 'The districts are inaccessible and cannot be climbed with ladders or ropes and the water seems insufficiently buoyant to float a boat,' complained a Chinese general who survived one onslaught.[48] The Southern Barbarians crowed in their war chronicles about how easily they overcame Qianlong's '250,000 men and 25,000 horses'. Their enemy was attempting to forge fast-flowing rivers using bulky sampans that hundreds of men had to carry through the jungle and were instantly shattered on rocks and in whirlpools. The Chinese were reliant on horses that found it impossible to pick their way through the dense undergrowth, while enemy troops battered down the thicket upon elephants that were also used as movable cannon batteries, the weapons fixed onto howdahs and fired from the animal's back. 'The noise . . . was as ten myriad fireworks, exploding at one time, rendering speech inaudible.'[49] The Southern Barbarians, who made gunpowder by distilling animal droppings, fogged the jungle with smoke, and in the blind confusion erected stockades from where they poured molten lead onto the heads of the advancing Chinese. Qianlong's finest soldiers were scalded, divided and driven into gullies 'like cows in a pound'[50] where, according to the Barbarians' chronicler, they 'perished pile upon pile'.

The Chinese body count soared, but the Emperor repeatedly sent his troops back into the fire-fight, and soon officers on the front line, fearing for their lives, began to report defeats as victories. It was only a matter of months before Qianlong found them out. 'These victories, I see, are all bogus. Is it not absurd that at the height of our power, having just crushed Zungaria and Kashgar, we should be thus defied by a petty state like Mien-Tien?' Qianlong asked. When the culprits were identified, his response was merciless:

> Marshall Akwei may deserve killing, but if he is to be killed it will be public execution. I am not going to let the Southern Barbarians make matters worse for the dignity of this country. I have given Akwei every chance and now I see it is hopeless to expect anything from him. He is hereby reduced to the rank of common soldier and will redeem himself by zealous service in the ranks. His two sons are exiled and will leave Peking this very day.[51]

When Têfuh, the Viceroy of Yunnan, tentatively suggested that the Chinese could not win, Qianlong banished him to a remote military station at Ili, on the Russian frontier, where he was made to serve as a minor official at his own expense. 'Oh, dear. Oh, dear,' the Emperor bemoaned in vermilion, 'I have made a mistaken choice once again. You dunderheads. Whom can I trust?' Dozens of generals were ordered back to Peking where they were 'allowed to commit suicide'. Qianlong's misery would be compounded. In 1766 Giuseppe Castiglione died and the Emperor devoted a plot of land in the Western Suburbs of Peking to him, inscribing on a tombstone two Chinese characters that recorded his appreciation of his work. Within two years, Qianlong's family also let him down. The Emperor's younger brother and son-in-law were sent to the front in 1768, during a third campaign. But the former took his own life after becoming trapped by an enemy advance, while the latter abandoned his line, leaving his troops to be butchered. More than 50,000 Imperial soldiers died of malaria and 22,000 troops were cut down in a single battle, one of many that lasted for more than 80 hours.[52]

The Emperor called on his most trusted and loyal general to turn around the haemorrhaging campaign. Ming Jui had been granted the title 'Purely Rejoicing, Recklessly Gallant, First Class Duke' in recognition of his bravery in the war to seize Sinkiang, had won many female admirers for his verse, *Rough Notes of Songs Murmured at the Northern Window* and now he charged towards the front. At first the general succeeded in rallying the Chinese troops, and the Barbarians' chronicler reveals his King's growing dismay at the Chinese advance. 'My generals are a joke. Let no one stop the Chinese. Let them come down even to my palace. When the Chinese arrive I shall cross the river with my four brothers and like mine ancestors shall smite them, though they come thick as grass, and cast them into the Irrawaddy,' King Sin-byu-shin declared.

But soon Ming Jui also succumbed to the jungle. Finding himself surrounded, the general seized a sword. 'Before committing suicide, he cut off his pigtail and sent it to the Emperor as a last token of affection,' recorded the *Shêng Wu Chih*.

Qianlong's courtiers, schooled in the Classics, were incredulous at the lengths to which their sovereign was apparently prepared to go to obtain a supply of shiny, green foreign stones that bore no resemblance to the Chinese Stone of Heaven. They had supported whole-heartedly the Western Campaign, as it had liberated Confucius' touchstone from the infidels. But the Emperor was now decimating his treasury in search of a mere bauble. In a barbed aside, Chi Yun, a Qing statesman and scholar, commented: 'I recollect that when I was young the *fei cui* jade was not regarded as jade but as merely usurping the name of jade. Now apparently it is regarded as a rare luxury, its price far exceeding that of real jade.'[53]

The Emperor's behaviour became increasingly erratic. He became convinced that China was in the grip of a 'soul-stealing' crisis. Rounding up 'master sorcerers', he accused them of clipping off the pigtails of Qing loyalists to steal their power, which was to be channelled into a spirit army bent on his destruction. In his private jade poetry too his grip began to waver. On one of the seven jade archer's rings that was displayed in the Emperor's cinnabar treasure box, he inscribed a telling verse:

> Once I wrote a poem about 'clearing doubts' . . . I called myself the Master of Providence . . . Many times [I] have succeeded when on the verge of failure . . . [But] too many things have happened in the past and I try not to recall them. Since the road ahead of us is still long, we have to be cautious and more diligent. We cannot rely on Providence . . .[54]

Qianlong could no longer rely on the heavens alone, but in 1769 he was thrown a surprising lifeline. The Southern Barbarians had succeeded in holding off the might of the Chinese Empire, but at a cost.

King Sin-byu-shin of Mien-Tien now proposed a cease-fire in return for trade. Qianlong would at last be supplied with green stones from 'the treasure well' in return for allowing traders from Mien-Tien access to Chinese markets. The Emperor hastily dispatched an official, General Kwese, to sign a peace pact, and he returned to Peking in 1770 with an assurance that mule trains laden down with panniers of stones were on their way. The Emperor was beside himself with joy. He ordered his historians to compile several volumes about his 'great victory' and impatiently waited for the tributary caravans to appear.

He barely had time to celebrate. Rioting broke out along the Sichuan border in a prolonged revolt that would cost £20 million to crush. While the Emperor's troops were fighting in the west, Shandong Province in the north was shaken by a Kung Fu scare. In 1774 an enigmatic herbalist and martial arts expert called Wang Lun confronted the alien Qing with a rag-tag army of 'peasants, travelling actresses and fish sellers' that believed they were blessed with magical powers.[55] Six years later Formosa became the seat of unrest, the Heaven and Earth Society taking up arms against the Emperor, whom they accused of greed and nepotism. And when it was placated, the Muslims of Gangsu Province, north of the New Territories, also attacked Qianlong's interests. And still there was no sign of the tribute from Mien-Tien.

Instead, Qianlong commissioned ever-larger carvings from Sinkiang jade. In 1778 he learned of a phenomenal boulder hewn from Mount Mirtagh. Weighing 5350 kilograms and 224 centimetres tall, this huge jade slab towered over the men he hired to transport it to Peking. It was loaded onto a specially reinforced wagon, 35 feet in length, drawn by 100 horses and pushed by 1000 labourers. They sawed through the mountains to create a path wide enough for the wagon to pass, cut a swathe through the forest, built bridges over the rivers and, in winter, sluiced the path with water to create an ice slide for their primitive heavy-goods vehicle. At best they covered five li a day (25 kilometres), so it would have taken them three years to travel the 1100 li (5520 kilometres) to Peking. There, the Ruyi Guan artist Chia Ch'uan was selected to create a three-dimensional model from a painting taken from an ancient Song catalogue.

Seven years after carvers first began chipping away at the mountain of jade, it was completed, and the finished work depicted lofty peaks down which rivers and waterfalls cascaded. Tiny figures of men hacking into the bedrock of a mountain could be seen working with hammers, spades and huge spikes to change the course of a torrent of water that threatened to engulf them. What had been carved was the story of a man credited with forming China's first Imperial dynasty, who was reputed to have ruled from 2205 to 1766 BC. Great Yu, it was said, had regulated the rivers and drained the land to hold back a flood of Old Testament proportions that threatened to submerge China. The mountain of jade was transported back to Peking and installed in the Palace of Peaceful Longevity in the Forbidden City, where it still stands today. It was engraved with columns of characters, Qianlong's jade poems that eulogised Great Yu. Only a stone of such monumental proportions could provide a fitting tribute to a Chinese Emperor who had saved his nation through resourcefulness and ingenuity. But a carving of such dexterity and scale, costing 15,000 taels (750,000 grams) of silver, also publicly demonstrated the economic power and reach of Qianlong, who was now fighting to hold back a flood of dissension and rebellion.[56]

One morning in 1785 the Emperor rose to be greeted by news of a messenger bearing gifts. Had the tribute from Mien-Tien finally arrived? Leaving his swallow's nest steeped in crystal sugar untouched, the Emperor rushed to his hall of audiences, his head filled with brimming panniers, but a single small leather pouch landed at his feet. It was a gift from a Chinese merchant returning from the Yunnan border and not the promised caravan from Mien-Tien. Qianlong retreated to his favourite shaded spot in the Garden of Peaceful Longevity, where a bronze dish was left out every night by eunuchs to gather youth-enhancing dew. He sat in the garden's centre-piece, a simple, carved wooden pavilion that sheltered a meandering water channel, shaped like an endless knot, down which he floated wine cups in homage to the ancient Spring Purification Festival. The gardens and pavilion recreated a Ming legend about 42 revered writers who had penned verses and drunk wine beside a spring. In the company of the spirits of China's greatest literary figures, Qianlong opened the pouch and found inside two small nuggets that glowed green with warmth and light and that were glassy to the touch. When he held them up to the lantern, they shone with a rare lustre that reminded him of emeralds.

Qianlong immediately ordered his Southern Masters to carve one of the stones into an archer's ring that was to sit at the centre of his cinnabar treasure box. When the ring arrived Qianlong dipped his brush into his jade inkpot and composed an eight-line elegy that would be inscribed around it:

> Green jade is rare and deep-green jade even rarer,
> It is the treasure among treasures.
> The archer's ring carved from this jade is more lovely
>   than the dark-green leek,
> Its colour is as bright as bamboo shoots.
> This treasure should not only be used by the Song people,
> Nor should it be the exclusive treasure of the Wei,
> It is a pity that I am old and no longer able to draw a bow.
> I hold the ring and feel deeply grieved.[57]

The Emperor's delight at finally owning even small pieces of this 'treasure among treasures' is evident. The *Book of Changes* states that 'Heaven is Jade' and so surely this rarest and most translucent of jades was the very essence of a stone of heaven. But equally clear is the 74-year-old Emperor's frustration that Mien-Tien had still failed to deliver its tribute. Was he now too old to force the wayward Southern Barbarians to honour their pledge? Was he now incapable of commanding a successful campaign against them? Was there something else lurking beneath his final morbid lines?

While travelling along the Karakorum Highway in 1998, in search of Qianlong, we came across a tragic tale that was said to be burning in the Emperor's mind as he sat beside the endless knot of water in the Garden of Peaceful Longevity. The shadow of an ethereal girl, a tantalising glimpse of a lost story that is barely referred to in the dust-dry pages of the Qing archives.

Near the oasis town of Kashgar, a resting-place along the ancient Silk Road where Uighurs once farmed besides Tajiks, where Kyrgyz once traded with Uzbek nomads, we came across a battered copy of the *Sinkiang Verses*, poems based on the folklore of Qianlong's New Territories that were published in 1892. One of them, the

Xiang Niang Niang Miao or The Temple of the Fragrant Woman, tells the story of how Qianlong became bewitched by a mountain girl who had 'skin like satin and sapphires for eyes'.

In the years following the tragic death of Fucha, the story of a child born smelling of the jujube tree's yellow flowers was traded like silk from the Pamir Plateau to the Levant, across the Land of the Blue Skies and along the desert plain with its fan of snow-capped peaks. It was said that her name was Xiang and that she was born to a family who for twenty generations had ruled the local clans. When the Western General Zhaohui waged war in Sinkiang, he also learned of Xiang. Her family had raised an army to assist Qianlong, as his troops became exhausted in the desert dunes that drained their rations. According to the Sinkiang poets, General Zhaohui rewarded his allies with a betrayal, abducting the flower girl as a gift for the Emperor. But Xiang had never travelled beyond the mountains, 'where she gathered wild mushrooms' and 'collected the strange-shaped egg-stones'. And when she embarked on a momentous 5000-kilometre journey from her village in the shadow of the Kunlun Mountains to Peking, Xiang warned her brother that the Forbidden City 'would be her prison' and inside its walls 'she would bury her joy'.

It took two years for General Zhaohui's procession to reach Peking, and when he presented Xiang to Qianlong outside the gates of the Forbidden City, the Son of Heaven was mesmerised by her fragrance, her Cupid's-bow lips and her heart-shaped face. As the only Muslim girl in court, Xiang Fei, as she was to become known, the Imperial Fragrant Consort, stood out from the swarthy Manchu women and the pan-faced Han who populated the Western Palaces. Unlike the concubines of the Hall of Concentrated Beauty, with their faces bleached by thick layers of make-up, Xiang Fei's skin was naturally translucent and, the poets of Sinkiang added, 'her cheeks blushed with the bloom of the mountains and valleys'. The Emperor was so smitten by his Kashgar girl that he commissioned his favourite artist to paint her dressed in a red silk Manchu gown. Castiglione's portrait shows Xiang Fei glittering with jade, bangles on her wrists, triple hoops hanging from her ears, a rosary pinned to her gown, her hair wound around jade ornaments. But according to the poets of Sinkiang, proud Xiang Fei ignored the Emperor's advances, sitting silently before a band of Uighur acrobats that had been hired to please her, refusing food spiced with peppers prepared by an Uighur cook.

The Forbidden City was set alight with stories of how Qianlong's romance with this perfumed consort from the western deserts echoed a thousand-year-old love story. During the Tang Dynasty an Emperor had become besotted by the Fragrant Pearl, a girl who was said to have been nourished as a child on rose petals, scented herbs and precious essences, who exhaled heavenly breaths as she entered the Imperial bedchamber.[58] But, it was said, Qianlong was unable to entice Xiang Fei into his Dragon Bed.

Behind the Emperor's back the flower girl was ridiculed for her Uighur dress, her prominent nose and, the poets said, she struggled to learn Mandarin and Manchurian. Isolated in the cold, alien environment of the Forbidden City and shunned by her fellow concubines, she slumped into a deep depression. The *Xiang Qi Lou Wen Ji*, A History of the Fragrant Woman Buildings, claims that the Emperor ordered the Jesuits to adapt his European-style Summer Palace as a residence for Xiang Fei. They painted friezes on the walls of the Fangwai Mosque and erected a new pavilion, the View of the Distant Lake.[59] Inside were mirrors designed to give perspective to a collection of paintings that captured views of Kashgar, the Kunlan Mountains and the Pamir plateau, scenes that were placed on runners, enabling them to be moved around like 'magic lantern slides'. Qianlong hoped that his stately pleasure dome would enchant Xiang Fei, and it was said that he ordered Castiglione to paint her again and again. In a second portrait she is shown dressed in armour; in a third, she is depicted as a European shepherdess; and in the fourth she appears standing beside Qianlong in front of the bamboo belvedere, as if they were contented lovers.

The more Qianlong fêted his captive from Kashgar, the more she retreated, and in 1785, she collapsed, gripped, the poets claimed, by a mysterious illness that defied palace physicians. When Qianlong sat down to write of his 'treasure among treasures', was he also then thinking of the flower girl, suffocating in despair; of an amorous campaign that had, to date, so miserably failed? 'It is a pity that I am old and no longer able to draw a bow, I hold the ring and feel deeply grieved.'

The desperate Emperor seized upon the second nugget of green stone that had sat, unused, in his leather pouch, and ordered his craftsmen to transform it into a brilliant memento of Xiang Fei's Uighur lands. What they produced was a pepper, an exact replica of the ones eaten by nomadic herders who had travelled from Persia down the Silk Road to Kashgar. The perfect pepper pendant, with a delicate tendril that glanced off its plump surface, appeared to glisten as if dampened by dew, and quantified Qianlong's love. The pepper was an ancient symbol of an Empress of China, and by giving one to Xiang Fei was he not telling his fragrant flower girl that he loved her as he had his tragic Fucha?

The pendant only served to remind Xiang Fei of her life in exile. On 19 April 1788, according to the poets of Sinkiang, after a final meal of ten tangerines, the fragrant flower girl died. The grieving Emperor ordered that she be buried with all the pomp and ceremony of an Empress of China, dressed in pearls, diamonds, rubies, cats-eyes and *fei cui* jade, her body encased in a lacquered coffin inscribed in gold with the words of the Koran. The body of Xiang Fei was carried by a cortege of 120 people back to her homeland in a final epic journey that took three years to complete. She was buried beyond the Sunday market, overlooking the Tuman River, in an ancestral vault clad in fired green *kashi* tiles, a windswept tomb that the local traders still call *Xiangfei Mu*.

The epic *Sinkiang Verses* enraptured Chinese readers, concluding that Xiang Fei had died of a broken heart. The Persian Pepper, an exquisite token of an Emperor's love, was locked away in a treasure store in the Forbidden City, a symbol of what Qianlong could not conquer, the delicate consort who had been trampled in the rush of his pursuit. Or so the storytellers would have you believe.

Two

Lord of the Mines

Amarapura. They used to say that when the sun rose above the purple mountains of Yunnan, a fountain of light welled up from the capital of a distant land that lay to the south-west. Refracted by a million flakes of gold, shimmering rays swirled high above a circle of stone battlements, magnified and reflected by mosaics that encrusted halls of ritual and honour. The sun crept up jewelled *htees:* finials adorned with thousands of tiny diamonds and silver bells that, when caught by thermals, showered the palaces of Earth, Fire, Water, Glass and Elephants in a silvered tinkling. Rising out of the Irrawaddy plain, this brilliant new tropical metropolis was known far and wide as the City of Immortals.

Every facet, prism and hue reminded its residents that this was the capital of Burma, a land ruled by the 'Lord of the Mines of Rubies, Safires and Spinels'.[1] Those who had not seen Amarapura for themselves were told of its gaudy glory by King Bodawpaya, scion of the Konbaung Dynasty, who took pleasure in sending boastful missives to world leaders that proclaimed his citadel one of the greatest, invulnerable wonders of Asia. One, sent shortly after the City of Immortals was erected by an army of slaves in 1783, advised the Governor General of India that Burma's shimmering new capital was 'illuminated and illuminating'. In it, Bodawpaya bragged of his 'Habitation of Angels, lasting as the Firmament, embellished with Gold, Silver, Pearls and the nine precious stones'. 'The Golden Throne,' he wrote, was 'the seat of splendour whence the royal mandate issues and protects mankind.'[2] But, the British were warned, 'do not call uninvited'.

Drawn out along a sinewy strip of South-east Asia, sandwiched between the vast empires of India and China, concealed by the folds of the Himalayas, Bodawpaya's nation brimmed with treasure. There were rubies and sapphires the size of pigeon eggs to the south; seams of gold and silver in the east; amber, coal and oil welling in the west. But the most precious treasure of all, buried beneath the impenetrable jungle of the north, was a secret mine that had never been seen by outsiders. Said to be the source of a strange and exotic luminous green gem that glowed as if lit by a hidden flame, legend had it that the jewels were guarded by many-headed *nagas*, mythical serpents that brooded over them as if they were their eggs.

The architect of the City of Immortals, the lord of these mines, King Bodawpaya had burned alive his brothers and their 'queens and concubines, holding their babes in their arms', to secure his ascension to the Lion Throne in March 1782.[3] Following the bloodshed that had accompanied his coronation, the incendiary monarch surrounded himself with Brahminical high priests and 'Masters of the Occult' who advised him to ring his city with an impenetrable psychic force-field. Bodawpaya inscribed cabalistic charms on square sheets of silver that he buried at strategic points around Amarapura's fortifications. He invoked *nats*, the country's spiritual guardians, to protect his wells, forests and mines. And leaving nothing to chance, he posted mortal armies along all of his borders, turning a bejewelled kingdom into a fortress that bristled with spears and *dahs*, the razor-sharp machete used by his troops in jungle warfare.

King Bodawpaya had every reason to worry. Whenever he climbed the tower that rose above his City of Immortals to sing out superstitious spells, his voice was carried over villas of vanquished kings, ruined palaces and pagodas that had fallen to foreign invaders, gravestones from many a battle, fields of ancient ruins that stretched away in derelict silence. Here before him was evidence of Burma's turbulent past that told how, for centuries, the kingdom's treasures had tormented other men's dreams, tempting Mongol warriors, Tartar warlords, Siamese princes and Moghul emperors to storm Burma's borders and steal its riches.

On this morning in May 1788, barely a month after Emperor Qianlong's beloved consort had died in Peking, Amarapura's royal apartments were teeming with anxious servants, their bare feet pattering along teak corridors, careful not to wake the princes of the blood and their minor queens. Outside, the lanes were choked with women, jogging along with panniers of mangoes, their cheeks smeared with *thanaka*, a sandalwood paste that prevented sunburn. Alleys were thronged with vendors sipping from thimbles of green tea, steaming bamboo towers of pork buns teetering behind them as thousands of soldiers and court officials, monks, high priests and sorcerers pressed towards the King's Hall of Audience, the Earth Palace.

From far across the Irrawaddy plain, over the great river that rushed 1000 miles from the Tibetan plateau, past the Sanda-Muni Pagoda and under the great gilded *pya-o*, an archway that framed the capital's Southern Gateway, horsemen galloped towards the capital. Princes from Burma's distant states threw up waves of dust as they passed lumbering elephants and troops of tumblers, all of them streaming towards the curlicue roofs of the Earth Palace. Extraordinary news was spreading through the city: the King was to make an announcement when the Baho Sigyi Drum, his regal alarm clock, struck 9 a.m. There was talk of a caravan being sent forth laden with gifts and a letter of friendship, a mission of peace bound for the 'Elder Brother' who sat on the Dragon Throne, a regal bid to end hundreds of years of bloody conflict.

A call from the watchtower behind the Earth Palace announced the approach of three officials who, it was rumoured, had been chosen to represent King Bodawpaya in Peking. Ye-myauk Shwe-daung, Thiya Kyaw-gaung and Ngwe-lu-saya rode towards the chamber in a winged chariot festooned with bunting and pulled by white stallions.[4] From the writings of a British officer who visited the court around this time, we know that they would have been dressed in flowing, velvet coats with flared cuffs, richly braided and lined with coloured silks under which they wore embroidered sarongs and curling Burmese court slippers. On their heads, drooping velvet conical caps, secured by a crown of beaten gold leaves and flowers. Piercing each ear were 'tubes of gold about three inches long and as thick as a large quill, which expands at one end like the mouth of a speaking trumpet'.[5] Draped across their bodies were gold-linked *tsalwes* that announced their rank and displayed their credentials as men of bravery, physical strength and diplomatic skills.[6] Surely they would need all of these attributes in the arduous months to come if the rumours of the journey they were about to undertake were true.

Their slippers discarded at the steps of the Earth Palace, the three barefoot envoys padded across the vast open-air hall with its cool marble floor and 77 lacquered pillars. Behind, courtiers, princes, minor queens and consorts all filed barefoot into the chamber, and bringing up the rear was the *Chaingeewoon*, master of the King's beloved white elephants, the rarest of mammals in Asia, the exclusive symbol of Bodawpaya. Above them all, the grandest *htee* in Amarapura, a gilded umbrella that signified the Burmese cosmic order, in which the Lion Throne that was positioned directly beneath it occupied the centre of the universe.

As the audience chamber settled, the whisper of *htees* filtered through the hall until two great gilt doors, covering an opening halfway up the rear wall, groaned. On either side were ritual vessels, encrusted betel-nut boxes, embroidered flags and regal flywhisks. Beneath were the *chinthe* and the *camari*, statues of mythical beasts tamed by the King, and arranged between them was a gathering of gilt page boys, their wooden arms raised in devotion to the father of the nation. As the doors swung back the King, with his great domed forehead that marked him out as a true descendant of King Alompra (a former vegetable-seller who had founded the now great dynasty), appeared to levitate, rising like a phoenix through the firmament, powered by wings of beaten gold.[7] 'His crown was a high conical cap, richly studded with precious stones; his fingers were covered with rings, and in his dress he bore the appearance of a man, cased in golden armour.'[8] He wore jewelled slippers, a mark of royal authority that explained another of his more obscure titles: 'Great Golden Feet'.

His subjects pressed their faces to the marble floor, their hands clasped above their heads in a *wai*, a greeting to an immortal ruler who appeared to have magically floated onto the Lion Throne. While Bodawpaya settled onto a plump scarlet cushion, the Royal Voice, an official who spoke on behalf of the regal deity, confirmed the rumours that had spread that morning. Bodawpaya was sending forth a caravan to the old enemy. The three envoys selected by the King were to embark on a punishing journey. The route had been chosen by the Brahminical council and now the Seredaw, the feared High Priest of Amarapura, dressed in a white robe and velvet cap studded with gold stars, revealed it. It was to be the ancient Thienni Road or Embassy Route to China, a name that they had heard before and one that filled them with dread. The King's envoys listened in dismay as they were ordered to find a way through the hostile and malarial jungles of the north-east, to navigate the gaping Kachin valleys, to ford the thundering Irrawaddy and Salween rivers before scaling the great purple mountains of Yunnan.

Burma's ancient chronicles had much to say about the Embassy Route. According to the histories painted onto *parabaiks* (lacquered bamboo books, which would later be translated into English by nineteenth-century explorers), it had been cut 1700 years ago by the envoys of King T'an. This Burmese monarch had sent along it 'conjurors who were able to transform their own limbs and to put on cows' and horses' heads' and 'precious things', gifts bound for Emperor Ho of the Eastern Han Dynasty in AD 97. Twenty-three years later King T'an had been rewarded with the title 'Chinese-pleasing pro-consul' and presented with 'gay silks, gold and silver' by the Emperor.[9] The route became a honeycomb of mule tracks that ran through the gorges and high passes of the Kachin Hills, miles of narrow footpaths, stepping-stones and bamboo bridges, used by Burmese and Chinese traders. It carried convoys laden with 'lead, opium, hams, honey, pears, candied oranges, leeches, chestnuts and dried fruit put up in small paper parcels of about a viss [3.5 pounds] each', and it was said that 'a traveller could trace his way by the fluffs of cotton torn by the mulberry bushes'.[10]

Now in 1788, as the three envoys would have known only too well, it was *terra incognita*. The Embassy Route had not been crossed by a Burman for hundreds of years. The maze of tracks that spilled out to the north and east of Amarapura was far beyond the suzerainty of King Bodawpaya, controlled instead by marauding tribes and bandits who worshipped mystical jungle spirits. Even if the three envoys survived as far as the Chinese border, ahead lay the glaciers and gorges of Sichuan, the mighty Yangzi and Yellow rivers and the dustbowl of the Shanxi and Hebei wastelands. The envoys would have known that their journey would almost certainly take months to complete, and surely they thought that their King had set them an impossible task.

The Seredaw called forward a sacred letter that the three envoys were to present to Emperor Qianlong if they reached Peking. Its message was almost crowded out by the Burmese monarch's titles: 'the Great Golden Feet, Lord of the Mines of Rubies, Safires and Spinels, Lord of the Golden Lion Throne, Lord of the Rising Sun, Lord of the Chaddanta and other white elephants and Suzerain of all umbrella-bearing Kings ruling over great empires and kingdoms in the west.'[11] Whereas court edicts were written on palm leaves, we know that this missive was made of beaten gold and weighed ten ticals. It was inlaid with three rows of 192 rubies, studded with several large uncut pieces of *fei cui* that were surrounded by thousands of sapphires and pearls.[12]

Waiting outside Amarapura's Southern Gateway, barred from entering the palace precincts with their weapons by a King who was paranoid about coups, was the envoys' military escort. News of the route they were to take raced through the 30 infantrymen who were to lead the expedition, halberdiers who were stripped to the waist and barefoot, their long hair tied into a top-knot. Armed with ancient French muskets and Burmese sabres, these wiry fighters could march through jungle for up to eighteen hours a day living on foraged vegetation, but even they were daunted by the prospect of opening up the abandoned Embassy Route. They passed the bad news back through the ranks to the cartographers, the engineers and the astronomers. Eventually it reached the two dozen cavalrymen from Cassay, modern-day Manipur, in their velvet frock-coats and muslin skirts, who sat astride stubby Pegu ponies, high up in the saddle, their bare feet slipped into short stirrups, a loose rein held in one hand. Famed for their agility and armed with only a single spear, seven or eight feet long, even the feared engine of Bodawpaya's war machine was silenced by the terrible news.

It took eight men to carry the golden letter to the gateway, now that it had been sealed inside an ivory cylinder for safe keeping.[13] Envoys Ye-myauk Shwe-daung, Thiya Kyaw-gaung and Ngwe-lu-saya followed behind and clambered onto the backs of their elephants. The Burmese shunned *howdahs,* preferring to take a commanding position behind the animal's head. Behind sat servants who had the unenviable task of clinging to the moving beast and holding aloft a gilded parasol to shield their masters from the sun.

The Baho Sigyi Drum boomed out across the city as the gifts bound for the Son of Heaven were brought forward. Eight young grey-skinned elephants tamed by the *Chaingeewoon,* each one carrying a priceless treasure wrapped in dried grass: a miniature Burmese pagoda carved in *fei cui,* inlaid with gold, small boulders of *fei cui,* panniers brimming with rough-cut stones, Persian carpets and Indian silks. Finally, a dozen manacled Chinese prisoners captured twenty years earlier, during the 1769 war, crawled forward. Feverish and malnourished, would any of them survive the tortuous journey that lay ahead?

King Bodawpaya retired to Amarapura's turrets and from there watched his adventurers halt briefly beside the Colossus of Gautama, a vast statue of Buddha before which priests prostrated nine times. But soon the party was enveloped in a billowing cloud of yellow dust that tore up from the plains, and the King descended to his private apartments.

🌑

The elaborate preparations for this expedition and details of its priceless cargo would be lost in the tumultuous upheavals that were soon to rock the continent. Disentangling the history of the Stone of Heaven, 210 years later, we discovered a decaying trove of documents, diaries, ledgers, minutes and telegrams in the National Archives of India that provided us with a spy-hole into Bodawpaya's long-forgotten world. These footsteps of an expanding Empire, abandoned by the British in New Delhi after India was given its independence in 1947, are today locked away in a crumbling tenement set back from Janpath. The broad, pink, tree-lined avenue sweeps through the heart of Luytens' Delhi like a river of time. On its banks are the whitewashed bungalows of the nation's political dynasties, the headquarters of Jawaharlal Nehru's Congress Party and the sprawling home of its current president, a former air-hostess from Orbassano, India's First Widow, Sonia Gandhi. Eventually you come across the wrought iron gates that lead to the document store.

As we passed through, two dust-covered labourers were demolishing an office block, armed only with a bent iron pole. Inside the lobby four men in their mufflers lay on a broken bench below a sign that read 'Scholars' Corner', muttering wildly in their sleep. The Reading Room appeared surprisingly spacious and well ordered, although it hummed like a defrosting morgue.

'You'll be wanting to study the files on the Burmans.' The Reading Room Superintendent itched beneath his woolly tank-top. He had been warned that we were on our way and combed his moustache with a forefinger dipped in *chai*. 'As scholars you are free to study the Burmans, only the Kashmiris are not allowed. But you will be beginning your study at the index,' he said, pointing in the direction of a wall of broken spines, volumes that teetered like vandalised telephone directories in an abandoned phone box. 'I will be warning you,' he whispered conspiratorially. 'These indexes are only saying what the Britishers were filing and not what we Indians are filing. We do not know what we have been filing and only you, the scholars, will come to know what we have been filing by requesting the files.'

We, the perplexed scholars, were to identify ten documents at a time from the broken indexes and list them on request forms that were to be handed to teams of copy clerks sitting behind Dickensian podiums. They slowly transposed them onto another set of forms that were then passed to filing officers who worked unseen in the four floors above. On the back of the request forms were printed seven reasons why a document might not be produced, a pregnant check box sitting by each. It was five hours before a trolley appeared loaded with folders and bound volumes, the squealing of its wheels rousing men and women who slept at their desks. A mob dashed for the gurney, pulling at the corpse of the British Empire, fighting over the paper remains of the Power and the Glory. A student from Madras clutching eight out of ten requested files basked in envious glances. But there was nothing for us on that trolley. Or the next one. Or the one after that. Thirty slips were returned to us, tattered and covered in an illegible scrawl.

It was only at the end of the second long week, that a requisition finally arrived; anorexic folders stamped 'Secret' that crumbled as we opened them. Inside was a treasure of information, written on paper splattered with inky thumb-prints, brittle as buried bones, on wax-sealed parchment, stamped by authorities. The vast majority of the New Delhi files that incorporated the administration of Burma up until 1937 had remained unopened since the day they were transferred, wholesale, into India's hands. Here were King Bodawpaya's bragging postcard to the Governor General of India and extracts from the *Burmese New Chronicle,* commissioned by him. Here were the memoirs of Father Vincentius san Germano, an Italian missionary, who arrived in Burma in the year that Bodawpaya ascended to the Lion Throne, and the journals of Michael Symes, a major serving with His Majesty's 76th Regiment, dispatched to Amarapura in 1795. In cramped handwriting that took days to decipher san Germano and Symes described the ceremonies of the Earth Palace and the court of the King. But here also were vast extracts from the secret Qing court annals that had been acquired in the nineteenth century by British intelligence officers, and they revealed the purpose behind King Bodawpaya's great expedition, as far as Emperor Qianlong perceived it.

⊠

As soon as he ascended to the throne in 1782, Bodawpaya had commissioned Twinthin Mahasithu, a palace scholar, to compile a chronicle. The King aspired to become the supreme ruler of Asia, and it would be the lessons of history that would enable his rise. But in 1788, while Twinthin was busy in the Glass Palace painting on *parabaiks,* Bodawpaya learned that his ambitions were being outflanked. The King of Siam, against whom Burma had waged war for the past four years, had sought and won the backing of the Dragon Throne. Qianlong had granted Rama I (the grandfather of King Mongkut, whose friendship with the English governess Anna Leonowens was the inspiration for the musical *The King and I*) a title, 'Prince of Siam', and with it came an assurance of military assistance against the Burmese aggressor.

There were other pressing problems. Burma's wealth of natural resources had been severely depleted by Bodawpaya's excessive military expenditure: repeated invasions of Siam and the suppression of uprisings in the ancient Kingdom of Arakan on the country's western borders in 1784. His troops were exhausted and his people hungry. For the past two decades Burma had ceased trading with the outside world. Despite his delusions of immortality, Bodawpaya now recognised that he, the 'Younger Brother', would also have to seek the friendship of the region's 'Elder Brother', Emperor Qianlong.

Although reluctant to share any of his country's priceless treasures, Bodawpaya decided to resurrect a plan drawn up by his brother. Nineteen years earlier, in 1769, tired by four bloody wars with China that had left hundreds of thousands dead on both sides of the purple mountains of Yunnan, King Sin-byu-shin of Burma, the second son of Alompra, had offered a 'contraction of friendship' to the Dragon Throne that it had been quick to accept. Qianlong had agreed to suspend hostilities with Burma if the King opened 'a jade, gold and silver road' that traced the Embassy Route, enabling green stones to pour into the Son of Heaven's workshops. On 13 December 1769 the King had signed a peace pact, that was 'conducive of conferring prosperity and happiness on both peoples', at the Palace of Honour outside the Burmese capital.[14] General Kwese, representing the Chinese delegation, had carried back to Peking news of the deal and a pledge that the contents of the treasure well were also on their way.

But the Konbaung Dynasty had made a promise it could not keep: the celebrated *fei cui* mines were beyond its control. Fortunately for the Burmese monarch Sin-byu-shin, rebellions against the Qing in Sichuan, Formosa, Shandong and Gangsu temporarily distracted Qianlong from his pursuit of the Stone of Heaven. Unfortunately for King Sin-byu-shin, he contracted malaria in 1776, and his death threw Burma into civil war. His nineteen year-old son Singu-min ascended to the Lion Throne and promptly put to death his younger brother and his uncle, the fourth son of Alompra. Bodawpaya, the fifth son, was sent into exile, but in 1782 returned to the capital city of Ava with an army to proclaim himself King. He rounded up Singu-min and his wives and children, who were executed at the start of a twelve-month reign of terror. Thousands of monks and children were arrested and burned alive on an immense pyre that had barely cooled when the King's Masters of the Occult warned him that the spilling of blood on the streets of the Burmese capital was a bad omen, 'akin to vultures sitting on the *htee*'. Bodawpaya decided to move five miles north and there on the right bank of the Irrawaddy he erected his glistening City of Immortals, Amarapura.

Now, in May 1788, Bodawpaya had dispatched his three envoys on the Embassy Route to the court of Qianlong, with a caravan weighed down with the haul of *fei cui* promised by his elder brother. Unfortunately for the envoys, the Seredaw's divination had not only landed them with the Embassy Route to China but had dictated that they leave Amarapura in the season of dust and droughts. As the expedition headed into the foothills, the temperature would have soared above 130 degrees Fahrenheit, and by the time it entered the jungles of the north, the simmering humidity beneath the canopy would have made breathing akin to inhaling warm soup.

On they pressed, towards the Chinese border through the purple amphitheatre of the Kachin Hills, a wild tract of parallel ridges and sheer gullies dubbed the 'forbidden belt'. The ranges ran like a giant scar through the barren landscape, before merging, at an elevation of 15,000 feet, at the Kao-li-kung Mountains. The entire region was carpeted in a gloomy jungle: giant teaks and conifers rising like pillars in a vast crypt. In places the vegetation would have become so dense that the envoys would have had to illuminate their path with lanterns. Had they read the accounts of itinerant Chinese traders, who attempted to explore the area in the ninth century, their discomfort would only have been heightened. We came across their sorry tales of losing their way for months in these perilous hills in the Ming Dynasty *Book of the Southern Barbarians* that also recorded the lament they used to sing:

> In the winter-time, we long to come home:
> But there is snow on the Kao-li-kung;
> In autumn and summer we long to come home:
> But oh! the heat of Ch'iung-tan [Valley];
> In the spring-time we long to come home:
> But we have no money left in our hands.[15]

When Kublai Khan's warriors had invaded in the late thirteenth century, his hardy soldiers had avoided the Kachin Hills, an area they described as 'impossible to pass' and 'shadowed by death'.[16] Marco Polo, who claimed to have accompanied them, wrote that 'the air in summer is so impure and bad and any foreigner attempting it would die for certain.' A Chinese annal known as the *Man-Shu,* thought to date to the Ming Dynasty, warned that the Kachin Hills should be avoided at all costs, even by those who were seeking jade:

> Of the Ho-t'an persons who go there and catch malaria, eight or nine out of every ten die . . . The whole area has malaria poison. In winter, grasses and trees do not whither. The sun sets at the level of the grasses. The various officials of the walled cities and garrison towns dread malaria and sores. Some desert their posts and stop in other places and do not personally attend to their official business.[17]

Qianlong himself alluded to the terrain in a Qing geography book 'in terms of horror vivid as those applied by the imaginations of Virgil or Dante'.[18]

At night the jungle hummed with mosquitoes that carried a virulent strain of cerebral malaria that quickly invades the liver, kidney, lungs and brain, stifling tiny capillaries, sending its victim into a rapid coma. They also carried blackwater fever that led to anaemia and ultimately death. And if travellers managed to avoid both of these as they slept, there were even more aggressive hazards that came alive in the day. Then the tiger mosquito set about its prey, carrying dengue, known then as breakbone fever, as it incapacitated the victim, causing excruciating pain in the joints and behind the eyes before haemorrhaging set in, blood seeping through the skin. The Golden Fly harried all, biting through cotton and even canvas, leaving behind tiny pinpricks that soon swelled into pustules. George Morrison, an Australian doctor who set out along the Embassy Route a hundred years after Bodawpaya's envoys, described how the 'exuberant vegetation' was 'throbbing . . . humming and buzzing with all insect life', deafening to 'unaccustomed ears'. When, having walked for miles, exhausted by fear and the death of some of their party, the dehydrated envoys of the King of Burma stumbled over a jungle pool that appeared sweet and refreshing, it too contained life-threatening bacteria. Cholera, dysentery and typhoid were ever present, inducing vicious bouts of diarrhoea and fever. And beneath every stone, concealed in the mud, lay buffalo leeches, parasites the size of a small cucumber that prized their way into every human orifice. Bodawpaya's expedition, armed with mystics and quacks, would have carried with them nothing that could have either prevented or salved the hazards of the jungle.

But there were more than parasites and bacteria lying in wait. The reason why the Embassy Route was no longer used, and why the expedition was so daunted by it, was that the land through which it passed had been taken over by tattooed hordes of Kachin, tribal marauders and assassins who guarded their territory from invisible tree-top lookout posts. Taller than the Burmans, the *New Burmese Chronicle* describes them as 'ferocious and intractable', fuelled by a cocktail of opium and rice spirits. The Chinese knew them as *Ye Jein*, the wild men who practised strange animist rites, spoke a language that few could understand, and who were virtually naked apart from a waistband of lacquered bamboo.

So warlike were these tribes that Qianlong wrote of them with respect when he was told by his front-line generals of their existence during the Burmese campaigns. 'When on an expedition they were not, like the Chinese, under restrictions imposed by health and distance,' the Emperor observed of the Kachin before considering whether it was possible to recruit them into his ranks. The lesson to be learned in war, Qianlong had advised his remaining generals, quoting from Sun Tzu's *Art of War*, was that 'attention should be paid to the enemies of your enemy. Barbarians should be used to fight barbarians. Do not waste resources in little wars.'[19] But by then his *fei cui* campaign was all but lost and the strategy he had gleaned from the ancient manual was never tested.

The Kachin lived in thatched long-houses that were ringed with wooden stockades protected by man-traps and rows of sharpened spikes that were disguised with foliage. The most savage were said to be the Lahpai clan, who occupied the jungles of the far north, where Hkakabo Razi, the highest peak in South-east Asia, rose to 5889 metres. The strongest were the Ithi clan, who populated the southern jungles. The 'treacherous Marip' who guarded the secret mines of *fei cui* lured treasure-hunters on, only to murder them on the road to the pits.[20]

According to Kachin lore, their eight tribes claimed an ancestral line to one of the eight great-grandsons of Ning Gawn Wa, the creator of the jungle, who married a female crocodile. But their true roots lay in the Mongol wastelands beyond China from where, thousands of years earlier, their ancestors had followed the streams south as they drained off the Himalayan plateau. Now the north-east of their territory was bounded by *Hukawng*, the Valley of Death, a place littered with thousands of cremation mounds and sacrificial pits – evidence, if any were needed, of their mastery at war. They had adapted quickly to life in the jungle and used opium paste, a form of cupping and a concoction of potent jungle herbs to ward off tropical diseases.

Outsiders were shunned by the Kachin, who drew their strength from the jungle that they believed was inhabited by *nats*. These omniscient 'messengers of the soil' hid among the thickets, watched from the skies, possessed wild animals and entered the tribesmen's homes.[21] They were said to be the spirits of those who had died violently and could assume monstrous shapes, bringing disease and destruction on all those who failed to honour them. The jungles would certainly have reverberated with the sound of wild incantations as the Kachin invoked the Great Spirit, the Evil One, the Glorious One.[22] And when a traveller heard the hell-raising screams he knew that the Kachin were about to go into battle, leaping on their quarry from the tree-tops, lopping off the ears of their victims, which were collected as trophies.

And given the fear that the Kachin generated, and the darkness of their jungle and its isolation, time would not change them. Eighty years after Bodawpaya's envoys crept into the lair of the Kachin, Captain Edward Sladen led an ill-fated British expedition into the same territory and narrowly escaped with his life. Sladen returned to London with a terrible tale, and in 1871 recounted the *manau* ceremony to an invited audience of fellows in the panelled lecture theatre of the Royal Geographical Society. In the RGS archives is a transcript of the lecture that begins with a description of how naked Kachin clansmen, their bodies caked in soot and chalk, gathered before their chief's house to perform the 'death dance', which began at dawn and went on long into the night. 'They are not Buddhists and it is hard to say of what religion they are,' Sladen proclaimed as he unveiled the horror. Dancing as one, in a crab-like motion, some tribesmen chanted while others beat enormous ox-hide drums. Dozens of bullocks, goats and chickens were brought into the arena and, with the murderous slice of a *dah*, their blood was spilt. As the animals' screams mingled with the men's ever-wilder shrieks, the

Jaiwa, the Kachin's High Priest, his headdress quivering with feathers and bamboo fronds, fell into a catatonic trance:

> He crouched down and began to work himself into a fury – stroking his head and face with both hands – tore his hair – sighed and moaned – groaned – and finally, his legs from the knee downward were made to quiver with a reverberation which repeated itself on the bamboo flooring with a sharp castanet-like sound which kept up incessantly during the remainder of the ceremony . . . his utterances, henceforth, were believed to be those of demons and *nats,* in a fury of anger which promised some violence.[23]

What was not revealed to the RGS fellows (Dr David Livingstone, Richard Burton and Charles Gordon among them) was that Sladen was forced to turn back when the Kachin honoured the 'promise of violence'. In his private journal that we found buried in the New Delhi archive is an admission that his expedition was ambushed in March 1868, two of his 'Panthay escorts' losing their lives.[24] If Sladen had known that the Kachin called him 'the white meat chief', would he have entered the jungle at all?

In 1788, Bodawpaya's three envoys planned to avoid the Kachin at all costs. They sent out scouts to scour the jungle for columns of rising smoke, footprints or the embers of a campfire. They littered the route with elephant tusks, blunt swords and pieces of buffalo flesh, symbolic gifts of peace and friendship.[25] They also carried with them tokens with which they intended to negotiate safe passage. British explorers would do the same 80 years later, loading their mule-trains with 'braces of muskets, boxes of gunpowder and pouches of lead shot, musk pods, amber beads, yards of silk velvet, rugs, needles, thread and scissors for the chiefs' wives'.[26]

Even if Bodawpaya's envoys succeeded in skirting around the Kachin, the jungle was filled with evidence of their existence. The tribes buried their dead in the trees as an offering to the *nats.* A body was encased in a bamboo wrap that resembled an enormous chrysalis and decorated with painted skulls, carved elephant tusks and bullock horns. Beneath lay thatched shrines on which had been scattered bones and horns, carved wooden totems and painted skulls. The wild jungle temples and treetop tombs must have terrified the Buddhist officials from Amarapura, who believed that if they came across a *manau* they would be instantly blinded.

Ripping their longyis on walls of thorns, losing their footing in the jumble of vines and bamboo, Bodawpaya's envoys would have struggled to uncover the remains of King T'an's once famous highway. They would have attempted to follow stream-beds, but that too posed a problem. We know from the field diaries of British officers who surveyed the same area in the early nineteenth century that elephants had difficulty picking their way between large boulders, and it would not have been unusual for the animals to fall or lose their loads.[27] Where the rivers were too deep or the current too fierce, the party would have been held up for hours while bamboo was cut and lashed together as rafts. A single bamboo with a diameter of just 10 centimetres can carry the weight of a 5000-kilogram elephant and, even though they had brought with them hutting tools, axes, swords and scythes, hooks and chains, it would have taken the halberdiers hours to break through a portcullis that rose 30 metres into the air, each shoot as wide as a dinner plate.[28]

It was a race against the onset of the monsoon, that would transform what remained of the path into a torrent of slurry, landslides sending boulders crashing down into the river valleys. And finally, bedraggled, starving and feverish, they emerged from the jungles after a gruelling journey of approximately three months. Jiang Liang-ji, the Chinese Imperial court's chief librarian, would later register their long-awaited appearance in the *Tung Hua Lu,* an Imperial history of the Qing Dynasty:

> Suddenly in the Summer of the year 1788 three high Burmese officers named Ye-myauk Shwe-daung, Thiya Kyaw-gaung and Ngwe-lu-saya appeared on the banks of the Salween with a submissive address written on gold leaf, a pagoda, rubies, jade, tame elephants etc. They said that King Meng Yun [Bodawpaya] had sent them to offer tribute. They said they had come via Thienni [the Embassy Route] because the Kaungton route was too hilly and too malarial for the passage of elephants.[29]

What the envoys were carrying and their intent is confirmed by an entry in the *Shêng Wu Chi,* a second Chinese court record translated in 1890 by William Warry, a fluent Mandarin speaker and an aide to the British consul in Shanghai:

> Accordingly, in 1788 the Burmese sent a golden letter, a gold and jade pagoda, eight trained elephants, rubies, foreign carpets, boulders of jade and other presents, to the frontier by the way of Thienni. They also returned the remaining Chinese prisoners. The King's letter was to the effect that he had not long succeeded to the Burmese throne and that he was profoundly conscious of the faults of his predecessors in levying a war against China and that he had long desired to send tribute, though trouble with Siam had prevented him from doing so.

Whether Bodawpaya's letter was as submissive as the Qing annals claim is open to question, but that it caused consternation when it arrived at the border is certain. When Viceroy Fukang of Yunnan heard of the appearance of Ye-myauk Shwe-daung, Thiya Kyaw-gaung and Ngwe-lu-saya he immediately rode to their jungle camp to challenge them, acutely aware of the human and financial cost of the Sino-Burmese wars and recalling the double-dealing of previous Burmese kings. The Viceroy found the men 'so shifty that he sent an officer to get a translation of their papers and see if the tribute really was there.'[30] Fukang concluded that the tribute mission was a Trojan Horse, and he jailed the three envoys in the border town of Shun-ning Fu while he sent word to the Son of Heaven, bragging at having intercepted a secret Burmese war party.

Qianlong was at Jehôl, mourning the death of his beloved Fragrant Consort Xiang Fei, when he received the news. The Son of Heaven could barely contain his anger and unleashed his fury in an Imperial edict dispatched to Yunnan on thick yellow paper, rolled up inside a piece of bamboo, encased in a yellow satin bag, tied to the back of a Fifth Rank Mandarin like a rucksack:[31]

> You, the so-called Viceroy are a ridiculous fool and a blockhead. I stopped the war in Burma . . . because the climate was so murderous. Moreover the Burmese had already become afraid and begged me to withdraw my troops, and I thought it best to further Heaven's manifest desire and save human lives. Meng Yun [Bodawpaya] . . .

was nothing to do with the crimes of his two predecessors. His advances are manifestly genuine and his ambassadors should have at once been sent to Peking. My viceroys are all in a state of panic and flurry when anything difficult occurs but are equally able to put on arrogant airs so soon as ever a man becomes submissive. I hereby convey my severe censure.[32]

What a terrible mistake Fukang had made. The Emperor immediately decreed that the three ambassadors be escorted to Jehôl in time for his birthday, 'at the beginning of the eighth moon':

> There will be an opportunity for the Burmese envoys to take part in the court banquets and see the display. But the envoys should press on with all speed. Let these orders go at 200 miles a day and sharp. The Burmese will leave at once for Peking as I directed. Report the exact date of their movements.[33]

Sprung from jail, Bodawpaya's men were now dispatched in the height of Imperial style, riding in sedan chairs that would take them on a 3333-mile trek across China. Although it was painfully slow compared to riding horseback, the Imperial sedan chairs ensured that the envoys would be treated with respect and given priority on the highway. No one 'who possessed any sense of self-respect' would travel any other way:

> Unfurnished with this indispensable token of respectability, he is liable to be thrust aside on the highway, to be kept waiting at ferries, to be relegated to the worst inn's worst rooms, to be generally treated with indignity or, what is sometimes worse, with familiarity, as a peddling footpad . . .[34]

Jogging through the Land South of the Clouds, along the narrow, flagged stone paths of the *Wuchi Dao,* China's ancient southwestern silk route, the envoys' chairs passed under 'grand memorial arches spanning the roadway', their 'columns and architraves carved with elephants and deer, flowers and peacocks', and 'the Imperial seven-tailed dragon of China'.[35] The Sino-Burmese wars had left Yunnan a blighted land of plague, famine and slavery, and the rocky landscape was dotted with bleak hamlets, their exposed roofs weighed down with stones and surrounded by starving cattle.

Plunging through narrow gorges, between poppy plantations and barren plains, the envoys passed caged children on their way to the slave market, putrefying heads in bamboo cages swayed atop poles in the breeze, and chained prisoners destined for execution, at best by beheading, at worst by 'the death of a thousand cuts'. Worn by centuries of use and surrounded by towering 300-metre cliffs on either side, the path was littered with ancient grave mounds, evidence of those who had succumbed to a tortuous route.

Eventually the envoys would have emerged into Sichuan, a province the size of France that the Chinese called the 'Heavenly Kingdom', a wild land of legends and ghosts. It was fringed by the Tibetan Plateau to the west, surrounded by soaring snow-capped peaks and criss-crossed by more than 80 mighty rivers. The Burmese must have been overwhelmed by its sheer size. As they skirted the base of Emeishan (one of the Middle Kingdom's four sacred Buddhist mountains, crowned with a golden temple) and crossed the Yangzi, 'the river of golden sand', they must have wondered if they would ever see Amarapura again.

Before them lay vast tracts of Chinese history: Shanxi Province, the crossroads of the trading routes from eastern China to central Asia, a region of deep ravines and vertical cliff faces. Once home to the Zhou Dynasty, who had conquered much of northern China by the third century BC, it had also been the territory of the Qin, who burst forth from this province to build the first dynasty to rule eastern China in the second century BC. The envoys would have passed by the ancient city of Xi'an, where a 2000-year-old army of terracotta warriors lay as yet undiscovered in the tomb of Shi Huangdi, the Qin's first Emperor.

Following the Yellow River into Shanxi Province, they would have been carried beneath ancient monasteries that clung to the cliff face, temples carved into the hillsides, caves that were the long-forgotten shrines of the Wei, who prayed to the gods for rain and once possessed a treasure that shone like a kingfisher's neck-feathers. King Bodawpaya's party ploughed on, across the Taihang Mountains and down into Hebei, the last province before Peking, with its monotonous southern plains. Scorched in summer, frozen in winter, the land would have been whipped by dust storms when they crossed it in the autumn of 1788. Having passed the *shisan ling*, the tombs of the

Ming, that were said to contain fragments of *fei cui*, the fatigued party eventually arrived in Peking, only to be sent north for a further 150 miles to Jehôl, where Qianlong was impatiently waiting.[36]

They followed the Imperial Highway that leap-frogged over China's Great Wall and up into the mountain tablelands that surround what is today the tattered mining town of Chengde. But only the Emperor was permitted to ride on the Imperial Highway, and the sedan coolies would have spent the last few weeks traipsing through mud. When they finally arrived in the gardens of the Imperial hunting lodge, with its lily-filled lakes and weeping willows, in early September 1788, days before the Emperor's seventy-eighth birthday, King Bodawpaya's envoys had been on the road for more than six months.

When Emperor Kangxi had ridden through Jehôl for the first time in 1703, it had been a wild and remote place, known as the 'fleeing-the-heat mountain villa'. Now its simple paths, hedgerows and thickets were dotted with temples, palaces and parks that had been built to remind the court, if not China, of Qianlong's conquests and the multicultural nature of his Empire. There was a miniature replica of the Potala Palace in Lhasa, a symbol of the Tibetan rebellion crushed by Qing forces in 1752 and an imitation of the Uighur plateau from where Xiang Fei, the Fragrant Consort, had been abducted. The untamed forest and glades were now a vast landscaped garden studded with hunting lodges, villas, 72 contrived beauty spots and a pool on whose waters a lucky crescent moon was permanently reflected, courtesy of some well-placed rocks.

The Burmese envoys were shown to a small guest-house in the north-western corner of the largest regal gardens in China, their *fei cui* gifts surrendered to household officials, their elephants given to the 'Grand Equeriz Department'. Their meeting with the Emperor had been fixed for the 'fifth day of the ninth moon', when they were expected to assemble in the gardens before the Emperor's palaces, several hours before dawn.

On the appointed morning the three envoys were roused from their beds at 2 a.m. and, after hurriedly dressing in their velvet coats and conical caps, followed an Imperial court official to where a temporary Hall of Audience, a large canvas marquee supported by lacquered pillars, had been erected on the lawn before the Emperor's Front Palace, a modest replica of the Forbidden City built from aromatic hardwood.[37] Beside it several more tents, of Manchu style, had been set up, their flaps decorated with muskets and sabres. Bodawpaya's envoys waited, shivering in the cold, their opened-toed slippers soaked in dew, surrounded, in the half-light, by small huddles of nervous princes, mandarins and court officials who talked in urgent whispers, their hands clasped inside their horse-hoof cuffs to ward off the early-morning chill. They would have just been able to make out the outline of the Misty Rain Tower and the follies and lakes that rolled out behind it.

At last, several hours later, as dawn rose above the Fragrant Garden House, music and distant voices broke the silence. A contemporary account of a meeting with Qianlong at Jehôl describes the scene that must have greeted the three Burmese envoys:

> He [Qianlong] soon appeared from behind a high and perpendicular mountain skirted with trees, as if from a sacred grove, preceded by a number of persons busied in proclaiming aloud his virtues and his power. He was seated in a sort of open chair, or triumphal car, borne by sixteen men; and was accompanied and followed by guards, officers of the household, high flag and umbrella bearers, and music. He was clad in plain dark silk, with a velvet bonnet . . . and on the front of it was placed a large pearl.[38]

The Emperor climbed from his 'open chair', swept into the marquee and ascended a cinnabar Dragon Throne. The wide-eyed envoys were ushered inside and directed to his right. Windows had been cut into the canvas to cast a golden glow onto the Emperor's face, and, kowtowing nine times before him, the Burmese envoys slapped their foreheads on the ground with suitably loud thuds. The Son of Heaven proffered his outstretched hand, each thumb encased in a jade archer's ring, each finger tipped by an elegant, elongated nail.

The envoys now called forward eight servants who strained under the weight of Bodawpaya's gold and jade letter, whose ivory case was smashed at the Emperor's feet. Qianlong motioned for a senior mandarin to accept the 'chieftan of Burma's' missive and grandly announced that Bodawpaya's 'prayers had been answered'. He then disappeared behind a yellow fly-sheet to compose an Imperial order in vermilion ink that would glisten with 'the dew of new words'.

The following day Bodawpaya was given the title 'Prince of Burma', subject 'to the payment of a decennial tribute' in the form of Burma's enviable 'products of the soil'. The deal was done: a Chinese rank in exchange for *fei cui*. Bodawpaya would now be on an equal footing to the Siamese monarch, and Qianlong would at last see the opening of the long-awaited Jade Road. The Emperor's feelings of remorse and gloom at the death of Xiang Fei, his Fragrant Consort, must have been lifted by the realisation of his *fei cui* dream. But the dour wording of the Son of Heaven's vermilion edict was intended to remind King Bodawpaya of his lowly status in the grand scheme of things:

> The display of loyalty and submission of presents are in the form in which a torrid corner prepares its duty as tribute. The encouragement and entertainment of vassal envoys are the mark by which the Imperial administration evidences its sublime tenderness. Taking cognisance of the fact that the frontier wilderness has only continued its ancient submission, the Emperor's majesty has now to refresh it with the dew of new words. Chieftan of Burma . . . Thou has manfully corrected the errors of the past . . . We rightly opine that all cause for war should forever cease. An Imperial decree reminds Burma of its insignificance and the significance of China. Respect this, and never fail to obey these, our Commands.

For several days the three envoys rested in the guest house by the North West Gate, visited occasionally by court officials who bore 'commands of commendation'. Others brought small gifts for Bodawpaya: 'images of Buddha, figured silks, jewels, curiosities and various vessels and dishes which the Country Chief shall respectfully receive, striving still more to be sedulously dutiful.'[39] But the prize gift that the envoys were to take back with them to Burma took several days to complete. When they were finally allowed to leave Jehôl, they were accompanied by a Commissioner whose duty it was to carry a poem written by the Son of Heaven for the Burmese King. Yunghwei, an attendant of the Imperial Grain Store, Colonel Pehfuh, a Manchu officer, and T'u Shu-lien, an Imperial magistrate, were deputed to guard the precious verse on its long journey and to carry with them 'an Imperial mandate, a gilt seal and a [white] jade *ruyi* sceptre'.[40]

⌗

No sooner had the Emperor accepted the King of Burma back into the Chinese family of tributary nations than he was confronted with the combined forces of King George III and the East India Company. Since Elizabethan times England had repeatedly attempted to engage the Celestial Emperor in commerce, but as the eighteenth century drew to a close England's presence in China was still limited to the southern trading port of Canton. While the Middle Kingdom kept foreigners and their wares at arms' length, Europe greedily consumed all that China had to offer, revelling in chinoiserie. The Orient fired the imagination of Western designers, and its influence could now be seen growing in the meandering gardens of the British aristocracy, rising in their pagoda-like follies, glazed onto their willow-pattern porcelain, pasted onto the walls of every respectable country house, echoing through the pages of popular literature. But it was Britain's greedy consumption of Chinese tea that was to trigger the mission of 1792.

While the beverage was unheard of in Europe before 1600, now £20 million worth of tea was annually bought from the Chinese who, in return, only purchased £800,000 worth of Manchester cotton, Derbyshire lead and Cornish tin. The East India Company was literally running out of silver. Between 1760 and 1780 the amount of British silver flowing into China rose from 3 million taels (150 million grams) to 16 million taels (800 million grams), much of which Qianlong lavished on his European-style palaces. George Staunton, 'Honorary Doctor of Laws from the University of Oxford, Fellow of the Royal Society of London', who was to accompany the delicate British trade mission to China, wrote in a preface to his account of the expedition:

> Until teas, of similar qualities with the Chinese, could be procured from other countries, in equal quantities, and at a reasonable price . . . no precaution was to be neglected, which could secure the usual supply of that article from thence.[41]

The British needed a diplomat of 'tried prudence' to present a convincing case to the Chinese Emperor. His Excellency the Earl of Macartney, Knight of the Bath, was chosen to represent the Crown.

A friend of Edmund Burke, Voltaire, Samuel Johnson and Sir Joshua Reynolds, Lord Macartney had excelled in complex diplomatic missions to the Court of Catherine the Great in St Petersburg, had survived capture by the French while serving as Governor of Grenada, and was already familiar with the idiosyncrasies of Asia, having served for six years as Governor of Madras.

The mission was trailed in a series of satirical cartoons published in London that lambasted impoverished Britain for going cap-in-hand to a nation of savages. Qianlong was portrayed as a corpulent sloth with cat-like eyes, his men behind him with sabres drawn, while the dandyish Macartney, powdered and bewigged, approached the Dragon Throne, a bedraggled union flag, a rocking horse and a hot-air balloon in tow.

'His Majesty's Embassador Extraordinary and Plenipotentiary to the Emperor of China' sailed from Portsmouth harbour aboard the man-of-war *The Lion* on 26 September 1792, having been instructed by King George III to establish 'a free communication with a people, perhaps the most singular upon the globe.'[42] 'Chinese civilisation,' the King wrote, 'had existed, and the arts been cultivated, through a long series of ages, with fewer interruptions than elsewhere'. It was Macartney's duty to change all that, 'in the pursuit of knowledge and for the discovery and observation of distant countries and manners'. He should seek important trade concessions, win access to more of China's ports and the right to station a British envoy in Peking.

Aware of the success of the Jesuits in the Chinese Court through the hydraulics of Father Benoist and the portraiture of Giuseppe Castiglione, this mission bent on 'a business of such delicacy and difficulty' was accompanied by Britain's finest 'products of the soil'.[43] Macartney filled the bowels of his troop ship, *The Hindostan,* with a trove of gifts from the King: 'a universe machine, a telescope, a globe of silver and gold stars, a celestial and earth lobe and a vacuum machine.' There were 'brass howitzers, mortars, muskets, pistols and sword blades', vases of a newly discovered substance, 'platina, or whitegold', Crown Derby porcelain figures and vases, clocks, portraits by Sir Joshua Reynolds, 'Parker's giant lens' and a gilded state carriage. All of which would sit well in Qianlong's 'cabinet of European curiosities'.

The Lion and *The Hindostan* sailed into the Gulf of Peking in August 1793, after a journey through seas 'of which there was no recorded account by European navigators'. Thirty Chinese Imperial junks were dispatched to relieve the British of their gifts. After gorging on shark's-fin soup and 'muddy wine', Lord Macartney set out on the rutted track that ran parallel to the Imperial Highway leading to Jehôl, in an English state carriage accompanied by a train of 1200 soldiers, mandarins, trumpeters and crowds of locals, waving them on. Swollen with pride, Macartney welcomed the bannermen carrying aloft messages of greeting, until he learned that they announced 'Embassador bearing tribute from the country of England'. Ma-ka-erh-ni, as the Chinese called him, and his gifts were immortalised in the *Ying-shih Ma-ka-erh-ni lai p'ing an* or Lord Macartney's Audience with the Emperor. In it the British were presented as a nation that had, like Burma, subjugated themselves to the Dragon Throne.[44]

Lord Macartney was encouraged by the delight of the Qing officials who received his gifts, only to be infuriated when shown a Chinese newspaper that reduced them to a ridiculous pantomime: 'Seven dwarfs or little men not twelve inches high . . . an elephant not larger than a cat, and a horse the size of a mouse . . . a singing bird as big as a hen, that feeds upon charcoal', apparently at least 50 pounds a day. The English were a 'carroty-pated race', the embodiment of the Foreign Devil: king of the underworld with his bulbous nose, startling eyes and hairy body.[45]

But all of these were minor irritations until the 'kowtow' question was raised. No one had ever been presented to the Son of Heaven without prostrating themselves nine times. The mandarins, whose conversation Macartney described as 'wonderfully supple', engaged him in polite discussions about knee buckles and garters, advising that it would be 'better to disencumber ourselves of them before we should go to court'. When the British envoy prevaricated, they only became more insistent and added a new act of subservience: he would also have to kiss the Son of Heaven's hand. Ever the diplomat, Macartney agreed to comply if someone of equal rank would kowtow and kiss a portrait of King George III.

When Qianlong finally received Macartney on 16 September 1793, the day before the Emperor's eighty-third birthday, a marquee had been set out on the lawns before the Front Palace at Jehôl. After being kept waiting in the dark for several hours, gathering dew, the British envoy followed the Emperor into the tent and bowed briefly before the Dragon Throne. Sitting on a cushion beside the Son of Heaven, Lord Macartney listened as the Emperor spoke of his satisfaction at the 'testimony which his Britannic Majesty gave to him of his esteem and goodwill, in sending him an Embassy, with a letter, and rare presents'. After a few false starts it all seemed to be going rather well. Qianlong conveyed his hopes 'that harmony should always be maintained among their respective subjects'.[46] But in response to Macartney's formal requests for trade, the Emperor's answers were vague. Instead of discussing terms, Qianlong distributed gifts:

> His Imperial Majesty gave, as the first present from him to His Majesty [George III], a gem, or precious stone, as it was called by the Chinese, and accounted by them of high value. It was upwards of a foot in length, and curiously carved into a form intended to resemble a sceptre. Such is always placed upon the Imperial throne, and is considered as emblematic of prosperity and peace.[47]

A drawing by William Alexander, the mission's draftsman, reveals that the present was an ornately carved *ruyi* sceptre, a token of esteem fashioned from jade from the Khotan mines, a symbolic gift that the Chinese understood as meaning 'May your wishes be fulfilled.' Staunton also received a jade *ruyi* sceptre that is today in the Victoria & Albert Museum in London, while Macartney was given 'some very curious and precious gems', which the Emperor told him were of great value, having been in his family for eight centuries. Of course, all the gifts were accompanied by a 'few stanzas' of Qianlong's verse.

Surprisingly, the British dismissed the Chinese presents as 'less valuable in the estimation of the receivers than in that of the donors'.[48] Macartney and his deputy clearly had no understanding of the historic value of China's touchstone, even though Sir Hans Sloane, colonial physician and Royal Society president, had displayed a Chinese jade bowl among 'Dr Sloane's curiosities and knick-knackery', a cabinet of foreign trinkets that formed the first collection of the British Museum when it opened in 1759.[49] The word 'jade' had been introduced to the British 30 years earlier when

Chambers Cyclopaedia first listed it. The envoys' ignorance of jade and the Chinese presumption that everyone knew that their gifts were priceless illustrated the collision of two intransigent powers, the former presuming they owned the world, the latter thinking it was the world.

Macartney had not made things easy for himself. Only one member of his delegation had even bothered to learn any Chinese, and it fell to George Staunton's twelve-year-old son to make a short speech to the Emperor. Qianlong beckoned George junior forward. 'Either what he said, or his modest countenance, or manner, was so pleasing to His Majesty, that he took from his girdle a purse, hanging from it for holding areca [betel] nut, and presented it to him.'[50] William Alexander used the moment to scribble a surreptitious portrait of Qianlong, resplendent in his jade archer's rings and jade court necklace. The British knew that their audience was over when 'some Hindoo [*sic*] embassadors from Pegu [Burma] . . . were introduced to the Emperor on the right hand side of the throne.' Staunton smugly noted that 'they repeated nine times the most devout prostrations and were quickly dismissed.'

Macartney and his men were entertained for several days in Jehôl and attended 'sumptuous banquets', rode with the Emperor's Chief Vizier, were shown his great jade mountains inscribed with poetry and celebrated Qianlong's birthday, where 'masters in the art of balancing their bodies upon a wire, while walking upon it' entertained the court. There were people 'tumbling and posture making . . . wrestling in long robes with clumsy boots', and musicians who 'affected most slowly and plaintive airs, not unlike those of the Highlanders of Scotland'. The climax came in 'a volcano . . . of artificial fire in the grandest style'.

But the real fireworks were reserved for when the British delegation returned to Peking, bumping along the rutted track that ran parallel to the Imperial Highway, closely followed by the Burmese delegation. Once they reached the capital 'a chair of state hung with . . . curtains' arrived, carrying a blunt Imperial letter. 'Impelled by your humble desire to partake in the benefits of our civilisation . . . your envoy crossed the seas and paid his respects at my court . . . To show your devotion you have also sent offerings of your country's produce,' Qianlong wrote to George III. 'As to what you have requested in your message, O King . . . this does not conform to the Celestial Empire's ceremonial system and definitely can't be done. The Celestial Empire, ruling all within the four seas . . . does not value ingenious articles, nor do we have the slightest need of your country's manufactures.'

And there it was. The British were doomed to run on a parallel track to the Emperor of China, who had swatted the approaches of George III like a fly. When he read the letter, Macartney knew that his mission had failed, but his private journals reveal that the ambassador's time had not altogether been wasted. Beneath the jade veneer Macartney had glimpsed the creeping decay that now surrounded Qianlong. 'I have seen King Solomon in all his glory,' the envoy wrote, recalling a puppet show from his childhood. At the time he had enjoyed it as 'a true representation of the highest pitch of human greatness and felicity' although as an adult he recognised it for what it was – a charade. China, he concluded, was 'an old crazy first rate man-of-war' that now only overwhelmed its neighbours 'by her bulk and appearance'. The Qing dynasty, Macartney predicted, was doomed to be 'dashed to pieces on the shore'.[51]

Three

A Jungly and Evil Place

Only legends succeeded in escaping from the noxious jungle that smothered the Kachin Hills, intoxicating myths that crept out of the dark land and slowly circumnavigated the world. Whispers that secret pits nestled between the twin peaks of Loi Lem and Loi Law passed from tribesmen to hermits who lived on the banks of the Uru River. Elephant trappers who stalked the *Hukawng,* the Kachin's Valley of Death, traded fables of how the road to the mines of *fei cui* passed beneath the shadow of *shwe-down-gyee,* the Great Golden Mountain. Stories of the mine's mythical guardians – half-man, half-snake – cruised on bamboo rafts, passed the whirlpool of Pashio and down through the defiles of the great Irrawaddy. Boarding ships at the river delta, the fantasies sailed out into the Bay of Bengal, docking in Calcutta or Chittagong. Ebbing and flowing with the Ganges, the saga of a wondrous mine that drew in adventurers who were never heard of again was carried against a tide of disbelief, across the dusty plains of central India. Galloping northeast on horseback towards the Karakorum Highway, on the stories went, transported by camel trains that ploughed the Central Asian steppe, now weighed down with terror and shot with the supernatural, the jungle floor was the lair of a many-headed serpent who brooded over her green stones like eggs. Traded by silk and spice merchants, the rumours were dispersed like the seeds of a dandelion clock, a fabulous story blown across the Levant.

Inevitably they reached the ears of East India Company representatives at Fort William, Calcutta, and treasure-seeking envoys were repeatedly dispatched from British India to a place first named by Ptolemy as *Survarna Bhumi,* the Great Golden Land. The Company men bore gifts of English state carriages, coin-making machines, sacks of silver, cucumbers, apples and oranges, with which they hoped to smooth their passage towards the treasures concealed in the north.[1] The minutiae of these missions were painstakingly recorded in elaborate hand that filled volumes of vast leather-bound ledgers that would later be discarded in New Delhi. Inside one, we found accounts for the sale of woollen socks that the Burmese nobles took to wearing beneath their slippers in the winter months.[2] In another, were admissions that more often than not the trade delegations of *kullas* (the derogatory term for foreigners used by the Court) were rebuffed and even humiliated. The British were ordered to remove their boots outside the Royal City, made to walk in stockinged feet, forced to kneel before the empty Lion Throne and *sheikoo* (kowtow) to an absent King. And in one volume of watermarked cartridge sheets sewn together with cotton, the right side of the pages densely inscribed with a leaning pen, the left abandoned to pencilled comments and marginalia, was captured the story of Michael Symes, a major serving with His Majesty's 76th Regiment, who was dispatched to Amarapura in 1795.

For once King Bodawpaya was present when a Company envoy was ushered into the Earth Palace. But while the courtiers were awed by the levitation of their winged monarch onto his Lion Throne, Symes saw only a portly man clambering up a concealed staircase. He 'seemed not to possess a free use of his limbs, being obliged to support himself with his hands on the balustrade'. Symes concluded that Bodawpaya struggled 'due to the weight of the regal habiliments in which he was clad. He carried on his dress fifteen viss, upwards of fifty pounds avoirdupois of gold. In his dress he bore the appearance of a man, cased in golden armour, [with] a gilded, or probably a golden, wing on each shoulder.'

He might have glimpsed the Lord of the Mines, but in a matter of days the Major was ejected from Amarapura, and it would take another seven years to negotiate his return. Then Symes experienced a different face of Burmese diplomacy. Bodawpaya exiled him to an island in the Irrawaddy, 'where corpses were buried and criminals executed', while he pondered Britain's request for a meeting.[3] During three months of waiting Symes greedily consumed the accounts of early European explorers that he had packed in his trunk. He pondered over the *Itinerary of Ludovico di Varthema,* a trader from Bologna who docked in Burma on 1 March 1505, recounting how the 'sole merchandise of these people is jewels'. Their monarch was so loaded down with gems that 'by light at night, he shines so much that he appears to be a sun.'[4] Here the 'gorgeous East with richest hand showers on her kings barbaric gold and pearl'. Symes pored over the journals of Ralph Fitch, the first Englishman to traverse Burma, in 1587, and must have read his account of the gem markets of the north where stones were so plentiful that they were sold by the fistful 'at most vile and base prices'. Perhaps he also took a moment to enjoy Fitch's explicit account of the eccentricities of the locals:

> the men weare bunches or little round balles in their privy members . . . They cut the skin and so put them in, one into one side and another into the other side; which they do when they be 25 or 30 years old . . . The greatest are as big as little hennes egges; some are of brass and some of silver: but those of silver be for the King and his noblemen.

Finally, as the monsoon broke, Bodawpaya's herald sailed out with word from the King. He 'did no business on wet days'. Symes was forced to retreat once again.

Bodawpaya had no need of trade agreements with the British, as by now he was making a fortune in a deal struck with the Emperor of China. So busy had Lord Macartney been in conveying the might and bluster of George III that in 1793 he had missed the story of the Stone of Heaven altogether. His aide George Staunton noted in passing 'some Hindoo embassadors from Pegu' who 'repeated nine times the most devout prostrations and were quickly dismissed'. But what Staunton failed to deduce was that these men were Burmese envoys and they carried a message of far more interest to the Dragon Throne than Britain's trove of mechanical toys. Bodawpaya was sending news that his army, dispatched into the jungles of the north, surviving a journey through a land of legends, had finally succeeded in brokering a deal with the 'treacherous Marip Kachin' who guarded the source of Qianlong's Stone of Heaven.

The Marip Kachin had won control of the Uru River valley in the centuries following the Mongol invasions of Mien, unaware that they had also secured a priceless treasure. The Kansi Duwa, the Marip Kachin leader, had used the smooth jade boulders that he found in river beds to cradle cooking pots on his campfire, until Bodawpaya's troops informed him of their value.[5] The matchmaker King introduced the jade aspirations of the Chinese Emperor to the tribesmen and within a matter of years stories began to pace the secret Kasa Naga Road that led from the mines, that the land of darkness was now flickering with campfires and lamplight.

A cordon of Marip Kachin guards sealed off the Uru River valley, but between the trees and over the stockades could be seen feverish shadows bearing staves and picks. Elephant trappers told how they saw wild men wielding burning bamboo rods in the undergrowth, shrieking as they hovered over pockets of land, the poles vibrating as if they were some kind of satanic divination instrument. Beside the campfires lay the corpses of slaughtered animals, they said, sacrificed to the jade *nats* who the Marip Kachin now believed inhabited the valley, vengeful spirits that sent scree tumbling. In the half-light men and women danced around chasms, sprinkling rice and goats' blood, ringing them with painted skulls and bones.[6]

It was said that the 'treasure well' was now a rancid gulag where thousands were dying. The Marip Kachin had refused to work the mines themselves and instead Bodawpaya had supplied them with Manipuri chain-gangs, the hostages of a war with his north-western neighbours. The prisoners excavated deep shafts into the mud and then were lowered into the darkness to chip away at black and green veins. Fires were lit at the very bottom of the mud shafts to dry out the walls, and those forced to work in the depths wrapped their faces and bodies in plantain leaves to fend off the searing heat.[7] Cave-ins buried alive hundreds of labourers, and as many were dying from a fever that also gripped Chinese traders who waited in a nearby village called Mogaung for the elephant convoys bearing stones. On the crumbling walls of a Chinese temple on the outskirts of Amarapura you can still see the names of more than 6000 merchants who died while trading *fei cui* in the Kachin Hills.[8]

The British however would not be kept at arm's length for long. After Bodawpaya's death in 1819 his wayward grandson, Sagaing Min, sent half-naked soldiers armed with spears and *jingals*, unwieldy hand-held cannons of Chinese design, charging into British sovereign territory along the borders of Manipur, Assam and Chittagong. Maha Bandula, the Burmese commander-in-chief, bragged that he would imprison the Governor General of India in 'gilded fetters' while the Burmese Crown Prince would take the throne of an insignificant little island he called *Bilat* (England).[9] Lord Amherst, the Governor General of India, responded in March 1824 with a declaration of war against a 'capricious and distasteful race', sending gunboats into Burma's southern port city of Rangoon, deploying troops along the Indian border.[10] The British might have appeared to be dressed for a field day in the Home Counties, with their scarlet tail-coats and shakos (black leather helmets with bearskin crests). But they picked off the Burmese with flintlock Paget carbines and bombarded their lines with the rockets of the Honourable East India Company Artillery.

A distraught Sagaing Min eventually surrendered on 24 February 1826, signing a peace treaty that ceded Assam, Arakan and the southern coast of Tenasserim to the British and recognised Manipur as an independent state. British troops took home trophies of the campaign. Captain Frederick Marryat seized the 'gilt figure of Gaudma', a striking seated idol that he donated to the British Museum, and the *Rath*, the King's state carriage. A buggy drawn by elephants and encrusted with more than 20,000 precious stones, it was lent to Bullock's Egyptian Hall on Piccadilly. Such was the scale of Marryat's haul that the Asiatic Society Rooms in London dedicated an entire exhibition to it in 1826. But the real prize was the right to establish a British residency in the Burmese capital, and on 22 August 1829 Major Henry Burney of the 25th Regiment, Bengal Native Infantry, caught his first glimpse of Sagaing Min's palaces as the *Diana* steamed round a bend in the Irrawaddy. The Burmese King had abandoned Amarapura after vultures landed on the *htee* and decamped back to Ava, the country's former capital. As the *Diana* docked, Burney noted how in the distance King Bodawpaya's City of Immortals, once said to be as 'lasting as the firmament', was now consumed by jungle.

Burney was a polyglot with years of overseas experience but he immediately tripped up, over his own shoes. The Major meticulously studied accounts of earlier Company envoys and noted how they had been forced to unslipper 'in the dirt and filth, or hard gravel of the public streets, a hundred paces before you come to the spot where the King may be sitting'. By his reckoning the distance the envoys were expected to walk in stockings had already been reduced from the Palace gate to the foot of the Hall of Audience steps, and Burney now hoped that 'with a little management the remaining space between the steps and the Hall itself may be dispensed with.'[11]

The Major's fixation with footwear threw his new residency into an immediate stand-off with Sagaing Min that lasted for ten months, during which Burney was reduced to spying on the court with a telescope from a hill outside. Days spent watching the King 'race ponies and his white elephant up and down the streets', the sloth of long Burmese nights, a boredom mediated only by intelligence reports about the King's gradual descent into madness. Sagaing Min, who had taken to drink, suffered from 'a wandering eye' and had begun to use his servants for spear practice.[12] Only in June 1830, after Burney threatened to leave Burma altogether, did the court finally agree to erect 'a small shed' outside the Elephant Palace, where Burney 'could unslipper in private'. On 17 June the Major was finally introduced to the deranged monarch as the 'Company King', and no sooner had he padded into the Earth Palace than he requested permission for his officers to travel into the jungles of the north, 'a portion of country hitherto unexplored by any European'.[13]

※

The details of Burney's forays into the wild north were themselves buried in *terra incognita*. The treasure trail through the New Delhi archives had petered out, and for weeks we received no documents at all, only piles of returned requisition slips that were covered in an unintelligible scrawl, the monotony of rejection compounded by the dull thud of a pole being whacked against the derelict office block outside the window. We sought out the Reading Room Superintendent.

'Of course it has meaning,' he reassured us, pushing the rejected slips around his desk like pieces of a jigsaw.

'What is this meaning?' he barked down the bakelite phone at the invisible men in the filing room, raging at them in broad Hinglish. 'Meaning, eh?'

He was trying.

'Never again. Never. They come here. And you are there. They go there and . . .'

But the handset at the other end of the line had been replaced long before, and even we could hear the buzzing of the discontinued tone as he raged on.

'Bloody fools. I will be reporting.'

The Reading Room Superintendent poked his finger through the skin on his tea and straightened his moustache. There was a shortage of bulbs, so the invisible men four floors above were moving them around the building on rotation, and currently the Burmans were in the dark. Their desks were too messy and they were 'lost in files'. Four of our requests were 'under search', not lost but 'maybe missing'. Two were 'possible secrets' that were never to be allowed down into the reading room. It was worth noting now that anything that included a map, a sketch or a likeness; or had any bearing on geography, topography or geology; that talked about borders or boundaries, the contiguity of two countries and their meeting at mountains, forests or valleys, was 'not allowed'. There we had it. We had been shown the field, and over the months to come we scrambled across it, and it was only the pedantry of the old Indian Civil Service filing clerks that saved the day. Every file had a duplicate and was cross-referenced to dozens of others, and soon we learned how to follow the paper-trail to track down material that had been missed by the modern-day censors, neatly folded paper packets, sealed with red wax and ribbon.

At last we found some of Burney's correspondence. His letters revealed that he had managed to make several trips up-river, disguising them as sight-seeing tours, and found that Bodawpaya's Embassy Route was still open and used by the Chinese. The Major observed 'a caravan of 1000 mules' arriving at an up-river settlement, bearing 'small panniers of bamboo work'. But while attempting a survey of a remote valley close to the Manipur border, through which flowed the Chindwin River, Lt McLeod, one of Burney's officers, struck a more fruitful seam. He sent back intelligence to Ava of something he called 'the much talked of serpentine mines':

> I have observed daily three or four boats going up and down the river. They are all bound for the Oroo [Uru] River . . . The noble serpentine is found on the bed of this stream at Mogaung, within one mile of which there are some hills from which it is also dug . . . Chinese merchants appear to monopolise this article . . . They come to the place above-mentioned annually and pay large sums of money for it . . . His Late Majesty employed 3000 men to procure some and they succeeded in transporting three large boulders of it to the capital, from which cups etc. were made.[14]

We know from his papers that Burney was well read and took a keen interest in the history of the country, so it is likely that he would have studied *The Itinerary of Ludovico di Varthema* and Fitch's account of his foray into northern Burma. McLeod's letter echoed their stories of a river valley brimming with stones, and Burney decided that the 'curious' trade on the Chindwin warranted further investigation. British India was already embroiled in a dispute between two rival 'Kakhyen' tribal chiefs in the north, and a forthcoming mission to mediate a settlement was secretly charged with investigating the source of this mysterious 'serpentine stone'.

In December 1835 Captain S. F. Hannay of the 40th Native Infantry was dispatched with Sepoy Supahee Singh on a mission to the Assam frontier with a 'sextant and artificial horizon borrowed from the Prince of Mukkhara'.[15] By January they had reached Mogaung, where they met Duffa Gam, one of the two warring chiefs, who recounted how his family had been butchered by his rival, Beesa Gam, who had also stolen 'a piece of noble serpentine stone as much as two men could carry'.[16] But before he had a chance to make plans to travel further north, Hannay was taken hostage by Mayouk Teza Naratta, the local governor and commander of a garrison of 800 soldiers, who insisted that the British officer return immediately to Ava.

When Burney heard of the crisis, he was at first perplexed. Until his court spies revealed the hand behind the crisis. 'A letter lately arrived here from the provincial government of Yunnan, remonstrating with the Court of Ava for having allowed an English officer to proceed to the northward and ascertain the route into China,' Burney wrote to William MacNaghton, the secretary to the Governor General of India, in Fort William. It had been followed by a deputation of Chinese merchants who had lobbied the Court against the British expedition. 'This remonstrance proceeded from a natural apprehension that the monopoly which they have long held of the whole trade to the north of Ava and of the produce of the serpentine mines might be disturbed by an English officer exploring the country.'[17]

Then a copy of a far more significant document, penned on yellow paper, marked with four seals and enclosed in a yellow silk bag bearing a dragon seal, fell into Burney's hands. Three Burmese traders, Nga Shue Ye, Nga Lo Tsan and Nga Lo-thank, had returned from Yunnan with a letter from the Chinese Emperor:

> With respect to younger brother's Empire. It is not proper to allow the English after they have made war, and peace has been settled, to remain in the city [Ava]. They are accustomed to act like Pipal Tree. Let not younger brother therefore allow the English to remain in his country and if anything happened, Elder Brother will attack, take and give.

Burney understood all too well Emperor Daoguang's reference to the pipal tree. 'Whenever this plant takes root, particularly if on old temples and buildings, it spreads and takes such firm hold that it's scarcely possible to remove it,' Burney noted in the margin for MacNaghton's benefit.

But the Emperor's warning had come too late. Hannay had persuaded his captors in Mogaung to allow Sepoy Singh to go on alone to the Assam border, trekking through the *Hukawng,* the Kachin's Valley of Death, while the British officer remained a hostage. The Burmese had insisted that Singh follow a circuitous route, but on his return the Sepoy bribed his guides to take him on a more westerly path through the *Pet Kai,* or Cook's Beak Mountains, that were populated by Naga tribes. 'Supahee [Singh] found them remarkably civil, in particular the principal chief,'[18] Hannay wrote to Burney. And it was this chief who revealed to Singh that he was standing on the secret Kasa Naga Road that unfurled towards *shwe-down-gyee,* the Great Golden Mountain, and eventually led into what the British called the 'serpentine mines'. The Sepoy made scrupulous notes:

The distance particularly between Mogoung and the Khyendwen [Chindwin River] is much more than the distance the map shows, but I have every reason to believe that the road is very winding and goes north as far as Nampoung Tsekain, and then strikes off nearly west to Kamain [Kamaing]. At Nam Santa commences the old Shan district called Tshay-yoma (meaning ten towns) which extends to the Khyendwen from Tainznoo to Phaho – the serpentine mines district.[19]

Hannay had also been busy in Mogaung. A merchant had been persuaded to part with specimens of a bright-green stone that the Captain also identified as serpentine, a material that the Burmese called *kyouktsein* and the Yunnanese called *Yü*. 'The Chinese choose pieces which although showing a rough and dingy coloured exterior have a considerable interior lustre, and very often contain spots and veins of a beautiful and bright apple green,' Hannay reported to Ava.

Burney immediately wrote to MacNaghton proposing 'that some pretext should be found for sending an officer from Assam to me here', enabling a British expedition to chart the secret Kasa Naga Road and investigate the mines.[20] Captain Hannay, who eventually returned unscathed to Ava, in July 1836, was ordered to Fort William to be debriefed, his field diaries, sketch maps and mineral samples dispatched ahead of him by express courier. But barely had the sweat dried on his brow than Hannay learned that instead of earning well-deserved leave, he was to immediately return to the jungle on a mission even more dangerous than the previous one, which had almost cost him his life.

Accompanied by Dr William Griffith, a 'hardy and active' scientist with a passion for exotic tea bushes,[21] Hannay was ordered to make an arduous overland journey through the North-East Frontier, beyond the British outpost of Guwahati, the capital of Assam, into no-man's-land. There they would attempt a jungle rendezvous with a British diplomat, Dr George Bayfield, Burney's deputy, who had been ordered to trek alone, up from the Burmese capital to the ancient Chinese stone pillars that demarcated the boundary between Assam and Burma. If Bayfield, a fluent Burmese speaker with some knowledge of the hill tribes and tropical medicine, managed to locate Hannay and Griffith, he would join them on the quest for the mines.

Bayfield, who had seen active service on previous postings as medical surgeon at Fort St George, in Madras, was a fluent reader of Pali and for the past three years had endured the hardships of Ava. Burney had a particular attachment to the resourceful doctor, as Bayfield had nursed him through several bouts of jungle fever and had found time to compile a verbose history of Burmese-British relations, a work that had earned the doctor a promotion and that today languishes, forgotten and mouldering, in the New Delhi archive.

If anyone stopped the three British explorers, they were to say that their mission was to placate the Beesa and Duffa Gams, to arbitrate in their dispute over a slaughtered family, the stolen serpentine boulder and contested territory at the border.

The Indian archive files give no hint of the foreboding that the three men must have felt after they were issued with their orders. Civil servants only wrote of an expedition propelled by the great 'spirit of inquiry' and brushed aside the dangers of crossing the baking plains and pinched hills of Assam that concealed tigers, snow leopards and head-hunting tribes. Without maps or any means of communicating with Dr Bayfield, it would be a miracle if they found each other at the ancient Chinese pillars. For Bayfield, a lone European officer, reliant entirely on Sepoy Singh's notes, it would be an even more precarious and exhausting 663 miles that would undoubtedly bring him into contact with the 'scowling savages' with strange fringed hair, 'exceedingly dirty and much addicted to drinking' – the feared Kachin.[22]

The files record how Hannay visited Fort William's 'shopping emporiums' to purchase a range of 'affluent articles' costing 1300 rupees, following the advice of Major Arthur White, British India's bombastic commanding officer at Guwahati. White, who would be responsible for escorting Hannay and Griffith to the frontier, had suggested that they buy gifts to 'charm the natives':

a few small articles of hardware – clasps, knives, large and small, scissors, needles, glass beads, all of which are of great importance to the Singpho [Kachin] chiefs . . . It would also be advisable for Captain Hannay to bring up about 12 red woolen chuddors and as many Muslim turbans and some rum.[23]

Hannay purchased 'a sextant, a false horizon, a nautical almanac for 1837, one large compass and one small pocket compass' while White requisitioned '150 Sepoys and five or six commissariat elephants' to accompany the mission into a region that he feared was gripped by a 'barbarous state of society'.

In Ava, the self-assured Bayfield was also shopping. He hired a *moonshee,* or Burmese clerk, two coolies and bought presents for the Kachins, including a 'gold ornament in the shape of a bugle'.[24] His men were to be dressed in scarlet 'to give them the appearance of the Company's troops and render them more formidable in the eyes of the Burmese'. They would also need shoes, as 'Burmah spikes are serious obstacles to bare feet' and each would have to carry a 26-pound pack that contained 'two hutting tools, two light *towrahs,* two felling axes, six *dahs* and six small native hooks'. They would also be required to stow the clothing and rations required by the expedition leader and his Sepoys:

> a loose bag dress made of light materials to be worn when actually crossing the hills, or other fatiguing duties, two blankets, a great coat for night use, one pair of mosquito curtains, two pairs light shoes, two pairs of white and two pairs of coloured trousers, two white and two check shirts, regimental cloth jacket and trousers, one flannel waistcoat, one regimental shakre, neckcloth and woollen night cap, one small metal plate, knife and fork, spoon and drinking cup. Eight seers of biscuit, eight seers of rice, one quart of spirits, 2 lb made up of ghee and salt.[25]

Accompanied by the 40th Regiment Bengal Sepoys, coolies, boatmen, servants and a 'liberated Assamese slave, who had found his way down to Ava in the train of a wandering fakeer', Bayfield departed from Ava at 11.30 a.m. on 13 December 1836 at double march. The doctor, with his entourage – 'me, my dog and musical boxes' – intended to cover 28 miles a day, despite the cloying humidity, the stiffness of his frock coat and the weight of his men's woollen shell jackets. How were they perceived as they sashayed across the Irrawaddy plain, their patent boots gleaming, the sun glinting off their sabres, the plumes on the officer's hat riding high above the elephant grass, a convoy of sashes and silk cords racing at a murderous pace, jogging past Burmese villagers who had learned to be languid in the unbearable heat?

Bayfield eventually arrived in the Mogaung Valley shortly after daybreak on 14 January 1837. 'Taking a gun and a guide', he marched for five days before reaching the gates of the stockade. Inside, more than 2000 Burmese troops, 'headed by the governor's elephants and ponies gaily caparisoned', surrounded the doctor, his crisp linen shirt caked in yellow dust and soaked with sweat. Something in their faces told him that all was not well. But before the doctor could retreat, he was 'surrounded by a crowd of people attracted by the presence of a white stranger', who pushed him forward to where Mogaung's Governor was waiting. Mayouk Teza Naratta, his reputation much enhanced by his detention of Captain Hannay eleven months before, was 'seated on a mat and a cushion at the head of his hall of reception'.

The Governor was jittery and for several days he prevented the doctor from leaving, stalling for time with stories of ambushes in the jungle, a slaughter on the path. The governor's guards sent on to arrange rice supplies in villages ahead all returned with news that, apparently, none was for sale. Instead of planning the route and accompanying the doctor towards the North-East Frontier, the Governor hid. 'My entreaties were of no avail. I could not persuade him [the Governor] to relinquish any part of the force that the King had given him for his protection and honour and as a means of enforcing obedience and respect from the Singphos of whom he was in some dread,' a furious Bayfield wrote to Burney. But his scribbled letters, sent almost daily, were delivered by foot messenger and would take weeks to reach Ava.

Instead of providing road-cutters and safe passage, when the Governor reappeared he engaged the doctor in incongruous conversations. Had Bayfield ever travelled to a 'large island three days sail across a narrow channel beyond China, inhabited by a very powerful race of men, five cubits high, with ears eight inches long and members generally of a still larger proportion'? The doctor 'confessed his ignorance' and instead unveiled his collection of musical boxes. But nothing would save him from the nightly honour of sitting at high table, participating in a pork feast, forced to chew on an 'uninviting black looking piece of the aforesaid unclean animal' that the governor had first 'torn to pieces with his finger [and] which had been a dozen times half down a mouth and throat'.

Finally, Bayfield could stand it no more and on 26 January, with no word from Ava, he decided to go it alone. He crept out of the stockade and into the jungle, leaving his supplies and baggage to follow, sending Governor Teza Naratta into paroxysms of fear. The doctor struck out at a 'double march' to make up for the time that had been wasted, pushing his men long into the night, when the steaming stillness came alive with the threat of ambushes, of marauding Kachin rebels rumoured to have occupied the track ahead. Now seven days later, he was in danger of missing his rendezvous with Hannay and Griffith and must have mulled over the disaster of being stranded in the jungle without supplies or ammunition.

What Burney had no way of conveying to Bayfield was that mad Sagaing Min had had a change of heart, having learned that Captain Hannay, a man that he had accused of intriguing with Duffa Gam, was to join the expedition at the Assam border. All hell had broken loose at Court and the King had threatened to shoot Hannay on sight if he ever set foot on Burmese soil, sending his orders on to Mogaung, where the Governor had become paralysed by fear of incurring his monarch's wrath. Burney dashed off a letter to Fort William warning that the Burmese were becoming increasingly nervous and sure to find out the true nature of the British expedition. A messenger was immediately dispatched from Fort William to intercept Hannay's party at the Assam border with new orders. 'Griffith and Bayfield must complete the mission alone.' But the letter would never arrive.

On 28 January Dr Bayfield's mood lifted as he spotted what Sepoy Singh had described as the Great Golden Mountain, but he also knew that he was now nearing the feared Kachin. 'Not to be taken by surprise, I had all our muskets loaded,' Bayfield scribbled in his journal, ever conscious that the absence of the Governor's promised troops made their life expectancy in the jungle that much shorter. He also had no guide, and one can only imagine him stumbling blindly through undergrowth, having to scale hills to see above the jungle canopy in vain attempts to glimpse the valleys of Assam.

For days that began at dawn and ended well after dusk, Bayfield waded 'wet up to the waist', sometimes the armpits, through 'tor-tuous rivers' and swamps, determined to make up time. But now the terrain began to slow down the expedition. 'Several of my party have severe colds and coughs, myself amongst the number,' Bayfield noted on 30 January. 'The natives attribute it to the drinking of the river water but it is more likely to be from constantly wading through it.'

The convoy passed under fringed, evergreen canopies, slicing through vines and bamboo with their bayonets and *dahs,* passing through rivers that 'abound with fish and jungles with elephants and many kinds of game'. By 3 February they were in the territory of the Marip Kachin and Bayfield at last began to flag, even though he had calculated that his party had made up for at least two lost days. 'Last night I was unable to lie down,' he wrote, obsessed by the thought that Hannay and Griffith would return to Fort William without him. 'I was kept awake by a cough nearly all night.' Not even the perfume from wild purple orchids that surrounded his camp could rouse the doctor from his funk.

The following day, no one could get out of bed. When they fi-nally hit the track at 10 A.M., they marched for only five hours. The noxious jungle was poisoning them all. The damp and humidity rotted their clothes and clogged their lungs. Their steady hands were tested by wild elephants and boars that charged from the un-dergrowth. Their nerves were jangled by the curdling screeches of brain-fever birds. Their noses were assailed by the rancid odour of musk beetles, crushed beneath their boots. Their skin crawled with blood flies and ticks. But anything or anyone that was observing the small party led by a bedraggled, fair-skinned man in a stained shirt and ripped twill trousers, did so in silence.

It was only a matter of days before they ran out of supplies, the Governor having made no arrangements to send on food, leaving them to forage for hairy figs that hung from vines above their heads. 'We have not yet received a single basket of rice,' Bayfield wrote on 8 February. 'The people are literally half-starved . . . and subsist upon young leaves, gathered in the neighbouring spot of for-est, and boiled with some rotten fish and salt, dignified with the name of *gnapie.*' Within a day his entries had become all the more stark. 'Three of the poor fellows have died, many have fevers . . . it is really pitiable to hear the incessant coughing during the whole night, and to witness the state of misery and want now existing among them,' the doctor scrawled.

Even though the Kachin had kept their distance from the crimson trail, they were very much in evidence. 'Cymbals and tom-toms' reverberated through the night. By 10 February even the stoic Bayfield was forced to admit, although only to his journal, that he now feared for his life. The doctor was by now utterly depressed by the ravages of the Kachin Hills, where the threat of a silent death from poisoned arrows constantly dogged the travellers:

> the wretched depravity and utter intellectual darkness of this people, the war of extermination in which some of them are constantly engaged, tribe against tribe, villages of the same race against each other, brother against brother, the strong against the weak, the ties . . . of friendship unknown by them, the brutalising effects of opium and spirits.

Bayfield pressed on, desperate to make his rendezvous and made up another two days, but the jungle was a labyrinth, and as often as not, the party ended up where they started: 'at 1 p.m. my further progress was arrested by thick jungle and after searching in vain for a footpath, I was reluctantly compelled to retrace my steps to the nearest water, distance 2½ miles, and halt for the night.'

The following morning the doctor was told that he had crossed over the secret Kasa Naga Road and learned that it hid 'secret subterranean passages that ran under the mountains'. Higher and higher his party climbed, shinning up spiralling paths in the foothills of the *Pet Kai* Mountains that rose to 7700 feet, elevations that he established by recording the boiling point of water. On 4 March the track had all but disappeared and the expedition slowed to a crawl. Bayfield and his men, who now knew that they were still two days late for the rendezvous with Hannay and Griffith, struggled on. All 'suffered much from leeches and dum-dum bites, of the former I have no less than 120 on my feet and legs which are swollen and painful, the itching occasioned . . . is intolerable', Bayfield scratched into his pocket-book.

The next morning they walked in silence, fingers of sunlight poking through the canopy. Then a cry from the trees high above ricocheted through the undergrowth like a rifle shot. Bayfield grabbed his musket and the party stopped dead in its tracks. He whispered for his men to run for cover and they ducked behind mulberry bushes, some face down in the crawling loam, the putrid smell of decomposition filling their nostrils. One of Bayfield's sepoys dashed back through the undergrowth with terrible news. 'A party of Nagas were observed to issue from the forest . . . they were carrying the baggage of a European officer.' It seemed that the head-hunters had claimed a British scalp, and Bayfield ordered his men to engage the treacherous tribes with 'a volley or two'.

Crouching in silence. Watching the thicket. Waiting for tattooed faces. Listening for the hiss of a poisoned arrow. And then two ragged shapes burst through a curtain of bamboo. Captain Hannay and Dr Griffith charged like bull elephants towards Bayfield. They were alive. If the good doctor was delighted at having stumbled across his fellow explorers after more than 70 days alone, his diary does not reflect it. Instead, the reserved Englishman dwelt on another impending disaster, news brought by Hannay and Griffith. Neither side had more than two days of supplies. Major White, who was to have restocked the party for its return to Ava, had turned on his heels and headed back to Guwahati, claiming a 'scarcity of provisions and the irruption of a party of Singphos in his rear'.

As the starving men considered their options, the Governor of Mogaung arrived on the scene, accompanied by local warlords and 1000 Burmese soldiers. Here, face to face around the campfire, were Captain Hannay and his former jailer, who had been ordered to kill him. Hannay was forced to retreat into British territory on the condition that Bayfield and Griffith would be allowed to go on alone. On 18 February they set off east-south-east towards Sepoy Singh's marker for the secret Kasa Naga Road, plunging down the sheer slopes of the southern *Pet Kai*.

It was the end of March before they spotted the outline of the Great Golden Mountain, but before them was an immense tract of teak jungle fogged by wood-smoke. They were in the 'jungly and evil place' that Hannay had warned them of, the territory of the Marip Kachin, who were 'exceedingly treacherous and deceitful and ready to commit murder on any grounds, either for revenge or for the sake of plunder'. As they inched forward Hannay's warning rang in their ears:

> the Kakhyns seem to carry their ideas that if a child or any individual of a family is drowned accidentally, the whole proceed in a body and cut at the water with their *dahs* or swords, showing the intent of killing. In the same spirit if an individual is either hurt or killed by falling from a tree they immediately hack it down and cut it into small pieces. It is thus they mutilate and cut up the bodies of their enemies, sparing neither age nor sex.[26]

Slowly Griffith and Bayfield moved south-east, their creeping paranoia compounded at night when, sitting inside a ring of fires, they listened to the bellow of elephants. Or was it Sladen's *Jaiwa* invoking the *nats*? For six days more they hacked through the jungle, covering a distance of 103 miles, before emerging at last at Kamaing, a settlement of 60 bamboo houses that Sepoy Singh had been told was the last outpost before the mines. It was 'a mean and paltry town' and only a small shed was reluctantly set aside by its chief for their accommodation.[27]

Soon Bayfield and Griffith were surrounded 'by all the village men, women and children', who listened slack-jawed as the British informed them that they intended to visit the 'far famed serpentine mines'. The chief, puffing on a silver opium pipe, his head wrapped in a silk turban, his face concealed by a ragged moustache, peered at them with snake eyes. He had listened to their entreaties for more than an hour and then swept away without uttering a word. For several days Bayfield and Griffith waited for a message from the chief, filling in time by strolling around the ramshackle town, seeing all it had to offer in an hour. They bought up supplies of rice and dried fish in the morning market and attempted to entice surly Shan and Chinese merchants into conversation, but all of them sat in silence, conspiring beneath sackcloth, their fingers entwined in a secret dance that neither man understood. At last Bayfield and Griffith found a lone trader sitting in the shade of a pipal tree, who accepted some gifts and talked about precious stones.

He told them that Peesae Nong, a Kachin warlord from the Marip clan, controlled the mines, but refused entry to Shan and Chinese traders and to all foreigners, who were forced to wait in

Mogaung for boulders to be dragged out of the valley by elephants, floated down the river on bamboo rafts and then auctioned on the bank. Before a sale, a thin slice was shaved from the surface of each rock, creating a small window to which the Chinese merchants would hold a candle in an attempt to glimpse what lay inside. (Was this why the Han poets described *fei cui* as a stone 'that glowed as if lit by a hidden flame'?) Then the haggling would begin. And Bayfield recalled the journals of Caesar Fredericke who had anchored off the Burmese coast in 1567. The Venetian merchant had witnessed a secretive sales method employed by gem dealers who 'have their handes under a cloth, and by touching of fingers and nipping the joynts they knowe what is done, what is bidden and what is asked.'[28] Nothing much had changed.

Only after the sale had been completed could the merchants crack open their boulders, roasting them over fires until the stones fizzed and split. A handful left the fire-pits wealthy men, but many more turned to drink. 'When the skin of jade is one inch thick, even the Immortals cannot guess what lies within', the Chinese used to say, but that didn't stop thousands of them from holding a light to the rock or running amok in a drunken rage when their boulders crumbled to dust.[29] China's passion had made the Kachin rich, as Bodawpaya had promised in 1793.

After seemingly talking for hours, the trader at last told Bayfield and Griffith what they wanted to know: how to reach the legendary valley of green stones. Drawing in the sand with a stick, he mapped the final stages of their journey. Two crosses marked the twin peaks of Loi Lem and Loi Law, between which they would have to pass along a wiggling line that represented the Kasa Naga Road. When it crossed the 'Ooroo Stream', drawn with dashes in the dirt, a four-day journey of 51 miles north-west, they would reach the mouth of the 'treasure well', marked with a cross.

William Griffith quickly copied the map into a pocket-book and on 2 April, having at last hired a willing guide and overcome 'slight opposition on the part of the village chief', the two men set off. Almost immediately their coolies, petrified by the prospect of trespassing in the Kachin's secret valley, protected as it was by wraiths and serpents, deserted. Bayfield and Griffith raced on alone through waves of labourers. Thousands of Shans, Chinese and Assamese, all of whom appeared to be heading at great speed in the opposite direction, carried with them huge hunks of serpentine. None of them would stop to answer questions.

Bayfield and Griffith began each day at 5 a.m. and, on the third morning, they entered a 'complete forest of wild plantains and some very fine teak', criss-crossed by 'numerous elephant tracks'. Every two miles forward their path split at least two ways, and they gambled on their route as they pressed towards the hidden valley. As the heat and humidity struck down their few remaining porters, they discarded their baggage by the path.

They spent the night of 4 April camped on a narrow plain bounded on the west by the Kawa-Bhoom mountains, and rose before sunlight at 5.27 a.m. marching north-west to a large open forest, their boots no longer blistering their feet, their damp clothes no longer chafing their skin. At 6 a.m. they stopped for breakfast, picking at rice and pork fat, as they had done now for months, but on this morning it tasted like a feast. And by 7.15 a.m. they were back on the road and 'commenced the tortuous ascent' through a bamboo forest, reaching the summit by 8.36 a.m. At a height of 2799 feet Bayfield and Griffith could spy the valleys below and glimpsed to the south 'the great lake Eng-dau-gyih', beneath which they had been told lay a sunken royal city of a long-forgotten king.

It was as if they were following in the footsteps of Sindbad on his second voyage. According to the tenth-century story-teller Abu 'Abd Allah ibn 'Abdus al-Jashyari, from the top of such a hill the sailor had spied a 'Valley of Serpents' that was 'exceeding great and wide and deep and bounded by vast mountains that spired high in the air'. Sindbad's valley was littered with diamonds and 'swarmed with snakes and vipers, each big as a palm tree that would have made but one gulp of an elephant'. In his story of 'perils and terrors' Sindbad had learned that local merchants 'take a sheep and slaughter and skin it and cut it in pieces and cast them down from the mountain tops into the valley-sole, where the meat, being fresh and sticky with blood, some of the gems cleave to it.'[30] And later it would be claimed that these stories woven by the merchants of Basra originated from the very spot on which the two Englishmen now stood.

Down the western slope Bayfield and Griffith stumbled, past giant cocoons hanging from the trees decorated with painted skulls, until they reached an alkaline spring where a handful of labourers were sluicing cakes of yellow dust off their burnished skin. Hauling off their shirts, both men plunged into the soft, sweet water. At 10.30 a.m., after a march of nine miles, Bayfield and Griffith reached the lip of a valley and looked down into a 'narrow strip about 20 miles in length and varying in breadth from 200 to 800 yards, bounded on the east by the Kawa-Bhoom'. All around were hills rising to 1000 feet and, according to the map in Griffith's pocket-book, this was 'the serpentine mine'.

But where was the great city of labour, the conscripted gangs of miners, the burning bamboo diviners and teams of diggers, and where were the green gems said to stud the sides of the valley? Bayfield and Griffith had slipped over the lip expecting to find the source of legends, the spring of myths, but all that they could see was the gaping jaws of a derelict mine. 'Nothing, in fact, like a pit or a shaft exists, nor is there anything to repay one for the tedious marches from Kamein,' the desolate Griffith wrote in his pocket-book. 'I did not see the manner by which they work or the tools they employ.'

The two explorers' dreams of discovery were dashed as they stood in a malarial vale of mud. While Bayfield half-heartedly mapped out their co-ordinates – latitude 25 and 26 degrees north and longitude 96 and 97 degrees east – Griffith slung a few rough stone specimens into his canvas bag. A handful of grubby Kachin teenagers, scavenging through a spoil heap, laughed scornfully. The mines, they cried, were finished. There were no more good stones. Everyone was leaving. 'The best sort is said to be getting yearly more scarce and the stone that the merchants willingly buy would not formerly have found a purchaser,' Bayfield noted, concluding that the 'far famed serpentine mines' had been worked to death.

There was nothing to do but climb out of the valley and begin the long journey back to Ava, made even more intolerable by bitter disappointment. They trudged back into the 'mean and paltry town' but that night, as they packed canoes to take them back down to Mogaung, the village chief appeared 'foaming with rage'.

He seized their boats and remaining bales of supplies. 'As he spoke he drew himself up to me [in] so threatening and insolent a manner, that I was compelled to put forth my hand and push him away,' Bayfield wrote. '[He] and one of his followers instantly drew their swords and flourished them about in so ominous a manner, cutting up the grass and earth . . . that . . . being totally unarmed, I considered myself in some jeopardy.' Even though they had seen absolutely nothing, the chief had been reprimanded for allowing the foreigners to travel to the mines.

Forced to 'surrender' their canoes, Bayfield and Griffith set off on 'a fatiguing march of 25 miles' before reaching Mogaung and, as they hacked their way through the undergrowth, the monsoon pitched into Burma on a clap of thunder. The two men emerged mud-soaked from the jungle after five days only to fall into yet another disaster. Mogaung, partially flooded, was being evacuated. Burma had descended into a 'state of rebellion'. In a palace coup, mad Sagaing Min had been ousted from the Lion Throne by Prince Tharawaddy, his brother turned jailer. There were reports that hundreds of court officials had been crucified and disembowelled. Now cut-throats employed by the Prince were said to be roaming the countryside. Mr Kincaid, one of Bayfield's colleagues in Ava, had been captured by 'roving bands and murdered'. And as the water rose and the rain poured, it slowly dawned on Bayfield and Griffith that they were marooned. Day after day they sat on the riverbank, soaked by the monsoon, waiting dejectedly for a boat. '11th: still no news. 12th: still no news. 13th: came to the determination to wait rather than retreat into Assam.'

There was even a story galloping around the stockade that Prince Tharawaddy had ordered his mercenaries to capture the serpentine mines, and now they were on their way to Mogaung. On 19 March the stockade finally erupted, a keg of paranoia set alight by whispers. Muskets were fired 'in a most disorderly manner', crowds thronged the muddy streets and, in the midst of the confusion, Bayfield and Griffith seized their only opportunity. They stole some oars and made a break for the river, leapt aboard the single boat that was waiting, only to see the boatman dive over the side and into the rapids, screaming that he dared not take them to Ava. And so the explorers set off from Mogaung alone, slapped by sheets of rain, all the time the Irrawaddy swelling, its waters rising 'by more than 18 inches every hour', concealing razor-sharp rocks that threatened to splinter their canoe.

They were swept through the Elephant and Cow Defiles 'at the rate of 12 and 15 miles an hour'. Every bank-side village was now deserted, every riverside town danced with fires set by arsonists, headless corpses floating by, strapped to bamboo rafts. The battered boat raced past the ruins of Amarapura that now crackled with fire, and finally, on 5 May, the dishevelled travellers floated into Ava as the crown was placed on King Tharawaddy's head.

British Resident Henry Burney was dumbfounded by Bayfield's reappearance at the capital after an absence of five months and two days. 'I was agreeably surprised to see my assistant Dr Bayfield and Dr Griffith,' Burney remarked in his usual dead hand. The very next day, after Bayfield and Griffith had been presented to the King, 'who received us in a most engaging manner and talked much affably and kindly', the entire British delegation was banished from court altogether, exiled to Rangoon from where, even armed with a telescope, nothing of importance could be spied.

Four

The Palace Plunderers

A sharp rap at the cracked lacquered door announced the arrival of an Imperial escort at the drab single-storey home in *Hsi-la hutong*, Peking's Pewter Lane. Inside, Little Orchid was waiting impatiently. The solemn sixteen-year-old, with a glossy mane, that coiled down her back like molasses, had been ready for the Emperor's envoys before dawn. Pacing the cloisters, rehearsing her kowtow, she had kept her family awake for hours with the click of her porcelain platform slippers on the flag-stone floor.[1]

Since childhood, she had jealously watched aristocratic processions entering the Forbidden City through its blind battlements, half a mile west of her home in the Tartar City, a maze of grey houses that were painted in dull shades by order, so that the Imperial court, wrapped in yellow and scarlet, appeared all the more brilliant. But on this day finally dawning, 14 June 1852, an Imperial procession was waiting outside her door and a unique opportunity beckoned. Xianfeng, the indolent nineteen-year-old Emperor, whose name meant 'Universal Prosperity', was about to complete 27 months of mourning for his late father the Emperor Daoguang. Court etiquette stipulated that the Son of Heaven should soon resume his physical life. The pageant of fertility was about to begin. A decree had been issued by Xianfeng's step-mother, the Dowager Empress, ordering all suitable daughters of Manchu aristocrats to present themselves at the Imperial Household Office.[2] Girls with buck teeth whose 'hairs are growing in the wrong direction' were instructed not to apply, but hundreds of others, who met the Imperial criteria, would soon clog the streets with their sedan chairs.[3] Only 60 would be permitted to enter the citadel, and this group would eventually be whittled down to a select group of 28.

Little Orchid's maids had dressed her in jewellery and silks borrowed from friends and family who all hoped to shine in her reflected glory. Fragrant oils would have been massaged into the girl's scalp to mask any lingering kitchen odours, and her thick, uncut mane had been tamed with rich pomade before being wrapped around the butterfly-shaped wooden frame of her headdress, its upper edge strengthened by a *bianfang*, a flat spatula of jade. Her winged coiffure resembled the fanned tail of a peacock, and the teenager's maids had adorned it with jewelled fruits and auspicious symbols of longevity, happiness and fertility. Peaches and pomegranates fashioned from pearls and coral, writhing fish, three-legged frogs and iridescent butterflies carved from Qianlong's Stone of Heaven. The confectionery of delight quivered with every step, accentuating her perfect Manchu features: a long, graceful neck; a high, wide forehead and an oval face that, according to a Chinese saying, shone like the moon.

Her young skin hidden beneath a thick pancake of white lead, her eyes dusted with a hint of rose, her lower lip painted with a glistening vermilion teardrop, the mask sprinkled with glycerine to stop it melting, she could have passed as a singer in the Peking Opera. The doors were opened and Little Orchid hoisted up her robe to step over a gutter clogged with duck fat and tea leaves. Flowing down to her ankles, covering her tiny hands with its horse-hoof cuffs, her shimmering silken robe was sown with a sea of tiny precious stones and seed pearls. Clambering awkwardly into the yellow satin sedan chair, Little Orchid was whisked to the Tiananmen Gate, where she would be introduced at court by her formal family title of Yehenara.

As the sun rose over the monotone Tartar City, a pall of yellow dust swept down from the Mongolian steppe. It was buffeted and blown out of narrow alleyways by a stream of yellow sedans that chased towards Tiananmen Gate.[4] Every door and window thrown open, thousands straining for a glimpse of the jostling chairs, strings of fire-crackers dancing from eves and gables, bearers blinded by gun-powder flashes and shreds of scarlet paper. Eunuchs called out names from a shortlist of candidates whose chairs were pulled through the scuffle towards the great Meridian Gate. Yehenara was among those welcomed by the chant, 'Li la, doula', 'Have come, have arrived'.[5]

Sixty girls emerged blinking from their curtained carriages and rustled over the five marble bridges that spanned the Jade Belt River, crossing the cobbled expanses of the Forbidden City's outer courtyards, their awkward platform slippers hung with fringes of pearls and jade.

Past bronze incense burners, storks, dragons and turtles that filled the air with plumes of fragrant smoke, through the Gate of Supreme Harmony, beside the gilded columns of the Son of Heaven's throne-room, the procession swung towards the Western Palaces. These were an intricate network of apartments, courtyards and flagstone corridors that promised a secret life of luxury for those who won a place inside. The Imperial candidates were entering the domain of butterball eunuchs who, in their make-up and gaudy robes, fussed and cooed around them.

As the doors closed behind her, Yehenara would have known that if she passed the forthcoming tests she would forsake her right to associate with any man other than the Emperor. Successful candidates would never again leave the Western Palace precincts unescorted and Peking would become a city of sounds: a crash of carts, the shrill of voices, a song of the lotus seller floating over the walls. In reality the Western Palaces were a prison that the eunuchs guarded as possessively as they did the glass jars that contained their severed testicles, bitter keepsakes of lives that had been taken away. To the Manchu noblemen, the future their daughters now vied for represented the ultimate privilege, but to one foreigner who learned of the customs of the court, the Western Palace appeared to him as a 'terrible dream in which a series of corridors opens up, then closes again, preventing you from ever getting out.'[6]

We know from the records of the *Nei Wu Fu*, the Imperial Household Department, that its staff were waiting to examine each girl astrologically, mentally and physically. In search of auspicious signs, Yehenara's horoscope of five lucky characters would have been studied, as would her genealogy and the circumstances of her birth. She would have been asked to read aloud from the Classics in

Manchu and Mandarin, before courtiers rubbed her face with wet fingers to ensure that she had not concealed 'celestial flowers' or pock-marks beneath her make-up.[7] The teenager's neck would have been inspected for signs of goitre – the disfigurement caused by iodine deficiency that afflicted so many Chinese in the nineteenth century. And then a midwife would have ordered her to lie on a couch. The physical examination was a feared and embarrassing test, and some in the West would later claim that to get through it, Yehenara demonstrated her resourcefulness:

> Yehenara wore a pair of valuable jade bracelets. Wise beyond her years, she knew that when she lay on the couch in the examination room, the practised hand of a midwife would discover in a second whether or not she was a virgin. When her turn came at last, she went into a theatrical tantrum and indignantly refused to be pawed over. As she did . . . she deftly slipped off the costly bracelets, and unseen by the eunuchs, dropped them into the eagerly waiting hand of the midwife. For an instant the two women's eyes met and locked in a glitter of mutual understanding. Finally, the elder nodded her head; and [Yehenara] was able to stand in line with the other selected maidens.[8]

We know from Ming and Qing sex guides that equally important to virginity was a concubine's ability to exude the right amount of *yin,* a primordial essence that was one half of the building-block on which the Chinese universe rested. The term that literally meant 'hidden' or 'dark' was said to have been identified in 2700 BC by Emperor Shen Nung and by the time of the Qing, it had also come to represent a woman's vagina and, more practically, a concubine's ability to become aroused and to arouse.

The *Yü-fang-pi-chüeh* or the Secret Prescription for the Bedchamber, an explicit sixth-century Daoist book, taught midwives that *yin* could be determined by examining a woman's vagina, breasts, hair, eyes and speech. 'A man should select for his sexual partners young women whose breasts have not yet developed and who are well-covered with flesh. They should have hair fine as silk and small eyes . . . Face and body should be smooth and speech harmonious,' it prescribed.[9] The *T'ai-ch'ing-ching,* an ancient book of physiognomy, was even more explicit:

suitable women are naturally tender and docile, and of gentle mien. They are neither too tall, nor too short, neither too fat nor too thin. The labia of the vulva should be well-developed. They should have no pubic hair and the vagina should be moist. During the sexual act their vagina should produce rich secretions and their body should move so that one can hardly keep them under control.

The didactic *Yü-fang-pi-chüeh* also ruled on what was not wanted in the bedchamber: women with 'dishevelled hair and coarse face ... protruding adam's apple ... and manly voice, a large mouth and long nose, eyes which are bloodshot or yellowish, long hairs on upper lips or cheeks resembling whiskers'.

Finally, having been poked, prodded and measured, Yehenara was among the 28 perfect specimens that were herded into the Manchu gynaeceum, where they were all paraded before the Dowager Empress, who awarded each of them a position in the Son of Heaven's seraglio. Every girl aspired to become a *huangguifei, guifei* or *fei* (Imperial consort, high consort or consort) as only women of these ranks could bear the Emperor's child. But most would become *bing,* Imperial concubines, who, like the *guiren, changzai* and *daying* below them, the lesser concubines, rarely slept with the Son of Heaven at all, and only then to arouse him before one of the senior members of his harem was carried into the bed-chamber.

Unfortunately for Yehenara, she was inducted as a *guiren,* in a palace where 3000 women and 3000 eunuchs serviced the court and the Emperor. Yehenara now received cat's-eye or *fei cui* jew-ellery, a pair of triple-hoop ear-rings, two bangles and a 108-bead necklace punctuated by three plum-size stoppers. Her name was in-scribed on a jade tablet that was placed in the Emperor's bed-room.[10] Every evening the Son of Heaven would turn over the name jade of his desired playmate and his eunuchs were dispatched to the gynaeceum to see that his choice was stripped naked, ensuring that she carried no weapon, before being bathed in perfumed oils and depilated.[11]

Yehenara and her competitors were stabled behind paper win-dows in rows of small box-like apartments around open court-yards, constantly waiting for the order to attend the Eastern Warm

Chamber. Although it could be years before she got her chance, if at all, she was always on call, ready to entertain the bored young Emperor.

The Qing annals state that within a few months of entering the Forbidden City Yehenara moved into the *Chang Chun Gong,* or Palace of Eternal Spring, an ancient teak villa with heated flagstone floors, where Xiang Fei, Qianlong's Fragrant Consort, was also said to have once lived. By the time Yehenara was enrolled as a *guiren,* Xiang Fei's story had become palace folklore, a morality play for concubines, all of whom dreamed of capturing an Emperor's heart. Such was the clamour for all things related to the flower girl from Kashgar that society ladies now demanded to be painted in the style of the Xiang Fei portrait by Castiglione, artists throughout the Middle Kingdom churning out scores of copies. The fragrant flower girl's story was also set to music. The *Flag Cloth Opera* had become one of the most popular of the 1000 plays and operas in the Palace repertoire, and we know from Imperial court records that Yehenara visited the *Chang-yin-ge,* or Pavilion of Joyful Music, where she would have been entertained by a tale of love, betrayal, jealousy and death.

The Flag Cloth Opera presented a very different story of the fragrant flower girl from that which had emerged during Qianlong's day. Claiming to be based on contemporary historical research, this version was a stark tragedy of a Muslim girl betrayed by a fellow concubine. As the cymbals shimmered in the Pavilion of Joyful Music and the players entered, the soughing of the seven-stringed *ch'in* floated down from the gallery to the audience below, reclining on Chinese *chaise longues.* It was 1760. Alone in the Western Palaces, frightened by the strange, cold citadel, the young country girl, played by a smooth-skinned boy, was befriended by Ying Fei, the Emperor's favourite consort, who was startled by her new companion's ethereal beauty and smell. The jealous Ying Fei hatched a plot, teaching the Fragrant Consort to stand while the Emperor sat and to talk before he had spoken, sure that Xiang Fei would be banished. But Qianlong laughed at the country girl's waywardness and loved her all the more.

When the Dowager Empress prepared to celebrate her seventieth birthday, Ying Fei struck again. She advised the naive Xiang Fei to embroider a pillow cover with a single phoenix in a tree, but the gift concealed a hidden message. The phoenix was the symbol of an Empress, but standing on its own in a tree it surely meant that she would die unloved. Xiang Fei was sentenced to death in the Emperor's absence and, as the Peking players' voices rose in a crescendo, she declared: 'If I die the Emperor will know the truth.' Grabbing a knife, she stabbed herself through the heart. As the curtain fell, the stage awash with tears and cries, the Emperor could be seen weeping over his beloved Xiang Fei, her body encased in a lacquered casket, her head-dress adorned with pearls, diamonds, rubies, cat's eyes and *fei cui*.[12]

Low-ranking concubines could only ever grasp a few fleeting moments to shine brightly enough to attract their Emperor's attention. Like fire-flies, most would burn out, abandoned in the Palace for Forgotten Concubines. So this rags-to-riches melodrama would have struck a chord with Yehenara, who, like Xiang Fei, was beginning her long climb from a position of disadvantage.

Hardly anything is recorded in the Imperial chronicles about her social pedigree and little is known about how she entered the race to the Dragon Bed. What we do know is that she was almost certainly born on 29 November 1835, probably the daughter of a midranking Manchu military official of the Blue Bordered Banner whose name was possibly Hui-cheng.[13] We found the girl from Pewter Lane listed in the Imperial archives as Yehenara, signifying that she was a child of the Yehe tribe of the Nara clan. Beyond that, claims about her antecedence vary wildly. Some say that a soothsayer called Fu oversaw her birth 'at the Hour of the Tiger' witnessing 'a great flash of light'.[14] The mysterious Fu examined the infant and found on her chest the outline of a fox, an ambiguous symbol in China that was seen as both good and evil, representing cunning and stealth.[15] For those who invested much in this dubious story, the fox-shaped birthmark linked the infant to an ancient prophecy. '[Qing] rule . . . would someday be ended forever by a great woman of the Yehenara clan bearing the mark of the fox.'[16]

Others would claim that her father died when she was three years old, leaving his family in penury.[17] One rumour spread by antiManchu scandal-mongers had the teenage Yehenara purchased from a Canton brothel as a sex slave for the Emperor.[18]

Some embellished this theme of licentiousness, claiming that Yehenara's father was addicted to gambling, his opium pipe and to sniffing the bound feet of Han Chinese prostitutes, an erotic delicacy of the time.[19] To finance his multitude of bad habits, he was said to have forced his young daughter onto the street to sing by the highway, often in tears, while her sister shoved a tattered Manchu cap towards passers-by. Even more fanciful was a claim that would gain ground in 1930s Shanghai that the teenager's pale white skin was evidence that she was the product of a secret tryst between her Manchu grandmother and a White Russian lover.[20] The only biographical account that stakes a claim to authenticity is written by her lady-in-waiting. 'I have had a very hard life ever since I was a young girl,' Yehenara was reported to have complained to her companion. 'I was not a bit happy when with my parents, as I was not the favourite. My sisters had everything they wanted, while I was, to a great extent, ignored altogether.'[21] Tarnished by so many salacious rumours, it is amazing that Yehenara got beyond Tiananmen Gate. There is no record of how she engineered her entrance, although at this time Qing officials were certainly open to bribery. Maybe her family had the money to pave their daughter's way, but it is more likely that her undisputed radiance won her the coveted place in the Western Palaces. 'A lot of people were jealous of me, because I was considered to be a beautiful woman at that time,' Yehenara was said to have gloated to her aide.[22]

⊠

The Emperor's concubines had little to do but chatter like mynahs in a *cloisonné* cage, but the eternal tick of the English clocks that Qianlong had placed throughout his palaces would have reminded Yehenara that time was of the essence. She must have been haunted by the prospect of ending up locked away in the Palace of Forgotten Concubines. So she chose to study. Sitting beneath painted mottos that urged, 'If you read all of the books you will understand the past and the future',[23] Yehenara began to immerse herself in the history of the Qing Dynasty, its calligraphy and the wealth of Imperial artefacts that surrounded her. Riveted by the stories of the Khotan fisher-folk, she was said to have even trained her fingers to feel the Stone of Heaven, blindfolded, learning to appreciate the smooth, hard skin of the jewel as it warmed in her palm. But the one story that truly bewitched her was that of *fei cui*, a jewel that had become so popular at court that it had now eclipsed Confucius' touchstone and become widely known as Imperial Green Jade.[24]

Yehenara's studies and investigations into Imperial Green Jade would certainly have brought her into contact with the iconography of Xiang Fei, the piles of portraits, some by Castiglione, of a pale-skinned girl with piercing blue eyes. It might have been now that she also uncovered the story of the Fragrant Consort's Persian Pepper. She undoubtedly knew that the pepper or *jiao* was a symbol of the Empress, whose apartments in the Palace were known as *Jiao Fang* or the Pepper Rooms and whoever possessed Imperial Green Jade, especially a piece carved into an Empress' emblem, would be edging ever closer to the realm of the Eastern Warm Chamber.

The occupants of the Western Palaces would have overheard the rumours that while Emperor Xianfeng desperately needed an heir, he led a life of fruitless debauchery. By all accounts he was a sickly man who by 1855 had only produced one daughter by Li Fei, his favourite consort. His Empress Niuhuru, an insipid girl two years younger than Yehenara, had failed to produce any children at all. It was rumoured that this Son of Heaven preferred the company of male opera singers to that of the women of the court.

Confined to the gynaeceum, Lady Yehenara would have been lucky to catch even a glimpse of the Emperor. But her meticulous attention to detail and her studious and radiant demeanour soon won plaudits from the court. In August 1855, the Qing annals reveal that Yehenara was promoted to *bing*, doubling her quota of eunuchs and handmaidens to four of each and earning the right to be addressed as Lady Yehenara.[25] Now she was able to stroll in the gardens of the Summer Palace and, according to one florid account, it was here that the Emperor found her singing in the summer of 1855:

> he heard from a grove close by a delicate voice trilling a Southern air. Greatly charmed, the monarch proceeded to make the acquaintance of the fair singer. This was his first meeting with Yehonala . . . She proved herself an adept flatterer, and was clever enough not to prove servile.[26]

It was not long before Xianfeng overturned Lady Yehenara's jade tablet. When a eunuch told her that her presence was required she would have recited the well-practised phrase, 'The Emperor's wish shall be granted.' Wrapped in a scarlet cloak, she would have been delivered *bei gong*, carried to the Emperor on the back of a eunuch, a tradition that dated to the Han Dynasty, when concubines were unable to walk unaided after their feet were unbound for sex.

The triumphant Lady Yehenara was deposited naked at the foot of the Dragon Bed. Behind a swathe of crepe curtains lay the Emperor, reclining on a heated kang, atop three thick mattresses of yellow brocade, beneath a rainbow of silk sheets draped with a coverlet of yellow satin, the air perfumed by sachets of lavender and jujube flowers. Framing the alcove were red banners that proclaimed his prowess in battle and in love, his fertility and longevity. Eunuchs were posted inside and outside the room that was now known as the Jade Chamber.

Etiquette required Lady Yehenara to crawl up the prone Emperor's legs, begging the Son of Heaven to share his 'celestial fireworks'. The scene that would have followed was intertwined with Confucian values and set in the philosopher's most virtuous stone. In the multitude of Chinese historic handbooks that would have been studied by Xianfeng, a penis was known as the Jade Stalk and a woman's vagina was the Jade Garden that a man entered through the Jade Gate to stimulate her Jade Veins and Jewel Terrace. And once the couple were in their rhythm, the concubine was expected to exude Jade Fluids from her Jade Fountain and the bedchamber would be filled with her Jade Perfume of love.

On this first encounter, Lady Yehenara would have been expected to know very little about *Fang-chung* or the Art of the Bedchamber. This hotchpotch of erotica, fertility and mysticism bound Imperial procreation in complex Daoist sexual rules that required Xianfeng to build his *yang*, his 'vital essence' or semen, that represented heaven, sun, fire and light. The stronger the Emperor's *yang*, the more powerful his Spirit of the Vale or fertility, that was also enhanced by the use of potions. In the final chapter of the *Tung-hsüan-tzû*, a sexual reference book from the Three Kingdoms and Six Dynasties (AD 221—581), instructions were given for an elixir whose main ingredient was powdered jade. The stone was ground up with stems of fresh *rehmannia lutea,* two grams of cinnamon, five grams of *glycyrrhiza glabra,* two grams of *atractylis ovata* and five grams of *kan-ch'i* or dry lacquer. Having been sieved, a 'square inch of the powder' was added to wine and consumed three times a day. Other concoctions used *boschniakia glabra,* a plant resembling an erect penis, or deer horn, also chosen for its phallic shape.

To arouse the Emperor and increase the power of his *yang,* explicit guides like *The Manual of Lady Mystery, Secret Codes of the Jade Room* and *Recipes for Nursing Potency,* some of which dated back to the Han Dynasty, were pored over. They all invoked the sixty-third hexagram of the *I Ching* that discussed the important matter of *chi-chi* or intercourse, the act of completion. But while the Emperor was supposed to *chi-chi* with as many concubines as possible, bringing them all to orgasm, he was not allowed to ejaculate. Every time he succeeded in containing himself while pleasing his partner, he increased his *yang* and added twelve years to his life – or so the Ming sexologists claimed.

To spice up what in theory could become quite a tedious exercise, the eight handbooks that made up the *Art of the Bedchamber* exhorted the Emperor to try out numerous exotic couplings. Elaborate variations on the missionary position included 'Reeling off silk', 'Flying Seagulls' or 'Winding Dragons'. If the Emperor wished to take his concubine from behind he could adopt the 'Three-Year-Old Donkey', the 'Jumping White Tiger' or the 'Dark Cicade Cleaving a Tree'. When the Emperor wanted his concubine on top he could ask her to perform 'Cat and Mouse in One Hole', 'Fluttering Butterflies' or even 'Phoenix Holding its Chicken'. The narrator, one Master Tung-hsüan, concluded that these positions were 'most effective indeed' and 'encompassed all possibilities'. He beseeched the practitioner to 'probe their wonderful meaning to its very depth'.

Lady Yehenara would have been encouraged to take an active part, but to ensure that Xianfeng savoured his *yang,* he would have been taught from the *Classic of the Immortals* to pinch his seminal duct on the verge of climax and 'inhale deeply and gnash his teeth scores of times, without holding his breath. Then the semen will be activated but yet not be emitted; it returns from the Jade Stalk and enters the brain.'

There were other inventive and compelling methods of restraining the Emperor, including a soft ring of flesh stripped from an eyelid of a sheep that was rolled down over his penis. The eyelashes that were still attached to the ring of flesh would stimulate a woman to climax, brushing against her clitoris, while gripping the penis so hard that ejaculation was impossible. Jade rings featured in the *Yüan-yang-pi-pu*, an album of erotic woodcuts, that showed a man wearing one over his member, held in position by a cotton harness that was pulled ever tighter between his buttocks by the concubine.

To compound Xianfeng's sexual responsibilities, gynaeceum rules dictated that the Emperor was only allowed to ejaculate seven times a year: three dates in spring, two in summer and two in autumn. Only on these days could senior concubines, consorts and the Empress be impregnated with the Imperial sperm. To conceive an heir, the auspicious copulation had to coincide with the first, third or fifth day after his consort's period – if it were the second or fourth day, his bed partner would conceive a girl, and after the fifth she would not conceive at all. To make matters even more complicated, the Emperor had to climax on the stroke of midnight. If he came before then, his child would die young. If he came after the allotted time, the baby would die in infancy. It's a wonder he ever *chichi*ed at all.[27]

What is abundantly clear is that all the rules and regulations surrounding the Imperial sperm were broken. As soon as the Emperor encountered Lady Yehenara in July 1855, he came and she became pregnant. It was a huge victory for the minor concubine, who immediately withdrew to the heart of the Western Palaces in the Forbidden City. There she underwent the nine-month regime of 'educating the unborn child', ordered to avoid raw, cold, sour or peppery foods and to refrain from riding in a cart or on a horse, and prohibited from drinking alcohol.

We know from the Qing archives that two months before Lady Yehenara was due to give birth, her mother was summoned from Pewter Lane to supervise her daughter's care. A symbolic 'pit of happiness' was dug outside the Palace of Concentrated Beauty in which the Imperial after-birth would be buried, and concubines serenaded Lady Yehenara with the 'song of happiness'.[28] Beside her

bed lay a pair of chopsticks, whose Chinese name *kuaizi* was a pun
on the phrase 'smooth delivery of an infant boy'. Above her door
hung a broadsword to protect the pregnant concubine from evil
spirits, and a symbolic 'childbirth hastening stone', possibly made
of jade, was placed under her kang. The clothing section of the Imperial Court Affairs Department ordered 75 'chih' of coloured
pongee, 81 'chih' of coloured lu'an silk and 3 bolts of white Korean
cotton that was made into 27 jackets, 4 short gowns, 75 bed sheets,
4 stomachers, 18 quilts and 12 mattresses. The General Affairs Section ordered two wooden tubs, two wooden bowls, one wooden
shovel and one small wooden knife. The Provisions Section pro-
cured a black felt blanket and an auspicious cradle.[29]

On the twenty-third day of the third month of the lunar calendar
in 1856 (27 April), Lady Yehenara's pulse suddenly became 'slippery and wet'.[30] According to the *Yi Fei Yi Xi Da A Ge* in the China
First Historical Archive, a document whose title translates as *Concubine Yi [Yehenara] Happy Delivery of Baby Tongzhi,* Lady
Yehenara gave birth to a large, healthy boy, an heir to the Dragon
Throne.

We know that doctors Luan Tai and Ying Wenxi attended to the
birth and, after inspecting the baby's facial expressions, prescribed
him with *fu shou dan,* a pill concocted from cinnabar, soy and
honey-water for happiness and longevity. A jade locket was tied
around the baby's neck and soon he would be christened with the
reign name Tongzhi or Perfect Ruler. The mother of the future Son
of Heaven was rewarded with an immediate promotion to *guifei*
and was now second only to Niuhuru, Xianfeng's vulnerable and
childless Empress. Lady Yehenara, the new Consort of Feminine
Virtue, blithely gave her infant son to a milk nurse and took a 'de-
coction for delactation'.[31] At the age of 21, she had secured power
by a stroke of sexual prowess and biological luck. Her trajectory
was celebrated in a poem written anonymously by one of her
courtiers:

> In the firmament of the Son of Heaven
> A brilliant new star has risen! —
> Supple as the neck of the swan
> Is the charm of her graceful form.

O beauty Supreme! O brilliant Star
Shining but for the Son of Heaven!
From thy glowing soul radiate
Love, daring, hope, intellect, ambition, power![32]

Ambition had driven Lady Yehenara thus far, and now she reaped the rewards of her new-found power. According to Customs Department records, she immediately placed orders for large consignments of Imperial Green Jade. She intended to assemble a collection that would be the envy of China. But the annals record that her requests were repeatedly refused. Regular Imperial Green Jade tribute missions from Burma that had begun in the twilight of Qianlong's reign had been interrupted by Muslim Panthays in Yunnan who had risen up against the Qing in 1855. They had closed Qianlong's Jade Road and thousands were put to the sword by the Imperial army. For Lady Yehenara this was all a minor inconvenience. Instead of importing Imperial Green Jade she began to fill her apartments with artefacts taken from Qianlong's sealed treasure stores and surrounded herself with over-fed Pekinese lapdogs.

Such an indolent paradise, as she recalled, could not last forever. 'I was lucky in giving birth to a son. But after that, I had very bad luck,' she was said to have told her lady-in-waiting.[33]

⬚

Qianlong and his successor Jianqing had met with no reprisals after rebuffing the British mission to China in 1793. But while they had both assumed that it was due to China's unequivocal dismissal of Lord Macartney, in reality Britain had been temporarily distracted by the Napoleonic wars.

No sooner had the Duke of Wellington blasted Napoleon's ambitions at Waterloo in 1815 than Lord Amherst was dispatched to Peking to renew British requests for reciprocal trade. While every British breakfast table was adorned with Chinese tea, porcelain and silk damask, British goods still failed to penetrate into the Chinese interior. But Amherst refused to kowtow before Emperor Jiaqing and was roundly ejected. In the face of Chinese intransigence, the British turned their attentions to an irresistible and illegal trade. The East India Company began secretly offloading chests of Indian opium at Canton. The Qing had previously controlled opium through a government monopoly, but within 20 years the demand had grown to 40,000 chests, that consumed 9 million taels of Chinese silver (450 million grams).[34] In 1834, when the East India Company was stripped of its monopoly by Parliament, dozens of trading houses like Jardine Matheson entered the fray, saturating the Chinese market with a product that they claimed was 'not a curse, but a comfort and a benefit to the hard-working Chinese'.[35]

By 1836 China was gripped by addiction and impoverished by the evaporation of its silver reserves, a situation to which Emperor Daoguang was surely referring when he wrote to mad King Sagaing Min, warning the Burmese monarch about the invasive British. In an attempt to clamp down on a drug that was being foisted on his people, Emperor Daoguang ordered the impounding of British opium chests. But in 1839, after a valuable shipment of 20,282 chests was confiscated, the British responded by unleashing their fleet, claiming an easy victory in the First Opium War in 1842. China was forced to sign the Treaty of Nanking, ceding Hong Kong to Britain's young Queen Victoria, and five ports were opened up to international trade. The British government won an indemnity of £12.7 million, and to compound the misery of defeat, Emperor Daoguang's mother died. After refusing food and water for one month, the Son of Heaven followed her to the grave in 1850.

The teenage Emperor Xianfeng had inherited a country that was wracked by crisis but chose to hide, idling away at the Summer Palace with his consorts and opera singers, leaving the critical business of ruling a nation now dangerously exposed to Prince Gong, his humourless and unimaginative brother. Both men failed to address the internal upheavals that beset China. By the time Lady Yehenara gave birth to the heir to the Dragon Throne, the Chinese masses were in revolt, rising up in messianic civil war led by a failed mandarin who claimed to be the brother of Jesus Christ. As Yehenara plundered Qianlong's storerooms, rebel leader Hong Xiuquan launched the Taiping Rebellion, a movement named after the Heavenly Kingdom of Great Peace that he claimed he would install after wiping out the Qing. His followers swept across the country, burning opium dens, slaughtering addicts and prostitutes, targeting Manchus or those with connections to the Imperial household, leaving the corpses of 25 million people in their wake and forcing tens of thousands of Chinese peasants to flee to Java, Hong Kong, Singapore and America. Xianfeng clung on, propped up by the determination of those around him, in particular Prince Gong and Lady Yehenara, who was becoming an increasingly powerful consort. But it was soon obvious to all, and particularly to the Western powers, that the Emperor was out of his depth. 'Xianfeng had not a single quality to redeem his defects, too unintelligent to realise that the Manchu dynasty, foreign in a land which was hostile to it, was running towards destruction if the trend of its policy was not completely changed,' wrote Henri Cordier, a French Orientalist.[36]

In 1856, the Emperor's troubles came to a head. Chinese officials boarded a 'scrambling dragon' or opium-running craft in the Pearl River at Canton and tore down its Union Jack. Even though the *Arrow* was not a British-registered vessel, London seized upon the act as one of Chinese aggression and declared war. When a French missionary was murdered in the Chinese interior, an isolated incident with questionable circumstances, France joined England against the Chinese, and Allied warships gathered off the Canton coast. Within two years the Second Opium War had depleted Xianfeng's forces and he was obliged to sign the Treaty of Tientsin, handing Britain and France the right to sell opium legally and to station envoys in Peking.

In London, newspapers crowed. British readers were advised that a woman held the true power behind the Dragon Throne:

> Completely violating the conservatism of the Chinese notions of female beauty, Hien-Fou [Xianfeng] formed a matrimonial alliance with the daughter of a Mongol chief – a lady remarkable alike for the physical accomplishments and the unchecked development of the means of locomotion. The Court soon became composed of women of the same race, who have entirely superseded those poor crippled beauties who formerly held sway there, and now have to retire with jealousy before a band of robust Amazons, whose amusement of riding, hunting, shooting, and even footraces, are shared by the Emperor himself. The wife of Hien-Fou is at once the object of his affection and his respect, shares the secrets of his state, and sits with him at the council table, where her opinions are listened to with the same attention and deference as those of her royal husband.[37]

When it came to ratifying the Treaty of Tientsin in 1859, the British and French dispatched dozens of warships that anchored off the Chinese coast, requesting permission to sail upriver towards Peking. The nervous Imperial court, now all too familiar with Allied diplomacy, requested that the delegations be sent overland. The British and French claimed provocation once again and attacked, but lost 400 men in the battle for the Taku Forts that guarded the Peiho River mouth. The British regrouped and dispatched Lord Elgin, former Governor of Jamaica and Governor General of British North America, as plenipotentiary to China in March 1860. A man of hardy Highland stock, Elgin was known among his men as the Big Barbarian. A photograph of him taken by Felice Beato, who accompanied the mission, shows him dressed in a greatcoat with fur collar and cuffs, his mane of powder-white hair untamed and windblasted.

That summer, a large body of British and French troops attacked the Chinese mainland, laying waste the port city of Tientsin. By August, Beato was sending home photographs of a massive British force encamped five miles east of the capital. His pictures, published in the *Illustrated London News,* were the West's first glimpse of the fabled Chinese Empire. It was a tawdry sight: cannon-scarred Chinese battlements and the corpses of Imperial soldiers strewn in the rubble of Taku.

A small party of British representatives struck out for Peking to negotiate Lord Elgin's safe passage, but on 18 September news raced back to the British camp that 20,000 Chinese troops had ambushed them. Harry Parkes, Britain's unofficial consul at Canton, Mr Bowlby, *The Times'* correspondent in Peking, Henry Loch, private secretary to Lord Elgin, and lieutenants Anderson, Phipps and De Normann, officers of the King's Dragoon Guards, had been shackled in iron collars and fetters. The Big Barbarian was incensed and ordered an immediate attack on Peking.

News of a thunderous Allied advance sent the Imperial court, that had decamped to the Summer Palace, into a blind panic. The terrified Emperor, his eunuchs already packing, announced that he was leaving, despite warnings from Prince Gong that to do so would dishonour him in the eyes of his people. By the time the Allied troops had reached the Palikao bridge on the outskirts of the capital on 22 September, a five-mile-long caravan of yellow satin sedan chairs, concubines, flags and banners was streaming out of the Summer Palace. As the British and French swarmed ever nearer, the Imperial procession sped towards the Tartar wastelands beyond the Great Wall, heading for the Emperor's hunting lodge at Jehôl. Lady Yehenara had stuffed her travelling chests with jewels, and we know that among them was Xiang Fei's precious Persian Pepper. But what the Imperial party took with them represented a tiny fraction of the treasures of the Dragon Throne that were left behind, guarded by twenty flatulent eunuchs.

The French and British headed for the Summer Palace, certain that the Emperor of China would not have deserted his post. On 5 October the Allies split and advanced separately around Peking's walls, planning to rendezvous outside the Summer Palace gates. Arriving in the early hours of 6 October, the French took up position, infantrymen behind sandbagged carts, cannons trained on the rococo gates, snipers in the trees. But it was a volley of fruit that came over the walls. The French soldiers were strafed with lychees and figs hurled by a huddle of portly unarmed men in make-up and silk robes, who screeched and hissed at the gathered might of the French Empire. A few shots fired above their heads was all it took to disperse the Imperial front line, and then General Comte de Montaubon, the French commander, ordered his men forward.

Before them, nestling in the lap of the Western Hills, in all its secret glory, lay the Emperors' stately pleasure dome, Yüan-ming Yüan, the Garden of Perfect Brightness, an eight-mile sprawl of hidden groves, meandering footpaths, a Jade Belt Bridge and goldfish ponds, all set around the elegant expanse of Lake Kunming. And to the east stood the extraordinary theme park, Qianlong's Oriental Versailles, something Europe had only read about in the letters of Jesuits. 'Each valley has its pleasure palace, small in relation to its own enclosure but in itself sufficient to lodge the greatest of our European lords with all his retinue,' Jean-Denis Attiret had written home in 1743.[38]

Here Xiang Fei, the Fragrant Consort, was said to have prayed in solitude behind the fretted marble veneer of Fangwai Mosque. On the verandahs of Wu Zhu Pavilion, inlaid with pearls and precious stones, she had taunted Qianlong, her besotted Emperor. Here she must have strolled, between the ornamental fountains and twirling topiary, homesick for the wild plains of her beloved Sinkiang. But now, as French officers peered through the gates, the only inhabitants to be seen were a litter of Pekinese puppies.

General Comte de Montaubon, Comte d'Herrison, his secretary, Baron Gros, France's envoy, and 'his aide Monsieur Bastard' strode across a large paved courtyard around which thousands of birds twittered nervously in cages hung from pine trees.[39] Through a reception hall paved with marble and painted in gold, azure and scarlet, they stalked into the Emperor's Hall of Audiences, their carbines cocked. 'Involuntarily we spoke in low tones, and began to walk on tiptoe on seeing before us such a profusion of riches . . . which their owner had abandoned in his flight as indifferently as a citizen closes the door of his house,' Comte d'Herrison wrote in his diary. Even the soldiers of the French Empire, immersed in the rococo splendours of Paris, were dumbstruck by the wealth of the Son of Heaven. 'The walls, the ceilings, the dressing tables, the chairs, the footstools are all in gold, studded with gems . . . In a room adjoining the throne room were gathered all the articles for the daily use of the Son of Heaven . . . his tea service, his cups, his pipes – the bowls of gold or silver – the long tubes enriched with coral, jade, rubies, sapphires and little tufts of many-coloured silk,' d'Herrison marvelled.[40]

The British didn't arrive until the next afternoon. They had been following a map drawn by Lord Macartney's draftsman William Alexander, who had only caught a glimpse of the Summer Palace on his way to Jehôl in 1793. His directions had sent Lord Elgin marching the wrong way. Now Sir Hope Grant, Elgin's eccentric commander-in-chief, who always insisted on playing his bull-fiddle before going into battle, and Sir Robert Napier, a swashbuckler with mutton-chop whiskers, who had led the attack on the Taku forts three months earlier, raced into the Summer Palace. Accompanied by the photographer Beato, the soldiers leapt off their mounts and took up defensive positions, but not one shot rang out. Elgin, Napier and Grant were perplexed and ordered the firing of a 21-gun salute to announce their arrival. But there was no response and the British congratulated themselves on having beaten the French to the plunder.

Grant proudly led the way through the vast chambers and would note later in his spartan journal how 'the principal palace was filled with beautiful jade-stones of great value, and carved in most elaborate manner.'[41] Others among the party, particularly the Chaplain, the Rev. McGhee, were more lyrical:

> If you can imagine fairies to be the size of ordinary mortals, this then was fairyland. Never have I beheld a scene, which realised one's ideas of an enchanted land before.[42]

But as they entered the Emperor's Hall of Audiences an alarming sight greeted them. 'Alas! Such a scene of desolation,' Elgin noted, stumbling over the French, who, for more than 24 hours, had fallen onto the treasures of the Qing in a frenzy of 'looting', a term the British had recently learned from their Hindi-speaking Sepoys, who used the word *lūt*, meaning 'plunder'.

The Big Barbarian demanded to speak to Comte de Montaubon. '[He] came up full of protestations. He had prevented looting in order that all the plunder might be divided between the armies ... But there was not a room I saw in which half the things had not been taken away or broken into pieces,' Elgin blustered.[43]

Perhaps he was mindful of the scandal that had overtaken his father, the seventh Earl of Elgin, who as British ambassador to the Ottoman Empire had secured permission from the Turks to remove marble sculptures and friezes from the Parthenon in Athens. Perhaps the British plenipotentiary was still smarting from the wrath of Lord Byron, who had chastised his father when the first shipment of marbles had arrived in London in 1802. Later, after a House of Commons select committee had criticised Elgin senior's conduct, he was forced to publish an explanation of his actions, and the British government reluctantly paid £35,000 for the looted haul. Although the ancient wonder of the world was duly put on display in the British Museum in 1817, the whole episode had been acutely embarrassing.

Now before his son's eyes, another great wonder was being quartered and ferreted away. French soldiers were running back and forth, weighed down with virtually everything bar the marble floor tiles. Qianlong's beloved English clocks, most of them manufactured by George Clarke of Leadenhall Street in the City of London, had been reduced to glittering rubble. Soldiers hurled eggshell-thin Imperial Green Jade cups off balconies, cheering as each one exploded in smithereens. A thick carpet of gleaming shards – jade, glass and porcelain – crunched beneath their boots. Outside the Palace of Calm Sea, a group of French privates wrenched at Father Benoist's magnificent bronze animal heads, seizing a monkey, an ox, a boar, a tiger and a horse.

Colonel Schmidt, Montaubon's chief-of-staff, pocketed a brush holder of spinach-green jade, commissioned by Qianlong in 1788, depicting King Bodawpaya's envoys on their first jade journey to China. From the Calm and Bright Park, Schmidt's officers carted off a twelve-pound double-dragon jade block inscribed 'Imperial Seal of Ching Ming Yuan'. In the Emperor's apartments, a Parisian officer spotted an exquisitely carved cinnabar treasure box depicting carp swimming among cherry blossoms in a turbulent pool. In it were seven rings of coloured stone, cold to the touch – perfect serviette holders, a fine gift for his father. Inside a Louis XIV-style cabinet glittered trays of Imperial Green Jade jewellery – pea pods, miniature aubergines, dragons and phoenixes, discs, triple-hoop ear-rings – waiting to be stuffed into pockets and shirts, gifts for anxious wives and girlfriends, who would welcome their men back at the quayside in Marseilles. Count Kleezkowsky, one of Montaubon's officers, grabbed a fistful of brilliant green stones – a carved dragon, a pair of triple-hoop ear-rings and an unusually large pendant that reminded him of a squid.[44]

A cry went up from a scout who had broken into the Imperial storerooms and found thousands of shimmering lengths of silk, satin, crêpe and brocade. Within minutes dozens were pulling and tugging. 'Hundreds were thrown down and trampled on, and the floor covered thickly with them, men were throwing them at each other, and all taking as many as they could carry,'[45] Mr Wirgman of the *Illustrated London News* telegraphed home. 'Some idea of the quantity of silk may be given by the fact that fowls, old pots etc. were wrapped in the most costly silks and satins.'[46]

Lord Elgin mulled over the scene, his black frock-coat dusted with China's heritage, his ears ringing with requests from his senior officers who demanded that they be allowed to take their share of the plunder. Mumbling regrets, he ordered his officers to fill only 'two or three carts with treasures'. But then, in one of the Emperor's ante-rooms, an officer spotted Elgin's signature on a discarded piece of paper. It was the Treaty of Tientsin, the document they had come to China to ratify, 'thrown on the ground by someone . . . in the heap of broken articles'.[47] What more justification was needed? Queen Victoria's soldiers swarmed through the Immense Ocean Observatory, the Hall of Harmonious Wonder, the Hall of National Peace, quarrelling over whatever took their fancy, while Felice Beato quietly put his camera away.

Lady Yehenara's chambers were stripped and vandalised, soldiers smearing her walls with facetious messages in the Emperor's vermilion ink. Two large Imperial Green Jade statues of kneeling boys that she used as pillows caught one soldier's fancy. Lieutenants Carnac, Cattley and McGregor, who had honoured themselves in battle and earned a mention in the *Illustrated London News,* gutted Imperial bolsters and charged through clouds of feathers.[48] A pantomime of British war heroes paraded in 'extensive wardrobes of every article of dress; coats richly embroidered in silk and gold thread, in the Imperial dragon pattern; boots, head-dresses, fans, etc.,'[49] Wirgman wrote. They chased one another around Qianlong's labyrinth, and officers of the 1st King's Dragoon Guards smashed the Sèvres looking-glasses in Qianlong's Chamber of Mirrors. In the library, Mr Wade spent several hours 'securing some valuable books and papers . . . for the British Museum'.[50] One of Qianlong's serenades to his Mongol wine-bowl, inscribed onto five jade books, was thrown into a kit bag. It would eventually find its way to the Chester Beatty Library in Dublin.

Among the wrecking crew was 26-year-old Captain Charles Gordon, of the Royal Engineers, who had already earned a reputation for reckless bravery during the siege of Sevastopol. The young hawk, with 'eyes that look you through and through and summed you up at a glance, eyes that told you of a stronger will than yours',[51] seized a fine, white jade boulder, carved with a mountain grotto scene, a gift for his mother that was wrapped in silk.[52] For himself, he chose a small, exquisitely carved green jade horse,[53] while Sir Hope Grant's staff officer, Garnet Joseph Wolseley, the youngest lieutenant colonel in the Empire, who would later be venerated as the moderniser of the British army, packed up the plunder.

Wirgman could barely contain his excitement: 'no pen can describe correctly the scene that has taken place there within the last two days. The immense quantity of loot of all kinds made it almost impossible to know what to take away. The jade-stone and china were of great value . . .'[54] Comte d'Herrison was equally breathless: 'the second night we spent in the Summer Palace was impossible, crazy, giddy.'

Only Sir Hope Grant, a man of few words other than 'charge', refused to join in the orgy. Instead he attempted to end the chaos. 'A general order from the British commander-in-chief that all articles taken by officers and men were to be sent for sale by public auction for the benefit of the army. The sale is to be divided as prize money on the spot,' the *China Herald* reported.[55]

Allied troops of every rank filed into a courtyard, where they were ordered to turn out their pockets and knapsacks. The Sikhs were placed in charge of 70,000 bolts of silk. British and French officers made pyramids from jade, porcelain, watches and clocks, jewellery, furs, enamels, carpets and a large number of mechanical toys. Before the sale could commence, Lord Elgin packed up two special shipments, one bound for Henry Cole's new South Kensington Museum on Old Brompton Road and another, containing jades and Imperial robes, destined for Buckingham Palace.

When the public bidding began, the courtyard echoed with the din of an improvised auctioneer's gavel, a pistol rapping on a teachest. An Imperial Green Jade brush washer, its bowl inscribed with a sign of the Emperor, 'four times ten thousand ages', went to a 'Mr Walkinshaw of Peking'.[56] Captain Charles Gordon purchased one of Qianlong's thrones, its 'cushions, embroidered with gold dragons, attracting general admiration', as a present for his corps headquarters in Chatham, Kent, where it remains today.[57] A copy of Qianlong's beloved Mongol wine vessel, which the British described as a 'large fish-bowl', weighing 134 pounds, was sold to T'ien-pao, a Chinese trader. Surely he was the only person at the sale who could read the Emperor's thoughts inscribed upon it: 'What I prize are worthy men.'

The *Daily News* reported that the auction continued for several hours, 'the whole sum . . . being somewhere about £30,000'.[58] Every soldier was rewarded with a payment of £4 and Charles Gordon wrote shortly after, 'although I have not as much as many, I have done well.'[59]

Amid the straining hands and flushed faces, only the Rev.

McGhee sounded a melancholy note. 'There was a sacrilege in devoting to destruction structures, which had been reared many, many hundred years ago. Every building was a repository of ancient and curious art . . . things which, apart altogether from their value, were full of interest from their beauty and rarity.'[60]

When news of the ransacking reached Prince Gong, he tried to appease the British by releasing his hostages. Harry Parkes and Henry Loch emerged from their cells on 8 October, only to set off for the Summer Palace, where they joined in the sacking. Six days later, De Normann, Anderson and two Sikh soldiers also arrived back at the British camp, packed in boxes and immersed in quick-lime. 'It was impossible to recognise them by their features,' Loch wrote. 'Poor De Normann we knew by his boots and a piece of leather coat he always wore.' Phipps and Bowlby of *The Times* were never seen again. When Loch told Lord Elgin of the fetid prison conditions, of the manacles that had cut their skin to the bone, how wounds became gangrenous and 'nails and fingers burst through the tightness of the cords . . . worms were generated', China's act of appeasement became Lord Elgin's excuse for one final act of revenge.

'After anxious deliberation, Lord Elgin decided to request the commander-in-chief to take the requisite steps for the destruction of the Emperor's palace of Yüan-ming Yüan,' wrote Henry Loch. 'Against the natural repugnance which must always exist in the mind of every educated person to the destruction of the beautiful, must be brought the consideration of the position in which the Allies were placed . . . No money indemnity could compensate for the insult inflicted.'[61] Captain Charles Gordon led the Royal Engineers through the halls and chambers, lacing their columns with explosive charges.

It was only the European Palaces that were chosen for destruction, as if Lord Elgin was infuriated by the grand folly commissioned by a Chinese Emperor who had snubbed Western interests, a creation that only days before had so mesmerised Comte d'Herrison. 'To depict all the splendours before our astonished eyes I should need to dissolve specimens of all known precious stones in liquid gold for ink, and to dip into it a diamond pen tipped with the fantasies of the Oriental poet,' he had written soon after entering the Hall of Calm Sea. Now he joined the ranks of men who watched beams folding, lacquered pillars crumpling, fountains of pulverised masonry spewing into the air. As a fire-storm swept through Castiglione's vision, Robert Swinhoe, Sir Hope Grant's interpreter, described how 'the sun shining through the waves of smoke gave a sickly hue to every plant and tree.' The sophisticates of France and Britain appeared to him as satanic voyeurs; the 'red flames gleaming on the faces of the troops engaged made them appear like demons glorifying in the destruction of what they could not replace.'[62]

In the race for the Great Wall, Lady Yehenara had forgotten her Pekinese puppies. Now packs of 'little Japanese dogs, something resembling a King Charles spaniel, were running about in a distracted state', until one was spotted by General J. H. Dunne of the 99th Regiment. 'A French soldier seized it by the tail but as it made some vigorous snaps at him he handed it over to my charge. I rolled it up in some yellow satin and gave it to one of my native servants to bring to the camp,' Dunne wrote on his return. The officer would later present the dog to Queen Victoria, who named her new pet 'Looty' and commissioned Friedrich Keyl, a pupil of Sir Edwin Landseer, to paint its portrait, a picture that was exhibited at the Royal Academy in 1863.[63]

The Rev. McGhee had climbed to the Pavilion of Precious Clouds, a spiritual eyrie from which all of Qianlong's cabinet of European curiosities could be seen, and he was dumbfounded by what he saw:

> Soon . . . you saw a wreath of smoke curling up through the trees . . . in a few minutes other wreaths of smoke arose from half-a-hundred different places . . . soon the wreath becomes a volume, a great black mass, out burst a hundred flames, the smoke obscures the sun, and temple, palace, buildings and all, hallowed by age . . . are swept to destruction, with all their contents, monuments of imperial taste and luxury . . . No eye will ever again gaze upon those buildings which have been doubtless the admiration of ages, records of bygone skill and taste . . . You have seen them once and for ever, they are dead and gone, man cannot reproduce them.[64]

As Yüan-ming Yüan burned, Harry Parkes, Henry Loch and Lord Elgin, 'a man who at that time was more powerful than even their own Emperor', galloped to Peking.[65] But Xianfeng was still cowering beyond the Great Wall, and it fell to Prince Gong to greet the

A painting of Emperor Qianlong by his European confidante, Giuseppe Castiglione
that shows the Son of Heaven, resplendent in Imperial Green Jade and silk, at the
peak of his Golden Age

These three images of Xiang Fei, Qianlong's Fragrant Consort, show how the flower girl's story captured the popular imagination. The original eighteenth century portrait by Castiglione (bottom left), which is here seen adorning a pack of Chinese postcards on sale in Beijing, now hangs in Madam Chiang Kai-shek's Manhatten apartment. At the end of the nineteenth century every Chinese lady of rank demanded to be painted in the image of the Fragrant Consort, as can be seen in this old tinted photograph of an artist's studio (left) and this nineteenth century copy (below right) which recently came up for auction in London.

香妃漢裝像

Top: Thomas Allom's evocative portrayal of the Forbidden City's imposing Western Gate gives some idea of the trepidation with which the first Western travellers must have approached the Emperor of China's realm.

Above: This cartoon of a dandyish Lord Macartney, cap in hand, dragging a sad collection of 'mechanical toys' up to the Dragon Throne reveals the derision heaped on this first embassy to China by some quarters of the British establishment.

Right: The start of Qianlong's 3,000-mile Jade Road from the Burma-Sino border at Yunnan, the Land Beyond the Clouds, to Peking.

Left: Felice Beato's images of the Allied assault on Taku Fort, in the mouth of the Peiho River, were the first photographs of China to be seen in th West.

The remains of the Burmese defences at Mindhla after the British Expeditionary force took out the Riverside fort, machine guns mounted on the prows of General Prendergast's steamers 'that appeared to King Thibaw's men to be flaming nagas spitting bullets like fire.'

The British officers who led the looting of the Summer Palace in 1860: (clockwise from top left) Lord Elgin, son of the aristocrat who stole the Parthenon marbles; Sir Hope Grant, who played the fiddle before going into battle; Sir Robert Napier, whose statue stands today on Kensington Gore; Charles 'Chinese' Gordon, who laced the columns of Qianlong's European palaces with explosives.

Right: King Thibaw's diminutive commander-in-chief, who emerged from the mist that masked the Irrawaddy in November 1885, aboard the King's golden war barge, to deliver Burma up to the British Empire.

Below: Thibaw, the last King of Burma, with his queens Supayagyi and Supayalat (right), pictured in the Mandalay palace studio that was staffed by a French photographer who claimed that he was as likely to leave each evening without his head as with a fistful of gems.

A victorious Hampshire Regiment, singing Christmas carols before Mandalay Palace in 1885, having evicted Thibaw from the Lion Throne.

Left: A Kachin warlord reclines in his silk robes with an opium pipe pressed between his lips.

Below: Kachin jaiwas or priests performing the 'death dance' at the manau ceremony that concludes with a bloody sacrifice to appease jungle spirits, as witnessed by Edward Sladen and so feared by every other traveller.

Below: After the siege of the foreign legations in 1900, Chinese and Allied soldiers wreaked revenge on Boxer rebels who had terrorised the Western community with their cries of 'sha kweitse' – 'kill the foreign devils'.

Dragon Lady, the Dowager Empress Cixi, adored having her portrait taken in her Imperial studio at the Summer Palace after being introduced to photography by the ladies of the foreign legations. In the second picture a thought bubble hovers over her head declaring her the Goddess of Mercy, her chief eunuch Li Lianying by her side.

The Dowager Empress Cixi invited the wives of foreign ministers to tea in 1898 in order to improve her public image at home and abroad. Here the ladies pose with the wives of Court mandarins.

British delegation. The 28-year-old signed the Treaty of Peking, agreed to the payment of £100,000 in compensation for the loss of a handful of British lives and sanctioned Frederick Bruce, Elgin's younger brother, as Britain's first chargé d'affaires to Peking, as a band played 'God Save the Queen'.

Victorious dispatches converged on London. 'Two of the gates of Pekin are in our hands. Parkes and Loch have been returned to us. Capt Anderson and De Normann have died from the effects of ill-treatment . . . Bowlby unaccounted for. The Emperor's summer palace taken and sacked, affording immense spoil. Emperor fled to Tartary. Forces to winter at Pekin and Tien-Tsin,' Elgin reported.[66]

But those responsible for the sacking would soon re-evaluate their actions. Elgin, who was rewarded for his Chinese adventures with the post of Viceroy of India, kept his personal journal blank from 14 to 26 October. Not a single word on the subject of loot was included in his frequent and detailed letters home to his wife. Instead, the British plenipotentiary revised history in later life: 'plundering and devastating a place like this is bad enough, but what is much worse is the wastage and breakage. French soldiers were destroying in every way the most beautiful silks, breaking the jade ornaments and porcelain etc. . . . War is a hateful business. The more one sees of it, the more one detests it.'[67]

In contemplating his own role as torch-bearer, Captain Charles Gordon, apparently haunted by his actions, admitted how 'it made one's heart sore to burn them.' He struggled in his private journals to reapportion blame: 'you can scarcely imagine the beauty and magnificence of the palaces we burned. In fact, these palaces were so large and we were so pressed for time, that we could not plunder them carefully . . . The French have smashed everything in the most wanton way, it was a scene of utter destruction, which passes description.'[68]

Within four years the young Captain would become famous throughout the Empire as the 'Chinese Gordon' who helped the Qing to put down the Taiping rebellion and who came to the rescue of the International Settlement in Shanghai. Then he would denounce the vanquished bandits for indiscriminate looting. 'There shall be no more sacking and burning of towns: I command soldiers, not robbers,' he would order.[69]

Henry Loch returned to Scotland, perhaps not fully recovered from his incarceration. His memoirs claim that nothing of value had been found by the Allied forces. There was, he wrote, 'no utter annihilation of works of art or learning'. Loch, whose own vast collection of Imperial artefacts, porcelain and *cloisonné* would soon be sought after by collectors around the world, concluded: 'nothing unique either in the shape of books or manuscripts was kept at Yüan-ming Yüan, and in the subsequent search for both, previous to the burning, very few were found, and certainly none of any exclusive rarity.'[70]

In Paris too there were denials. The *Moniteur* reported that General Montaubon had not seen any looting at all. However, in 1862 the same paper advertised an unusual sale from 'the Palais d'Eté' at the Hôtel Drouot, where certain bronze items – fountainheads, a monkey and an ox – were among the prize lots. A sizeable Chinese collection requisitioned by the forgetful General was also put on display by Empress Eugenie in her Chinese salon at Fontainebleau.

While the victorious Allied troops wintered in Peking, their plunder and stories flooded Europe, a glittering cargo of Oriental treasures and tales that would go on to found almost every major public Chinese art collection established in the late nineteenth century. More than 60 per cent of the estimated 1.6 million jades that had been displayed in the Yüan-ming Yüan converged on London, Paris and later New York.[71] With the profits generated by the Great Exhibition of 1851, Henry Cole, a fellow of the Royal Society of Arts and aide to Prince Albert, opened the South Kensington Museum in 1857 on a site nicknamed 'Albertopolis' by journalists. Four years later, an elaborate Oriental Court in the East Cloister opened, displaying the contents of packing cases dispatched by Sir Hope Grant's men. *Harper's New Monthly Magazine* fêted the exhibits as exuding 'the romance of the East'.[72] It was a display that would 'revise, correct and estimate the traditions of the Oriental world',[73] although the museum catalogue advised that the Chinese people were 'an effeminate . . . degenerate race, softened by luxury and too great facility for enjoyment'.[74]

America followed the British lead, and by 1870 museums were opened in Boston, Washington DC and New York, each displaying a share of Imperial Chinese pieces that had once graced Qianlong's cabinets in the Yüan-ming Yüan.[75]

Motivated by the diaspora of stories and artefacts, wealthy private individuals also began collections. One would-be American connoisseur who came to Europe on a shopping trip, recalled: 'many objects had found their way into the shops of dealers in antiquities . . . but many were still held by members of the [Chinese] expedition. I found the same pieces had been carried to Frankfort [sic], Amsterdam, Dresden, Berlin and Vienna. At St Petersburg, Moscow and Constantinople I also obtained some beautiful specimens that had come out from China.'[76]

In Massachusetts, Heber Bishop, a twenty-year-old business school graduate with aspirations to revolutionise the sugar industry, vowed, as he set off for Cuba, to reassemble Qianlong's precious jade collection as soon as he had made his fortune.

In London, James McNeill Whistler bought his first Imperial treasure in 1863. The blue-and-white plate whose seal denoted that it had once belonged to Emperor Kangxi inspired the painter to incorporate pieces from the Summer Palace in his portraits. An Imperial blue-and-white vase and a cinnabar lacquer cup can be seen on the mantelpiece behind Joanna Hiffernan, Whistler's mistress, who sat for his *Symphony in White* that was completed in 1864 and today hangs in Tate Britain. Charles Freer, a businessman from Detroit and a close friend, was inspired to follow Whistler's example and began acquiring Imperial jades that would in time form one of the largest private Oriental collections in America. Among Whistler's London circle, Dante Gabrielle Rossetti also began to purchase and employ Oriental jewellery in his work. In *The Beloved,* the Pre-Raphaelite beauties wear lavish head-dresses and necklaces that are surely inspired by the Imperial court. One woman appears to be draped with jewels that glisten a brilliant green.

In Paris, a mysterious parcel, containing several pieces of exquisitely carved translucent green stones – a pair of triple hoops, a dragon clip and a large squid-like pendant – arrived at the jewellery workshops of Eugène Fontenay.[77] The jeweller, 'a man of rare intelligence, much spirit and very sure taste', was only too happy when

Count Kleezkowsky, so recently returned from his expedition to China, commissioned him to set the stones for his wife. From them Fontenay created the first suite Western jewellery to be made from the Burmese stone. 'It has the reputation of being more luminous than any other known piece ... The possessor of this Collection has failed to see its equal, and believes it to be unique.'[78]

The Emperor's Stone of Heaven also found its way to a laboratory in Lyon where Professor Alexander Damour analysed a handful of bright-green gems taken from a Louis XIV-style cabinet. Damour had already read of *jade imperiale*. An article written by the artist Alfred Jacquemart published in *Le Gazette des Beaux Art* six years earlier had described Imperial Green Jade as 'a peerless gem almost rivalling an uncut emerald'. Damour, a minerologist who had been studying Chinese jades since 1846, immediately recognised that this stone was completely different to the waxy samples he had obtained from the mines of Khotan. When he compared both stones under the microscope, he discovered that the brilliant green one had large, interlocking crystals and sheered when it was split, while the waxy jade was made up of rope-like fibrous crystals and broke open like a sugar cube.

In 1863 Damour published his findings, naming the stone from Khotan, the treasure of Confucius that had been carved for thousands of years, 'nephrite'. But the brilliant green stone, so desired by Qianlong, that besotted Lady Yehenara, was not 'serpentine', as the British had mistaken it, nor was it 'chrysoprase', as it was known to the French, nor was it 'stone of the flank', as it was named by the Spanish in 1565. Damour's new green stone was to be called 'jadeite'. He announced that the only source in the world was a secret mine in northern Burma to where the British were now advancing.[79]

Five

'The Far Off, the Strange, the Wonderful, the Original, the True, the Brave, the Conquered'

For once the Baho Sigyi Drum was silent. In the Presence Chamber, a lofty hall to the west of the Glass Palace where the ear-boring ceremonies for the princesses of the court were held, King Mindon lay in a fever, fanned by his daughters and queens, ringed by a court of mumbling astrologers and wailing priests.

In July 1878, Burma's most revered monarch had been struck down by dysentery, and his once-famed 'bright black eyes that twinkle up into quite a Chinese obliquity when he laughs' were dulled.[1] King Mindon had once prided himself on a lavish moustache and solid physique but, wracked by cramps, his grey hair thinning, the architect of Burma's Golden Age now melted into the cotton sheets that clung to him like a shroud. Only his great domed brow marked him out as a true descendant of King Alompra's Konbaung Dynasty.

King Mindon had brought stability and vision to a kingdom crippled by conflict from the day that Bayfield and Griffith had fled the jadeite mines. After King Tharawaddy deposed mad Sagaing Min, a wave of terror had crashed over the country and Tharawaddy too had succumbed to insanity, eviscerating his palace servants, offering their livers to the *nats*.[2] His son, King Pagan, had seized the throne in 1846, only to send Burma hurtling into a second war with the British. It culminated in a humiliating surrender in 1852, after Captain Tarleton, commander of the gunboat *Medusa*, led a British assault on the Burmese capital. The southern port city of Rangoon was ceded to the British, along with the remaining provinces of Lower Burma. The booty that filtered back to London included the embroidered jacket of a Burmese commander nicknamed 'Bandoolah Junior', son of the general who, in 1824, had bragged that he would clap Lord Amherst in gilded fetters. Lined with yellow silk, decorated with gold thread, sequins and braid, it reappeared on a stall in Portobello Market in Ladbroke Grove, west London, in 1993, complete with a label bearing Tarleton's name.[3]

In the fall-out of this second, disastrous Anglo-Burmese war, Mindon had deposed his brother King Pagan, and in 1853 set in motion an age of enlightenment. He dispatched peace envoys to London, Paris and Rome. He exchanged Burma's system of barter for coinage, weights and measures, connected the sinewy country's distant towns and cities by road and telegraphy, and built a sparkling centre of Buddhist learning at his new capital, Mandalay.

Completed in 1857, the gem-studded pagodas and pavilions were laid out beneath a towering hill that the Burmese believed was filled with gems. His palaces were enclosed by 6666 feet of crenellated walls and surrounded by a tree-lined moat almost 25 feet wide. Twelve enormous gates interrupted the crimson boundary, four of them at the cardinal points. Between them dozens of watch-towers peeped over, glinting with gold-tipped finials. To the north were the gardens of Queen Alé-nan-daw, her palm-lined waterways and grottos; to the west, her audience rooms, the Queen's glittering Lily Throne and her outdoor spa shaded by cloisters. Dominating the skyline, its golden eaves flaming in the setting sun, was King Mindon's palace, above which towered a golden stupa, rising over Mandalay like Mount Meru, the mythological escarpment that Buddhists believed was the axle around which the world rotated. Although within sight of Ava and Amarapura, Mindon's new Mandalay was built to distance his reign from the excess and defeats that had dogged his predecessors. It was not just a royal city but a divine imprint of the star-filled heavens, and only bare feet could walk across it.

But nothing could raise Mindon from his fever, and on 1 October he 'migrated to the country of the Gods'. Obituaries encased in ivory tubes were dispatched around the globe. Queen Victoria, addressed as the Konbaung Dynasty's 'Royal Friend!' was the first recipient, followed by her British Foreign Secretary and her Viceroy of India, the office-bearers of the 'Hat Wearing Nation'.

Within three weeks another flurry of telegrams rained down on the British 'Royal Friend!', announcing the coronation of an unknown nineteen-year-old prince: 'His Great and Excellent Majesty who has sovereignty over all umbrella-bearing rulers of Thuna-paranta, Tampa-dipa and other great eastern realms and countries. The Burmese Rising Sun King, Lord of the Saddan Elephant, Master of many White elephants, Lord of Existence, Great Just Ruler etc. etc.' Then came his curriculum vitae. The new monarch had 'passed at three different times, brilliant examinations in sacred literature. Wishing Your Excellency etc. etc.'[4]

But who was this new King Thibaw that hardly anyone in Burma and certainly no one outside the country had ever seen? We returned to the New Delhi archives in search of another paper trail that we hoped would lead to Mandalay. The reading room superintendent moistened his finger with tea and straightened his moustache as he saw us approach with fistfuls of graffitied request slips.

'No. No. No,' he insisted, chasing us away from his desk. 'I will not be helping you. I must be referring you to the DDNAI.' And with that he dashed for the staff canteen, sheltering behind the unexplained acronym.

There was no one else, so we roused the men in Scholars' Corner, the small bench on which weary students slept, and they pointed to a curtain. Behind it we found the Deputy Director of the National Archives of India, a melancholic academic who complained of being trapped in the 'labyrinth of Janpath'.

'How long have you been here?' he asked, looking sympathetically at our forms. 'God be saving us all. Please print in your newspaper, your book, whatever you are writing,' he implored. 'It is a national disgrace. We are so sorry to abuse you. Scholars come from afar and we write rubbish on their forms. We have no money and hundreds of thousands of files to keep, mostly in the dark, many of them in a horrible mess. What are we to do?'

He stood up and the crumbs of history fell from his lap. 'We cannot go forwards and cannot conserve the past.' His round face gleamed like polished brass. 'Every night I'm off home to my wife and I say to her, "Look, I am covered in history and there is nothing we can be doing." Many of the files that you will view, and I promise you that you will see the files, will be finished by the time that you have read them. Vanished, poof – into thin air. Destroyed. Powder and dust.'

He banged his fist down on a pile of manuscripts and broken words flew through the air, covering his hair and hands in a thin film of Empire.

Within hours files that had been 'missing but not lost', that were 'secret if not missing', manuscripts that had been stranded in the darkened galley of the document store, appeared on our desks, and soon we began to weave together the strands of King Thibaw's history.

❈

While Mindon lay dying in the darkened Presence Chamber, Alénan-daw, his wife, the Queen of the Middle Palace, plotted succession. She secured political backing from the *Hlutdaw*, the Burmese Council of Ministers, and announced Thibaw, her stepson, as heir-apparent. This unworldly teenager, one of the most junior and least impressive of 82 princely brothers and sisters who were vying for the throne, was epileptic and there were rumours that he was also illegitimate. He had spent most of his life tucked away in a monastery outside the city, in the company of a revered Buddhist scholar named Yanaung, and knew nothing about palace politics. But then again, a weak sovereign increased the power of a constitutional government, something that the members of the *Hlutdaw*, who had travelled to Europe at Mindon's behest, clearly appreciated. No sooner had Thibaw's status been ratified than Alé-nan-daw announced his marriage. The pasty-faced monk wed Princess Supayalat and Princess Supayagyi, his own half-sisters, the daughters of Alé-nan-daw, in a double wedding that secured the Queen of the Middle Palace's position as Dowager.

No sooner had King Mindon died than Alé-nan-daw and the newly crowned Queen Supayalat placed a curious order for several yards of red velvet carpet with Maria Denigre, a French weaver working in Mandalay.[5] One month later, in January 1879, some of Mindon's children were spotted by Robert Shaw, the British Resident, selling 'brilliant green stones' to Mulla Ibrahim, an affluent merchant. On 15 February, the storm finally broke in two nights of long knives. Assassins hired by the Dowager Queen chased down King Thibaw's fraternal rivals to the throne and bagged them in the newly made velvet sacks before beating them to death with sandalwood clubs. It was sacrilege to spill the blood of Burmese aristocrats, but Maria's thick red fabric absorbed it and muffled the screams.

Robert Shaw advised Fort William that his spies had seen members of the royal family being thrown into a large hole that had been dug in the jail-yard:

> Their outcries were stifled by the hands of their executioners grasping their necks until they were strangled. Others were killed with bludgeons, which in the hands of half-drunken men, often required to be used repeatedly before the victims were put out of their pain. Infants were taken from their mothers' arms and their brains were dashed out against the wall.

By the next dispatch, Shaw's normally elegant hand was racing at such speed that the nib perforated the paper. The pit had become so full that, in the middle of the night, eight cartloads of bodies had been driven out of Mandalay and dumped in the Irrawaddy.

The jail-yard grave was filled in, but several days later stiffened hands and tortured faces burst through the topsoil. Hysteria tumbled through the palace, but no doubt gas produced by heat and decay had inflated the putrefying corpses, thrusting them upwards as if they were escaping from the grave. Queen Alé-nan-daw ordered in the royal elephanteers, who trampled the grotesque tableau until nothing more than the ox-blood earth could be seen.

The British were unnerved by the Mandalay massacre, concerned that Burma would soon erupt once again, dismembering British interests even before they had had time to take root, endangering the thousands of Britons who were now stationed in the Kingdom. But the military were committed elsewhere. British troops had occupied Kabul in November, invading Afghanistan over the high Indian passes to counter Russia's attempts to exert political influence over a country that lay along the North-west Frontier. Rather than get embroiled in another military conflict, Fort William advised Robert Shaw that he should concentrate on intelligence gathering.

But the representative was struggling with Burney's legacy and had no direct access to the King. No British representative had met a King of Burma since 1876, as they were still refusing to remove their shoes. In hundreds of telegrams that flew between Mandalay,

Calcutta and London, the British postured and ranted as Michael Symes had done before meeting King Bodawpaya. The British shoe was hard to unlace and lace. Bare feet were demeaning. It seemed impossible to resolve the diplomat's problem, even though British merchants were happy to unslipper. 'Now it really is not so bad to go a few yards in one's stockings,' Mrs Ellen Rowett wrote in *Frazier's Magazine*. 'One can put on two or more pairs of stockings and even slip a thick cork sole inside.'[6]

The Empire's view of Mandalay was filtered through intermediaries, and as Shaw warned Fort William, making policy from second-hand intelligence was like 'striking a piece of money at the bottom of a basin of water'. While Britain maintained an occluded vantage-point on a hill outside the court, feeding off rumours that Thibaw was a bloody tyrant who had orchestrated the killings of his brothers and sisters, a reporter from *The Times* interviewed the new King face-to-face. Thibaw appeared to be completely daunted by the task of ruling, a dim-witted boy barely able to grow a moustache and with no sign of the Konbaung Dynasty's regal forehead. As the stubby youth fiddled with his ceremonial sword and sweated beneath his golden armour, he blamed his mother-in-law for everything. 'You English think that I killed all my relatives, but it is not so,' he whispered. 'I was under guard myself. The reason that I was not murdered was that before the King died he told the Queen I was the quiet son.'

Before Shaw had a chance to resolve the shoe question and meet Thibaw for himself, he contracted rheumatic fever and died on 15 June 1879. His untimely demise would prove disastrous for the new King, as his place was taken by Colonel Horace Browne, a British warmonger, with his eye on the King's oil wells, teak forests and legendary gem pits.

Browne had an agenda of his own: to seek revenge for his previous encounter with the Burmese, one that had begun with fanfares and ended with beheadings. His log for that fated expedition records that in 1875 his party left Bhamo, a river port north of Mandalay, at the same time as a Burmese tribute mission, the first for more than twenty years, that was carrying to Peking 2000 viss of jadeite (7000 pounds). Although Browne had been sent to gather intelligence on the reopening of Qianlong's Jade Road, his dispatches soon dissolved into a tirade that displayed his prejudices. A local warlord, conferred with a Golden Umbrella by the King of Burma, who had offered to help Browne, was the 'dirtiest and most repulsive man we have yet seen'. Others were 'dogs' or 'savages'. A guide who was to escort the Colonel to the Chinese border reminded him 'of a dressed-up monkey in a circus'. Luckily, a member of his party had come with eau-de-Cologne, 'without which it would have been quite impossible to sit anywhere near these people.' When villagers accepted the money Browne offered them, they were 'Jewish skinflints' bagging a pound of flesh, 'if such an animal as a Shylock with the nasal development of a gibbon can be imagined'.

Then on 22 February Browne's expedition was attacked. Ignoring repeated warnings from the locals, his party had pressed on into dangerous territory, and Augustus Margary, his translator, and five Chinese servants were decapitated, their heads abandoned on a wall. As Margary's body was transported to Rangoon, Horace's *Odes* and *Satires,* a compilation of Milton's poetry and three pieces of rough jadeite in his pockets, Browne returned to Mandalay. There, in June, he filed a compensation claim for 918.12 rupees for the loss of his waterproof, umbrella, dress uniform and cashmere coat.

Fifteen years later, the bigoted Browne was the eyes and ears of the British, and he immediately set about regurgitating rumour and misinformation:

> In the Palace the ignorant, arrogant and drunken boy king is surrounded by a set of parvenu sycophants, the men of massacre and bloodshed, all of them ignorant and savage enough to urge him on to further atrocities.

The Colonel claimed that Thibaw had secreted bottles of French brandy in every cold stone parapet. He executed officials caught playing marbles. Using a wholly unrelated incident in Afghanistan, Browne, with his fairground hall of mirrors, raised the stakes. Sir Louis Cavagnari, his staff and 75 soldiers were slaughtered at the British Residency in Kabul following a mutiny that erupted on 3 September. Browne, who was clearly a graft from the same pipal tree that Emperor Daoguang had warned against in 1836, advised that Mandalay too was about to become hostile.

Within weeks the British Resident in Upper Burma was recalled, and now there was no independent means of confirming Browne's analysis, no direct links with the court or the King, only a vacuum to be filled with prejudice, gossip, innuendo and self-interest. The accidental monarch was being drawn towards a collision with the cantankerous juggernaut of the British Empire.

British intelligence from the court of King Thibaw was left in the hands of Giovanni Andreino, an Italian former postman whom Robert Shaw had dubbed 'an illiterate organ-grinder who could hardly write his name'. And even Andreino's information was second-hand.

Mrs Mattie Calogreedy Antram, the widow of a Captain of the Irrawaddy Flotilla Company, had become an informal adviser to Queen Supayalat, whom she met once a week in the Lily Throne room, accompanied by two French Catholic nuns, sisters Theresa and Sophia. Mrs Antram was brimming with gossip: the Queen called her husband 'Maung Maung', he knew her as 'Su Su'. The royal marriage started promisingly with Supayalat taking the upper hand by shouldering aside her ugly older sister. But then Thibaw took to being entertained by a harem of girls who were called to his chambers by electric buzzers that sounded in their rooms. When Su Su discovered that her husband had fallen in love with one of his harem, Mi Hkin-gyi, the daughter of the Minister of Mines, she acted with brutal efficiency. In March 1882, she abducted Yanaung, Thibaw's religious instructor, whom she accused of procuring her husband's girlfriends, rolled him up in a straw mat and had him clubbed to death by four drunks.[7] Two months later Mi Hkin-gyi, who was by now heavily pregnant, 'was beaten to death in the presence of the Queen [Supayalat]'.[8] Missionaries who had heard of the events at court from the Catholic sisters sent telegrams to London that called for a military assault on the Burmese court, a 'fountainhead of depravity'.

Antram also revealed that Thibaw was running out of money. She had obtained copies of accounts that showed that the King and Queen had been spending more than 4 million rupees a year on Chinese silks, French perfumes, jewellery and spirits. Soon their poverty became more public. Thibaw and Supayalat began granting audiences to tourists for 200 rupees per ticket, transforming the monarchy into a side-show. Felice Beato, who had recently opened a studio in Rangoon, sold photographs of the King in his Mandalay Regalia, his Queens sitting demurely by his side, their legs tucked beneath them 'like Punjabi tailors'. The Royal snapshots were in such demand that Queen Supayalat had a studio installed in the palace staffed by a French photographer, who quipped that when he 'took a picture of the King or Queen it was an even chance whether he would get a handful of rubies or have his head cut off.'[9]

While the palace gossip was entertaining, it did not provide the evidence, as Colonel Browne had suggested, of a Burmese tyrant bent on destroying the British Empire. But in May 1885, in a fiery swish of satin and crinoline, Mrs Antram sought out 'the illiterate organ-grinder' and gave him a parcel of secret documents. She had stolen them from her common-law husband, a French engineer, after he returned from a trip to Paris with a new wife. They purported to show that the French were preparing to steal a march on the British in Burma. The French government was said to have secured Thibaw's permission to establish a bank in Mandalay, build railroads and, most significantly, survey the northern reaches of Burma for gems.

Andreino stirred the pot by leaking another letter that revealed how Frederic Haas, the new French consul, had secretly met Burmese courtiers without his shoes on. Further, the letter revealed a plot. 'The French government is in the position to supply any amount of arms and ammunition . . . The Burmese received the information with great joy,' it stated.

Britain's Chief Commissioner passed on news that a new contingent of 'capitalists from Paris' had been spotted in Mandalay. 'They have applied for permission to travel all over the country and search for mineral deposits . . . swelling themselves like the frog in the fable.'[10] The news was confirmed by Edwin Streeter, a watchmaker and diamond merchant, based in the City Bank Building, Holborn Viaduct, in London, who had overheard a conversation 'while at breakfast in his hotel in Paris' between French merchants who claimed to have secured concessions from Thibaw to mine gems. Burma was about to be crushed like a peppercorn between jockeying Imperial powers.[11]

But when the British finally threatened war, it was not over gem concessions. The Burmese court fined a British trading company 2.3 million rupees (£153,000) for illegal logging, a punishment that threatened to bankrupt the firm and see a French competitor steal its contract. So the 'Royal Friend!' sent King Thibaw an ultimatum. Dispatched on the steamer *Ashley Eden* on 23 October 1885, it demanded independent arbitration over the Bombay Burma Trading Company logging dispute. But more significantly, a new British Resident was to be installed immediately in Mandalay (with his shoes on) who would be given full access to the King and control of Burma's foreign policy.

Queen Supayalat, who was five months pregnant, ordered the *Hlutdaw* to prevaricate. She was certain that she was bearing a son and had no intention of handing his future kingdom to the *kullas*. But the British were already reducing it to tables and graphs. The forestry industry would realise an estimated 1,350,000 rupees annually; the sale of royal lands would raise 800,000 rupees; 2.3 million rupees would be generated through taxation; the legendary jadeite mines were worth 800,000 rupees a year. Although Burma would run at a loss of 2.3 million rupees for the first 10 years, it would then become a profitable wholly-owned subsidiary of the Indian Empire, civil servants had concluded in secret dispatches.

❖

Before the Burmese had a chance to reply, General Harry Prendergast, a ramrod British commander and veteran of Afghanistan, received orders to advance up the Irrawaddy. The Conservative Party was facing a General Election in late November 1885. A speedy victory, Randolph Churchill, the foreign secretary argued, would add a new territory to the Empire's portfolio, a new market for exports, a distraction from the glum news of the stagnating domestic economy. Prendergast's political officer was Colonel Edward Sladen, a decorated veteran of the Second Burmese War, who had been wounded by a poisoned arrow, and also survived the relief of Lucknow in 1857, having served in India with Sir Hope Grant. Now, on 14 November 1885, Sladen, with his delicate features and clipped moustache, stood on deck as the expeditionary force swept up the Irrawaddy. It was a rapid and ruthless advance. Telegrams flew between Fort William and Whitehall as the Burmese frontier defences fell at Minhla and then at Gwaygyaung. Burmese troops abandoned their positions *en masse* as British boats steamed into view, machine-guns mounted on the prows that appeared to Thibaw's men like flaming *nagas* spitting bullets. Although the Burmese outnumbered the British by more than two to one, their flintlocks and muskets had to be loaded with a rod, each shot taking an age to prepare, while the British breech-loading rifles blasted out eight rounds a minute. Before he even glimpsed Mandalay, General Prendergast telegraphed an urgent request to army command. Was he permitted to sack Upper Burma? The Foreign Office mulled over Prendergast's request with the Chinese war still uppermost in its thoughts. 'It will not do for our troops to simply sack the palaces as the French did in Peking,' the Foreign Office concluded. Eventually it was agreed; the General's men could take booty, but it was to be a systematic operation bound by orders and precedent. Civil servants referred Prendergast to the recently published *Manual of Military Law* and particularly to the chapter entitled 'The Customs of War:

> The property of the enemy, whether public or private, found on the field of battle, in a camp taken by assault, or a town delivered up to pillage are the spoils of war and can legitimately be considered booty.

Seven days later the General was within striking distance of Mandalay. Several amateur photographers were within the ranks, W. W. Hooper and Robert Blackall Graham among them, hanging over the rails of the lead boat to record for posterity the fall of Burma. A staccato telegram wired by a correspondent from *The Times* described how a golden warship emerged from the heavy mist that clung to the Irrawaddy, pulled by 44 oarsmen, bearing a flag of truce and a letter:

> Burmese government cannot believe that British government would take Upper Burma. Burmese government has welfare and prosperity of English people at heart. Kingdom of Burma need not be occupied . . . His majesty is inclined to be well disposed in mind and heart, straightforward and just . . .

Within hours the commander-in-chief of Thibaw's army, a sparrow-like man dressed in a conical velvet cap, held by a crown of beaten gold, clutching a palm-leaf fan, rowed out to greet the 'British War Vessel' with news of King Thibaw's unconditional surrender. On 28 November British troops disembarked from their steamers, clambering over the wreckage of Thibaw's sunken fleet, and marched towards the royal city, from where a terrible wailing could be heard. On the parapet of Mandalay's spiral lookout tower the soldiers from the Hampshire Regiment spotted a pregnant woman, screaming and slapping her distended belly. Edward Sladen was called over and recognised the distraught Queen Supayalat, but the King was nowhere to be seen.

The man from the Calcutta *Daily News* accompanied the soldiers as they surrounded Mandalay. 'Troops landed, marched, colours flying, bands playing, three columns, through city to palace, which was occupied without resistance,' he filed. For the rest of that afternoon Prendergast and Sladen stood impatiently at the palace gates, passing notes to the few remaining royal servants in an attempt to persuade the King to come out. Eventually, at 1 p.m. the following day, the gates opened and Prendergast and Sladen, accompanied by the ever-present man from the *Daily News,* entered the palace precincts, the first British party to do so in nine years.

Their path was littered with upturned carts and abandoned panniers, out of which spilled gold bars, silver betel boxes, jadeite boulders, ruby caskets, necklaces, tea sets, idols and mirrors. Thibaw had obviously been packing, and beside the cases of treasure stood 50 elephants and 200 ponies that were to have carried the Royals into the northern jungles, if Supayalat had not refused to leave.

Inside the empty Hall of Audiences, the forlorn couple sat unattended on the Lion Throne, the King dressed in his regalia. Before them stood the protective ranks of the *chinthe* and the *camari,* statues of mythical beasts tamed by the King and gilt pageboys, their arms raised in devotion to the father of the nation. While the Queen pressed for concessions as she hugged her unborn heir, Thibaw sobbed. 'I surrender myself and my country to you,' he told Sladen, who spoke Burmese and Hindi. 'All I ask is, don't let me be taken away suddenly.' The *Daily News* filed an on-the-spot report:

> British had interview with King and Queen. I was present. King fairly dignified manner, short, stout, unintelligent looking. Queen with slight, young, rather clever face, good looking except for very hard evil mouth. She constantly whispered suggestions to Thibaw during interview.

Thibaw was terrified of his own people, Sladen wrote in his log, of being abducted by a lynch mob. He asked if Sladen would place a European guard in the palace to protect him and his property. 'Sentries were dropped as we passed through the several state apartments of the palace,' Sladen wrote before pocketing the keys and asking Hooper to take his photograph, standing beneath a golden umbrella, a perplexed Burmese court official at his side.

A young captain, Charles Adamson, one of the first to enter the palace, recorded with glee that 'where barefooted ministers used to walk to pay obeisance to the centre of the universe', British soldiers 'in their heavy boots tramped in and out'. Adamson was surprised by the chaotic state of the palace, 'heaps of arms and helmets formerly belonging to the King's soldiers, palm leaf records, lumps of jade, huge mirrors, gilded and jewelled chairs . . . scattered about promiscuously throughout the rooms and passages.'

Magnificent Mandalay, built as testimony to the omnipotence of the Konbaung Dynasty, appeared to the man from the *Daily News* as little more than a ramshackle tombstone for the Kingdom of Burma:

> Royal family almost deserted, even food said wanting; saw white elephant near in splendid house also unattended. Very ordinary really with just two, small, imperceptible dirty white spots behind its ears.
>
> Palace wonderfully effective, distinct, closer, rather tawdry, tall carved wooden roofs profusely gilden coloured; interior mass of small detached buildings look like gold caskets inside, also much gold colour as usual Asiatics, dirty, neglected in places. King ordinary dress; Queen splendid diamond and jade necklace, nothing definite arranged yet as to future of country; late afternoon two bullock gharis conveyed the King and Queen. Populace generally perfectly unconcerned.

One short telegram to encapsulate the demise of thousands of years of Burmese monarchy. Where the Mongol hordes, Chinese Imperial armies, Siamese monarchs and Moghul emperors had failed, a small band of men in khaki and pugarees had succeeded. The 'King of all Umbrella Wearing Nations etc. etc.' had been driven with his two inconsolable wives, the Dowager Queen, five leading ministers of state, 16 princesses and maids of honour, and 43 followers into exile on bullock carts. Pulling up at the Irrawaddy pier, the Royal party, Queen Supayalat weeping, accompanied their cumbersome trunks and packages aboard the steamer *Thooria* bound for Rangoon, ascending the gangplank along a corridor of British troops, followed on board by two companies of the Liverpool Regiment. Left behind were Thibaw's two white elephants, one of which would die from starvation after its keeper fled, and the other would be fought over by the New York Zoological Society and London Zoo. Eventually it was penned in Phayre Gardens, Rangoon, the public symbol of a tethered nation. As the *Thooria* pulled away, Thibaw turned to see the Union Jack fluttering over his Great Golden Land and heard the British salutes thundering across the divine imprint of the star-filled heavens.

One week later, the Royals were on the move again as the sun set over Rangoon. The sullen King and his pregnant Queen were deported from Burma on the *IGS Canning* along with their cumbersome baggage train, which a welcoming party in Madras, where Thibaw arrived four days later, attempted to investigate. Asked to itemise all of his possessions, the deposed monarch simply wrote: '1 King, 2 Queens, 2 dauters [*sic*], 2 nurses, 2 assistant nurses, 13 maids of honour, 1 King's herald, 1 clerk, 1 Chamberlain, 9 interpreters.'

Temporarily installed in The Mansion, Thibaw and Supayalat struggled to adjust to life in exile, believing that it was only a matter of time before they would be allowed back to Burma. One morning they woke to find that the zinc pipes had burst, flooding the house, and a glass chandelier had plunged to the floor. These were inauspicious signs, but not as worrying as a letter that arrived, bearing critical news. 'The Head of the Umbrella Bearing Nations etc. etc.' was now to be known as 'the ex-King' and was required to live on a pension of 3000 rupees a month. Deputy Inspector Cox of the Madras police reported how Thibaw refused to leave the house for a week, ranting and crying, muttering about shoes. He complained 'that time hangs heavy on his hands and repeatedly asks when Sladen will return his property'. When, on 25 March 1886, Supayalat gave birth to a third daughter, it must have finally dawned on the exiled couple that the end of the Konbaung Dynasty was in sight.

Within a fortnight the ex-King's entourage was at sea again. On the suggestion of Sir Charles Bernard, the Chief Commissioner of Burma, the Royal party was transported to an Indian village so sodden in the monsoon and so parched in the summer that few knew of its existence. The Governor of Madras thought it a harsh place. 'Ratnagiri seems very desolate and cheerless, not somewhere to spend the rest of your life and I believe the climate of northern India is trying for the Burmans,' he wrote. Lord Dufferin, the Viceroy of India, had to be advised where Ratnagiri was and suspected that it was 'dreary'. But on 10 April, the Royal party boarded the SS *Clive,* muffled in furs. They were led to the quarter-deck that had been screened off and carpeted. The King and Queen shuffled toward two deckchairs, but as the ship weighed anchor and careened in a squall, jadeite and diamonds spilled from their pockets, brilliant green stones rolling across the deck like marbles. The King and Queen seemed blasé to the point of sedation, according to sailors aboard the vessel, they were two barely recognisable figures, plump silhouettes of a monarchy sailing into extinction.

The SS *Clive* arrived six days later on the west coast of India, and the ex-King's retinue was transported to a cliff-top villa that had been bought from a Colonel Godfrey. The old man's retirement home, at the end of a rutted dirt track that overlooked the Arabian Sea, was to become Thibaw's prison, frugally furnished with a handful of pieces from Mandalay: a Cleopatra sofa, a deer-horn hat stand, a teak table supported by carved elephant legs. Everything else was garage-sale stock sent down from Bombay. Now certain that the British would execute him, Thibaw spent his days sitting on the roof, refusing to come down, writing letters to his 'Royal Friend!' in London. In one, composed in August 1886, the ex-King asked for the treasures he had entrusted to Edward Sladen and implored Queen Victoria, as if she were a schoolma'am and he the errant pupil:

> My spirits are low. I can only compare Ratnagiri to the wild villages of the Kachin and Karen, there are a great many snakes and scorpions. I have only a small brick house to live in and am guarded by a party of Sepoys. I wish to be allowed to return to my country on any conditions that the British government may make and that if I misbehave myself in any way, I will be willing to be sent back and placed in confinement.

Attached to the letter was a five-page list written in a child's hand that quantified the personal wealth of the Konbaung Dynasty. Thibaw demanded the return of his regalia: crowns, *tsalwes* of diamonds, emeralds and rubies, worn across both shoulders. He then listed a trove of precious boxes cast in gold and set with jadeite, golden hand basins and twenty jadeite necklaces belonging to 'Su Su'. There were nine ruby rings, gold bracelets and a diamond belt, royal crests set with precious stones, his gem-encrusted caps, clocks and the Queen's court dress. It was a dazzling inventory of jewels: a wild duck with rubies for eyes; an infant's cradle of spun gold; caparisoned trappings for the royal elephants and horses; seven swords whose handles and sheaths were inlayed with jadeite and rubies. Finally Thibaw asked for 21 lacquered boxes that contained his collection of silks, and his Royal bed. Pinned to the inventory that had been abandoned in the New Delhi archives was the original typed reply: 'We have failed to discover . . . the items Thibaw has requested. The property cannot be restored and we have been liberal in allowing the ex-King to take with him what he has.' The Dowager Queen, inconsolable after being separated from her two daughters and sent to live in the southern Burmese town of Tavoy, also demanded to know what had happened to the treasures that she had entrusted to the engaging Sladen. Her pencilled inventory, delicate curlicue Burmese letters drawn with short controlled strokes, was prefaced with a letter to the Viceroy of India in which she accused Sladen of stealing her jewels:

> I entrusted them to him. Colonel Sladen said: 'The government will not take possession of the Royal Family property; we only want the king and his kingdom. Believe me, these valuable articles cannot get lost, your highness can at pleasure take them back any time.' So saying, he personally locked the box, then shut and locked the door.

An inventory that ran to six pages itemised the contents of trunks that contained diamond ear-rings the size of door-knobs and rubies the colour of pigeon's blood. There were gold anklets shaped like dragons and a diamond casket in which she had pinned a portrait of the Prince of Wales. The letter and the list ended up on the desk of Sir Donald Mackenzie Wallace, private secretary to the Viceroy. 'The identification and recovery of the Queen's possessions is hopeless,' he advised London, suggesting that the Queen Mother's pension be raised by 50 rupees a month 'in settlement of the property claim'. But the Foreign Office declined for compelling reasons that we uncovered in the New Delhi files.

■

On 11 December 1885, General Prendergast had sent a telegram to Calcutta confirming that his men had in their possession 'treasures and valuables, consisting of jewels, large quantities of silk and other stuffs'. When the Hampshire Regiment had gathered for 'a Divine Service' on Christmas Day outside one of the royal palaces and sung 'Hark the Herald Angels Sing', a moment captured by Hooper, they had much to celebrate.[12] A prize committee was to be formed by Lt Col Budgen, and in the New Year he was to hold a series of auctions in Burma and in India. The boxes of silks requested by Thibaw were sold off in Rangoon for 14,000 rupees. An unknown number of artefacts and items of jewellery, dismissed by the British as 'palace waste', including solid-gold icons that surrounded the Lion Throne, were sent to the Hamilton Mint in Calcutta where they were melted down, the bullion realising 211,000 rupees. Even Burmese bullets were smelted into ingots that were sold for 19,906 rupees. A haul of jadeite boulders that the British had initially mistaken for 'a rockery in the southern gardens of the Mandalay palace' was given to Gillanders, Arbuthnot & Co., who reported that a sale in Hong Kong had only raised 3170 rupees.[13] When later challenged by auditors to explain the dismal amount, the jeweller claimed to have lost the receipts and the matter was closed. In all, 99 boxes of booty were taken by the armed forces from Mandalay, and Lt Col Budgen valued the army's haul at 900,000 rupees, of which 477,000 was divided among those who had participated in the Burma Campaign.

While Thibaw wept atop his Ratnagiri roof the British attempted to balance the books. Edward Grant, chief superintendent in the office of the Comptroller General in Rangoon, advised Calcutta that 'a large quantity' of items listed as prize property had disappeared before the government auctions took place. 'There are numerous articles of considerable value that I have not been able to trace,' a perplexed Grant wrote. But the Government of India refused to investigate.

Despite Foreign Office claims that it would prevent a repetition of the Summer Palace débâcle, British soldiers had filled their pockets with 'loot and bizarrerie' in the days following the ex-King's deportation as they rampaged through Mandalay. They had stripped the Hall of Audiences, defaced Royal bedchambers, swum in the Queen's spa and looted the monasteries. Lt Col Raikes dismantled a gilded shrine, sending the gold supplicants that sat around a miniature copy of the Lion Throne back to Somerset, where they remained until after the Second World War, when they were acquired by the Victoria & Albert Museum, where they stand today. Captain Truscott seized a seated lacquered Buddha that he later gave to Exeter City Museum and Art Gallery. No one knows who prised the large ruby from the forehead of the 'Gautama of the Incomparable Pagoda' or who torched the treasury.[14] But thousands of unique parabaiks were destroyed on the pyre, although a consignment of them, including two manuscript boxes, ended up in the British Museum.

There was no attempt to hide the trophies of war, and Hooper was recruited to take snapshots. Officers of the 2nd Madras Lancers, who had transformed a monastery into a billet, piled up golden statues, spears, jewelled betel boxes and court regalia on tables beside their army-issue camp beds, pith helmets and holstered pistols. On the back of one photograph Hooper wrote: 'The contents of the room in the picture here given consist principally, as is seen, of what may be designated loot.'[15]

A second series of equally candid photographs were deemed to have overstepped the bounds of respectability. Hooper, a Provost Marshal with the military police, was criticised by *The Times* for taking snapshots of Burmese looters being executed by a British firing squad. The outcry led to a court martial during which General Prendergast attempted to defend Hooper by claiming that 'The prisoners were blindfolded and did not know they were being photographed.' Hooper was sent home, along with his sepia prints that, bound by a publisher in gilt and red leather, became a best-seller.

Stories soon began to circulate about buried treasure. So many had looted so much that some of the haul from ransacked Mandalay was thought to have been hidden in the gardens of the palace. James Mobbs, an estate agent from Onslow Road, Southampton, contacted the Earl of Kimberley claiming to act on behalf of a Burma veteran who was prepared to disclose the location of his secret stash. 'The items were buried,' Mobbs wrote. 'I am perfectly willing to do anything you may wish to obtain their recovery but I require first to know what remuneration you are willing to pay me.'[16]

He claimed that William White, a.k.a. Jack Marshall, a 30-year-old soldier whose eye had been closed by a sabre scar while serving in Burma with the 2nd Queen's Royal West Surrey Regiment, 'currently employed in Kent as a farm labourer', could lead the British to the plunder. But the Foreign Office buried Mobbs' proposal, preferring to lose Thibaw's jewels rather than pay for their return.

Many of the missing items had secretly been dispatched to Queen Victoria. Acting on the orders of the Viceroy of India, three crates left Rangoon on 27 March. The consignment was routed through Liverpool, arriving there on 13 May, before being sent to the India Store Depot, Belvedere Road, Lambeth, from where it was eventually delivered to Windsor Castle. The boxes themselves had been ambiguously labelled, the contents misleadingly valued at only 10,000 rupees, and no inventory was provided.[17]

Owen Burne, head of the India Office's Political and Secret Department in London, received a second consignment of more than 120 hand-picked items, including jadeite carvings and a hoard of jewelled boxes. Sir Charles Bernard oversaw the covert exports with zeal:

> Items for Her Majesty the Queen-Empress, Windsor Castle, England: Thibaw's best crown, in a large gilt box, three emeralds and other stones including jade from Thibaw's second crown, envelopes containing jade, loose stones etc. which have dropped off the crown, necklace with diamond peacock and gold comb. Two handsomely carved elephant tusks from palace at Mandalay. A solid gold figure of Buddha from the palace. I am also sending home boxes of rubies, jade, diamonds and sapphires, many kinds of stones etc. These are for examination and sale.

Bernard forgot to mention that he had also shipped part of Mandalay to London, after the Governor General of India took a fancy to a pavilion 'which was rather an obstruction to free passage and ventilation'. But his clerk noted on file:

As a characteristic specimen of Burmese architecture it seemed worthy of a place in the South Kensington Museum . . . The Prince of Wales hearing about it directed for it to be sent hence . . . Sir C. Bernard has, on his own initiative, added a second small pavilion of the same kind and both are at the moment on the way home.

So many parcels converged on London that Alfred Phillips, an auctioneer and jeweller, and Edwin Streeter, were hired to value the Burmese haul. It was stored, temporarily, at the South Kensington Museum. One hundred items, including the King's regalia, were valued at £21,198.10s.0d, in a report that, echoing Henry Loch, concluded that the Mandalay treasures were of 'little or no intrinsic value'. Boxes of jadeite bangles and rough jadeite boulders were put into storage, as no one understood their worth. Burne ordered some of the haul to be sold off to the highest bidder, and the remainder was sent as a hasty addition to the Colonial and Indian Exhibition that displayed 'the far off, the strange, the wonderful, the original, the true, the brave, the conquered'.[18]

❧

On Tuesday 4 May 1886, days after the ex-King of Burma arrived at his cliff-top prison in India, Queen Victoria officiated at the opening of the Exhibition, seated on a looted throne of hammered gold that had once belonged to Ranjit Singh, the Maharaja of Lahore. The Albert Hall resounded to the national anthem sung in English and Sanskrit, and a new verse by Alfred, Lord Tennyson was read aloud, imploring the sons of Britain to 'be welded each and all, into one Imperial whole, one with Britain's heart and soul.'[19]

Illuminated by 9700 'electric glow lamps', the Colonial and Indian Exhibition shimmered behind the Albert Hall, on a site bought out of the proceeds of the 1851 Great Exhibition. Stuffed elephants charged through papier-mâché jungles. Wounded bears sought refuge in wooden caves. Glassy-eyed cheetahs stalked gazelles grazing on a plaster savannah. And in the Imperial Court a 'catalogue of ethnic people' had been updated to include the residents of Upper Burma and their vast expanse of treacherous jungles that concealed hidden treasure over which now optimistically fluttered the Union Jack:

> The conquests of the last few months have . . . extended the British dominions. Upper Burma is, however, too imperfectly known to justify an attempt being made in this brief ethnological catalogue to include the tribes, which have so recently become British subjects.

In the Upper Gardens were Thibaw's private apartments that had been reconstructed in Kensington by 'Hormusjee, a Parsi carpenter'. Inside were 'the ex-King's hat and slippers' that 'drew large and admiring crowds'.

The shilling programme, on which a strident Britannia ruled over a docile lion, paid tribute to Caspar Purdon Clarke, Keeper of the India Museum, the exhibition's architect. It also thanked 'J. L. Kipling, principal of the Mayo School of Arts in Lahore', who had obtained Ranjit Singh's golden throne, while his son was presumably dreaming of sitting astride the great gun Zam Zammah.[20] It thanked the 'native princes and nobles', the Nizam of Hyderabad and the Maharaja of Mysore, but there was no mention of King Thibaw.

When the great exhibition drew to a close, Alfred Phillips was hired again on a £25 honorarium to determine the future of the Burmese exhibits. The majority of them, including the regalia, the pavilions and a gold betel box shaped like a goose were handed over to the South Kensington Museum. Of the remaining items, two cushions that a humorous Burman had embroidered with peacocks trampling a lion and a unicorn were presented to Queen Victoria and the Prince of Wales.

Two years later, dozens more missing items turned up at the International Exhibition in Glasgow. Robert Gordon lent Thibaw's teak bed, complete with mattress, bolsters and pillows, the frame 'covered with gold, mirror and red lacquer work'. John Conbrough lent a collection of Pali manuscripts and a gilt umbrella. Jadeite and gold jewellery was contributed by General E. H. Power. The gangplank from 'Thibaw's Royal Yacht' was anonymously lent and Edward Sladen displayed the *tsalwe* awarded to him by King Mindon during happier times.

What of Sladen? Only months after the conquest in Mandalay, the British Government asked the Colonel to retire after 40 years of military service, despite his entreaties to stay on. In March 1886 a farewell dinner was held for him at Mandalay Palace, where dozens of officers dined on salmon, pigeon, Burmese chicken and salami, finishing up with *poudin à Sladen* while the 1st Madras Pioneers played extracts from *The Mikado*. His after-dinner speech was an untidy set of thoughts that he clearly revised several times before the soirée. 'Now that I am on the point of shuffling out of harness,' he wrote, 'my greatest regret, gentlemen, is that I am leaving at a time when matters are unfortunately far from settled . . . I leave Mandalay with many regrets.'[21]

Seven months later Sladen received a knighthood, but was his role in the pillaging of Mandalay among his regrets? When the Government of India had received letters from Thibaw and his mother-in-law accusing Sladen of theft, Sir Charles Bernard had quietly warned the Colonel 'to be discreet'. When the ex-King and his mother-in-law became more insistent, a second letter, via the United Services Club in Pall Mall, politely demanded a response:

> The court officials tell us that on the morning of the 29th November they were present when a large quantity of jewels and other valuables were made over to you by the ex-King. Sir Charles Bernard thinks that you may be able to help us. Could you give us any information as to what became of these valuables? PS May I be allowed to congratulate you on your distinction, also Lady Sladen, whom I would like to be remembered to. I hope you have been enjoying your rest in England.

Sir Edward rounded on the allegations, claiming that in November 1885 Mandalay had been 'in chaos' and that he had been forced to work under 'exceptional circumstances'. But although Sir Edward was now seen through the lens of his brilliant negotiated victory, he had not always been held in such high regard. The New Delhi archives contain a series of secret reports that detail how in 1869, Sladen, then a political agent, had been recalled from Mandalay, after being accused of having lost his mind. 'Captain Sladen . . . is evidently suffering from nervous excitement and irritation, with threatening symptoms of paralysis. He should be strongly recommended to take leave at once,' one medical report concludes. He had mistranslated letters from Mindon, claiming that the King had used a 'tone of insolent defiance' when there was none. He had advised of an imminent Burmese war that was not threatened and never materialised. He had suffered from hallucinations and extreme paranoia. A more explosive issue surfaced in 1881, when the Indian Government was confronted by a Burmese woman, his children's former nurse, who claimed to have given birth to his illegitimate child. This time Sladen escaped punishment by accusing the woman of blackmail.

The gentlemanly disciplinarian evidently had a history of succumbing to stress and temptation. A private note, discarded in a file of personal correspondence gifted to the British Library, appears to confirm a third deviation from the righteous path. On an undated sheet of plain paper, torn from a notebook, Sir Edward began to write, in the same black, spidery hand that distinguished his letters and journals, a list of artefacts and jewellery that he had acquired 'during the first few days of the surrender'. They were taken from the palace itself and also 'from my followers who had reclaimed them from other looters . . . I merely took these items to prevent them from being looted and if required will surrender them to the prize committee.' The note begins by listing maps, umbrellas, spears, fans, silver caskets, a large gem-encrusted state chain, a French writing-desk, Burmese gongs and three photograph albums, before petering out. It was never completed or submitted to Sir Charles Bernard.

※

While Sir Edward searched his conscience, the British stepped into the ex-King's jewelled slippers, dismantling his legacy. Mandalay Palace was renamed Fort Dufferin after the Viceroy of India, whose title was extended to 'Lord of Dufferin and Ava'. The Baho Sigyi Drum was dispatched to Rangoon Museum and the gilded thrones in the ex-King's palaces were sent to Calcutta. The *Hlutdaw*'s hall, that once had 'powers of life and death, that could make or mar a man's fortunes', was now home to 'a superintending engineer, and a horde of plodding clerks engaged in the filling in of forms with as much zeal as if they were building an empire'.[22] The golden monastery where Thibaw had won his only mark of distinction under the tutelage of the rapacious Yanaung now held Sunday services. The few remaining Burmese monks at Salin Kyaung Daik monastery watched in bemusement through one window as British riders chased balls with mallets, while through another came the crack of a rifle discharged at a makeshift range. Thibaw's Royal Barge, its prow a seething *naga,* was towed to the edge of a new gymkhana ground and transformed into a floating refreshment stall. The ex-Queen's Lily Throne room chimed at dusk as ice cubes tumbled into crystal and paper-skinned British ladies sat with their blazered husbands toasting the Empire in the Upper Burma Club. A band chugged out serenades while tall men studied the lie of the billiard table. The 'swish of the soda-water bottle and the spluttering of fans' were drowned out by the bragging of adventurers in striped sports jackets who boasted of the fortunes they would make in the jungles of the north.[23] A bored baronet set on finding the legendary mines searched the notice-boards for news of a departing expedition.

Burma was, after all, the Great Golden Land and treasure was on everyone's mind. When on 10 February 1886, General Prendergast convened a meeting aboard the steamer *Mindoon* to plan the future of the 200,000 square miles of new British territory, he resolved that an expedition into a 'rugged and little traversed route' that was 'rich in mines' should embark immediately. Thanks to the French mineralogist Alexander Damour, the British now knew that it was jadeite that lay in the Kachin Hills, a Stone of Heaven prized by the Qing, who were said to be willing to pay a fortune for even the smallest pieces.

Sir Charles Bernard advised caution: 'The area will become an important trading centre but is populated by Kachins who even owed the Burmese government very little authority.' But the first hostile element to wipe out the British troops was the perilous climate. General White, the expedition's leader, had warned against embarking during the monsoon, but, anxious to proceed, the British Government had ignored him. By June, White had established a garrison in Bhamo, and very quickly he found himself marooned. 'Troops available are suffering dysentery, recovering from cholera, will lose more if we march,' White cabled, as the rain lashed his new stockade and fever claimed a quarter of his men. When intelligence arrived in Mandalay that the Chinese were moving in on the pits, White and his depleted forces were ordered on.

No sooner had they left Bhamo than they encountered Hannay's 'masters of war'. Bogged down in mud-pools that soaked their dyed khaki drill uniforms, White's men were pinned down by invisible snipers who jeered and screamed through the day and night. The General dispatched urgent messages. He needed at least 600 more rifles and 800 ponies. 'The road is a mountain track, infested with robbers who live on blackmail . . . All around is dense jungle and forest.' In a matter of weeks White's expedition was reluctantly re-called. Bernard sent an expeditious telegram to Calcutta to explain the retreat: 'It is decided that the jade is to be left for the present in the hands of the Chinese lease-holders until a geological survey of Upper Burma can be carried out.'

In November 1887, Captain Charles Adamson, who had re-corded with glee how British boots stomped across Burma's her-itage, began to assemble another expedition. But as we raced through the New Delhi files, the paper trail abruptly vanished. Someone had gone through the archives and ripped out every refer-ence to Adamson's journey down to the requisition orders for men and munitions. It wasn't until several months later that we found a 63-page manuscript in the Oriental and India Office archives in London that trumpeted the success of 'a great journey north'. It was Adamson's personal account of the expedition that had been filed in a box of miscellaneous nineteenth-century Indian river journeys.[24]

It began on a triumphal note that mocked General White's mis-erable campaign: 'If any credence had been placed in the difficulties and dangers that we were informed had to be faced, it is certain that our expedition would never have started.' But despite his bravado, the Captain was leaving nothing to chance. He requested as his deputy Captain Triscott, an old friend and veteran of the Burma War. He called up 50 rifles from the Cheshire Regiment, 100 rifles from the Kilat I Gilzais Regiment, 25 men from the Mounted In-fantry and 500 from the Military Police. He demanded 2 mounted gun batteries, 350 baggage mules, 2 elephants, 3 steam launches, 33 'large country boats' and a party of surveyors who were to en-sure that they would find their way back to Mandalay. He recruited a medical field unit and a Roman Catholic pastor and hired 'Suffer Ally', 'a Musselman who had a wife in every important place', a man who had worked in the jade mines, to negotiate safe passage with the tribes. His secret weapon was Po Saw, 'a man of great in-fluence among the Kachins', coming from 'one of the noble families of Mogaung', who was given nine months' advanced wages to open a jade road. Finally, there was William Warry, the British Government's Chinese advisor, a former consul from Shanghai who had translated the annals of the Qing court. It was Warry who would negotiate with Chinese traders *en route*.

But Adamson encountered problems even before he left Bhamo. Suffer Ally bashfully admitted that he had in fact not visited the mines for many years and claimed to have forgotten the way. No one else in Bhamo was willing to accompany the British. 'The Chinese were afraid of losing a vast fortune represented by their monopoly, the Burmese knew they would lose their illegal gains, and the Kachin who listened to the Chinese and Burmans believed the English were no more than demons,' a disconsolate Adamson wrote. The Captain turned to more reliable sources. But Sepoy Singh's notes on the Kasa Naga Road were incomplete. The Kachin's constant warring had swallowed up many of his landmarks. Bayfield's journal was 'meagre', his map had disappeared and Griffith's log lingered on botany and ethnography.

So the Captain plunged into the darkness like Bodawpaya's envoys, with fanfares and a show of force. 'As the column marched out of Bhamo on 27 December [1887] it made a great impression of the natives. With a line of infantry marching one behind the other it stretched for two miles,' wrote Adamson.

Without local help it took the Captain's men nine hours to forge the Taiping, a tributary of the Irrawaddy that was a quarter of a mile across. The baggage mules had to be unloaded and forced to swim in an exhausting operation that was repeated the next day. As December ran into January, the convoy climbed hand-over-fist to a ridge from where Adamson saw for the first time what lay ahead: a range of jungle-clad mountains and valleys through which no paths appeared to have been cut. What had happened to Po Saw and his nine months' wages?

Adamson's men pushed on, encountering the 'dreaded whirlpool of Pashio', a torrent of water so extreme that they had to halt for a day to build a platform across it. Vultures swooped overhead and the tracks of wild elephant herds filled the men with dread. In his journal the Captain comforted himself with the vision of European settlers transforming a wild landscape into neat fields of wheat or maize once he had pacified the Kachin. The soldiers cheered themselves by the campfire singing each other to sleep. A bass from Cheshire filled the jungle with 'The Farmer's Boy' and taught the captain music-hall tunes that he had never heard before. 'Two lovely black eyes, Two lovely black eyes', they sang as they crawled through the land of the head-hunters without glimpsing the sun for days at a time. Only when Adamson came across a stream in which his men could cast a line did he find time to relax. Sitting on the bank, he cheered Captain Armstrong, the commander of the Cheshire Rifles, who snagged 'a very fine fish with large scales weighing 16 pounds'.

Finally, the expedition drew into Mogaung and found the Shan and Chinese residents heavily armed and living in terror of the Kachin, who were camped just beyond their ramshackle 'teak palisade'. Not a night passed without raiding parties breaching Mogaung's defences. 'Villagers keep their valuables and gemstones either buried in the ground or in their boats for protection,' Adamson noted, as rumours swept through the town that the tribes were massing. 'Monday 16th: cold and foggy, thermometer going down to 45 degrees,' one short entry records. 'We had a council of war.'

William Warry advised the Captain not to leave Mogaung without securing permission from the Kachin. Letters were sent on ahead advising the tribes that here was a friendly mission from Mandalay. For three days the jittery British stalked around the market 'displaying our large guns'. But when a message returned from the Kachin it was a warning and not an invitation. On 26 January, having waited for ten days, the impatient Adamson decided to ignore William Warry and press on across the rice paddy into a swamp so deep that the expedition had to bridge it with grass mats. But at least they were on the move again. 'The men were in high spirits; and the idea of entering an absolutely new and unknown country with the additional excitement of the chance of having a fight added much to the charm of the march we were commencing.'

The men wriggled across the swamp but their pack animals, weighed down with provisions and munitions, slipped between the bamboo warp and weft, some of them drowning in the treacherous slurry. For three more days they followed the Endaw River, through yet more marsh and across fields of unbending grass that towered above them. Ten men at a time would 'throw themselves at the blades', battering out a path. At last, they reached a clearing where men were carrying boulders suspended from poles like snagged wild boars. By now the British column, caked in mud and sweat, was barely recognisable. 'Faces . . . were as black as if they had been down a coal mine'. Every village they marched through bore the scars of Kachin treachery: razed huts, torched rice silos, tree-trunks soaked in blood and hung with bones.

Only when the exhausted Captain eventually reached the Uru River did he perk up. It reminded him of home, a day spent with friends on the riverside. It was 'as clear as crystal and so alive with fish that they rose to the surface in the evening like trout in an English stream.' But Suffer Ally, pointing to the hills that towered above, pulled him from his reverie, screaming for the convoy to dismount. 'The mines are there,' Ally cried, pointing north to the mist-covered ridge. 'Over here, hurry hurry.' And from the jungle came the sound of sluicing water, metal staves striking rock, picks and hammers breaking stone; a faint glimmer of fires licking giant boulders and smoke creeping through the trees.

Adamson's officers dashed into the undergrowth. The jewelled legends of Burma, a secret valley brimming with precious stones, blown like the seeds of a dandelion clock across Central Asia into Aristotle's study and through the Library of Alexandria, had at last been carried back to the Kachin Hills in British packs.

But before they could revel in history, the forward party returned. 'Men with arms' had blocked their path; 'they were not well received', and 'thinking that discretion was the better part of valour returned to base'. Adamson readied for battle. 'It was no light thing to be responsible for the loss of life incurred by forcing our way into the jade mines.' Captain Triscott called forward 100 men, bayonets fixed. 'This was a most anxious day,' Adamson wrote in his journal. 'Should we arrive at the jade mines without bloodshed or should we have to fight our way there and be harassed the whole way on our return journey? I was confident we could fight our way . . . but we were well aware we could suffer severe loss.'

Then, moving slowly along the opposite bank of the river, appeared 'a large body of men grasping a pair of elephant tusks.' At the front was the Kansi La, the Kachin warlord who ran the jade mines, and behind him were 12 *sawbwas* or chiefs accompanied by

100 bodyguards. Both sides circled. British rifles were raised. The Kachin were swathed in fur and fleece, armed with muskets, bows and spears. Then slowly and simultaneously everyone sat down, forming a circle outside the canvas flaps of Adamson's tent. The perplexed Kachin warlords, made rich by the jade they traded, were presented with mirrors, a mule and a buffalo by Adamson, who informed them that they were now British subjects. When they cast aside the gifts, the Captain ordered a demonstration of fire-power. 'One of the officers had with him a small Martini-Henry carbine, and with this he took a shot at a large kite sitting on a tree at the opposite side of the river . . . To the surprise of us all and especially the Kachin . . . the kite was knocked over.'

A murmur passed along the ranks of seated tribesmen, and Suffer Ally advised Adamson that his party was allowed to proceed. Through an abandoned bazaar they marched, then across an open plain where they spied 'about a dozen men on the far side . . . who on seeing us disappeared into the jungle'. Further on they came across 'blocks of white stone of all sizes, some of which were tinged with streaks of green. When we attempted to buy some jade as mementoes of our journey, the people mistrusted us and hid the most valuable pieces away.' But none of this spoiled Adamson's mood, and the Captain reflected on the success of his mission, almost giddy with excitement:

> We had arrived at the famous jade mines. With exception of Lieutenant Bayfield, who had reached them in 1838 [sic], we were the first Europeans to get there. We were absolutely looking at the mines which for the Chinese have from time immemorial been considered the most valuable possession in the world.

Adamson had seen the jade tract 'not in the position of a person admitted by favour' but 'as those who were there by right and who had come to take possession of their treasure in the name of the British people'. Overcome by patriotic fervour, he ordered Suffer Ally to translate his message from Queen Victoria, his words echoing the ethnological catalogue displayed in the Imperial Court of the Colonial and Indian Exhibition. What a terrible mistake!

☓

Secret letters and telegrams that flew between Mandalay, Fort William and London within weeks of Adamson's meeting with the Kansi La reveal how the braggartly officer ignited a conflict that engulfed the Kachin Hills and pitched the British into a bloody war. The *Hukawng* Valley was a testament to the wrath of the Kachin, filled as it was with the graves of conquered peoples, but had Adamson ever studied its history?

The night after the Captain had proclaimed the Kachin British subjects, they fell from the trees with poisoned arrows and *dahs*, hounding his column out of the hills, chasing them all the way back to Bhamo, taking the lives of four men in skirmishes that filled the jungle with screams. Adamson had been betrayed by his 'man of influence'. Po Saw, recruited at vast expense as Britain's jade roadcutter, had lured the expedition into a Marip Kachin ambush.

Never before had the Kachin been so directly threatened, and in the months following Adamson's retreat the *Ye Jein* went on the rampage. They attacked traders and fleeced travellers, boarding and looting Burmese and Chinese boats sailing between Bhamo and Mogaung. The British responded with a brutal and repressive campaign based on the Highland Clearances of the early nineteenth century. In 22 battles huge swathes of the rain-forest were dynamited, 639 Kachin houses were razed, 46 villages were obliterated, and silos containing 509,000 pounds of rice were destroyed. But still the Kachin fought on, invoking the *nats* with wild incantations before slaughtering 21 British officers and 3 privates.

William Warry watched the bloodshed with a heavy heart. He had read Qianlong's commentary on the Burmese war in which the Emperor, versed in Sun Tzu's Art of War, had recognised the strengths of the tribes. Warry had continually warned Adamson of the dangers of crossing them. 'Neither China nor Burma has exercised any active control over these Kachins. Like his prototype, the highlanders of Scotland of the last century, and other savages or semi-savages, he will go on thieving and cattle-lifting, murdering and plundering here and there for years to come,' Warry had advised Calcutta.[25]

Sir Herbert Thirkell-White, Bernard's chief secretary, privately conceded that the mines were now well beyond the Empire's grasp. 'We hold the country only up to the foot of the mountains, which is inhabited by Kachins . . . I think that any attempt on our part to exercise control over them and make ourselves responsible for their doings would be unwise,' he jotted in his private log.

By the end of the century the closest the British had got to the legendary jadeite mines was the outpost of Myitkyina, a dismal town on the 'borders of savagery', 'a military outpost in the heart of the enemy's country', built on the banks of the Irrawaddy, 60 miles north of Bhamo. For six months of every year it was cut off by the monsoon, leaving its British guard to 'fight upon occasion for its life'.[26] The 400 soldiers stationed there were responsible for taxing the jadeite trade, but the Empire only raised five rupees a year. It was hardly worth maintaining the garrison, and when William Warry visited, he discovered that Chinese and Kachin merchants were also reaping vast profits from a new business:

> The Kachin and Chinese carry opium to the mines to sell to the miners for 28 rupees a viss [1 pound] . . . and carry back jade but only a small proportion now passes through Myitkyina . . . our control over these areas is as poor as it was in 1886. I think we will never understand the workings of the Kachin or have the better of the jade trade.

Six

An Imperial Side-Show

Lady Yehenara was in mourning, her hair wrapped in white cotton bands, her silk robes exchanged for sackcloth, the vermilion teardrop on her lower lip scrubbed off. No sooner had she settled into her plump new role as mother of the heir to the Dragon Throne than her Emperor had slumped into a decline. Hearing of the razing of his beloved Summer Palace while still in exile at the hunting grounds of Jehôl, Xianfeng had taken to his Dragon Bed. On 22 August 1861, in the Hall of Refreshing Mists and Waves, he 'passed away at the *yin* hour' (between 3 a.m. and 5 a.m.). The story that raced to Europe was that Lord Elgin had broken his heart.

But the Imperial medical files tell of a less romantic demise. The 30-year-old regal dilettante caught a cold in the spring 'which caused a relapse of his old illness'. The Son of Heaven was plagued by 'diarrhoea in the sixth month that expended his vital energy'. All treatment proved hopeless and Xianfeng's condition 'seriously worsened on the 16th day of the seventh month'. The Emperor complained to his ministers: 'I cough more and more often, spitting phlegm with traces of blood.' His symptoms suggest that he had in fact contracted tuberculosis, a disease that would not be identified for another 21 years.[1]

Within hours the Imperial court was in panic. Disparate Qing factions huddled behind screens and in courtyards in Jehôl's arbours and pavilions, sending spies stalking down the corridors of the palace, seeking out support and eavesdropping on others who also sought control of the Dragon Throne.

Shuttered away in the Pine and Crane Chambers, the tearful Empress Niuhuru clung to Lady Yehenara as silhouettes of intrigue flitted past the paper panes. The Imperial consort knew that she must quickly exploit her position as the mother of the heir, or succumb to the dismal consequences of the Emperor's untimely death. Surviving consorts were often encouraged to commit suicide as a show of mourning, and even if they avoided that fate, they were banished to the Palace of Forgotten Concubines, the frugal chambers of the Forbidden City. Lady Yehenara's son was only five years old and a Regent would have to be appointed to rule on his behalf until he reached his majority. Whoever became Regent controlled China and the destinies of Lady Yehenara and Empress Niuhuru, whose tears were the only ones of genuine sorrow shed by so many in Jehôl that day.

Lady Yehenara showed her hand first. She confronted the Grand Councillors of the Qing court with an extraordinary claim that on his deathbed Emperor Xianfeng had appointed her Regent. But the eight Grand Councillors, led by Su Shun, rejected her bid and countered with one of their own. Su Shun offered Lady Yehenara and Empress Niuhuru symbolic titles and ceremonial seals in exchange for their support for his clique. But no sooner had Su Shun bestowed on Yehenara the title Dowager Empress Cixi, Empress of the West, and made Niuhuru Dowager Empress Ci'an, Empress of the East, than he locked them up, insisting that they relinquish all control of the young heir, or starve to death.

Prince Gong, Xianfeng's ambitious younger brother, was in Peking when he heard of Su Shun's *coup*. Enraged that he had been overlooked as Regent, he immediately set out for Jehôl, where he convinced his brothers to support an alternative plan. The two Dowager Empresses would become co-Regents while he assumed the position of Prince Advisor to the heir, who was to be enthroned on 11 November.

Released from their locked chamber, the Dowager Empresses Cixi and Ci'an fled Jehôl with Prince Gong on 1 November, bearing the body of the dead Emperor and the new proposal, completing the arduous ten-day journey to Peking in just under one week. The next morning the capital was secured by heavily armed troops before an edict was issued that accused the Su Shun faction of treason. It was proclaimed in the name of the heir to the throne and authorised by the ceremonial seals that Su Shun had given as a sop to the

Dowager Empresses. Six days later a crowd gathered in Peking's Vegetable Street to witness Su Shun's execution, a humiliating public death for an ambitious nobleman. On 11 November 1861, swamped by heavy yellow silk robes, his horse-hoof cuffs dragging on the ground, the diminutive heir appeared in the Hall of Supreme Harmony. Prince Gong lifted the boy onto the Dragon Throne, where he was christened Tongzhi, 'Perfect Ruler', as the Forbidden City echoed to the chime of bells, the crack of ceremonial whips and the rolling of drums.

Within days a double blackwood throne had been installed behind a yellow curtain in the East Wing of the Hall of Mental Cultivation, a chamber perfumed by the pomegranate, peach and cherry trees that blossomed in the courtyard. Hidden from public view, the Dowager Empresses sat side by side, twinned in power, identically costumed and bejewelled with jadeite. In front of the curtain sat the boy, astride his miniature Dragon Throne, within earshot of the whispers of his co-Regents, who could see everything that took place beyond the yellow curtain in carefully positioned mirrors. Only Cixi's closest ladies-in-waiting and senior eunuchs were permitted to look upon her face, but visitors would soon talk of the 'gravelly voice' that floated out from behind the yellow curtain.

While Emperor Tongzhi warmed the Dragon Throne, the court of the Qing was now stealthily transferred to the Hall of State Satisfaction, that stood behind it. There the Dowager Empress Cixi reclined on an ebony bed, her head resting on cushions stuffed with herbs and dried flowers, one ear hovering over a neatly scooped-out hole that ensured that nothing would ever again escape her attention, even while she napped. While Ci'an, who could not read or write – described in the Qing annals as 'amiable and friendly without thinking deeply' – retired to the Eastern Palace, Cixi relished her new-found status, littering the Hall of State Satisfaction with jadeite plates bearing sugared lotus-seeds, pickled walnuts, lychees and persimmons. She puffed on English cigarettes through a jadeite holder, court officials darting around her bed bearing edicts across which she would run her jadeite nail protector, blessing documents that she favoured with Su Shun's fateful seal.

Cixi's satin robes were now Imperial yellow and her head-dress bore a 'a beautiful phoenix in the centre made of purest jade' that, symbolising immortality and invincibility, could only be worn by an Empress.[2] Her shoulders were covered by a 'transparent cape of 3500 pearls the size of canary bird eggs', fringed by 40 jadeite drops and held at the throat by jadeite clasps, that a lady-in-waiting would later describe as 'the most magnificent and costly thing I ever saw'.[3] Cixi wore six Imperial Green Jade bangles carved into candy twists, triple-hoop jadeite ear-rings and a 108-bead court necklace made from Qianlong's Stone of Heaven. And on her shoulder was pinned the fragrant Xiang Fei's Persian Pepper, the symbol of an Emperor's love and a consort's rise to power.

While Cixi relished authority, Emperor Tongzhi swiftly outgrew his coronation robes. By his early teens it was said that he had become as debauched as Xianfeng, sharing his father's love for opera singers and as feckless as Daoguang, his grandfather, who had cried himself to death. 'He appears to have been living awfully fast . . . women, girls, men and boys, as fast as he could one after the other,' wrote Robert Hart, an Irishman who had recently been appointed Inspector General of Maritime Customs, an office imposed on Peking as a result of the 1860 treaty.[4] Prince Gong, whose own son was accused of accompanying the sixteen-year-old Tongzhi on nightly escapades over the walls of the Forbidden City to Willow Lane, the capital's brothel district, eventually came up with a solution. On 12 March 1872 the *Peking Gazette* announced that the Emperor was to marry a Mongolian girl of the A-lu-te clan, two years his senior. In only a year, Tongzhi would come of age and Prince Gong hoped that the wedding would settle him into a life of study before he assumed the full powers of an Emperor of China.

Cixi's appetite for the Stone of Heaven now matched that of Qianlong, but the Jade Road to Yunnan was still under attack by Panthay rebels and the traffic from Sinkiang that supplied the court with nephrite had also been halted. In 1865 Yakub Beg, a Muslim rebel leader, had proclaimed himself Emir of Yarkand and Kashgar, and for the next twelve years ruled over the nephrite mines. Cixi attempted to import the Stone of Heaven through Canton. Imperial edicts from the 1860s and 1870s show how she repeatedly ordered her southern customs officials to purchase jadeite with taxes collected from foreign merchants.[5] But the Stone of Heaven hardly ever left Burma by ship, and the annals show that customs officials failed to meet her demands.

In her frustration, Cixi dreamed up an ambitious plan. Filed in the New Delhi archives are copies of the few Burmese *parabaiks* that survived the British rampage in Mandalay, translated by William Warry, who saved them from the pyre. When we cross-referenced them with the Qing annals stolen by the British from the Summer Palace, we discovered how the inventive Dowager Empress set about replenishing the Forbidden City's jadeite stocks.

In 1873 she dispatched an Imperial caravan to Burma, the land of 'ferocious freebooters', with orders issued in her wayward son's name to reopen Qianlong's Jade Road.[6] Cixi's ambassadors carried letters to King Mindon that informed the Burmese monarch of the new order in China: 'the conferring of titles on the two Dowager Queens for governing the Empire during the minority of Emperor Tông kyi, for educating and bringing him up and for finding him a consort.'[7]

Accompanied by a 1300-mule caravan that carried gifts of 'fruit and some hams', the Imperial ambassadors were directed to take the Embassy Route. Although little is said by the Chinese about the journey, the Burmese court recorded the arrival of Cixi's caravan in Mandalay on 23 February 1874. China's ambassadors were mounted 'on elaborate gold and silver howdahs, on top of elephants, accompanied by artillery, cavalry and infantry'. It was 'a magnificent procession from the banks of the Irrawaddy', and 'when the ambassadors arrived at the palace . . . three cannons were fired and royal letters were read and His Majesty [Mindon] was transported in joy as if the two masters had met.'[8]

The British witnessed the Chinese procession too. Captain Crawford Cooke, resident at Bhamo, informed Fort William of celebrations held at court on 26 March that were 'far greater than that shown to any European or other Oriental mission'. Shut out from the discussions, Cooke advised London that Cixi's emissaries 'went to the palace and did little but smoke opium and then returned to China'.[9]

In fact strategic alliances were being planned in Mandalay, and jadeite was about to seal the pact. Like Bodawpaya, King Mindon realised that by steering Burma into China's sphere of influence he could protect his kingdom from its neighbours. In Bodawpaya's day it had been Siam that had worried the court, but now it was the British. On 4 November 1874 King Mindon acceded to Cixi's demands and dispatched a reciprocal caravan. Eight servants were needed to carry a weighty letter to the Emperor of China that was cast in gold and inlaid with rubies and jadeite, bearing the Burmese monarch's glittering new titles: 'Lord of the Rising Sun. Possessor of jade, gold and silver mines. Etc., etc.' Mindon professed to be 'impressed with the deep favours conferred by your heavenly dynasty'. He thanked his neighbour for the privilege of being allowed to enrol as a tributary of 'the territory of Yu', the kingdom of Jade. 'All within the realm join with one voice in the cry to his Imperial majesty. Happiness, Long Life, Male Issue,' he wrote, piling on the flattery, concluding that he was 'overcome with pleasurable feelings of extreme gratitude. Yours, etc., etc.'

Seven high-ranking Burmese officials, led by U Tha Pu, steamed up the Irrawaddy towards Bhamo, their baggage animals following behind, loaded down with hams, walnuts, opium and, more significantly, '2000 viss of jade [7000 pounds] in three large boulders, and 210 catties of jade etc., etc.' Colonel Horace Browne and his translator Augustus Margary were on their secret mission to chart the Jade Road when they bumped into the Burmese convoy in Bhamo.

The Burmese had been forced to halt in the river port for a month after three elephants promised by the Kachin failed to arrive. Although Colonel Browne deduced that the King's envoys were bearing jadeite, the pompous British officer had no idea where U Tha Pu or his cargo was heading.

Delay followed delay. When the Burmese eventually got out of Bhamo they were stopped again for seven days in Momauk, where 69 Kachin chiefs insisted on being entertained. For three days they were stalled at Mandaung, 'occupied in distributing looking-glasses, glassware things and betel boxes among the wives of the Kachin chiefs. Etc., etc.'[10] After a further 'eight-day halt necessitated owing to a misunderstanding which arose between Lasi and other Kachin chiefs regarding the entertainment and departure of the Burmese ambassadors', U Tha Pu and his delegation eventually reached the border village of Thantaya. There they were greeted with salutes of cannon fire and some dreadful news: 'the Emperor Tôn kyi had died.'[11]

Conflicting rumours flew towards Yunnan. U Tha Pu heard that the Dowager Empress had had a hand in the death of the Emperor, a poisoned handkerchief placed by her on his pillow, a story that took root in the *New York Times* that reported a 'mysterious' death in Peking. Others claimed that the wayward teenager had succumbed to syphilis as a result of his Willow Lane expeditions. But the Imperial medical files tell another story. The diaries of Weng Tonghe, a senior court official who attended Tongzhi on his deathbed, describe how the Emperor's face 'was covered with dense eruptions'.[12] The medical files of the court concur and describe almost day by day the gradual decline of the 'Perfect Ruler' as his body bubbled with infected pustules. 'Hidden skin eruptions, laboured breathing and headaches,' physicians Li Deli and Zhuang Shouhe noted, before prescribing dried reed root. 'Condition highly serious. Smallpox germs in bodily channels.'[13] On 12 January 1875 Tongzhi had breathed his last, dying in a side-room of the Palace of Heavenly Purity less than two years after attaining his majority.

Once again the Imperial court was thrown into spasms. Within 24 hours of her son's death, Cixi summoned Xianfeng's brothers and presented them with a *fait accompli*. The Dowager Empress announced that she had adopted a relative's three-year-old son and the infant was to be placed on the Dragon Throne. By adopting her nephew the Dowager Empress could continue as Regent even though the act trampled on the Qing's sacred rules of succession.

The court was enraged and a rival faction headed by another of Xianfeng's brothers, Prince Tun, responded with surprising news. Empress A-lu-te, Tongzhi's forgotten widow, was apparently pregnant, so all decisions on succession would have to wait nine months. The jadeite tribute bound for the Emperor of China was to be held at the Yunnan border until the court had identified the new recipient of King Mindon's largesse. Cixi's plan appeared to have been frustrated.

Within days another rumour spread through Peking, picked up by customs chief Robert Hart. Empress A-lu-te was critically ill after apparently swallowing gold dust, an ancient method of suicide.

Privately there were many who accused Cixi of the poisoning, but in the absence of evidence her adopted son, who would reign under the name Emperor Guangxu, 'Overpowering Light', was confirmed as heir.

Regent once again, Cixi immediately dispatched a decree to the Burmese border, where U Tha Pu and his jadeite haul had been holed up for 50 days. 'A letter arrived announcing the accession of Emperor Kunsi [Guangxu]. We had an escort from the governor and Chinese mahoots,'[14] U Tha Pu wrote. The Governor of Momein, who received the Imperial edict, ordered 'General Lee-See-Tahi' to secure the path ahead.

The British now became entangled in Cixi's jadeite dreams. Colonel Horace Browne's ill-fated expedition ran into the Chinese forces assigned to protect U Tha Pu. An eyewitness to the murder of Margary and his five servants, whose heads were abandoned on a wall, cabled Mandalay, reporting: 'Chinese attacking party was advance guard of an army of 3000 sent by order of the Governor of Momein to annihilate the British party, of this there is no doubt. Chinese commanded by nephew of Lee-See-Tahi.'[15] But the British would never know that the executions had been ordered after Margary unwittingly strayed too close to Cixi's priceless jadeite caravan.

As London made unsuccessful representations to Peking, Emperor Guangxu ascended to the throne on 25 February 1875, swamped by his yellow silk robe, his cuffs dragging on the flagstone floor, while in a distant corner of the Forbidden City his predecessor's poisoned widow was still fighting for her life. When A-lu-te's death was finally announced the following month, it was a brief postscript to what must have been an excruciating demise.

Envoy U Tha Pu finally reached Peking by palanquin, riding in the rutted mud beside the Imperial Highway, on 6 September and was received in the Hall of Conquered Nations, where he presented the infant Emperor with King Mindon's salutations. 'As the sunflower bows under the sun so does all mankind turn with adoration towards the Imperial person,' the Burmese monarch had written.

Within weeks, assured of a steady supply of the Stone of Heaven, Cixi ordered the reopening of Qianlong's Imperial workshops, closed by his austere son Emperor Jianqing in the 1820s. They would churn out thousands of pieces of jewellery and trinkets, highly polished and exquisitely carved, many cut from her favourite boulder that came to be known as 'silk melon skin green'.[16] Soon she was changing outfits several times a day to show off her latest acquisitions, and wherever she went, retainers would trail behind like her Pekinese. 'Each eunuch carried something in his hand . . . clothes, shoes, handkerchiefs, combs, brushes, powder boxes, looking-glasses of different sizes, perfumes, pins, black and red ink, yellow paper, cigarettes, water pipes . . . This procession . . . made one think of a lady's dressing-room on legs,' wrote Yu Derling.[17]

The author was the Dowager Empress's First Lady-in-Waiting. Educated in France before being enrolled into the Imperial household, Yu Derling would later marry Thaddeus White, an American diplomat, and would be encouraged by curious Western friends to spill her secrets about life behind the palace walls. As keeper of the Imperial jewellery, it was Derling who first revealed to the outside world that Cixi ordered the construction of a treasure hall to store her Stones of Heaven. It was 'lined with shelves on three sides' and on them were placed 3000 'ebony boxes, all containing jewels', each bearing a number and a yellow label listing its contents.'[18] No one was allowed into the locked chamber without the Dowager Empress's permission, and she slept with its key around her neck.

But Cixi ordered so much jewellery that she lost track of what she owned, a situation that was exploited by courtiers and retainers, including Prince Gong and her Chief Eunuch. The brooding Li Lianying, who was said to have secured Cixi's favours by offering to carve a piece of flesh from his thigh as a demonstration of his devotion, became so rich in Cixi's employ that he secretly bought a palace outside the citadel, filling it with stolen jewellery and, miraculously, a family.[19]

'It is harder to guard against a thief in the family than against an outsider,' an old Chinese saying goes, and Li Lianying soon became the conduit for Chinese agents who supplied a growing number of British dealers with Imperial jewellery and artefacts stolen from the court.[20] In the muddy *hutongs* of Liu-li-chang and Langfang, outside the Tiananmen Gate, rickety wooden shops sprang up that began to export hundreds of cases of jadeite and nephrite, said to have been purloined from the Imperial palaces, to London, Paris and New York, feeding a market kick-started by the Allied plunder of 1860.

William Lever, the soap baron, who had visited an exhibition of 'bits and pieces from the Summer Palace' in Manchester in 1879, was among dozens of wealthy entrepreneurs, including J. P. Morgan, Charles Freer and Alfred Nobel, who would collect Imperial jadeite. Later raised to the peerage, Lord Leverhulme would leave his Oriental legacy to the British people in the Lady Lever Art Gallery that he built in his model village of Port Sunlight on Merseyside.

The awakening of interest in Orientalia coincided with a sea change in British culture. The Great Exhibition of 1851 had brought the masses into close proximity with the plunder of Empire. Now art itself was redefined by new movements like Whistler's 'Aesthetes' and William Morris's 'Arts and Crafts' that broadened its definition to include decorative objects and interior design, influenced by the artistry of Chinese craftsmen whose work was flowing to the West.

Sensing the growing demand, a former warehouse manager borrowed £2000 to open a shop on Regent Street in 1875, the year that Cixi received her first jadeite haul from Burma. Arthur Liberty pulled in the crowds with ornaments, fabric and *objets d'art* from the East, and within a decade he had moved into the Tudor-beamed former headquarters of the East India Company, where the shop still stands today. The Eastern Bazaar in the basement sold curiosities and jadeite ornaments from Peking to a fashionable clientele including Dante Gabriel Rossetti, Frederick Leighton and Edward Burne-Jones. But the shop's wealthiest patron was Heber Bishop, who at the age of 36 had made his fortune in the sugar plantations of Cuba and multiplied it by investing in the railroads that were connecting America's east coast to its wild west.

Bishop visited Liberty's with Mary Cunningham, his society bride, in 1878. He had already begun to fill his palatial home in Irvington, overlooking the Hudson River, with Qianlong's jades:

> I was fortunate in finding some exceptionally fine objects of jade that had been brought from China to New York and Boston . . . the loot of the Imperial Summer Palace . . . I resolved upon a special visit to England and the continent of Europe, where I knew that most of the beautiful pieces had been taken by members of the returning Anglo-French expedition.[21]

Moving on to Paris, the sugar millionaire's purchases included Countess Kleezkowsky's jadeite suite and a large jade wine bowl, writhing with dragons, sold to him by T'ien-pao, the Chinese dealer who had bought it from the Allied prize auction. 'Having secured all the finest specimens obtainable in Europe . . . I went to China,' wrote Bishop, where he was introduced to Dr Stephen Bushell, a young medical officer with the British legation. A self-taught connoisseur of Chinese art, Bushell was hired by Bishop to hunt out jadeite artefacts that had graced the Summer Palace. He scoured the antique shops of Liu-li-chang whose owners, despite the threat of execution, peddled stories and artefacts that were said to be the Son of Heaven's legacy. Inveigling his way into the secretive world of the jadeite workshops, the persistent Bushell became the first foreigner ever to see the secretive carvers of Peking, whose closely guarded techniques had not changed for centuries. He would later commission the artist Li Shih Ch'uan to paint delicate watercolours of them at work and was soon playing a central role in the export of China's treasures.[22] In the early 1880s Philip Cunliffe Owen, the director of the South Kensington Museum, hired him as an agent. The medical officer dispatched hundreds of carefully packaged antiques to London, where they were catalogued by Caspar Purdon Clarke, keeper of the Oriental Collection.

Cixi's treasures may have been leaking out of the Forbidden City, but within its walls her power had increased. In April 1881, at the age of 44, Empress Ci'an collapsed and died. Once again there were rumours of a poisoning, the fatal dose was said to have been administered by Cixi in a doctored biscuit. And once again nothing was proved. Having outlived her lover, her son and his wife, the opportune demise of her co-Regent now completed Cixi's rise. The Empress of the West was appointed sole Regent to the young Emperor Guangxu, who was kept a virtual prisoner in the Forbidden City and was required to call his adopted mother *chin baba* or 'dear father'. Cixi's eunuchs now addressed her as 'His Majesty' or *Lao Fo Yeh,* 'Great Old Buddha', as she took control of palace symbolism that represented the old Imperial patriarchy.[23] Where her Ming and Qing predecessors had carved, painted and gilded dragons flying above the phoenix to establish the supremacy of the Emperor over his Empress, Cixi had the scenes inverted so that the phoenix dominated the Forbidden City. She summoned her mandarins daily to join her in a game of 'Eight Fairies Travel Across the Sea', an Imperial 'Snakes and Ladders' played with jadeite counters. The object was to race across the Empire and to claim the Dragon Throne, avoiding banishment from the Middle Kingdom. 'You will never catch my fairy,' Cixi chided her opponents, and, of course, she always won.[24]

Daily she took to touring her palaces dressed up as the Buddhist Goddess of Mercy, dispensing small jades and silks, trailed by bundles of Pekinese puppies, including her favourite, Shui Ta or 'Sea Otter', named after his fine silky pelt, a dog that came from the same stock as Queen Victoria's trophy, Looty.[25] When Prince Gong cautiously advised his protégée that her increasingly eccentric behaviour and profligacy was causing concern outside the palace walls, Cixi banished him as if he were a jadeite counter. The following year, to celebrate her fiftieth birthday, she refurbished the Palace of Concentrated Beauty, the hall in which she had given birth, with 630,000 taels of silver (3 million grams). Three years later she embezzled an estimated 30 million taels (1.5 billion grams) more, money raised by the Qing aristocracy to refit the navy, that she spent on constructing a retirement complex in the rubble of the Summer Palace. The Empire was facing mounting threats from the 'dwarf pirates' of Japan who had already attempted to take Korea from the Dragon Throne in 1882 and 1884, when the French had also clashed with the Qing over Indo-China, sinking a significant part of the Chinese fleet. While the nation demanded a fighting force, Cixi built the Hall of Jade Billows, the Hall of Delight and Longevity and the House of Fragrant Herbs. The spending spree was seemingly endless and on her sixtieth birthday she frittered away an unpublished sum on restoring the Palace of Peaceful Longevity, to which Qianlong had also retired in 1796. Through an Imperial edict, overseen by Fu Kun, a senior mandarin, Cixi let it be known that she would only accept birthday presents made of jadeite.[26] The Empress of the West instructed her eunuchs, as Qianlong had done before, to collect dew in a bronze plate that was mixed with powdered jade into an elixir of life, and she drank milk provided by lactating peasants whose own infants were starved.

Prince Gong had warned Cixi of the problems amassing outside the walls of the Forbidden City, but was she even aware that a sprawling foreign legation quarter squatted south-east of the Tiananmen Gate? Did she know that her parents' grave was now covered by a racecourse at the eastern end of the foreign legations?[27] While the Empress of the West indulged her jadeite whims, foreigners had been carving up her Empire. By 1898 the Russians had seized Manchuria, the French taken Indo-China, and Formosa and Korea were in Japanese hands. What remained was now wracked by famine, and a secretive lobby of academics slowly emerged that began to campaign against the excesses of the Qing. The *ming-shih* bombarded Chinese citizens with propaganda, portraying Cixi as a 'false empress', a 'murderous thief who deposes the sovereign and usurps his throne', a woman who had pillaged Imperial treasure-houses to feed her unhealthy desire for jadeite.[28] The Empress of the West was a wanton harlot who used the Stone of Heaven to 'give rein to her libidinous desires'.[29]

Kang Youwei, who masterminded the smear campaign, also sent letters to Edwin Conger and Sir Claude MacDonald, the American and British ministers in Peking, railing against a 'licentious and depraved palace concubine'. The revelations were explosive, and when George Morrison, the man from *The Times,* learned of them from MacDonald, he could not resist cabling the lurid tittle-tattle back to London. A doctor by trade, Morrison had come to journalism late after publishing a pompous account of his solo trek from Shanghai to Rangoon, a book slated by William Warry, who concluded that he had 'passed through the country practically with blinkers on'.[30]

Nevertheless, the trans-China expedition caught the attention of C. F. Moberly Bell, *The Times'* manager, who invited Morrison to tea at the Athenaeum Club in London. There Bell was regaled with ripping yarns – how the doctor had once carried a New Guinea spear embedded in his thigh for five months before a surgeon in Edinburgh had restored his 'power of locomotion'.[31] Bell was impressed, and dispatched Morrison to China, a place that the doctor quickly concluded was merely a pawn in the greater Imperial game. Too lazy to learn Chinese, boasting that his vocabulary was limited to the Mandarin for 'by jove' and 'the devil you are', he hired Edmund Backhouse, a linguist who had flunked his English course at

Merton College, Oxford. Backhouse claimed to have been a friend of Ellen Terry and Oscar Wilde, but had been forced to flee university and England after running up debts of £20,000.[32]

He would translate and augment Chinese gossip that Morrison would file as fact. Cixi, whom neither of them had ever seen or met, was now the reptilian ringmaster of a Chinese sexual circus, a perverted dominatrix who devoured her partners, assaulting them from behind with 'instruments' of Imperial Green Jade. In London, Paris and New York the palace tales titillated an audience that was quivering with sexual uncertainty. Oscar Wilde's trial in 1895 had forced into the public consciousness alternative notions of manhood, and the clamour among women for the vote terrified Victorian society. Is it surprising that male writers and artists now began portraying women as vampires? As Bram Stoker unveiled Dracula and Edvard Munch completed a series of dark oils and lithographs that depicted libidinous maidens draining the life-blood out of their male conquests, Cixi was transformed into a blood-sucking Dragon Lady. In one French journal she was caricatured as an Oriental witch, wild feathers flying from her severe black head-dress, wielding a knife in bony jadeite-clad fingers, her enemies' heads bleeding on spikes.[33] Women like the Dowager Empress were as dangerous as Loïe Fuller, the American dancer who metamorphosed on stage into a bat, and as tantalising as Sarah Bernhardt, who modelled herself as 'half-bat' in a parody of the chauvinism of the age.[34]

The Times meanwhile, fêted Morrison for his 'unfailing accuracy', his ability to distinguish 'between what was true and what was false' in what the West saw as the inscrutable mire of Chinese life.

Cixi was oblivious to it all, but Emperor Guangxu, who in June 1898 granted an audience to Kang Youwei, the anti-Qing propagandist, was drawn in. Persuaded of the need for reform, he issued dozens of decrees and sanctioned a plot to remove his adopted mother. But the climate of reform would last only 100 days, as Guangxu's plans were intercepted by Yuan Shikai, a young general who revealed them to Cixi's allies. The Emperor of China was arrested by his mother and forced to beg her forgiveness. While he lived out his remaining days under house arrest, the *New York Times,* ignorant of proceedings in the palace, accused Cixi of torturing, poisoning and even killing the Son of Heaven. In fact this punishment was reserved for the leaders of the *ming shih*, who were all rounded up, apart from Kang Youwei, who escaped to Hong Kong.

The 63-year-old Cixi, shaken by Guangxu's treachery, now went on a charm offensive. Having previously damned all foreigners as 'long-nosed barbarians', she decided to trample on another centuries-old tradition and, in May 1898, horrified her Grand Councillors by emerging from behind the yellow curtain to greet Prince Heinrich of Prussia, the Kaiser's brother and Queen Victoria's grandson. Then she announced that she had invited the ladies of the foreign legations to tea.

On 13 December the wives of the Japanese, Russian, German, Dutch, French and American ministers were deposited at the gates of the Imperial City, led by the statuesque Lady MacDonald, all of them resplendent in ostrich feathers and bone corsets except for the Japanese representative, who wore a satin kimono.

By all accounts Cixi was nervous and was said to have spent two hours choosing her jadeite jewellery and gown before settling on a phoenix-and-dragon coronet, a phoenix hair ornament, dragon hairpins and a peacock-blue robe embroidered with hundreds of phoenixes, each one with a two-inch string of pearls hanging from its beak. 'I want to look nice, and be amiable, but these people make me angry. I know [they] will go home and tell people about me, and I don't want them to have the wrong impression,' Cixi told Derling.[35]

The Empress of the West sat on an immense cinnabar throne in the Hall of Imperial Supremacy, the 'sad-eyed, delicate-looking' Emperor Guangxu beside her on a smaller throne. Incense smoke wreathed around a large carved dragon's head that, clinging to the ceiling, appeared to snarl down at the women from the West. The hall was 'crowded with gaudily-dressed and gaily-painted ladies-in-waiting, pink and yellow were the predominant colour, their cheeks and lips vying with their petticoats,' according to Lady MacDonald, who, with her blond curls spilling onto a chiffon gown, wrote as if she was reviewing Ladies Day at Ascot.[36]

Prince Ching, Cixi's chief minister, led each woman forward, and Lady MacDonald reported how the Dowager Empress, who 'might in another part of the world pass for an Italian peasant', studied them 'with the keenest interest'. What would the society hostess have said if she had understood Mandarin? 'How is it that these foreign ladies have such large feet?' the Dowager Empress asked. 'Their shoes are like boats and the funny way they walk I cannot say I admire. Although they have white skins, their faces are covered with hair. No matter how beautiful they are, they have ugly eyes. I can't bear that blue colour, they remind me of a cat.'[37]

Cixi played the gracious host and presented her foreign visitors with gifts. 'With a few words of greeting Her Majesty clasped our hands in hers, and placed on the finger of each lady a heavy, chased gold ring, set with a large pearl,' Lady MacDonald later wrote in *The Empire Review*.[38] Although he had not been invited, Morrison used his forensic reporting skills to discern that the British delegate had won particular favour and that Cixi had 'patted her [Lady MacDonald] playfully on the cheek'. Following a 24-course tea party accompanied by a brass band that played European waltzes, Cixi presented jadeite bangles and antique pendants. Were these the only Imperial pieces to be legitimately acquired by Europeans? Sarah Conger, the Bible-thumping American minister's wife whose favourite colour was black, recalled: 'Her Majesty seemed greatly pleased and waved her hand towards the richly draped and cushioned kang. At the back was a shelf filled with beautiful jade. She took a small jade baby boy and tucked it into my hand, with actions saying "don't tell".'[39]

Until Madame Plançon presented the Dowager Empress with an unusual gift, nobody outside Cixi's circle of retainers and this handful of European women even knew what the Dowager Empress looked like. A report that was recently rediscovered in a Forbidden City storeroom reveals how the wife of the Russian minister gave Cixi a framed sepia print of Tsar Nicholas II and his family. The hand-written note, found behind the Russian frame, records how Cixi was intrigued by the magical image and rewarded Madame Plançon with a jadeite pendant.[40] She immediately ordered a photographic studio to be erected in the Summer Palace, where artists made an artificial lily pond, complete with fake flowers, in which Cixi sat on a throne before a painted backdrop of a bamboo forest where water appeared to cascade from a pool. Cixi is dressed as the

Goddess of Mercy, a thought bubble floating above her head, bursting with auspicious sayings, while Li Lianying stands to her left, his hands clasped in supplication, his head-dress a tremble of pompoms like that of a pantomime dame.

Later the studio was abandoned in favour of location shots. Punting through real lilies, on a lake outside the Forbidden City, Cixi is captured seated precariously on her cinnabar throne, shaded by an enormous parasol, watched over by ladies-in-waiting and eunuchs who attempt to steady the boat. Sea Otter, her beloved Pekinese, shuffled into almost every shot, as did Li Lianying. Today these photographs provide a unique record of Cixi's jadeite jewellery, her jadeite talons extending four inches beyond her fingertips, her phoenix and dragon hairpins clearly visible on her head-dress, pendants suspended from her neck, a rosary pinned to her robe. And within a matter of years these sepia images would be all that Cixi had to remind herself of a trove of Imperial Green Jade that had taken almost a lifetime to assemble.

While the Dowager Empress retreated into her fictional China, an Empire painted as a Garden of Eden, her subjects cast as grateful subordinates, the reality was starkly different. In Shandong Province, the land of the legendary Water Margin, a Chinese Robin Hood saga where 108 bandits fleeced the powerful to feed the peasantry, poverty had raised a real grass-roots movement that now turned on the West. Missionaries, who had flooded into famished China as a result of Lord Elgin's treaty, offering rice in exchange for souls, were singled out as the harbingers of China's ills. Christianity interfered with *feng shui,* its spires stretching skywards casting unwelcome shadows over auspicious Buddhist sites and shrines. And soon superstitious peasants came to believe that famine and flood had also been caused by European magicians.

Millions joined a powerful, secret cult called the *Yihequan* or 'Society of Righteous and Harmonious Fists', named after the kickboxing techniques they employed. Sweeping through every province, the Boxers, as they were known to the West, presented a fearful sight, dressed in red turbans stained with their own blood, and armed with rusty flintlocks, spears, tridents and double-edged swords. With their high-pitched cry, *'Sha! Sha!',* 'Kill! Kill!' they devilled Victorian missionaries and paraded placards declaring: 'Death and destruction to the foreigner and all his works!'[41] British newspapers that reported 'The Crisis in China' also published adverts for 'Foreign Devils Pioneer Cigarettes', whose logo was a baggy-kneed Chinaman twiddling with his queue.[42]

What was Cixi to do? Should she support a home-grown movement that was attempting to rid China of a foreign scourge, or should she bow to international pressure, having emerged from behind the curtain, and condemn the Boxers as terrorists? While she vacillated, Li Lianying regaled her with stories of how native converts had been drugged and sodomised by missionaries, who 'take the poor Chinese children and gouge their eyes out, and use them as a kind of medicine'.[43]

It was a difficult decision, and so the Empress of the West went on holiday. While she relaxed in the Summer Palace in the early summer of 1900, mulling over China's future, the *North China Herald* reported news of a public execution in Taiyuanfu that sent shock-waves through the foreign legations. A congregation of British missionaries had been seized by a mob and beheaded, as had their children. 'Mrs Lovitt was wearing her spectacles and held the hand of her little boy, even when she was killed.'[44] One hundred years later the Catholic Church would propose the canonisation of the Boxers' victims, and the Chinese government would respond by claiming that they 'deserved to die . . . for bullying the Chinese people'.[45]

In Peking, the 'Corps Diplomatiques' was thrown into panic and, as rumours of a wave of red-turbaned terror converging on the capital spread, all foreigners were recalled to the legations. Morrison revelled in the uncertain times, on 28 May rescuing two women who were trapped at the American legation's summer villa in the Western Hills – Harriet Squiers, wife of the US First Secretary, and Polly Smith, an unmarried heiress visiting from New York. At the beginning of June Sir Claude MacDonald ordered the battening down of hatches. 'Deep trenches were cut, earthworks thrown up, and barbed wire entanglements laid down. The final stand was to be made at the British legation. No question of surrender could be entertained, for surrender meant massacre,' wrote Morrison, spoiling for a fight.[46]

On 12 June 'the most awful cries were heard in the city', 'demonical and unforgettable'; the shriek of the Boxers, 'Sha kweitze', 'Kill the foreign devils', mingled with 'the groans of the dying'. Morrison regaled Mr and Mrs Squiers and Polly Smith over a dinner of anchovies, preserved Californian fruits, macaroni and coffee with stories of 'awful sights . . . Women and children hacked to pieces, men trussed like fowls, with noses and ears cut off and eyes gouged out.'

While Sir Claude attempted to rally a ragtag army of soldiers and gun-toting diplomats, Edmund Backhouse retired to his bed with his Goodrich Pocket Chinese-English dictionary, complaining of an unspecified leg injury.[47] Then the Japanese chancellor was hacked to pieces in the street, and the imperious German minister, Baron von Kettler, who had beaten a young Boxer to death, was shot. On 29 June Imperial troops fired into the legations and '900 souls' gathered in and around Sir Claude's home, no doubt reliving stories from India, where so many had perished at Lucknow.

Sir Claude, a Sandhurst-educated career soldier and diplomat who had seen service in Cairo, Zanzibar and Niger, appointed himself supreme commander and made Herbert Squiers his chief of staff. Commandeering the 'strategically important' palace of Prince Su, they seized 'all his treasure and half his harem', artworks, jades, jewellery, porcelain and cash boxes containing £20,000 that was set aside to build a commemorative memorial to the siege if they survived.[48] 'For the first time in war, art was a feature in the fortification. Silks and satins, curtains and carpets and embroideries were ruthlessly cut up into sandbags,' Morrison gleefully reported.[49]

On the journalist's suggestion, Prince Su's garden was transformed into a refugee camp for 2000 Chinese Christian 'brothers and sisters', who had converged on Legation Street seeking refuge. 'Half starved, covered with soot and ashes from the fires, the women carrying on their breasts horribly sick and diseased babies',[50] they were left to forage for 'twigs and leaves', while a swift liberation of the legation's general stores provided Westerners with 'tinned beef, Liebig's extract and Stilton'.[51] The well-stocked wine cellar at Auguste and Annie Chamot's Hôtel de Pékin was similarly drained and the ladies took to quaffing champagne to 'calm one's nerves'.[52]

Morrison moved into a room at the back of Lady MacDonald's home, next door to Mrs Squiers, her new-born baby and her children, Bart, Herbert and Fargo. He was welcomed by Polly Smith, who shared their lodgings and had by now taken a shine to the 'dirty, happy and healthy hero'. By the end of June, with no sign of a rescue party, the Allies debated pulling down an 'unimportant' corner that abutted the British legation, a potential weak spot in Sir Claude's defences. 'Such desecration, it was said, would wound the susceptibilities of the Chinese government,' Morrison wrote, shortly before the Hanlin Library, 'the most sacred building in China', was set alight. 'It was necessary to continue the destruction and dismantle the library buildings. An attempt was made to rescue specimens of the more valuable manuscripts, but few were saved for the danger was pressing,' the journalist claimed as he and Edmund Backhouse gathered new Chinese libraries for themselves.

The following morning Robert Hart dispatched a letter to Tientsin: 'Foreign community besieged in legations. Situation desperate. MAKE HASTE!' It would be their last communication with the outside world. Soon London was awash with stories of how the legations had 'fallen victim to Chinese treachery and ferocity'.[53] On 17 July The Times reported that 'The last heroic remnants of Western civilisation in the doomed city were engulfed beneath the overwhelming flood of Asiatic barbarism.' The Illustrated London News published photographs of the MacDonald girls – Ivy, aged six, in a white astrakhan hat and coat, and Stella, three, in her favourite broderie anglaise dress – beneath a headline, 'Probable Victims of the Peking Massacre'. Grief boiled over into outrage and a memorial service was planned at St Paul's Cathedral.

But in Peking the foreign legations were far from silent. Hundreds of innocent Chinese civilians were being beheaded or bayoneted by the Allied defence forces, who had been instructed to save ammunition. By night Sir Claude and Lady MacDonald hosted black-tie dinners, Stella and Ivy safely tucked up in bed, their guests fed on curried pony, culled from the legations' polo stables, the mansion resounding to arias sung by the wife of a Russian banker. Life took on a surreal quality: a new-born baby was christened 'Siege'; Lady MacDonald played tennis while Sir Claude practised his batting strokes; the German First Secretary drowned out Chinese death rattles with his grand piano while Polly Smith and George Morrison promenaded through the legation garden.

When, in August, news reached the Dowager Empress that 16,000 Allied troops were marching on Peking, she decided to flee, ignoring the advice of her ministers. But before leaving the Forbidden City, Cixi found time to settle a score. Li Lianying was ordered to seize Zhen Fei, Emperor Guangxu's favourite Pearl Concubine. There was no room for her in the escape party, and as she would be raped by the Allies if she remained on her own, Zhen Fei would have to embrace a time-honoured fate. In truth, the spiteful Empress of the West had become jealous of the Pearl Concubine and the influence she wielded over Emperor Guangxu, and when the Imperial party fled Peking, the girl's jadeite jewellery was discovered scattered around the mouth of a well near the Gate of Spiritual Valour.

Travelling twenty miles a day westwards along the Great Wall, southwards through Shansi Province and on to Xi'an in neighbouring Shensi, the Imperial party camped out near a hot spring. It was the first time the Dowager Empress, who had disguised herself as a peasant, had witnessed the poverty of the Chinese interior, but the tears that she shed were for the treasures that she had left in Peking.

'I had a very hard time, travelling in a sedan chair, from early morning, before the sun rose, until dark,' Cixi complained to Derling. 'Some of the chair carriers ran away. Some of the mules died suddenly. It was very hot, and the rain poured down on our heads.'[54]

Relief finally reached the foreign legations on 14 August, when a vanguard of Sikhs and Rajputs blew the sluice-gate of the Imperial Sewage Canal. Outside the legations the 'bodies of [Chinese] soldiers lay in heaps', and the Rev. Arthur Smith reported that 'huge pools of stagnant water were reeking with rotting corpses of man and beast.'[55] When Polly Smith rushed out to welcome the rescue party with Harriet Squiers, General Gaselee, the British commander, jumped down from his horse and exclaimed: 'Thank God, men, here are two women alive.' The *Illustrated London News* reported: 'When the troops reached the British Embassy they asked if they had come to a garden party, for there was the indomitable Sir Claude Macdonald, clean shaven, in spotless flannels; his wife and other ladies, in summer toilettes, by his side.'[56]

The Allies' forces now 'looked on Peking as a prize of war' and exacted their revenge, conducting summary trials and beheadings on every street corner.[57] 'Survivors who remained cowered like whipped hounds in their kennels' and posted signs on their doors: 'Noble and Good Sirs, Please Do Not Shoot Us'.[58] Scooting around the execution sites, dodging the rolling heads, the liberated foreigners plundered with gusto. Morrison reported how Backhouse, who had miraculously recovered from his sprain, had been arrested inside the Imperial treasury by Japanese soldiers 'on a charge of blackmail, looting and robbery'.[59]

'Lady MacDonald was out with the small force left behind in Peking and devoted herself most earnestly to looting,' one British soldier wrote home.[60] Three jade seals belonging to Cixi and Guangxu, carved with entwined dragons, were liberated by drunken Cossacks who sold them to an Irish-American journalist for a bottle of brandy. Later, when a British auctioneer advertised them as 'the property of the Empress of China' a row broke out in the House of Commons over whether they should be returned to Peking. But when it was revealed that the seller was not a British citizen, all political objections evaporated and in January 1902 Oscar Raphael, a wealthy collector of Orientalia, bought them at a sale in Covent Garden, later bequeathing them to the Fitzwilliam Museum in Cambridge.[61]

Meyrick Hewlett, a junior diplomat with Sir Claude's mission, paid a British soldier a silver dollar for a replica of Qianlong's famed wine bowl, in which the subaltern had been washing his feet.[62] Auctions and bazaars sprang up throughout the capital, including one large jamboree in the British legation garden at which a flushed Lady MacDonald supervised the bidding. 'A collection of Chinese things lay spread out on the tiled floor . . . All the legation people, amongst them Lady MacDonald, sitting on a chair, and a number of other English men and women thronged around this display of valuable articles . . . A sergeant held up each article in turn, and the bidding was lively, but prices were low, there was evidently a glut in the market,' wrote William Oudendyk, a Dutch diplomat who attended the sale.[63] 'The value of the treasures taken in Peking is set down at between half and three quarters of a million,' trumpeted the *Illustrated London News*.[64]

Sir Claude acquired ten jade books belonging to Qianlong, while Lady MacDonald gained a rare seventeenth-century jade incense-burner, a duck-shaped jade incense-burner, jadeite clasps carved into hydras, jadeite spoons carved with birds' heads and a cinnabar box carved with Imperial dragons.[65]

'A large Sikh' approached Polly Smith outside the ruins of the American legation and said, '*Mem-sahib* give me two dollars, I give *mem-sahib* nice things.' When Polly handed over her cash, the Sikh deposited into her arms 'an exquisite gold-mounted *cloisonné* clock and two huge struggling hens'. Baron von Rahden, a Russian admirer, arrived at Polly's door loaded down with sable coats, and a Belgian soldier, who was also nursing a crush, presented her with a tortoise-shell bracelet set with pearls that he had hacked off the arm of a dead bannerman. 'The rumours come in that now the whole of Peking is being looted, and worse, and each Legation, closed up in its little compound, feels like a little question-mark of respectability, surrounded by a whole page of wicked, leering horrors,' Polly wrote piously in her diary.[66]

In the weeks that followed, more than 20,000 Allied troops converged on Peking, and General Gaselee had the city divided into zones to ensure that the plundering parties acted in an orderly fashion. The Russians were given the Southern Ponds hunting park, from which they looted one of Qianlong's carved cinnabar thrones, presenting it to Mikhail Girs, the Russian ambassador, who shipped it to Moscow among a vast haul of diplomatic treasure.[67]

On 18 August Sir Claude MacDonald proposed that the Allies raze the Forbidden City. But the Japanese and Russian commanders protested, and instead a victory parade was proposed, 'lest the Chinese, with their infinite capacity for misrepresentation, should infer some supernatural power had intervened' to save its sacred halls from the torch.[68] On 28 August, watched by a handful of eunuchs who had been too old or unfit to run away, the parade entered through the Meridian Gate, led by the 'lumbering, bony figure of Sir Claude MacDonald, in an ample grey suit of tennis clothes and a rakish Panama slouch hat'.[69] The French Minister, 'in a garb which combined the requirements of the Bois de Boulogne on a Sunday with the convenience of tropical attire on a weekday', accompanied Edwin Conger, dressed 'in white cottons and military gaiters'. But having entered the towering walled city, who could resist taking a souvenir?

From the Hall for Worshipping Buddhas, where Cixi prayed, a senior officer carted off a five-piece bronze altar set that had once belonged to Qianlong's father. In 1999 it would reappear at a Christie's sale in Hong Kong and fetch more than £100,000. A British diplomat pocketed three carved jades, including a reclining water buffalo, that were later bequeathed to the Fitzwilliam Museum in Cambridge.[70] Another diplomat took the enamelled telescope that Lord Macartney had presented to Qianlong in 1793. Today it is on show in the National Maritime Museum in Greenwich.

George Morrison assured his readers that the Imperial suites had been spared as he broke into Cixi's bedchamber with a British diplomat's wife, to find a tableau that revealed the haste with which the Dowager Empress had fled:

> On the rich coverlet of the bed lay an embroidered coat of black satin; beneath, a pair of Manchu shoes. Nearby were two large boxes of silk handkerchiefs, overturned . . . a handful had been hurriedly snatched from each . . . on a long table . . . were dozens of foreign clocks, some handsome, others hideous, all ticking cheerfully, regardless of the ominous silence around.[71]

Morrison helped himself to Cixi's jade prayer books and an ornament from her bedside:

> I succeeded in looting a beautiful piece of jade splashed with gold and carved in the form of a citron, the emblem of the fingers of Buddha . . . Sat in the Throne of the Emperor . . . everything that could be looted being taken away by . . . ministers and others . . . So back home very tired with my priceless jade.[72]

Morrison was sporting an embarrassing injury, a gunshot wound to his buttock, but it did little to slow down his appetite, and in his diary he calculated that he had stashed loot worth £3000. On 13 October *The Times* dedicated a whole page to his story that Cixi was to blame for the destruction of her own palaces. 'An ancient sage of China foretold that China will be destroyed by a woman. The prophecy is approaching fulfilment. What can be thought of a nation, which destroyed its own most sacred edifice, in order to wreak vengeance upon the foreigner?' Morrison asked, referring to the razing of the Hanlin Academy, without so much as a mention of the Allies' role or the bounty he had taken from its blazing shelves.

As the foreigners packed up their spoils, Morrison wrote to Moberly Bell in London: 'Sir Claude is leaving on Thursday. I personally am very sorry. He acted exceedingly well during the siege and was an example to all the other ministers, especially to the French minister [Monsieur Pichon], who was a craven-hearted cur.'[73]

So many Imperial artefacts disappeared in the days following the victory parade that General Gaselee was forced to lock the Meridian Gate. But a steady stream of officers and diplomats obtained permits from his office, and the Imperial household was systematically picked clean, Cixi's 3000 jewellery boxes among the spoil. Sarah Conger, who obtained an admission ticket in September 1900, wrote that 'nothing had been molested'. But Lieutenant General Lineivitch, a Russian commander awarded the Cross of St George for his part in the relief of Peking, took '10 trunks full of valuables from the looted Peking palaces' back to his post in Amur.[74] Julien Viaud, a French naval officer who kept at his side a case of Evian water to ward off 'native diseases', also obtained an entry pass and described Cixi's Western Palaces as a 'terrible dream in which a series of corridors opens up then closes again, preventing you from ever getting out'. Viaud, who wrote of his adventures under the pseudonym Pierre Loti (stories that won him entry to the Académie Française), revealed only to his wife the treasures that he acquired while in the Chinese maze:

> It is fun to open cupboards and chests every day to explore the marvels there . . . For company I have a great jade goddess in a golden robe, who was meant to ensure the safety of the Chinese emperor. I left home with a single suitcase. I will return with a huge load of baggage.[75]

In the chaos, the Summer Palace was forgotten until October, when, as a token gesture to the Chinese, Major Noel Du Boulay, the son of a Winchester School house-master, was called to 'take stock of the contents'. Major General E. G. Barron ordered: 'If he finds they have been wantonly damaged or flagrantly plundered he will record the fact in writing.'[76] Du Boulay, who took snapshots of the abandoned rooms, complained that he had been brought in three months too late:

We found all these buildings . . . completely swept of small ornaments, hundreds of small stands being left which presumably had
each held a small object such as a vase or a piece of jade. In many
cases small screens, clocks, artificial flowers etc, had been damaged
by the removal of inlaid pieces of jade, etc. In all the rooms, I think
without exception, were boxes in which were roughly packed a
number of articles.[77]

Members of the multinational force under Du Boulay's command
also abused their position to further plunder the Summer Palace.
The Italian contingent placed in charge of the Dowager Empress's
private apartments graffitied her walls with ribald comments and
sacked the chambers, leaving them 'in utter chaos'.[78] Edmund
Backhouse, who had been taught by Du Boulay's father, was employed to create an inventory and used his office to secure a private
collection that, he boasted, consisted of 600 pieces, valued at
500,000 taels or £80,000:

with the aid of trusty Manchus, I caused the removal of bronzes,
jades, porcelains, ivories, paintings, calligraphy, cloisonné, lacquer,
tapestries, carpets and about 25,000 vols . . . It included one enormous block of jade most beautifully carved and dating from 1420,
which was as dear to the Empress as *la pumelle de ses yeux*.[79]

Backhouse was referring to yet another copy of Kublai Khan's wine
bowl, a piece that subsequently disappeared, although his books and
calligraphic scrolls, that would later fill 29 crates, weighing 45 tonnes,
resurfaced at the Bodleian Library in Oxford, when he attempted to
buy a seat as Professor of Chinese studies.[80]

While Du Boulay blamed most of the thefts on acquisitive bannerman, an endless stream of illustrious visitors were admitted to
the Imperial chambers. Count von Waldersee, the German commander, popped in for a quick tour, followed by Sir Ernest Satow,
Sir Claude's replacement as head of mission. Satow dined at the
palace with General Gaselee, who suggested a 'handsome [jade]
screen standing behind the throne might be sent to the Queen'. Edwin Conger viewed the apartments. The Germans took back gifts
they had given to Emperor Guangxu.

Backhouse's completed inventory claimed that a palace complex that had once housed millions of Chinese artworks now contained only 865 items, including just 33 pieces of jade.[81] But photographs taken by Du Boulay as keepsakes of his time in China inadvertently confirm that the looting continued during his tenure. Many of the bronzes, clocks, pieces of jadeite and jades depicted in them fail to appear on his inventory. Instead, an assortment of Imperial artefacts, remarkably similar to the ones pictured, were later obtained by the Victoria & Albert Museum, the Wallace Collection and the British Museum in London and the Metropolitan Museum of Art in New York.[82]

Dozens of public and private collections would benefit from this second Imperial diaspora. When Polly Smith finally left Peking with the Squiers and their children, the First Secretary crammed his US Army schooner cabin with piles of looted jadeite. Even more followed him home. On 3 September 1901 the *New York Times* reported:

> H. G. Squiers started for home today . . . He takes with him a collection of Chinese artefacts, filling several railway cars, which experts pronounce one of the most complete in existence. Mr Squiers intends to present the collection, which consists largely of porcelains, bronzes and carvings from the palaces, bought from missionaries and at auction of military loot, to the New York Metropolitan Museum of Art.[83]

When the *New York Times* approached George Story, the Met's curator, for a comment, he turned on the reporter, claiming that the institution 'does not accept loot'. It was an 'outrage' that Squiers, a gentleman and art connoisseur, had been besmirched with the stigma of fencing stolen goods.[84]

Auguste and Annie Chamot, whose wine cellar had kept legations residents afloat during the siege, smuggled a haul of jadeite back to California, including a screen that had once belonged to Qianlong and a head-dress worn by Cixi. They displayed the treasure at their sea-front villa, built with a 200,000 US dollars indemnity that they squeezed out of the Chinese for damage to their hotel, but they would lose everything in the San Francisco earthquake of 1906.

When the US Army transport *Grant* arrived in San Francisco in September 1901, bringing soldiers home from the Allied Relief, customs officers discovered a secret haul. Mr L. A. Kent examined Marine Lieutenant Wise's leather suitcase and found ten book-size jade tablets inscribed with Oriental characters, wrapped in silk. Kent was advised that they were spirit tablets, memorials dedicated to Emperor Shunzhi, the first Qing Emperor. The following June, Lieutenant J. B. Schoeffel arrived on the transport *Hancock* and in his bags were found five jade seals, one of them belonging to Emperor Xianfeng and a second to the unfortunate A-lu-te. Schoeffel had also stashed away ten jade spirit tablets and thirty 'jade stones', including several pieces of the Dowager Empress's jadeite jewellery. Days later, two more spirit tablets were found aboard the transports *Sherman* and *Sheridan*: one dedicated by Qianlong to his mother and another to his father. A third was found aboard the *Logan*, hidden in a typewriter case belonging to a Sergeant Bronson. Fifteen months later three more jade tablets surfaced in the bags of a Captain A. V. P. Anderson, who claimed to have purchased them 'in good faith' from a Russian officer serving in China. All of the tablets had been stolen from the Temple of Heaven where they were once used by the Emperors to worship their ancestors, but where Allied boots now trampled mud through the hallowed halls and courtyards.[85]

Despite the wealth of customs reports and queries from the Chinese Embassy in Washington, all but two of these items vanished. Only one, the spirit tablet dedicated to Emperor Shunzhi, was ever returned to Peking.

Many found their way into the display cabinets of Abraham Livingstone Gump, an antique dealer in San Francisco. Gump turned his attention to Oriental art after the family's stock of Italian marble, French gilt clocks and European bronzes was destroyed in the San Francisco earthquake. Abe, as he was known by clients, claimed to be able to discern the quality and provenance of jade by touch alone, which was lucky, as he was blind. He sported an exquisite jadeite cabochon that he said had come from a necklace once worn by an Emperor and boasted in his memoirs of how he stocked his Oriental Room:

Soldiers and marines returning from tours of duty in China came into the Gump store with treasure secured during the Boxer uprising. There were solid gold boxes, set with uncut jewels, gorgeous embroideries, and other finery indicative of luxury almost beyond the comprehension of practical Americans. Neither their temporary owners nor the purchasers had any idea of the real value; but their very strangeness lured San Franciscans with their suddenly well-filled purses.[86]

One of Abe's most profitable purchases was Xianfeng's seal that he sold on to the Seattle Museum in 1935. When, ten years later, Hugh Alexander Matier, a 'scholarly amateur Orientalist', rediscovered it in the museum's vaults, he told *Time,* in an article that was headlined 'Yehonala's Loot': 'I nearly dropped my spectacles. It was the long lost seal of the Emperor.'[87] But Abe Gump then claimed not to remember where it had come from.

※

By the time of his death in 1902, Heber Bishop had gathered more than 900 Imperial jade and jadeite artefacts, and he bequeathed his collection to the Metropolitan Museum of Art. Following to the letter the instructions contained in Bishop's will, the Met constructed a replica of the Louis XV ballroom in his apartment at 881 Fifth Avenue to house the collection. Sir Caspar Purdon Clarke, who had received a knighthood for his contribution to art in Britain before becoming director of the Met, supervised the mammoth task of assembling the installation. He clearly did not hold with George Story's views.

Everything about the exhibition was extraordinary, including the two-volume catalogue that accompanied it. Weighing in at 125 pounds, only 100 copies of *Investigations and Studies in Jade* were printed on hand-made paper fashioned from 'pure white cotton rags', fastened using glue from 'pure Singapore Buffalo hide', printed using a typeface designed in Scotland that was destroyed as soon as the job was completed. Printer Theodore Devinne heralded it as 'the largest single presswork that had ever been attempted'. Each massive volume, lavishly illustrated with Li Shih Ch'uan's hand-coloured paintings, was bound using Levant leather, two skins chosen for each volume from the 900 that had been purchased. The limited editions, that required the strength of two men to be lifted, were gifted to the Prince of Wales, the Queen of Holland, the Kaiser of Germany, the Tsar of Russia, the Mikado of Japan and even the Emperor of China himself. No doubt Guangxu would have been interested to learn of how his legacy had been stolen, packed up and shipped to the United States.

Here was the scaled-down replica of Qianlong's wine bowl with its inscription, 'What I prize are worthy men'. Bishop assured his readers that it was 'the largest piece of finely carved jade known to exist'. Here was Colonel Schmidt's brush-holder carved with a scene from King Bodawpaya's tribute mission to China, and the double-dragon seal stolen by his men from the Calm and Bright Park. Here were the two kneeling jadeite boys that Cixi had once used as pillows, stolen from her bedchamber by British soldiers. Here was the Imperial Green Jade brush-washer, its bowl inscribed with a sign of the Emperor, 'four times ten thousand ages', that was sold to a 'Mr Walkinshaw of Peking'. Here was Countess Kleezekowsky's jadeite jewellery set by Eugene Fontenay in Paris. And here were dozens of jadeite *ruyi* sceptres, belt hooks, necklaces and Qianlong ornaments. Only two items were not ascribed to Chinese loot, one of them 'a portrait of Mr Bishop, 1898, nephrite, made in France by A. Berquin-Varangoz'.

The Bishop bequest opened in 1906 and entranced New York. George Frederick Kunz, of Tiffany and Co, pronounced it 'the finest collection of jade that exists anywhere in the world', and after seeing Countess Kleezekowsky's jewels, he took some new ideas back to Tiffany's workshop, that had produced the first Western collection of jadeite jewellery eight years earlier.

❋

When Cixi returned to the Forbidden City in the autumn of 1901, a long tattered ribbon of colour breezing into a desolate grid of dust and rubble, would she have even recognised her Peking? A city that had once been filled with the songs of traders, a rabble of markets and tea-stalls, was now deserted, 'not a single shop was open for business and scarcely a dozen persons were to be seen'.[88]

Riding through the smoking remains of the Middle Kingdom in her sedan chair, would she have glimpsed through the thick velvet curtains the Stars and Stripes that hung from the battle-scarred walls of the Imperial City? As she passed through the outer Qian-

men Gate, her sedan chair halted to allow the Empress of the West
to pay her respects at a small shrine, an intimate custom once only
practised by returning Emperors. Stunned by the destruction all
around her, only the click of a shutter alerted Cixi to the silent ob-
servers above her, a crowd of diplomats and their wives peering
down from the ramparts with cameras:

> the Empress Dowager looked up at the smoke-blackened walls and
> saw us: a row of foreigners . . . The eunuchs seemed to be trying to
> get her to move on . . . [but] she stopped once more and, looking up
> at us, lifted her closed hands under her chin and made a series of lit-
> tle bows. The effect of this gesture was astonishing . . . from all
> along the wall there came, in answer, a spontaneous burst of ap-
> plause. The Empress Dowager appeared pleased. She remained there
> a few minutes longer, looking up and smiling.[89]

The observer was an Italian resident who concluded that 'the return
of the court to Peking was a turning point in history.' The Dragon
Lady and her Imperial retinue, once so impervious to the world outside its walls, so acquisitive and invincible, was now no better than
a side-show, playing to a foreign crowd. As Cixi climbed back into
her sedan chair, she was swept towards the Five Towers of the
Phoenix, passing a Union Jack that fluttered to her right, triumphantly marking Sir Claude MacDonald's mansion, standing
like a headstone over the charred remains of the Hanlin Academy.
Soon she would be forced to compound the misery of China's defeat by signing an International Protocol that would extract indem-
nities from the country's purse totalling 450 million taels, then
worth £67.5 million.

Yu Derling claimed that Cixi spoke only once about the looting
of Peking, when she uncovered a few broken treasures in the rubble, including a jade Buddha that had been presented to her by a
Burmese monk. Its face and arm had been slashed by an Allied
sabre, but she insisted that it be dusted down and reinstated on its
old podium adjacent to where Qianlong had housed Kublai's
Khan's wine bowl. 'I don't intend to have it repaired as I don't want
to forget the lesson I have learned and this is a good reminder,' Cixi
was said to have told Derling as the icon was raised once again onto
its plinth. But for the Qing, it was far too late for lessons.

Seven

Twilight in the Forbidden City

When the towering doors of the Eastern Flowery Gate groaned open shortly before dawn on Buddhist All Souls Day in September 1909, a giant galleon, with sails billowing from 99-foot-high masts, glided into a silent city wreathed in mist and mourning. The ship floated past noblemen and their wives who had thrown open their double doors to watch open-jawed as ghostly sailors, dressed in court robes, steered a course north towards Coal Hill. They appeared to drop anchor on open ground but then torch-bearers raced forward, flames engulfing the hull within seconds, revealing the galleon to be nothing more than a card-and-cloth illusion. The spirit ship had been designed to bear the Dowager Empress's soul to 'the place of the nine springs', carried aloft among the cracking embers and flakes of soot that now rose in spirals above Peking.[1]

One month later, Cixi's mortal remains left the Forbidden City as the capital hunched under a charcoal sky. She was now leaving not in haste, as in 1860, or in the guise of peasant, as in 1900, but triumphantly borne in a golden casket that would be carried on a 125-kilometre journey north-east to the Imperial necropolis. George Morrison reported meticulously on the procession, having failed to alert London to the Dowager Empress's death on 15 November 1908, as he had skipped Peking to go hunting.

Prince Chun, the newly appointed Regent, led a bodyguard of Qing princes and members of the Grand Council. Behind them 'rode . . . a smart body of troops, followed by a large number of camels whose Mongol attendants carried tent poles and other articles for the erection of the palaces wherein the coffin rests at night at the different stages of the four-day journey to the tombs.' A procession of 'gaudy honorific umbrellas presented to the Old Buddha on the occasion of her return from exile in 1901' followed, as did the Dalai Lama and his maroon-robed contingent from Tibet and a weeping Li Lianying, who brought up the rear dressed in sackcloth.

'No such pomp and circumstance,' wrote Morrison, 'has marked the obsequies of any Empress of China since the funeral of Empress Wu.' It was a typically obtuse statement, as the last woman to rule China was the Empress Wu, 1200 years before Cixi. Wu, who had also risen from the ranks of concubines, had ordered that hundreds of servants be buried alive in her mausoleum. Cixi's celestial attendants who accompanied the spirit ship were, like it, cut from paper and were burned beside her catafalque before it left Peking.

The coffin followed a trail of yellow sand that wound its way across the Hebei plains towards the shoulders of the Changrui Mountains, where the Qing had erected their city of the dead. Down the Avenue of Immortals the catafalque was carried, past statues that lined the route: silent warriors guarding the citizens of the Qing Dong Ling, stone mandarins administering the dead, a menagerie of kneeling dragons, lions, camels, elephants and unicorns blessing the divine way as they all had done for more than 300 years. Finally the path ran down to the Imperial burial ground where 5 Emperors, 14 Empresses and 136 Imperial Consorts had been interred. Here, between cherry and cypress trees, lay 86-year-old Qianlong's elaborate underground palace, whose interconnecting corridors ran deep into the Changrui foothills like a pharaoh's vault until they reached the marble chamber that he shared with his beloved Fucha. To the west was the tomb of Emperor Xianfeng, dead at 30 after giving Cixi a son. Tongzhi, the smallpox victim, who had died aged 19, was shunted to the south-eastern perimeter. Intended as a lasting memorial to the power and longevity of Manchu rulers, the Qing Dong Ling now served as testimony to the greed and excess of Qianlong's feeble descendants.

Cixi's catafalque was carried along her newly built Sacred Way under her Dragon-Phoenix gate and over her seven-arched bridge towards her Precious Citadel, the elaborate fortress embossed with dragons that she had commissioned as a headstone for her subterranean burial chamber. Everything about her death, like her life, would now be encased in riches and mythology. Inside her golden casket, her body was cradled on a mattress of gold thread. Edmund Backhouse would later claim in *The Times* that it was seven inches thick, 'woven with an embroidery of pearls'. A jadeite pillow carved with lotus leaves was placed under her head, and another, carved with lotus flowers, rested beneath her feet. Her shoulders were enclosed by her famous cape of pearls, a demon-quelling wand clasped in her hand, its shaft made from a translucent jadeite stalk. In her mouth, Peking jewellers claimed, was a ripe black pearl as large as a nugget of coal, that prevented putrefaction and fed her spirit on its journey to the after-world. Around her neck hung a court necklace that an American millionaire would later boast had stop-beads the size of plums. In her hair butterflies fluttered in the draft, their wings a lattice of kingfisher feathers and jadeite splinters that Derling claimed had been designed by the Dowager Empress herself. In all, more than 33,560 pearls and 3660 rubies, sapphires, emeralds and cat's eyes had been sewn onto Cixi's funereal robes, and fistfuls of gems were sprinkled over her body, filling in the spaces around her casket. The Dowager Empress was literally 'buried in precious stones'.[2]

The coffin itself was sealed in a vault perfumed by 350 jadeite incense burners. Altar vessels contained her hair and nails. Gold and jade Buddha statues stood beside jade horses that appeared to canter through the everlasting gardens that were flecked with coral and jadeite leaves. There was even an Imperial larder stocked with watermelons and cabbages wrought from the Stone of Heaven, one vegetable concealing a tiny crystalline cricket, nestling between the leaves. Two sets of heavy stone doors sealed the treasure house, providing an inviolable sanctuary for Cixi's soul and an indestructible memorial to her reign. The Qing archives stated that it cost 2.7 million silver taels (135 million grams) to relocate Cixi from the Forbidden City to the necropolis, while only '459,940 taels, two mace, three candereens and six li' (23 million grams) had been spent on burying Emperor Guangxu, in a comparatively spartan ceremony that had taken place the previous May at Xi Ling, another Qing cemetery in the Western Hills.[3]

When it was announced on 16 November 1908 that the Emperor of Overpowering Light had died the day before his adopted mother, a rumour raced up and down the decaying crimson corridors that the poisonous Dowager Empress had struck again in one final act of petulance. The exotic tale of betrayal gripped Britain and America, where even the generalities of Chinese court life were still completely misunderstood. The *New York Times* published an obituary for Cixi that described her as Ci'an, the Empress of the East, illustrating the piece with a picture of one of Emperor Tongzhi's consorts. Because of Morrison's absence from Peking, *The Times* failed to report the deaths at all until he caught up six weeks later.

The truth behind Guangxu's demise lies in a nameless doctor's confidential medical notes, written with the candour of a man who was confident that no one else would read them. Guangxu 'dreams of fighting, premature ejaculation a problem, mental vagueness, spontaneous laughter without reason, occasional murmuring to himself'. *Hong Yu Gao,* a jade ointment, was prescribed to moisten his dehydrated sinuses, and Herbal Treatment for Calming the Mind was brewed as tea. But by 12 November his doctors had given up. So was it poison? The Emperor's medical file reveals a man of sickly demeanour, possibly weakened by syphilis, who at the age of 37 was also dogged by chronic arthritis and an incurable fever. Perhaps his beloved Pearl Concubine still haunted him; her bloated body sunk in the waters of the well. Perhaps the Emperor, who had narrowly escaped execution at the hands of his adopted mother, was kept awake by phantom assassins who stalked him in the day and through the night. If Guangxu was poisoned, it was by fear of the Dowager Empress and not by *Chin Baba*'s hand.[4]

Cixi's demise in a neighbouring apartment was an ugly affair. Imperial physicians Zhang Zhongyuan and Dan Jiajyu found that the indomitable Old Buddha had developed a urinary tract infection, her throat was blocked 'by excessive sputum' and her shrunken tongue had become trapped in the cavities of her rotten teeth. They prescribed an Imperial *Ginseng-Poria Pill* that was diluted with child's urine and a Modified Jade Cosmetic Powder to relax a persistent tic that contorted Cixi's face in violent spasms. As she slipped in and out of consciousness *Scorpio and Bombyx Batryticatus,* a concoction of warm millet and two crushed scorpions that had been milked of their poison, was dropped on to her blistered lips. Finally, the woman who had exorcised the words 'death' and 'finished' from the vocabulary of the Imperial court, had pushed her doctors aside and summoned Prince Chun.

Guangxu's long-faced brother, a malleable Qing loyalist who had sailed to Germany to apologise for the death of Baron von Kettler after the siege of Peking, later recalled how, when he left court, he sped to Pei Fu, his mansion in the extreme north of the Imperial City. Prince Chun's aged mother collapsed when she heard that Cixi had appointed him Prince Regent. His servants hoisted up their robes to dash for a doctor as the family gulped down cups of ginger tea, an infant scattering guests, wailing as he ran. The inconsolable Pu Yi, Prince Chun's two-year-old son, had also won a new title. He had been proclaimed heir apparent by the dying Cixi and was now 'resisting the Imperial Edict'.[5] Pu Yi later recalled spitting at the circling eunuchs, pulling at their hair and scratching their waxy skin as they dragged him to the Forbidden City.

The heir apparent never forgot his first and only meeting with the Dowager Empress as she lay on her death-bed, the odour of disease masked by clouds of incense that filled the room with a cloying mist. He was taken to the Forbidden City on 13 November 1908, dressed in a new yellow skull-cap and ankle-length robes, over which he wore a vermilion jacket with dangling yellow silk cuffs that came down to his knees. He wriggled around in the unfamiliar swathes of fabric until the crowd parted to reveal 'a drab curtain through which I could see an emaciated and terrifyingly hideous face'. The boy quivered, began to pant, a nasal gurgle swelling into a fire-alarm wail. Cixi bellowed for some candied *haws*. But the hysterical Pu Yi would not be comforted and threw the sweets onto the floor. 'What a naughty child,' the Dowager Emperor rasped, 'take him away.'[6]

Pu Yi would later claim to have no memories of those funereal days when Peking was as silent as the grave. He also remembered little of the ceremony that was staged on 2 December 1909, two days after Cixi's body was interred. The capital had been sheltering from a freezing gale as the commanders of the Palace Guard and the ministers of the Inner Court clattered into the Forbidden City. The storm that hurtled down from the Mongolian steppe grazed the three-year-old infant's face, his body swaddled in a thick fur-trimmed jacket. Carried in a palanquin encased in yellow silk to the Hall of Supreme Harmony, he was lifted onto the Dragon Throne that towered many feet above him. Thousands of Qing retainers and loyalists kowtowed in sombre rows, proclaiming his reign name, Hsuan Tung, filling the corridors and courtyards of the Forbidden City with their voices.

The palace eunuchs later recalled how, as Prince Chun bowed before his son, the three-year-old began to twitch and fidget, irritated by the sails of Imperial yellow silk that flapped around him in the snow-bearing draughts. 'I want to go home,' Pu Yi had screamed, his legs kicking in the air. Prince Chun raised his head and whispered hoarsely to his son: 'Don't cry. It'll soon be over.' A murmur of horror ran through the hall, palace retainers terrified by such ill-chosen and inauspicious words.

Pu Yi was enveloped in a 'yellow mist' – the colour of the citadel's glazed tiles, of his sedan chair and its cushions, of the lining of his hats and clothes, of his waist-band, of the plates and bowls, of his window curtains and even of his pony's bridle. Wherever he stumbled, a procession emerged. A eunuch from the Administrative Bureau, 'whose function was roughly that of a motor horn', ran twenty paces ahead, clucking like a football rattle to warn of the Emperor's movements. Ten more eunuchs 'walking crab-wise' flanked the path, and two more held a canopy over the boy Emperor's head. Behind was a weaving trail armed with an umbrella, a chair, fans, food, first aid equipment and a walking medicine chest: 'Essence of Betony pills for rectifying the vapour, Six Harmony Pills for stabilising the centre, Gold Coated Heart Dispersing Cinnabar, Onmi-purpose bars, anti-plague powder, the Three Immortals beverage to aid digestion'. And finally, bringing up the rear, was the Imperial yellow chamber pot.[7]

From his nursery the Son of Heaven could hear a disembodied Peking, the cry of his subjects, the rumble of a woodenwheeled cart, the song of his sentries patrolling the moat, but dressed in his dainty cloth socks appointed with golden dragons, he had no idea what it all meant. The Emperor was breast fed until the age of eight, clutching at the nipple of a nurse born to a farming family from Hebei, who had fled to Peking after being made destitute by high taxation, floods and famine. The milk nurse's parents had been forced to sell her into marriage, and when her husband died of tuberculosis, Mrs Wang had lined up to express for the Imperial household. Every day she was force-fed bowls of unsalted, fatty meat until she 'was transformed into a dairy cow'.[8] It was in her third year of plumping up the Son of Heaven that her own daughter died of malnutrition, with food shortages besetting the provinces and the capital. However, it was another six years before she found out, and only then by the cruel slip of a eunuch's tongue, by which time no one cared what Mrs Wang felt, as Pu Yi was drinking from a jadeite cup.

By appointing a child of Yehenara stock to the throne, Cixi had assured her clan's continuing hold over China, but she hadn't reckoned on the weakness of the Regent. Mesmerised by his new-found wealth, Pu Yi's father went on a spending spree, ordering foreign motor cars that he raced around Peking, installing a telephone in his mansion. But when he decided to embrace the twentieth century by exchanging his Manchu gown for a Western collar and shirt, it took a member of his family to point out that his flapping shirt-tails belonged inside his trousers.[9]

The Forbidden City was a rudderless ship, but it carried on as if it were at the centre of an eighteenth-century Confucian state bound by Imperial largesse. The power vacuum was filled by the Nei Wu Fu, the Imperial Household Department that maintained 48 offices, 600 staff and at its height spent more than 6 million taels (300 million grams) of silver cosseting the boy Emperor's 1100 eunuchs. Officially Chang Chien-ho, Pu Yi's chief eunuch, and his senior staff were only paid eight taels (400 grams) of silver and eight catties of rice a month. But somehow they managed to don a new fur gown every day and purchase sea-otter capes that were far too expensive for the Qing gentry, whose homes were rapidly sliding into dereliction.

Oblivious to the flood, famine and exorbitant taxation that was crippling China, every month the Imperial kitchens would order two tonnes of beef, lamb and pork plus 388 chickens and ducks for the child Emperor, his mother the Dowager Empress Lung Yu and her four frail consorts. But even these provisions were apparently insufficient for the cooks to sate the Imperial family of six. In the same period, the kitchen sent out for an emergency batch of 4786 chickens and a school of fish and shrimps. If the cooks were corrupt, so were the Imperial clothiers. In one month tailors stitched up the Son of Heaven with 11 fur jackets, six fur inner gowns, six fur outer gowns, two fur waistcoats, 30 padded waistcoats and as many trousers. Although the cost of the Emperor's new clothes has been lost, a chit survives for 2137 taels (106,850 grams) of silver for buttons, thread and pockets, that surely must have been deep.[10]

Even George Morrison noticed the rot. He wrote to his foreign editor Valentine Chirol, warning of 'the eunuchs and their hangers on who remain to poison the whole body politic with their corruption, intrigues and spendthrift extravagance.'[11] The profligate *Nei Wu Fu,* its retainers and eunuchs, were beginning to enrage disgruntled Chinese taxpayers, and rebellions now rumbled in the south and central provinces, galvanised by the leaders of fledgling movements that all called for a 'New China'.

The Imperial Court thrashed like a leviathan, concealing its vast wealth in the folds of its mythical skin, to which clung thousands of Imperial retainers. Prince Chun had no idea how to tame it or how to analyse the mood of the Chinese people. Now more than ever he needed an advisor and ally, but one of his first actions as Regent was to remove from the Imperial inner circle Cixi's loyal lieutenant Yuan Shikai. The powerful commander of the Peiyang Army, a force assembled out of the decimated ranks of China's army after its defeats by the Japanese in 1894 and 1895, had secured favour by betraying Emperor Guangxu in 1898, revealing his plot to depose the Dowager Empress. Yuan Shikai became the first Han Chinese to be elevated to Grand Councillor in a Manchu court, but when Prince Chun forced him to 'retire and attend to a leg injury' in a misguided effort to cauterise his ambition, the officer graciously retreated from court with his Peiyang Army.

The Son of Heaven would later claim that his only memory from his first three years on the Dragon Throne was one day in February 1912, in the Mind Nurture Palace, where Qianlong's *cloisonné* jar with its 36 blades of grass was still on display. Sitting on a dark-wood kang, he recalled seeing his mother, the Dowager Empress Lung Yu, sobbing into a handkerchief, 'a fat old man kneeling before her on a red cushion, wiping tears from his face'. The distended figure was Yuan Shikai, back at the court again with terrible news. Mutinous regiments had seized local arsenals. Several provinces had declared independence. The First Chinese Revolution had pitched China into chaos. Yuan Shikai, who had magnanimously agreed to aid the Qing in their hour of need and had quelled the uprisings in the Yangze region, was shedding crocodile tears.

What Pu Yi had witnessed in the Mind Nurture Palace was his own abdication. Yuan Shikai warned Lung Yu that if Pu Yi did not appease the destructive forces gathering in China by standing aside, the people would wrench him from the Dragon Throne as the revolutionaries had done to Louis XVI. So in the shadow of an illusory guillotine, on 12 February 1912, more than 2000 years after the first Emperor ruled China, the Dragon Throne was vacated to make way for the President of the Republic.

According to George Morrison, Yuan Shikai looked nervous at his presidential inauguration, 'fat and unhealthy, the flesh hanging over his collar'.[12] China's corpulent new leader immediately moved into the Forbidden City, setting up court in the southern apartments, from where he requisitioned the remnants of Imperial China, displaying them around the T'ai Ho Tien, Chung Ho Tien and Pao Ho Tien throne rooms. After bestowing on himself the office of President for Life and head-hunting George Morrison as his political advisor, he ordered the emptying of the Imperial treasure houses at Jehôl and Mukden. The Imperial family had lost virtually all of its Peking treasures to the Allies, but these distant places were still brimming with jadeite, nephrite, bronzes and ceramics. After dissolving his tame parliament and neutering the opposition, Yuan Shikai transformed the Wu-ying and Wen-hua audience halls into elaborate museums that displayed his stolen Imperial credentials.

So many treasures arrived at the presidential apartments that Zeng Guang Ling, a curator, was appointed to organise the loot. Among the jadeite and bronzes that he found in 1914 in the Raha Xing Palace at Jehôl was a painting of a fair-skinned, blue-eyed woman dressed in armour. Curator Zeng identified the warrior as Qianlong's Fragrant Consort and inscribed a new version of the Xiang Fei story onto the back of the canvas.[13] The girl from the New Territories who smelled of the jujube flower had married Hou Jing Zhan, an opponent of the Qing, but when he died in battle she was taken to Peking as a prize, curator Zeng wrote. There, Qianlong had attempted to win her hand with gifts of honeydew melons and grapes. But Xiang Fei secretly vowed to avenge her husband's death and when Qianlong invited her on a hunting expedition, she cornered him in the forest, lunging at the Emperor with a sword. But Qianlong side-stepped her thrust and Xian Fei returned to Peking, where, according to curator Zeng, she took her own life.

Two years after the President hung the painting in the Shu De room of the Western Flowery Gate, he shocked Peking by reviving the Winter Solstice festival at the Temple of Heaven, where Emperors of China once prayed for the atonement of their subjects. Yuan Shikai would have proclaimed himself Emperor, having already chosen the reign name Hung Hsien, 'Triumphant Forever', if it were not for another revolution that broke out in the central and southern Chinese provinces. Warlords loyal to the republican cause forced him to retreat back to the office of Life President of the Republic.

Pu Yi had been all but forgotten. He was shuttered away in the northern section of the Forbidden City where his only privileges were access to the Imperial Garden and library. He was now the subject of 'The Articles Providing for the Favourable Treatment of the Great Qing Emperor after his Abdication', an infant pensioner, bound by an eight-point contract, the state maintaining its political prisoner on an annual budget of 4 million Chinese dollars. It was perhaps lucky that he was too young and too well insulated from the outside world to hear the tragic news that arrived from the Southern Barbarians.

☒

At midnight on 16 December 1916 ex-King Thibaw had died in Colonel Godfrey's retirement home at Ratnagiri, his heart and kidneys having failed. Thibaw was survived by Supayalat, four daughters, a two-cylinder DeDion car and debts of 22,009 rupees (then worth £1467). To help meet Thibaw's obligations to 45 tradesmen and 23 servants, the Indian Government sequestrated his car. Its engine exhausted, its chassis buckled, the Royal motor was taken in a bullock cart to Bombay, where it was auctioned off for only 500 rupees (£33).

What had become of the scions of the Konbaung Dynasty? In the years following their arrival, Ratnagiri had experienced a gold rush.

The tailor who once stitched longyis now made suits from Chinese silk. The mango-seller with her parchment hands wore a ruby ring. Sadhus who once paraded in torn dhotis clinked and tinkled up and down the dirt track known as Thibaw Palace Road. What the British had dismissed as a sentimental haul of mementoes, the baggage train that Thibaw had taken from Mandalay, had gradually been frittered away to pay for a monarch's life in exile.

We know from an inventory hidden under Thibaw's bedroom floor that the ex-King smuggled out of Burma a small fortune: 'flat pieces of jade', gold bars, bags of diamonds, ruby slippers, emerald caps, a bathroom set studded with diamonds. Even his servants' luggage concealed treasure: 100 gold ladles, a child's silver tea set and 32 jadeite boulders. But the ex-King and his queens had never learned to budget or to haggle, and within ten years all that was left was a mattress of pearls, half a dozen silver vases and bills for more than 300,000 rupees (£20,000). An Indian Government investigation found that between 1885 and 1888, Thibaw had raised 40,004 rupees (£2666) by selling jadeite, diamonds and rubies and had bought silks, suits and shoes, artificial flowers and scent from Ludha Ebram & Co., Bombay. He had purchased cigars, magic lanterns, compendiums of games and cologne from Treacher & Co. He had ordered a grand piano from Soundy & Co. Alarmed at his profligacy, the Indian Government had passed the 'ex-King Thibaw Act' in 1895 that had prevented him from entering into binding agreements with anyone. They had postered Ratnagiri with warnings to local merchants not to trade with the ex-King.

When he died in penury his passing became a lingering farce. The ex-Queen Supayalat pleaded for her husband's body and that of her sister, who had died four years before, to be returned to Mandalay and entombed in King Mindon's mausoleum. But the British categorically refused. They were becoming increasingly concerned about the Young Men's Buddhist Association of Burma that called for an end to the brutality of the colonial police and the bias shown by the judiciary. The Burmese were expected to address British and Indian officials as *thakin* or 'master', remove their sandals and supplicate themselves in their presence, while the British kept their shoes on when visiting sacred Buddhist sites in Rangoon. By 1917 a YMBA 'no footwear' campaign had achieved widespread sup-

port, marking the start of a period of political agitation. 'In Ratnagiri the [bodies of] the ex King and Queen are harmless, in Burma
they might set the country ablaze,' wrote Denys Bray, a British bu-
reaucrat.[14]

As the First World War smothered Europe, Thibaw was forgotten. For three years his embalmed body lay unburied in a guarded
storeroom while his family sold their mirrors, chairs and cupboards
to keep the household afloat. Eventually, on 19 March 1919, the
growing scandal of the ex-King's corpse was interred in 30 minutes.
But Supayalat refused to attend, distraught at the prospect of a
King of Burma being buried in unconsecrated ground, although the
New Delhi files reveal that she was forced to sign a document ap-
proving the release of her husband's body. Instead, her third and
fourth daughters stood beneath a temporary awning that was surrounded by eight honorific umbrellas and eight drummers who serenaded them with a sombre tattoo. The princesses draped scarlet
velveteen covers over the coffins of the ex-King and his senior
Queen, and followed them through the haze of orchards sticky with
the caramelised scent of mangoes. Thibaw's mausoleum had been
built by the Public Works Department, 'five furlongs from the
palace grounds, close to the Ratnagiri-Kolhapur road', on a pau-
pers' funeral ground that the Indian Government had been given
for free. 'Happily they are now safely entombed and we can only
hope that no ill will betide from their not having received the full
ceremonial,' a relieved Denys Bray confessed, in a report to the
Bombay government.

The Second Princess immediately penned a letter to the authorities in broken English. The four daughters of an extinct Kingdom
had been 'brought up with fishermen, wild beasts, unmanly servants and false leaders'. They were ankle-deep in the odium of their
failed father. 'Must I be a labourer in the street or a servant in any
men's service to whom I think fit? We are improperly settled, we are
poor, we are to face the creditors,' she wrote, and the British cut her
annual pension to 300 rupees.

So Thibaw's daughters took their revenge against the high-
handed British in the only way they could. Bombay was warned of
an emerging scandal. 'The Third Princess is in a highly excitable
and neurotic state and cannot be trusted out of doors alone [lest]

she compromise herself with the first man she meets . . . Unless she is married at the earliest date, she will either lose her reason or follow in the footsteps of her eldest sister and cause another scandal,' a report warned. Within months British doctors had diagnosed the Third Princess as schizophrenic, giving a name to her racing pulse before it brought shame on the local government. But they had already mis-fielded Thibaw's eldest daughter, Phayagyi, and the scandal that the letter referred to was causing considerable consternation. The unmarried Phayagyi had given birth to Tutu, a baby girl, following a seven-month affair with Gopal Bhaurao Savant, the ex-King's former chauffeur, a married Hindu.

It was all too much for the Government of India. Thomas Cook & Sons were hired to arrange for Supayalat, now aged 57, and all but her second daughter, who refused to leave India, to be shipped to Rangoon. On 16 April 1919, they were searched 'to ensure that the body of the ex-King was not being surreptitiously removed' and then marched aboard the steamer *Arankola*, their luggage restricted to five carts. The illegitimate baby Tutu was left behind. In preparation for their arrival, posters were pinned up in Rangoon and Mandalay: 'The Government of India is not responsible for and will not assist in the recovery of debts incurred by the ex-Queen or any of her daughters.' There was to be no victorious homecoming after 30 years in exile, no secret baggage train of jadeite to buoy their fortunes, and when the once Royal family disembarked at Rangoon they barely raised a crowd, let alone a column inch. 'Bathos rather than pathos attends her [Supayalat's] return . . . a curious welcome to a lady who once ruled the court of Mandalay and nominal lord with a rod of iron,' the *Statesman* reported.[15] The fiery Queen of a once Great Golden Land was now relegated to barrack-room ballads:

> By the old Moulmein Pagoda, lookin' lazy at the sea,
> There's a Burma girl a-setting', and I know she thinks o' me . . .
> 'Er petticoat was yaller an' 'er little cap was green,
> An' 'er name was Supi-yaw-lat – ges' the same as Theebaw's Queen.[16]

✣

In China, Yuan Shikai's regal aspirations had been drowned in a urinal. In 1917 the *faux* emperor's bloated corpse was discovered in his toilet, apparently poisoned by gluttony. Royalists immediately raced around Peking gilding the case for the return of the boy Emperor. In the vacuum, Pu Yi was lifted back onto the Dragon Throne on 1 July, only to be pushed off it twelve days later after a republican general ordered his aircraft to shell the Forbidden City. Although only one bomb actually exploded, it was enough to burst the monarchist chimera, and the confused Son of Heaven was sent back to his library to listen to the city of sounds.

No one was willing to extinguish the office of Emperor altogether, 'the yellow silk chord that republican China retained to bind together her past and future'.[17] It was the Republic that decided to find a tutor for the Son of Heaven, maybe hoping to transform him into a constitutional European-style monarch, in case one was ever needed.

On 3 March 1919, Reginald Fleming Johnston entered the Forbidden City through the Gate of Spiritual Valour, the crumbling northern entrance, into a land of 'pompous make-believe'. An Oxford graduate who had served in Asia for twenty years, he sipped tea in the Mind Nature Palace, his pride ever so slightly swelling at the prospect of greeting a palanquin that carried an Emperor of China. What Johnston saw when the carriage arrived was a sulky-lipped thirteen-year-old with a sombre face, a lonely boy eager to learn, with no knowledge of English and only a shaky understanding of politics and geography.[18] When Pu Yi saw Johnston, he noticed his cornflower-blue eyes, greying hair and faultless Chinese. He was also reminded of the story of a General who had advised the Imperial court in 1900 that Englishmen were fitted with iron rods, and if knocked down could not get up.[19]

But Pu Yi warmed to his tutor. Over the next four years he donned European clothes, chose a name out of Johnston's list of British monarchs and obtained a pair of glasses, despite protests from his eunuchs that God's chosen ruler could not be myopic. Henry Pu Yi learned English, cut off his own queue when a barber refused and, despite howls of opposition, installed a telephone in the Forbidden City. The eunuchs claimed that it demeaned the Dragon Throne. Perhaps their real fear was the access it gave Henry Pu Yi to the outside world. Johnston, who told friends that he would not balk if asked to perform the kowtow before his pupil, swapped his morning coat for sable robes and eventually donned the cape and hat of a first-grade mandarin. He delighted in Henry Pu Yi's gifts of jadeite sceptres, brilliant green plaques and translucent plume holders that he would eventually take back to Scotland, where, sitting in his Imperial robes in a room filled with the Stone of Heaven, he would reflect on his days with the Emperor of China.

Outside the Emperor's time capsule China was a shifting mess of semi-autonomous states ruled by warlords whose armies had grown out of the mutinies of the First Chinese Revolution. In Manchuria there was Chang Tso-lin, the Old Marshal. In Shansi Province, Feng Yuxiang, the Christian General, a soldier from the age of eleven whose men were all urged to become Protestants. Yuan Shikai's powerful Peiyang Army was now divided into two factions, one in the Yangze Valley and the other in the North. In Yunnan it was Lung Yun, the Dragon Cloud commander, who ruled by means of the wealth he had gained taxing the Burmese jadeite trade.

As these warlords fought over the Empire, the Qing nobility's *hutongs* that surrounded the Forbidden City became impoverished, 'weeds grew in the great courtyards, roofs leaked and their stables were emptied'.[20] Some, like the family of Prince Gong, Cixi's confidant, fled the capital altogether, his walled palace sealed and its treasury left in the hands of stewards. Others, like the family of Prince Ching, Guangxu's chief minister, secretly began to sell Imperial jadeite gifts, and a few, like Prince Chun, used the money quietly to campaign for Henry Pu Yi's reinstatement. The finest pieces of jadeite, items that could be easily concealed in the dangling sleeves of a Qing gown or in the side-pocket of any army backpack, flooded onto the open market.

If life in the Forbidden City appeared to proceed with normality, it was only because the Imperial Household Department had begun selling the Stone of Heaven. In the absence of hard currency, Henry Pu Yi met his obligations with jadeite: sending 300,000 Chinese dollars' worth of palace treasures to Japan in lieu of financial aid after an earthquake; paying a vet's bill at the Peking Police School with a 'jadeite wristlet'.[21]

Eventually an honest member of the household staff confessed to Johnston that the Son of Heaven was being swindled. 'The *Nei Wu*

Fu would only sell to a small and exclusive ring of dealers whose close relationship with the palace staff enabled both sides to come to an agreement,' Johnston confided to his diary. Nothing was sold for its intrinsic value, only by weight. The price agreed was well below the actual value and the sale figure recorded in the household accounts was even less than that. The difference was then divided up between the eunuchs, some of whom were now earning more than one million taels of silver a year, then worth £200,000.

The eunuchs were also selling stolen treasures. In April 1921 Johnston came across a brawl in the apartments of Chuan-Ho, one of Emperor Tongzhi's consorts, who had just died. Eunuchs who, a few days earlier, had been in tears over their mistress's body, had broken into her apartment, stolen her jadeite collection and now argued over its division. 'The affair created a scandal in the city,' Johnston wrote later, 'not because of the actual thefts but because the thieves struggled amongst themselves for the booty and caused an uproar, which, in a chamber of death, was regarded by the household officials as unseemly.'[22] When the *Nei Wu Fu* failed to investigate, Johnston concluded that it too was complicit in the break-in. Fraud and theft was easily concealed by the elaborate dance of ritual and etiquette, and no one really knew what had been sold or stolen, as the Imperial treasures had never been catalogued.

Johnston told his pupil how on one occasion he had ridden out of the Tiananmen Gate and come across clusters of antique shops, some of which were run by palace eunuchs who made no effort to conceal their trade. If the tutor had ridden a little further into the Chinese City he would have been shocked. Barely a quarter of a mile from the Tiananmen Gate was a low-rise labyrinth that snaked between Zhengyangmen and Dashalan Street. Langfang was now one of the city's most prosperous quarters, 'hawkers vying to trade there with their large wicker baskets packed with ice, mulberries and cherries'. According to a popular Chinese saying, 'Langfang's east and west sides are for wealth and distinction; its south for fish and fowl, birds and flowers but its glittering centre is a jewel of jade'.[23]

Divided between the unmade lanes known as Langfang One and Two there were now more than 6000 lapidaries who filled the air with the growling of their water benches. It had been Muslims who had traded lapis from Afghanistan, turquoise from Persia, cat's eye from Ceylon, moonstone from Syria, and now in Peking they kept their abrasive wheels spinning by hammering at the treadle, grinding and regrinding new and old jade. Inside specialist shops like the *Tei Yuan Shieng* store, glass cabinets were filled with antique and new ornaments made from nephrite mined in desolate Khotan and Yarkand. But Tieh Bao Ting, the owner, kept his best business up his sleeve: exquisite ornaments and jewellery with a satin sheen whose brilliance and clarity marked them out as Burmese jadeite. Mr Tieh, whose father had abandoned farming to start the business in 1895, dressed in sombre Confucian robes and was regarded by his peers as 'strong and firm, like wisdom'. The most knowledgeable of Langfang's 40 jade dealers, Mr Tieh's word, the Chinese said, was worth more than gold.[24] And his name meant 'The Iron Pavilion of Treasures'.[25]

So many destitute nobles and corrupt officials arrived at Mr Tieh's lacquered doors that his vault was soon overflowing with pawned jadeite heirlooms that bought the farmer's son a new title, 'The Jade King of Peking'. Mr Tieh sold the Emperor's jewels to the new republican elite, to the warlords and occasionally to foreign antique dealers who were lucky enough to be admitted to his secretive inner court. It had been the Jade King and his regal circle that had handled Prince Gong's legacy in 1913 on behalf of Yamanaka & Co., a Japanese dealer who had shops in London and New York. Before the sale the Gong family, whose fortunes had dwindled after the death of Cixi's Chief Minister in May 1898, ordered their servants to open up their abandoned mansion to potential buyers, where, according to the catalogue, everything, including a half-smoked cigar, was left when they fled. Later Prince Gong's treasures, including emerald green jadeite buckles, screens, court necklaces and brush-holders, and a delicate vase the colour of 'moss entangled in melting snow', were shipped to New York, where they were auctioned at the American Art Galleries on Madison Avenue.[26]

Stories of princes and equerries scurrying through the night to rendezvous with bank managers, swapping rice sacks of jadeite for hard cash, drew dozens of agents for foreign dealers into Peking. One of the few Westerners who claimed to have access to the hocked haul was Ed Newell, a buyer for Abe Gump's Oriental showroom in San Francisco. Newell was mesmerised by treasures that he was told had leaked out of drawing rooms and dressing tables:

> The Empress Dowager had held many foreign audiences but even those who had been in her presence had seen only the audience rooms. No one had any conception of what artisans of the court had wrought during the centuries of absolute monarchy. But these were just a few of the treasures suddenly available . . . in the loot offered in the Peking market.[27]

Abe sometimes joined his agent, stalking China for raw jadeite. 'As a jade hunter he wished he could venture into the Kachin Hills but that was impossible of course,' his biographer wrote. Instead the two men scoured Langfang. Newell and Gump were a double act, the former armed with his employer's huge jadeite ring that he wielded like a shotgun, comparing it to every stone he was offered, the sightless Abe armed with a reputation for apparently being able to deduce antiquity and value with his fingers alone.[28]

But such was the demand for jadeite that the Jade King was forced to venture into the Kachin Hills to keep his 130 carvers occupied. He dispatched agents to buy newly mined stones that were smuggled out of the pits on the backs of elephants, avoiding British tax collectors. Having been forced out of business by anti-Qing revolutions, the mines were resurrected by the new market, but it was Chinese and Shan consortiums that now controlled all but four of the pits.[29] The *Ye Jein,* the wild men of the Kachin Hills who had once spilled blood to prevent all from gazing on their hearthstones, who had filled Burma's dark heart with wild incantations, who had spun stories of *naga* guardians and demonic armies, had lost control of their treasure valley.

The Kansi La, the Kachin warlord who had run the mines when Captain Adamson arrived in 1888, had died of malaria, despite the opium balm he had used to ward off mosquitoes. Although Sinwa Nawng, his son, inherited the valley, he lost control of everything apart from his opium pipe and a note that Adamson had thrust upon his father. The Captain had signed the tattered document, a draft of which we found in the New Delhi archives, the ink still bright although the paper was a moth's wing. 'You are hereby informed that you are under the orders of the officers of the British courts and according to the hill tribes customs, their orders must be carried out as they were under the Burmese King,' it stated. However, Sinwa Nawng could not read and had long forgotten his father's stories of how, after listening to the order, the Kachin had risen up against the British, forcing Adamson to flee through volleys of lead shot and the great Empire to change its course. Now only two Kachin sold to Mr Tieh's agents: Tingnan Kumjha, the late Kansi La's son-in-law, and Sao Krim, a man who was shunned by his own people for sleeping with his grandmother.[30]

When Henry Pu Yi began to hear stories about the Langfang trade at the age of seventeen, he took to wandering through the palaces, searching for legendary treasure stores that he had heard about as a child. One day, in the summer of 1922, as he paced the purple corridors, dodging palace retainers, doubling back on himself, he found himself alone. Down one darkened passage, an oil lamp in his hand, he brushed aside an unfamiliar curtain to find timbered doors 'plastered closed with strips of Imperial sealing paper'. Holding the light up high, he traced the rust-coloured ink with his finger and translated a smattering of words from the obscure Manchu script. It appeared to be the Palace of Established Happiness, a storeroom that had been sealed by the Dowager Empress Cixi shortly before her death. The Son of Heaven forced open the door. Clearing a curtain of cobwebs from the shelves, he pulled a lacquered trunk onto the floor, one of dozens that had been stacked around the room, and picked the lock. His face shone as he pulled out ancient calligraphy scrolls, golden idols, ivory carvings and cases of jadeite ornaments. His hands ran greedily through the glittering strings of beads. He threw gleaming pendants around his neck. He tried on a long-forgotten consort's head-dress. And into his pocket went a pair of translucent jadeite hairpins on which dragons stared through pearl eyes with ruby-red flames flickering from their nostrils, and something smaller, simpler but even more brilliant – a pepper pendant that glistened as if coated in a fine spray of dew. Then he carefully repacked the remaining items, closed the timbered doors behind him and charged back to his apartments, tears streaming down his face. 'The discovery made me wonder how much I really had,' Henry Pu Yi wrote. 'What should

I do about these enormous stores of treasure? How much of it had been stolen? How could I prevent further thefts?' It now dawned on the boy Emperor that he was a prisoner of an empty title.

The disconsolate monarch immediately demanded that he be taken on a treasure tour of his citadel, but for days the nervous Imperial household stalled. Instead, the *Nei Wu Fu* came up with a plan to distract Henry Pu Yi. It was time for the Emperor to marry, and within a month a double wedding was announced. Henry Pu Yi was to take Wan Jung as his Empress and Wen Hsui as his consort, in a celebration that would be held in the Palace of Heavenly Unity, where Tongzhi had died in 1875.

The fourteen-year-old Wen Hsui quietly entered the Forbidden City on 30 November 1922 as *fei,* the rank awarded to Qianlong's now legendary Fragrant Consort. She would wait for the wedding procession bearing Wan Jung, the woman who would become Empress. On 1 December a caravan of Qing courtiers, 72 dragon and phoenix parasols, 30 pairs of palace lanterns and golden pavilions 'containing the Imperial patent for the new Empress and her clothing', emerged from the Forbidden City. Accompanied by a Republican band and mounted police, seventeen-year-old Wan Jung was borne aloft by eunuchs in the Phoenix Chair from her house in Hat Lane back to the citadel, on her head a glittering crown of jadeite and kingfisher feathers. Henry Pu Yi, Wan Jung and Wen Hsui were showered with gifts by republicans and Qing aristocrats, many of which were later found to have come from the Imperial storerooms via Langfang. On their wedding night, as Wan Jung slept, thieves broke into the Palace of Earthly Peace and prised the Stones of Heaven from her wedding crown, replacing them with green glass.[31] Within days, Henry Pu Yi noticed that the lock to the Yu Ching Palace store had been smashed and a window had been forced open behind the Palace of Cloudless Heaven. Enraged at the eunuchs' contempt for his authority, the Emperor demanded an investigation, ordering the *Nei Wu Fu* to make an inventory of everything in the palace.

It was the fire brigade from the Italian legation that first noticed the soot-laden canopy hanging above the Forbidden City on 27 June 1923. But by the time they had fought their way through the Peking traffic and protocol, the Palace of Established Happiness,

Cixi's tinder-dry treasure store that Henry Pu Yi had discovered the previous summer, had been reduced to a smouldering pile. The blaze spread to adjoining rooms that were also piled high with Imperial artefacts, and the Italian crew fought for hours to contain the flames. But as the fire chewed through ancient gables and columns, spewing smoke over the capital, hundreds of Europeans and Chinese raced to the scene. Many were allowed in by the palace guard to help with the operation to save the Forbidden City and many of them helped themselves to souvenirs from the embers of the gutted rooms. Henry Pu Yi was inconsolable. An incomplete inventory for the Palace of Established Happiness showed that at least 6643 items had been stored there and only 387 had survived the fire. Among those artefacts known to have been lost were 2685 gold Buddha statues, 1157 religious paintings, 1675 altar ornaments made of jadeite and gold, 435 pieces of ceramic and an unknown quantity of jadeite carving and jewellery. It was surely the most valuable pile of smoking cinder and sodden ash in China, and when combed for precious metals by a merchant, who bought the right to clear the site, 17,000 taels of melted gold (850,000 grams) were recovered from the ruins.[32]

Like the young princes in the Tower, Wan Jung and Henry Pu Yi were now hostages to their retainers in a royal citadel that was also their jail. Locked in their bedchamber, surrounded by plotting eunuchs who whispered in corners and watched their every move, Wan Jung guarded her sleeping husband armed with a wooden club, and a loaded gun now lay beneath Henry Pu Yi's pillow. Terrified and isolated, they hatched a plan. The Zhou dynasty had begun the practice of employing eunuchs in 1122 BC, and on 15 July 1923 Henry Pu Yi ended it. The eunuchs were called to a meeting where they were surrounded by a borrowed Republican guard that marched them out of the Forbidden City, many of them clutching small glass jars that paid testimony to their years of service.

The Emperor and his wife rattled around the eerie citadel, dust-laden winds whipping across courtyards, spiralling columns of Mongolian sand scattering the steppe over tables and kangs in every hall and chamber. Moss covered the cobbles, weeds clambered over the marble phoenix and dragon friezes, and the jade river was a stagnant belt of slurry. Paper panes flapped, torn and stained, silk blinds that had once shaded the Western Palaces were laddered and mouldering, while the Son of Heaven surrounded himself with invoices, chits and ledgers, attempting to discover what had happened to his treasures. The *Nei Wu Fu* had raised 5 million Chinese dollars by stealing gold, ceramics, bronze and jadeite, and now there was no trace of the money or the artefacts. Dozens of courtiers and retainers were implicated in the thefts, including Jung Yuan, the Emperor's father-in-law.

Everyone appeared to have been conspiring against him from the day that he was lifted onto the Dragon Throne. Casting around for a way out of his prison, Henry Pu Yi approached the only man he trusted. Reginald Johnston was asked if the Emperor of China could be given asylum in the British legation before being smuggled to England. But the plan was deemed too politically sensitive, and instead Johnston suggested that his pupil retire to the rural idyll of the Summer Palace. Here was a semblance of freedom, the punts of Lake Kunming, the rolling western hills, the sacred groves and secret arbours. Henry Pu Yi reluctantly agreed and dispatched Johnston to prepare for his arrival, while he readied himself for a life outside the Forbidden City.

The Son of Heaven called in Pu Chieh, his brother, and over a six-month period they dodged the palace guard, breaking into Imperial store-rooms, where they quietly sifted through Qing treasure chests. Picking out the smallest and most precious items, they resealed the trunks and waited for sunset. Under the cover of darkness Pu Chieh, his robes bulging, his cuffs hanging heavy, his bag weighed down, slunk out of the palace, making his way through the empty streets to Pei Fu, his father's mansion. Soon 'antiques, calligraphy, gold, over a thousand hand scrolls, 200 hanging scrolls, 200 Song Dynasty books and cases of jadeite' had been transported to the Peking mansion and on to the port city of Tientsin. 'The things we took were the very finest treasures,' Pu Yi recalled.

On 23 October 1924 news that Feng Yuxiang, the Christian General, had sprung a *coup d'état* in Peking reached the Forbidden City. The warlord dissolved parliament and ordered the execution of the republic's corrupt treasurer, sending the nobility and republican ministers into flight. Most, like Dr Wellington Koo, the foreign minister, escaped to the foreign legations, that arranged for them to travel on to their concessions in Tientsin. Only Henry Pu Yi and Elizabeth (the name Henry had given to Wan Jung) remained calm. On 4 November Reginald Johnston was summoned to the palace and the Son of Heaven produced a small box. He asked Johnston to pick a farewell gift, and his tutor chose a large cabochon ring 'containing an exquisite piece of green jade' that had belonged to Tuan K'ang, the elder sister of Guangxu's tragic Pearl Concubine. The next evening, wearing the Stone of Heaven on his right hand, the Imperial tutor opened his journal, pulled up the dangling cuff of his Mandarin robe and wrote a lament to the House of Qing: 'the long twilight in the Forbidden City was deepening into darkness.'[33]

When a member of the household burst into the Palace of Accumulated Elegance at 9 a.m. the next morning to report that soldiers loyal to the Christian General had stormed the Forbidden City and were demanding the arrest of the Son of Heaven, Henry and Elizabeth were eating apples. They calmed their retainers and called forward the General's envoy. The Emperor placidly agreed to sign an article that abolished his title, reduced his annual pension to 500,000 Chinese dollars and evicted him and his retinue from their citadel. They were given only a few hours to pack what they could carry, and at 3 p.m. a five-car convoy swept out of the Tiananmen Gate and into the Imperial City, where the Son of Heaven blinked like a mole, staring wide-eyed at a capital that he had only seen once before.

As the motorcade weaved through the crowded *hutongs,* nobles and hawkers were transfixed by the sight of an Emperor of China being steered into oblivion. Elizabeth's only comfort was the dull weight of something small but priceless concealed in her belt. At Pei Fu, the Son of Heaven was met again by the Christian General's envoy.

'Mr Pu Yi, do you intend to be Emperor in future or will you be an ordinary citizen?'

'I had no freedom as an Emperor and now I have found my freedom. From today onwards I want to be an ordinary citizen,' Henry Pu Yi replied as Prince Chun threw his hat to the floor.

'It's all over, it's all over. I won't need this again,' the former Regent spluttered.[34]

Within hours a small group of artists and historians slipped into the Forbidden City to search the ex-Emperor's private apartments. None of them had ever dreamed of setting foot inside Emperor Yongle's citadel and Chuang Shang-yen would later relate to his family what he saw.

※

In 1999, we met Chuang Shang-yen's son in a small gallery in Taipei, where he was dismantling an exhibition of his father's calligraphy. By his death in 1980, the curator had become a world authority on Chinese art, and his own brushstrokes and poetry were now in great demand. Chuang Ling recalled his father's stories of the depressing dereliction that had transformed a regal axis around which the universe revolved into a crumbling pile.

Brushing away the dirt that caked every window, the curators had found storerooms with their doors pulled from their hinges, rooms full of stained and faded satin, silk and linen that clung to broken kangs and chairs, and everywhere the cloying odour of urine and damp. The courtyards were choked with weeds; the ceilings were sodden and murals peeled from the walls like protruding tongues. When Chuang Shang-yen entered the Palace of Accumulated Elegance he found a half-eaten apple lying on a wooden stool. Secretly smelling its browning flesh, he wondered if it had brushed the lips of the last Emperor of China.

'The storm of 5 November 1924 blew me out of the Forbidden City and dropped me at the crossroads,' Pu Yi later wrote, and in the weeks following his eviction rumours reached the ex-Emperor that Chinese radicals were planning to assassinate him. In the confusion of a new life in a strange city, everything took on an air of menace, and Henry Pu Yi slipped his government to seek sanctuary in the Japanese legation. Borrowing a diplomatic bicycle, he could not resist pedalling into the city he barely knew at the dead of night. When he had been thrown out of his palace he had written of his immense relief at having been released from a meaningless title. But more telling is his vivid recollection of those lonely midnight bike rides to the moat of the Forbidden City, from where the distant view of the turrets of the Mind Nurture Palace, the blurred silhouettes of its eves and buttresses, reduced him to an uncontrollable rage. Tears streamed down his face, his heart racing with 'a desire for revenge and restoration'.

On 23 February 1925 the ex-Emperor fled Peking altogether. A Qing general in Tientsin had donated Chang Garden, a mansion with three acres of land, whose driveway the soldier swept as a mark of loyalty to the Dragon Throne. Henry Pu Yi immediately began cashing in the palace treasures that had been hidden in Tientsin by his brother, depositing the money in foreign banks and investing it in real estate. Elizabeth Wan Jung was given an allowance of 1000 Chinese dollars a month, Wen Hsui 800 dollars, and both women supplemented their income by secretly selling jadeite to the Jade King in Langfang.

Henry Pu Yi spent 'incalculable sums', selling Imperial artefacts to buy British cars, French clocks, German watches and diamonds. Qianlong's and Cixi's Stones of Heaven paid for herringbone suits bought from Whiteway, Laidlaw & Co., fashioned in the style of sporting men who graced the pages of *Esquire*. Pawned bangles, carvings and hair ornaments perfumed and powdered Henry Pu Yi in Max Factor, and bought him two imported Alsatian puppies with which he would stroll down to Tientsin's Country Club, where the British committee had permitted him to play golf as a 'special Chinese'. Such was his immersion in the modernity of the West that Henry Pu Yi agreed to divorce Wen Hsui, his consort, who had become desperately unhappy in her 'empty marriage' and had disappeared while on a shopping trip to Peking. As a judge signed the decree absolute, the first time an Emperor had been dumped by a consort, Henry Pu Yi passed an edict that stripped her of her title. Wen Hsui became an outcast, never to re-marry, and at the time of her death in 1950 she was a primary school teacher.

Such was the scale of his conspicuous consumption that he drew dozens of opportunists to his court, all promising to restore the Dragon to his throne. They cajoled him into paying them dollars and jadeite to mount fictitious campaigns that always fizzled out after the first crack of a rifle, if the chamber was even loaded. Chang Tsun-ch'ang, a Shandong warlord with 'the physique of an elephant, the brain of a pig and the temperament of a tiger', was among the first to come to the new court in Tientsin.[35] Henry Pu Yi had heard of Chang's successes in pushing back the forces of the Christian General and now heaped money and jewels on him to continue the good work. But Chang was an unreliable lieutenant whose father had been a trumpeter and his mother a practising witch, until she was sold by her husband to a grain merchant when he ran out of money. In Shandong, Chang, who had been a bandit before becoming a soldier, amassed a 100,000-strong army that included companies of White Russian mercenaries, known as the 'soldiers of misfortune', and battalions of children armed with specially shortened rifles, who were led by his teenage son. His troops specialised in 'opening melons', splitting the skulls of their enemies, whose broken heads were hung in garlands from telephone poles. The man who Henry Pu Yi bankrolled as the scourge of Nationalism soon became more familiar to the Chinese people by his nickname: the Dog Meat General.

The next to arrive at Chang Garden was a Tsarist officer, driven by the Soviet Red Army into China, who offered his guns for hire. 'I cannot remember how much money I spent or how much jade and jewellery I gave away in trying to win the friendship of military men and buy them over,' Pu Yi later wrote. 'But I do know that the one who got the most was the White Russian Semionov.' His name was actually Ataman Seminov, a mercenary who had no real army but a small band of soldiers who raped and killed on the border while their leader grazed in Peking, Tientsin, Hong Kong and Japan, duping potential financiers, including the British, French and American governments as well as Henry Pu Yi. Seminov met the ex-Emperor for the first time in October 1925 and must have talked a good fight, as he left Tientsin with 50,000 Chinese dollars in cash and gems. Within weeks, Henry Pu Yi had opened a special bank account for him with a deposit of 10,000 dollars. The same amount in jadeite and scrolls was given to Liu Feng-Chih, a military strategist.

'Although there was no end to the number of treasures Liu Feng-chich took away there was no sign of action,' the disgruntled Henry Pu Yi wrote. There were so many people who benefited from his increasingly desperate acts of generosity that he was barely able to remember all of their names. An English journalist who may have been called Ross was paid to start a pro-Imperial newspaper. A nameless Austrian who claimed to be a diplomat was hired as a foreign advisor. 'Batch upon batch of defeated generals and failed politicians flocked to the concessions and the number of my protégés increased.'

Ultimately, it would take a very personal statement of rejection to bring to an end Henry Pu Yi's attachment to China's Dragon Throne. On 2 July 1928 armed men closed off part of Zunhua County in the shadow of the Changrui Mountains. Posters pasted up in the villages warned everyone to stay indoors. Ten days of persistent and alarming rumours pricked the champagne bubble of Henry Pu Yi's playboy court. Then large quantities of Imperial jadeite, gold and pearls of a quality rarely seen on the open market began to appear in Langfang. *The Times* commented on a mysterious £6.25 million Imperial fortune that was being secretly touted among an elite circle of socialites and compradors. The ex-Emperor immediately dispatched a team to investigate.

The stone warriors, mandarins and mythical menagerie were now standing in a smouldering savannah. A firestorm appeared to have razed the countryside surrounding the eastern necropolis and only the rain that lashed Qing Dong Ling had extinguished the flames. The Imperial investigators raced towards the mausoleums and saw the gaping gateway to Qianlong's subterranean tomb. The storm had flooded the catacombs and so they plunged down into the dark, wading through the silt that now carpeted the marble-clad passageways, torches pushed ahead of them, fearful of what they would find. Down they went, 54 metres beneath the Changrui foothills, into the heart of the Qing, every sharp intake of breath bouncing off the slippery walls, inching forwards through the four mammoth marble gateways that had sealed Qianlong's contract with death in 1799. Something had shattered the stone rods that had locked the doors from the inside. Short of breath, they slid into the burial chamber, their lamps flickering over the dripping walls, handkerchiefs tied over their mouths and noses in a futile effort to keep out the stench of urine and faeces that had been sprayed around the vault. Where they expected to find evergreen jadeite gardens, funerary treasures, the legendary 99 tonnes of silver that the Emperor had smelted to clad his death, there was nothing. Inching forward towards Qianlong's burial casket, their heads full of vengeful ghosts, they discovered a battered lacquered box, prized open with blunt force. On their hands and knees, the investigators scoured the chamber until their fingertips ran over bones – all that was left of Qianlong, hauled out of his coffin and scattered around the domed vault.

When the Imperial investigators approached Cixi's tomb, relief washed over them; the gateway was intact. But as they climbed to inspect her Precious Citadel, the tower that capped her mausoleum, they found flagstones prized from the terrace and a rope dangling into a tar-black hole. Reluctantly they dropped down into the Dragon Lady's grave, and here too the towering marble doors had been ripped from their hinges by an enormous blast. Gingerly they felt their way into the Dowager Empress's vault, and the puny beams of their flashlights passed over a crumpled pile of ripped linen slumped in the corner. They poked at the heap and leapt back as a naked corpse rolled out, a shrivelled and leathery form slashed and bludgeoned by swords and clubs. Edmund Backhouse would later claim that Cixi's hair had been ripped from her head by furious hands fighting over her jadeite butterflies. Turning the body over, the investigators reeled as a gaping face stared back at them from which the pregnant black pearl had been prised. 'The complexion of the face was wonderfully pale, but the eyes were deeply sunken and seemed like two black caverns. There were signs of injury to the lower lip,' concluded their official report.[36]

Pu Yi wept with rage. 'The report gave me a shock far worse than the one I received when I was expelled from the palace,' he wrote. Qing retainers, loyalists and even republicans, still steeped in Confucian values, expressed universal revulsion at the desecration of a monument to a family's ancestors. Buoyed by public support, Henry Pu Yi dashed off a letter to the new Nationalist government in Nanking, demanding an immediate investigation.

But there was no response, and Henry Pu Yi 'smouldered with hatred', vowing to abandon China altogether, taking his dynasty back to the northern plains and mountains from where they had first ridden down to crush the Ming in 1644. The Dragon, as Reginald Johnston was so fond of calling him, was now heading for a Manchurian lair.

◼

On the night of 10 November 1931 a car slipped out of Tientsin and sped to a concrete wharf on the Peiho River. Henry Pu Yi was leaving China in the boot of a convertible, and the waterway that had borne Macartney and Elgin to Peking would now ferry the scion of the Qing to his ancestral steppes. The ex-Emperor boarded a small motor launch guarded by Japanese soldiers that quietly slipped its mooring and chugged towards the sea. They had surprise on their side and had taken no chances, fitting the boat with sand-bags and armour-plating, as it would have to elude the Nationalist positions dug into the riverbank. Soon enough the ex-Emperor's party was called to a halt. 'I lay on the floor paralysed as if all my nerves had been cut,' Henry Pu Yi recalled, as he shrank from the sounds of rifle-shots. Its lights doused, its throttle floored, the tiny craft lurched forward, swerving away from the Nationalist forces, and by midnight the ex-Emperor had reached the ruins of the Taku Forts. Henry Pu Yi clambered aboard *Awaji Maru*, a Japanese mer-chant ship that slipped anchor to sail across the Yellow Sea, dock-ing at Liaoning, the southernmost province of Manchuria, three days later. For a nervous week he waited before his party continued on by train, not north into the Manchu heartlands but south to Lushun, the southernmost tip of the peninsula, a crag dwarfed by towering seas that would conceal the ex-Emperor until his new al-lies were ready for him.

Henry Pu Yi had swapped his Chinese court for a Japanese deal and on 24 February 1932, after three months spent hiding in the cramped Yamato Hotel, he learned over dinner that he was to be-come a head of state once again. The ex-Emperor of China boarded a train steaming north, through the hunting-grounds of Mukden, and on 8 March 1932 stepped down from his carriage in Changchun, a mountain town in Manchuria. Dressed in top hat and tails, he was declared 'chief executive of Manchukuo'. He had walked into the prison of another empty title, the puppet leader of a Japanese state seized from the Chinese the previous year while hundreds of miles down the Chinese coast, a vision of chrome illu-minated by jadeite was rising out of the detritus of the Qing.

Eight

Whore of the Orient

Rail hands polished the sooted panes, porters threaded their over-laden luggage carts between waiting passengers: a German opium smuggler whose papers stated that he sold Western pharmaceutical products; an English hotel-keeper, attempting to smuggle her Pekinese onto the train in a picnic basket. Reclining in an upper-class car, Henry Chang, a brutish warlord pitted against the Nationalist forces that had occupied the old Imperial capital, travelling incognito with a bounty of 20,000 Chinese dollars on his head. In the next compartment, Hui Fei, his estranged consort, robed in a silk cheongsam, who sat opposite a blonde wreathed in raven-black feathers, heading for the Grand Hotel. One carriage beyond, the zealous Dr Carmichael sweated over a missionary Bible, fighting to expel the vision of the two temptresses he had spied climbing into their carriage. And finally, bantering through an open window, his men at ease on the platform, was Captain Donald Harvey, a British Army surgeon on an eleventh-hour mission to save the Governor of Shanghai.

With 'a toot toot from the engine, the sigh of released air brakes', the train jerked forwards, scattering cows and chickens, boards on carriage doors flashing its route and destinations: Peking, Tientsin, Pukow and onwards. As the express fell into its rhythm, Captain Harvey looked back, catching the mysterious blonde's eye, sharing with her a glimmer of recognition. 'The past has reached out and subtly touched both of them. The years have rolled up like smoke.' The Captain tried to recall the last time they'd met. Something was amiss. The blonde appeared different. 'Have you married?' he blurted out. 'No!' she snapped. 'It took more than one man to change my name to Shanghai Lily.'[1]

Theirs would be a tempestuous journey into a China wracked by civil war. A British officer pitted against the 'yellow swine' in defence of European womanhood. A consort bent on revenge for a life lost to a sadistic master. A hostage crisis that would end in bloodshed. When the train eventually limped into its final destination, four hours late, newsboys called out that day's sensational headlines. 'All about Shanghai Express hold-up!' they screeched. 'Rebel leader killed by Chinese girl!' And it finished with a blush of romance outside a jewellery shop: Captain Harvey and Shanghai Lily entwined in an indiscreet clinch. The promise of an assignation. The Grand Hotel. That night. At 7 o'clock.[2]

The screenplay was provided by Jules Furthman, the 'Shanghai Express' had been hired from Santa Fe Railroad, camouflaged and crawling with Chinese extras who waved wooden rifles and tin-foil bayonets on a Los Angeles sound-stage. Josef von Sternberg, the expatriate Austrian director, had cast as his blonde heroine Marlene Dietrich, the *émigré* daughter of a German policeman. His Chinese warlord was Warner Oland, a Swedish actor who claimed that Mongolian ancestry had blessed him with an Asian air, while Hui Fei was played by Anna May Wong, the Californian-born granddaughter of an immigrant lured to the States in 1848. 'A China was built of papier-mâché and into it we placed slant-eyed men, women and children who seemed to relish being part of it,' the director told Hollywood reporters as his movie scored a box-office hit. Von Sternberg's *Shanghai Express,* with its pot-pourri of Oriental and Occidental passengers that steamed into American movie halls in 1932, transported a wide-eyed audience on a journey to an Asian oasis of feverish prosperity. Neither they nor the director had seen Shanghai for themselves, but all were intoxicated by stories of the adventurers and débutantes, playboys and chancers who were by now making the journey for real.

They arrived on the steamers of the Blue Star Line, the French Mail and the Peninsular and Oriental that anchored in Hongkew harbour after being buffeted for weeks on the Pacific or gliding through the Suez Canal. They disembarked in a city that boasted the world's longest bar and shortest street. Here, Californian evangelist Aimée Semple MacPherson fished for sinners, while W. H. Auden and Christopher Isherwood toasted them all.[3] Margot Fonteyn nervously débuted at the Lyceum Theatre, tutored by George Gontcharov, a White Russian refugee from the Bolshoi, while Mary Pickford and Douglas Fairbanks Junior shopped for jadeite and shoes.[4] Bertrand Russell lectured, George Bernard Shaw 'ate two lunches in one day', Noël Coward caught flu while Aldous Huxley was mesmerised by the pace of a city that had no time to sleep: 'so much life, so carefully canalised, so strongly flowing – the spectacle of it inspires something like terror.'[5]

Clutching *All About Shanghai*, the guidebook of the moment, they were exhorted to sample the 'bawdy and gaudy', a 'contradiction of manners and morals', to view a 'panoramic mural of the best and the worst of Orient and Occident'. Here was a chance to march in 'the Big Parade of Life', to experience an 'incomparable city'. 'So, this is Shanghai! Let's take a look!'[6]

Stepping off the gangplank, the new 'world tourists' rallied on The Bund, a waterfront, seven and a half miles long, that rivalled the Queen's Necklace of Lights strung along Bombay's seafront. Above the landing stages sashayed 'the prettiest of Celestial demoiselles, with their dark almond eyes which hardly deign to notice you while passing swiftly by like a cloud of gorgeous butterflies'.[7] Along the quay the tourists paraded past a stone effigy of Sir Harry Parkes, 'envoy extraordinaire', who had survived the Qing jail in 1860. On they went, ogling the new Cathay Hotel that had been voted 'the Claridge's of the Far East'. By the Customs House, with its statue of Sir Robert Hart, whose desperate missive to the Allied forces in 1900 had been mistaken for his last words, and on to the Grand Hotel, to catch a glimpse of where Shanghai Lily had intended to rendezvous with her Captain.

They promenaded by the towering palaces of plenty, flanked by public gardens whose notice-boards displayed the enclave's few rules: 'No Dogs or Chinese'. At No 3 The Bund, the lucky among them would obtain a two-week pass to enter the bastion of unofficial government, the Shanghai Club, where the elite jostled for elbow-room at the 110-foot Long Bar, sipping gin slings and champagne, secure in the knowledge that not even 'Special Chinese' were admitted here. Others would make do with the Canidrome, where Buck Clayton and his Harlem Gentlemen played the Hawaiian hula, the Russian mazurka and the Paris apache, accompanied by 'dusky crooners and torch singers'.[8]

'Keep moving, if there is but one night; start at Love Lane and finish at Blood Alley,' the guide encouraged. By now it was the small hours and, pungent and cacophonous, Shanghai reeked of French perfume and night queen. 'The symphony of lust; the swaying of bodies; the rhythm of abandon; the hot smoke of desire; joy, gin and jazz.'[9] It was the City of Blazing Night, a bazaar that promised a 'life Haroun-al-Raschid never knew, with tales Scheherezade never told . . . Sultan Shahriyar'.[10] But as the city ran into the dawn, here was also 'the bitter end of the long trail for many wastrel souls'. Immaculate Chinese beauties and their spent foreign beaux stepped over opiate children offering sex for a dollar, impoverished slaves to the 'Whore of the Orient', where one in thirteen women had a price, as did as many men. And if the tourist tasted too much, the guide recommended Dr J. Duncan, 'specialist in venereal, genito-urinary, piles', who offered a discreet service from his surgery on the North Sichuan Road. Americans escaping Prohibition called it Whoopee Town, but the Chinese knew it as 'a city of 48-storey skyscrapers built upon 24 layers of hell', and their life expectancy was 27, the same as in thirteenth-century Europe.[11]

⊠

Hugh Lindsay, the leader of an East India Company party in search of 'the great emporia of the East', was the first foreigner to spot a clutch of dirty, low-slung houses clinging to China's coastal mudflats in 1832, 'greatly resembling Holland'. Eager to 'engage the natives in trade', Lindsay ordered HMS *Lord Amherst* to drop anchor, but the Chinese chased him back to the dock with streaming red banners that warned of 'a barbarian ship hovering up the coast'. With 'six large guns . . . laid down on mud-banks upon each side of the river', the HMS *Lord Amherst* was run out to sea, just sixteen years after the vessel's namesake had been seen off by Emperor Jianqing.[12] Lindsay reported back to London that Shanghai, 'a name which had hitherto been scarcely . . . heard in Europe', was a miserable fishing village that provided anchorage for junks, sampans and scrambling dragons that plied the China seas.[13] But it was bound by the Whangpoo and Yangze Rivers. The latter was the third longest river in the world, whose silted currents ran 3915 miles from the Tibetan plateau through twelve provinces, and it could provide the British with a lucrative tongue of commerce. Ten years later, the British secured their prize, forcing Emperor Daoguang to sign the Treaty of Nanking as penance for losing the First Opium War. 'British subjects . . . shall be allowed to reside . . . without molestation or restraint,' the treaty decreed.[14] The new settlers would pay no taxes and be exempt from Chinese laws. Within weeks of opening for business on 17 November 1843, 50 British taipans, representing Jardine, Matheson, Butterfield and Swire, the opium trading houses of Britain's new Crown Colony of Hong Kong, had docked along the Whangpoo's muddy tow-path with their wives. Soon they were joined by a party of Persian Jews, one of whom, Elias Sassoon, would tell anyone who listened that he was a direct descendant of King David.

For hundreds of years, Elias claimed, his family had been Sheikh bankers, wearing 'robes of gold tissue' as they rode to the palace of the Pasha, until the early nineteenth century, when his father, David Sassoon, had been forced by pogroms to leave Baghdad. Moving to London, the family had begun trading spices, opium and silk, making dazzling social progress, boasting two baronetcies and sons at Eton and Oxford. While Sassoon senior lured the crowned heads of Europe to his court in Ashley Park, a new ancestral seat in Surrey that had once been used by Oliver Cromwell as a bolt-hole, Elias began buying up agricultural sites on Shanghai's mudflats at £90 an acre.[15]

In his flowing Persian robes Elias was the most conspicuous entrepreneur in a town that rapidly attracted 50,000 residents, who hid (from China's 'wars and alarums') behind the protective walls of the International Settlement and the French Concession. Few ever ventured into the gloomy passages that sprung up around them, a Chinese quarter that was rumoured to be infested with 'low characters and mangy dogs', and so few foreigners would learn of the glittering green stones that were secreted in its inhabitants' dangling sleeves. Instead, the Chinese quarter was a place to be reviled. One visiting New Yorker, who landed in 1868, found it to be 'exceedingly filthy, so much so that I would not think of taking a lady into it, even in a sedan chair'.[16] But for tens of thousands of impoverished peasants made homeless by rebellion, famine and flood, the shanty offered a refuge and employment. Alone, destitute and disorientated by the thick local dialect, new arrivals were inducted into secret societies, labourers, factory workers and rickshaw coolies swelling the ranks of the *Qing Pang*. The Europeans called it the Green Gang, and it was said that new members were initiated in joss-house ceremonies that extracted oaths of loyalty by spilling blood.

Among those to become ensnared by the Green Gang was the orphan Du Yuesheng, a gangly teenager with a domed shaven head, thin lips and pan-handle ears, who had crossed the Whangpoo River some time after 1888 to escape poverty and an abusive uncle. After a brief and unhappy career as a vegetable hawker and petty thief, Du swore allegiance, cultivated an obligatory opium habit and began to hang around the home of Pockmarked Huang, the Green Gang's Number One boss, who enjoyed a bizarre dual existence as the French Concession's police chief.

Having ingratiated himself with Huang's mistress, a former brothel-keeper, Du was employed to transport opium from Shanghai's Hongkew harbour to the dens run by the secret societies. Within months he had expanded the Green Gang's interests into gambling and protection rackets, monopolising a secret trade in jadeite, making so much money for his employer that he was promoted to second-in-command. Du swapped his cotton pyjamas for the silk robes of a Confucian businessman; cut his fingernails into elongated claws, sported a jadeite rosary on his chest and took to wearing patent leather boots that tapered into gleaming rapier points.

Europeans who caught a glimpse of his sphinx-like brow and sallow, opiated skin as they rattled through the Chinese quarter in their rickshaws, took back to the International Settlement stories of a devilish apparition that did his reputation no harm at all. Perhaps they saw in Du Yuesheng what Sax Rohmer would see in his Dr Fu Manchu. The Green Gang officer was certainly 'tall, lean and feline, high-shouldered, with a brow like Shakespeare and a face like Satan'. He too had 'the long, magnetic eyes of the true cat-green', and invested in him by the Western merchants and their wives was 'all the cruel cunning of an entire Eastern race'. Rohmer had asked his readers to 'imagine that awful being, and you have a mental picture of Dr Fu Manchu, the yellow peril incarnate in one man'. Shanghailanders needed little persuasion that in Du they had found the real thing.[17]

Rohmer, who had worked as a journalist in the City of London, found his inspiration in the Limehouse back-streets among the newly arrived Chinese who had slipped ship in the docks. His *Fu Manchu*, that was translated into every European language, encompassed Western fears of the strangers from the East whose 'fingers and slim white arms [were] laden with barbaric jewellery'.[18] The Chinese Diaspora would reach out across the world, taking with it handfuls of an unfamiliar and hypnotic stone, leaving an imprint wherever it sought shelter. Some of those who fled were destitute farmers, some rebel soldiers, but all dreamed of returning, loaded down with riches to reclaim their native villages from the corrupt Qing court.

One of those who fled across the Java Sea, smuggled in the bottom of a junk, was Oei Tjie Sien, the son of a petty government official from the port city of Amoy, who had fought with the Taiping rebels. Oei docked in the northern Javanese port of Semarang in 1860 and survived by selling rice to the Dutch. After several years he had saved enough money to marry and launch a business. As Heber Bishop had done in Cuba, Oei did in Java, refining sugar and his fortunes. By the time his son came of age, Oei was a wealthy man and had built the Eagle's Nest, an Oriental mansion furnished with kangs and jade screens imported from China, set in hundreds of acres of sugar cane plantations on the outskirts of Semarang. 'It was immense and gloomy, built in Chinese style with a series of separate pavilions linked together with what seemed like interminable miles of corridors, lined with fat-bellied earthenware vats filled with rice and tobacco, a rather obvious sign of prosperity,' his haughty granddaughter Hui-lan would recall.[19]

Some, like Charlie Soong, the twelve-year-old son of a farmer from Hainan Island, off the southern Chinese coast, would sail on from Java to the United States. He arrived in Boston in 1878 at the height of anti-Chinese feeling, riots burning from coast to coast, fuelled by white working-class talk of the 'yellow peril'. The first Chinese, like Anna May Wong's grandfather, had been drawn to America in 1848 by gold, and when the seams were spent, thousands more sought work on the railroads that stretched from California to Utah and beyond. The industrious Chinese in America would be caricatured as the Limehouse dockhands had been, C. W. Doyle, an expatriate British surgeon, creating the character of Quong Long, an evil gangster whose name bore an uncanny similarity to a Qing Emperor.

Charlie Soong had no intention of being ridiculed, forced down a pit or into a chain-gang, and promptly found another avenue, announcing that he had discovered God. Methodist missionaries welcomed him to their fold and dispatched him to university in Tennessee to learn how to save China's lost souls. In 1886, dressed in a three-piece suit, his hair neatly pomaded, Charlie returned to China, sailing up the Whangpoo to take up a position as minister at Shanghai's Southern Methodist Mission. With his Dixieland accent, he soon found favour with one of Shanghai's most illustrious Christian families, whose ancestors had been converted by the pioneering Jesuit missionary Matteo Ricci in the seventeenth century. Within years Charlie had married his patron's youngest daughter, constructed a New Orleans-style home near Hongkew harbour and fathered three daughters, Ai-ling, Ching-ling and May-ling. The family man secured a loan from his wealthy in-laws, lavished his daughters with jadeite and began printing cheap Chinese Bibles in his spare time.

Restless with the humiliating business of winning Buddhist souls, he soon cast around for another outlet for his entrepreneurial skills. When he was approached by the *Hung Pang* or Red Gang, Charlie Soong resigned from the Methodist mission and accepted a senior position immediately. Unlike its Green Gang rival that controlled blue-collar labour, the Red Gang was an elite anti-Qing triad of compradors and merchants with political aspirations. And it was through them that Charlie met the head of one of China's fledgling republican movements at church in 1894. Sun Yat-sen, the son of a village watchman from Canton, a Christian convert who had been schooled in Honolulu, persuaded Charlie to fund his Revolutionary Alliance. The Soong homestead would become the party's unofficial headquarters.

Charlie's daughters were sent away to Wesleyan College in Georgia where, according to their teachers, Ai-ling showed a flair for economics, Ching-ling for literary criticism and May-ling lost herself in the tales of Peter Rabbit. When Sun Yat-sen was forced into exile after an uprising against the Qing in Canton was crushed, Charlie combined a visit to his daughters with a much-needed fund-raising tour of the United States on behalf of the exiled revolutionary, whom Ching-ling praised in the Wesleyan College magazine.[20]

Charlie returned to China, followed swiftly by his secret fighting fund, while Sun Yat-sen secured another Chinese benefactor. Aboard a French steamer in 1906, he was introduced to Chang Jen-chieh, the crippled son of a silk merchant from China's coastal province of Chekiang. Chang had grown up closeted from China's rebellions and his parents had invested him with Imperial values – not the typical background for a budding revolutionary. But Chang, a precocious child educated by a private tutor, who had learned calligraphy and the Classics, had been mocked for his deformed feet that engendered a duck-like waddle, transforming him into a disruptive teenager. Taking up horse-riding to avoid ridicule, he would chase down peasants in the local market, until his exhausted parents secured him an appointment at the age of 25 as attaché to the Chinese Embassy in Paris.[21] Chang was quickly bored by diplomatic life and irritated by sniping Europeans, who called him 'Quasimodo' behind his back. He began to roam Paris's smart arrondissements alone lingering outside the window display at 13 Rue de la Paix. Here, in the velvet cases, Chang observed the West's new obsession with the East. 'Parisian women cast envious glances at Cartier's display, with their new collections of bracelets that join jade with lapis, jade with sapphires and jade with topaz.'[22]

Chang persuaded his father to part with 300,000 Chinese dollars, with which he established the Ton Ying Company that sold jadeite jewellery, earning him a new nickname, Curio Chang.[23] Soon branches had opened in New York and Shanghai, and his enterprise brought him into contact with a circle of European intellectuals, radical literature and ultimately, aboard a French steamer, Sun Yat-sen. The rabble-rousing leader of the Revolution-ary Alliance fired the jadeite dealer with his talk of free enterprise, of a new and modern China, and Curio Chang agreed to donate half of the Ton Ying Company's profits to Sun Yat-sen's cause.

While Curio Chang was providing jadeite collateral for the Rev-olutionary Alliance, another misfit from his home province of Chekiang, the awkward son of a salt merchant from a village in the shadow of Tiger Killing Mountain, was kicking up dust. Chiang Kai-shek had become an uncontrollable child after villagers took to mocking his strangely elongated head that they liked to say was shaped like a giant peanut. His mother recalled how he spent most of his childhood weeping hysterically, banging his skull on the kitchen floor, until he discovered Sun Tzu's *Art of War*.[24] The fifth-century BC military manual advised Chiang Kai-shek, 'If you wish to feign confusion in order to lure the enemy on, you must first have perfect discipline; if you wish to display timidity in order to entrap the enemy, you must have extreme courage; if you wish to parade your weakness in order to make the enemy over-confident, you must have exceeding strength.'

Forced into an arranged marriage at the age of fourteen, Chiang Kai-shek fathered a son but abandoned his family in 1907, sailing for Japan. There he took a concubine, had a second child and en-listed in the Imperial Nippon Army. But an ardent supporter of Sun Yat-sen convinced the nonconformist Chiang Kai-shek to convert to republicanism. On a trip to Shanghai in 1908, he joined the Rev-olutionary Alliance and was introduced to none other than Du Yuesheng, the Green Gang officer with his ghoulish sneer.

The Chinese Diaspora fired the West's literary imagination. Hav-ing sampled the jadeite artistry that flowed out of Peking, concealed in knapsacks and tea-chests, Western writers now encountered the East face-to-face. Jules Verne had taken his readers up into a hot air balloon, to the centre of the earth, from the earth to the moon and then 20,000 leagues under the sea, as well as whisking them around the world in 80 days. But it wasn't until 1883 that he set them on a course to a fantastical place where princesses and consorts fought, loved and died in the Palace of the Purity of Jade that featured in his *Tribulations of a Chinaman*. Two years later H. Rider Haggard, the son of a British barrister, played on public appetite for loot and conquest by dispatching his characters on imaginary travels to secret mines and valleys of death. And by 1902 the West's wander-lust was being sated by first-hand accounts of the Orient's busted treasure houses, courtesy of Pierre Loti. A member of the Allied Relief, Loti had transposed the sacking of the Imperial Court into *The Last Days of Peking*. Such was the demand for his story that it was reprinted 50 times and the author, compelled to revisit his Oriental theme, penned a play about a Chinese princess's unrequited love, *The Daughter of Heaven*, that premiered on Broadway in 1912.[25] Driven by fiction and packed onto *Around the World in 80 Days*-type cruises, chic world travellers were transformed into 'four-minute guests' who zeroed in on the Paris of the East, by now searching for a piece of this 'Stone of Heaven'.

Among them was Elias Sassoon's brash young nephew Victor, whose P&O liner docked in Shanghai's Hongkew harbour shortly before the First World War, at a time when the city's population had swelled to more than one million. Born in Naples in 1881, interrupting his parents' Grand Tour, Victor Sassoon had cruised through Harrow and Cambridge, where he had graduated with second-class honours and a flirtatious reputation. His family had made their fortunes from opium and Shanghai real estate. The regular parties they threw at the family's London home, 46 Grosvenor Place, had transformed Victor into a genial host. In a mansion filled with Louis XIV furniture and Chinese art, he had regaled David Lloyd George, Edward, Prince of Wales, Charlie Chaplin and T. E. Lawrence with tales of his travels. Now in Shanghai, Victor Sassoon discovered Nanking Road and its emporiums filled with a strange green stone. But Victor was oblivious to the political events racing past the shuttered windows of the Shanghai Club where he stayed.

In Peking, supporters of the boy Emperor Pu Yi had been struggling to cling on to power. Sensing the time was right, Sun Yat-sen had returned from exile, and in December 1911 declared himself the provisional President of a Chinese Republic. But without an army he was unable to command unanimous support among the fractious anti-Qing factions, and for two months the Imperial dynasty held out until a momentous day in February 1912. Then, Yuan Shikai, commander of China's Peiyang Army, arrived at the

Forbidden City in Peking and forced the boy Emperor Pu Yi to abdicate. After elbowing aside his presidential competitor, Yuan Shikai declared himself the head of the new Chinese Republic.

Sun Yat-sen was forced to accept a position in Yuan Shikai's government as Director of Railways but set about reorganising his political allies into the Guomindang (KMT), the Nationalist Party, appointing Charlie Soong, the former Bible salesman, as his aide, and Ai-ling, Charlie's eldest daughter, as his secretary. While President Yuan Shikai surrounded himself with jadeite treasures stolen from Jehôl and Mukden, the Nationalist trio travelled the countryside in Imperial style, requisitioning a Dragon Train that had been built for the Dowager Empress Cixi. Its walls were lined with yellow silk, its floors carpeted with Persian rugs, its carriages decorated with Imperial Green Jade and its toilet cast in gold.[26] But Ai-ling abandoned her post to marry, and moved into a mansion in Shanghai's fashionable French Concession, on the Route de Seiyes. Among the notable guests at her frequent garden parties was Du Yuesheng. Now the nominal head of the Green Gang, his newest recruit and sidekick was also invited to the party. Chiang Kai-shek had returned to Shanghai in 1912 and had sworn a secret blood oath.

Only a surprise wedding in November 1914 broke up the revels. Sun Yat-sen had recruited Ching-ling, Charlie Soong's second daughter, and promptly eloped to Japan with her, despite a 40-year age difference. Furious, Charlie denounced his best friend and his daughter, turning his attentions to May-ling, the youngest, grooming her as if she were his heir. Beautiful Mood (as her name translated) graduated from Wesleyan College and was admitted to Wellesley College, Massachusetts, where she adopted an English middle name, Olive, and dazzled her American friends Florence, Hattie, Flossie and Eloise with her curious green Chinese jewellery.[27]

In Semarang, the sugar baron Oei Tjie Sien was losing control of his wayward granddaughter, who had just turned fourteen. Hui-lan ran rings around the plantation's 40 Javanese servants, racing through the gardens in her bare feet, ripping 1000 US dollars dresses on the thorns, while they trailed behind, hampered by their cumbersome silk sarongs. She was already 'harder to handle than a thousand men' and her mother, Bing Noi, encouraged her unruly behaviour. Renowned in London's Bond Street for buying gems by the kilo, Bing Noi constantly showered Hui-lan with lavish gifts, including an 80-carat diamond 'as big as a fist' that the ungrateful teenager complained 'thumped against my chest, hurting me'.[28] Perhaps Hui-lan's only steadying influence was Miss Elizabeth Jones, an English governess. Miss Jones introduced a new regimen to the Eagle's Nest: cocoa and three rich tea biscuits at 11 a.m., Roman history, readings from Shakespeare and lessons in deportment before lunch, copies of the *Tatler* after supper. 'I pored over the illustrated magazines. I wanted to be a débutante and have parties and balls given for me. For the first time I became really conscious of Papa's wealth, and I thought it a shame that my beautiful clothes and jewellery and education should go to waste,' Hui-lan gushed in her memoirs.

When Hui-lan's father announced he was leaving his wife for one of his sixteen concubines, the self-styled teenage 'heiress of the moment' seized the opportunity to lure her distraught mother to Europe. Haunted by phosgene, the continent was recovering its dead from the Western Front when Hui-lan arrived in Paris at the age of nineteen. There she acquired a Great Dane, a bulldog, an 'extravagant wardrobe' and a Daimler, 'dazzling white with scarlet cushions'. In 1919 she docked in London, where she hopped between 'an outrageously expensive' house in Berkeley Square, a mansion in Wimbledon 'which boasted a superfluous white and gold ballroom' and her teenage bolt-hole, a villa in Curzon Street.

Between parties, there was shopping to be done. Hui-lan visited Liberty's exhibition of 'some of the finest and most beautiful specimens of [Imperial Green Jade] in the world', its catalogue, whose cover displayed a Qianlong poem, fêting the Stone of Heaven as 'the most precious gift of the immortals'.[29] London was by now awash with jadeite stories. Writing for *Connoisseur* magazine, Mrs Delves Broughton introduced society to a stone that shone as 'brilliantly as the truth', claiming that a 'modern mandarin' would pay 1000 ounces of silver for jadeite bangles that glowed like emeralds.[30] The *Illustrated London News* trumpeted: 'it's all the rage'. Jadeite, it claimed, owed its popularity 'to its romantic association with the gorgeous East and prehistoric art and to the beauty of its delicate colour'.[31] But the paper missed another good story that week. The Victoria & Albert Museum had just acquired Emperor Qianlong's cinnabar throne from George Swift, a British wholesale potato dealer who had bought it from Spink & Co., cable address: JADEITE LONDON. Spink obtained the throne from Mikhail Girs, the former Tsarist ambassador to Peking, who had brought it to Britain after fleeing the Bolshevik revolution of 1917.[32]

The British establishment had officially welcomed jadeite two years earlier when the Burlington Arts Club staged London's first exhibition. Its catalogue fêted Qianlong's kingfisher gem as 'the most treasured stone of all', down-playing the sacking of the Summer Palace and the Forbidden City. But here on display were Sir Claude MacDonald's jadeite incense holder, sceptre, fluted bowl, clasps and buckles and a jade book inscribed in Qianlong's hand. Here was Lord Allendale's green jade horse 'that was previously the property of General Gordon'. Here was Cixi's controversial jade seal, bought for a bottle of brandy and sold on to Oscar Raphael in 1902. Lady Sackville loaned eight jade plaques that had been taken from Cixi's apartments in 1900. Miss Ionides loaned a haul of jadeite jewellery that had once been stored in wooden cases, in a room locked with a key that hung around Cixi's neck. The show had even carried a royal warrant. Buckingham Palace had lent an Imperial jade carved tray lined with yellow satin, two silk jackets and a brocade robe embroidered with dragons that had been gifted to Queen Victoria in 1860, a royal collection augmented by General Gaselee, the British military commander in Peking, in 1900.

While Hui-lan's new circle of friends, Lord Brook, the Earl of Callodan and the Marquess of Dufferin and Ava, were mesmerised by the Stone of Heaven, their exotic Chinese heiress had seen it all before. Hui-lan was more interested by an offer from the *Tatler* to be photographed for its society pages.

Dr V. K. Wellington Koo, China's ambassador to Washington, was at home when he flicked through the magazine and gazed upon Hui-lan's face. Perhaps Dr Koo was intrigued by the small story beneath the portrait that alluded to Hui-lan's enormous wealth. The courtship was brief and business-like. In November 1920, at the Chinese legation in Brussels, Dr Koo bagged his heiress. Hui-lan's father sent her a 65-bead jadeite necklace that he had acquired in

Peking's Langfang Lane from the Jade King, Mr Tieh. He had been told that it had once graced the neck of Dowager Empress Lung Yu, the mother of the last Emperor of China.[33] Not to be outdone, Hui-lan's mother bought her daughter 'a Rolls-Royce limousine and a £10,000 gold and silver dinner service, both of which [Mamma] considered essential to my proper début in diplomatic circles.' The car would cost Hui-lan's father dear. His ex-wife 'coolly ordered another for herself and a third for my sister', before sending the bill to her estranged husband.

Dr Koo was soon dispatched 'to the Court of St James' and his wife's grey and silver Rolls-Royce, the Crystal Palace, became famous throughout London for its exceptionally large windows, custom-made so that Hui-lan Koo and her jadeite necklace could shine more brightly. 'Isn't she sweet? Isn't she a darling?' those who pressed their faces against the panes were said to utter as she 'threw them kisses'. Dressed in jadeite and an ankle-length ermine coat, Hui-lan Koo moved into Claridge's, where she befriended Princess Alice of Monaco, a long-term resident, who, she claimed, never emerged from her bedroom without wearing a choker of egg-sized pearls. When Hui-lan learned that she was to be presented at Buckingham Palace, it was Princess Alice who coached her in etiquette. But on the day, Hui-lan forgot herself and ogled the Queen's jewels:

> She glittered from the hem of her diamente-[sic] studded gown to the tip of her crown where the Koh-i-noor flashed in triumph. With each breath, each movement of Queen Mary's body, tiny rainbows blazed from the facets of her diamond dog-collar, then darted down the row of brilliants, strung across her regal bosom.[34]

Hui-lan Koo's London days were brought to a sudden end when her husband was appointed China's Foreign Minister in 1921. Her grey Rolls-Royce was packed off to Peking, where she bought Chen Yuan Yuan's Palace, a 200-room Imperial mansion built for a favoured concubine of the last Ming Emperor. Hui-lan was intent on becoming *Fu-jen,* the Number One Lady of China. Her pink-and-gold ballroom was filled with Qianlong's jade screens, Imperial lampshades and cinnabar furniture, her pavilions with dogs and children. Hui-lan adored Pekinese and her favourite, Pao-Pei, and 'his wife' Ching-Ming, were given their own living quarters, while

Hui-lan's two infant sons were relegated to a house at the bottom of the garden.

'The dull chores of motherhood' were kept at a distance while Hui-lan updated her breeding stock with puppies sent from London by her friend Sir Hugo Cunliffe-Owen, whose own pets were the progeny of Cixi's looted dogs. When Chinese newspapers, their pages filled with famine and war, learned that Hui-lan's 'babies' enjoyed an enviable lifestyle, they turned on her. 'I was horrified to read that the food I gave the dogs would keep three Chinese villages alive,' Hui-lan recalled, and so she sold all but three of her litter to American tourists for 1000 Chinese dollars apiece.

But Hui-lan Koo's social aspirations were about to be eclipsed. May-ling, Charlie Soong's youngest daughter, had returned to China in 1917, after ten years in America, dressed for the occasion in Imperial jewels acquired for her by Curio Chang. She threw parties at her father's Shanghai mansion on Avenue Joffre and invited his Green and Red Gang associates. 'People vied with one another in entertaining. Those were the days when families would celebrate birthdays with enormous feasts that lasted several days, importing famous actors by the troupe. China proper seemed very far away,' wrote Emily Hahn, who filed for the *New Yorker*. But only six months after the partying began Charlie Soong was dead from stomach cancer. His demise was kept from all but the family's closest friends, and after a brief period of mourning, May-ling returned to the social circuit, climbing yet another rung, having inherited millions of Chinese dollars, while thousands of miles away a third heiress was being promised the world.

One of Barbara Hutton's earliest memories was the day she found her mother dead in the New York Plaza Hotel. Dressed in a gold-and-white evening gown, her favourite double strand pearls around her neck, an empty vial of strychnine in her hand, her body lay beside a copy of the New York *Sun,* open at a page dominated by a photo of Barbara's father stepping out with a Swedish actress.[35] Days later, Barbara Hutton's grandfather, Frank Winfield Woolworth, the 'five and dime king', dressed her up in a white ermine coat, matching hat and muffler, and took her for a ride in his express elevator. From the top-floor balcony of Manhattan's Woolworth Building, a high-rise Gothic palace of Tiffany lamps, gargoyles and gold leaf, 'Woolly' promised Barbara that one day she would be the Princess of his vast retail court. When F. W. Woolworth died two years later, in 1919, his cathedral of commerce was no longer the tallest skyscraper, but Barbara Hutton, his seven-year-old granddaughter, had inherited his fortune of 28 million US dollars, becoming one of the richest little girls in the world.

With her platinum curls, black velvet eyebrows and mournful eyes, it was not long before Barbara was the darling of café society. At fourteen, she owned a multi-million-dollar duplex apartment on Fifth Avenue, a stone's throw from where Heber Bishop had once lived, and also a 125,000 US dollars private train carriage, its walls lined with silk, its floor covered in Persian carpets, walk-in wardrobes filled with *haute couture* and cases stuffed with jewellery. But it was not until she befriended Abe Gump in San Francisco that Barbara discovered the world of jadeite. According to a school friend, the blind Abe Gump taught Barbara 'how to tell a genuine court piece from a counterfeit, how to appraise jewellery by touch rather than sight'.[36]

At boarding school, Barbara pinned laminated National Geographic maps to her bedroom wall, shunned school pinafores in favour of Chanel and studied Chinese art and the illustrated magazines. *House and Garden* would have advised her that jadeite was 'an inviting field in which to exercise a hobby'.[37] A sumptuous catalogue invited her to visit a Fifth Avenue 'Collection of Jewels Created by Messieurs Cartier from the Hindoo, Arab, Russian and Chinese'.[38] Barbara would certainly have read of the auction of Mrs Emelie De L. Havemeyer's Qianlong bedroom suite, which she had somehow obtained in Peking and reinstalled in her Madison Avenue home. And, of course, everybody had heard about the sale of Prince Gong's jadeite heirlooms. But what the schoolgirl returned to, week after week, was an advert in *Harper's Bazaar* that promoted a 447-guinea four-month world cruise on the *Empress of Britain,* illustrated with pictures of the ruins of the Summer Palace and the Forbidden City. In the small ads were clues as to what lay in wait when the cruise ship anchored in Shanghai. The Ton Ying Company and the Mei Tsung Hwa Kyi jewellery store were there to sell Barbara Imperial treasures, and if she was willing to brave the Chinese quarter, there were the three emporiums in Horse Lane, 'where practically all jade dealers and brokers meet daily from 9 to 3 except Sundays'.[39]

What Barbara wouldn't have read in the pages of *Harper's Bazaar* was the story of a parallel Shanghai, a viper's nest that many in the International Settlement were also oblivious to. In June 1916, shortly after the corpulent Chinese President Yuan Shikai fell into his toilet, a heavily guarded mansion, tucked between the jade emporiums of Nanking Road, became a secret meeting-place for Nationalist revolutionaries. While China was torn apart by rival warlords, Sun Yat-sen plotted a KMT comeback, bankrolled by the jadeite dealer Curio Chang, who sent his wife, five daughters and vast Imperial collection to New York, mindful of the potential fallout.

Sun Yat-sen realised that to achieve his revolutionary goals he needed an army of his own, and he cast around for extra finance. The West and Japan refused to help, but then a tailor-made solution proffered itself in July 1921. Spies working for the Green Gang's Du Yuesheng learned that at the Shanghai Girls School on the Street of Joyful Undertaking, an assistant librarian from Peking University, a Soviet Agent, a Dutch Communist and a Russian trade union official had secretly formed the Chinese Communist Party (CCP). Mao Zedong and his comrades also needed allies to overcome the feudal armies of the warlords. In 1924 the CCP and KMT joined in a marriage of convenience, and Moscow agreed to finance Sun Yat-sen's fighting force.

Sun immediately dispatched 'one of the budding heroes of the KMT' on a secret mission to the Soviet Union, a young revolutionary who had been proposed for the job by his new mentor, Curio Chang.[40] Chiang Kai-shek, the peanut-headed Sun Tzu scholar, had become one of the jadeite dealer's closest friends, and three years earlier had taken a new teenage wife at Curio Chang's behest. Chiang Kai-shek had divorced his village wife, abandoned his concubine and married fifteen-year-old Jennie Ch'en at Shanghai's Great Eastern Hotel in December 1921. Curio Chang had officiated, his eldest daughter Therese had been the chief bridesmaid and her sisters Yvonne, Suzanne, Georgette and Helen had sailed from New York to be flower girls.[41]

When Chiang Kai-shek returned from Moscow he established a

KMT military academy at Whampoa, but within months Sun Yat-sen was dead. In March 1925, with Curio Chang at his side, the KMT leader died of liver cancer in an army cot at Hui-lan Koo's Peking palace. Within hours the KMT/CCP coalition was thrown into panic, factions huddled behind screens and in courtyards, secretly plotting to wrestle control of China, while Sun Yat-sen's body was borne on a catafalque to the Temple of the Azure Clouds in the Western Hills. There it would lie forgotten for the next four years.

In Shanghai, one of the coalition partners secretly began plotting a *coup*. Du Yuesheng's Green Gang had by 1925 all but merged with the Red Gang, giving the godfather a standing army of more than 20,000 gangsters who controlled 80 per cent of the city's labour force.[42] The CCP, with its plan to unionise the workers of Shanghai, had proved a constant irritation, and Du was not about to let go of the empire he had fought so hard to build.

The Green Gang boss was now chief executive of the Black Stuff Company, a cartel of extortionists who demanded up to 10,000 Chinese dollars a month from every opium *hong* in the French Concession. He was chairman of the Opium Pipe Company that supplied Shanghai's pharmaceutical needs, ringing in profits of 100,000 dollars a month.[43] If an opium den attempted to hide from him, Du simply called in the French Concession police. He was a prominent member of the French Municipal Council, president of two banks, chairman of Cheng Shih Middle School, counted Baron Rothschild among his friends and sold jadeite to foreigners through his Mei Tsung Hwa Kyi jewellery store on Rue du Consulate.[44] He delivered coffins to the homes of adversaries but was described in Shanghai's *Who's Who* as a 'well-known public welfare worker'. Cadaverous and menacing in his tortoise-shell tinted glasses, Du even inveigled his way into the European cocktail circuit, thrilling foreign guests with his reputation as 'the killer of a thousand men'.[45] Ilona Ralf Sues, a representative of the Anti-Opium Information Bureau, was one of the only foreign writers ever to interview him, and wrote: 'I had never seen such eyes before. Eyes so dark that they seemed to have no pupils, blurred and dull – dead impenetrable eyes . . . I shuddered.'[46]

Du Yuesheng, whose *alter ego* was soon to be played by Boris Karloff in Hollywood, an evil mastermind who would capture his screen heroines with drugs, hypnotism and a fiendish array of traps, made his move in July 1926. He propelled Chiang Kai-shek into the party's chair with Curio Chang's backing. While the new Generalissimo Chiang Kai-shek publicly announced a Nationalist assault on China's northern warlords, Du Yuesheng put into action his secret plan to expel the CCP. When a general strike was called by the Communists in March 1927 in support of the KMT's military campaign, it was publicly backed by Generalissimo Chiang Kai-shek. More than 5000 armed CCP pickets took to the streets, buoyed by news that Nationalist troops were heading for the city to aid them.[47] The Generalissimo urged the strikers to remain on the streets until 4 a.m. on 12 April when the Green Gang's thugs, wearing coded arm bands, were unleashed. Hundreds of CCP members were decapitated, their heads carried through Shanghai on bamboo poles and on platters. Within days thousands more were dead.

Hui-lan Koo missed it all. She was busy shopping in Peking, a place that foreigners now referred to as the Old Curiosity Shop.[48] She scoured Lin Li-chang with Senhora de Freitas, wife of the Portuguese minister, and Langfang with Señora Garrido of Spain, Madame de Martel of France and Sir Ronald and Lady Macleay, the British minister and his wife. 'All foreign residents in Peking had a mania for collecting Chinese treasures but being Chinese I usually managed to outstrip them,' Hui-lan bragged. 'I bought every piece of exquisite jade I could find . . . I peppered dealers with questions.' She taught her foreign friends that old and new jadeite were as easy to distinguish as 'a teenage virgin and an old widow'. She bought court necklaces from 'higgledy-piggledy' shops, 'each round bead the size of a nickel', and pairs of antique jadeite bangles costing 30,000 Chinese dollars a piece. Her car 'was guarded by four soldiers ferociously armed to the teeth, who stood on the running board, clinging precariously by specially made handles'. Trailed by eight vehicles 'crammed with ladies-in-waiting, amahs, young girl attendants and men servants brought along to serve tea and delicacies', they surely must have been mistaken for an Imperial convoy.

Was it then a surprise that Hui-lan Koo befriended Yu Derling, who had now recast herself as Princess Yu, the Jade Princess. She had left the Forbidden City in 1907, where she had served as the Dowager Empress's lady-in-waiting and now told everyone that her father was Lord Yu Keng of the White Banner. 'Princess Yu' became Hui-lan Koo's 'darling' and 'godmother to her youngest son'. Despite her dubious title, her royal connections were real enough. She introduced Hui-lan Koo to a sister-in-law of the deposed Emperor who 'came often to our palace and was an exquisitely improbable sight in her shimmering Manchu robe and exotic headdress'. Through these Imperial connections Hui-lan began to fill her jewellery chest. 'As [Manchus] grew progressively poorer they sold their jewels first, then furniture, robes, and furs but never, short of actual starvation, could they be induced to part with their magnificent Pekinese dogs,' Hui-lan Koo sympathised.

Generalissimo Chiang Kai-shek had also been secretly brokering important new relationships. In the summer of 1926, at the height of his northern campaign, the Generalissimo and his wife Jennie had received an invitation to dine with Ai-ling and May-ling, Charlie Soong's daughters. Jennie failed to understand her husband's apparent delight until he spelled it out for her. 'You must be sensible and realise how very important it is to me to get closer to the Soong family,' the Generalissimo said. 'I have position, but I lack prestige. I want the names of Sun, Soong and Chiang to be linked together tightly.'[49]

What Jennie did not know was that the year before Chiang Kai-shek had secretly proposed to Ching-ling, Sun Yat-sen's widow, but the offer had been rejected as tasteless and ill-timed. Jennie was no match for the 'chic and aristocratic' Soong sisters, who 'looked as if they had stepped out of a Shanghai fashion book'. Over roast pigeon breast and jellied consommé, they grilled her mercilessly. 'Have you bought much jewellery, Mme Chiang?' asked Ai-ling. 'You can afford it, you know.' After dinner, as Jennie strolled around the garden, she overheard Ai-ling's indiscreet tones: 'How can she ever qualify to be the wife of a budding leader? Something must be done about it.'[50]

Weeks later, Ai-ling made the Generalissimo a lucrative offer. If he would marry her little sister, she would rally the might of Shanghai's bankers behind the KMT. Chiang Kai-shek hastily accepted and went home to tell his wife. 'I now ask you to help me. After all, true love is measured by the size of the sacrifice one is willing to make! Step aside for five years so that I can marry May-ling

Soong . . . It's only a political marriage . . . I call upon your patriotism to help the country.'[51]

Five months later, on 19 August 1927, Jennie exiled herself from China, sailing on the SS *President Jackson,* accompanied by Curio Chang's daughters, and while she stayed below deck, May-ling and Chiang Kai-shek were introduced to the press at a Shanghai garden party. 'The Generalissimo is going to marry my little sister,' Ai-ling told a reporter from the *New York Times* which carried the story the next morning. When Jennie disembarked in San Francisco, she was mobbed. Newspapers around the world were carrying an Associated Press story that quoted the Generalissimo as claiming that he 'does not know the Madame Chiang Kai-shek mentioned in dispatches'. Jennie, he claimed, was an impostor.[52]

The Soongs staged a wedding banquet at Shanghai's Majestic Hotel on 1 December 1927. In the lobby Green Gang henchmen frisked 1300 guests before the newlyweds repeated their vows in the ballroom, in front of a looming portrait of Sun Yat-sen. The bride wore a white-and-silver georgette gown, a veil of Chantilly lace and, as the American tenor E. L. Hall sang 'Oh Promise Me', accompanied by a White Russian orchestra, thousands of rose petals fell from the ceiling. The entire diplomatic community turned out for the third Madame Chiang Kai-shek alongside Du Yuesheng and Curio Chang, who presented her with jadeite gifts. Henry Luce, publisher of *Life,* fêted it as the union of 'Gissimo and Missimo', and the local press described May-ling as the new and undisputed Number One Lady of China. Hui-lan Koo was beside herself with jealousy that would only increase when the KMT won control of Peking in June 1928, establishing a new government in Nanking with the Generalissimo at its head and *Fu-jen* May-ling at his side.

Barely one month later, the Generalissimo and his new wife made their move on China's Imperial legacy. A KMT column, acting on behalf of the central committee, cordoned off the Imperial necropolis in Zunhua County. Notices pinned around the Qing Dong Ling were signed by the commanding officer Sun Dianying, whose identity was confirmed by eyewitnesses. At midnight on 2 July, Sun Dianying ordered his corps of engineers to surround the entrance of Emperor Qianlong's tomb, where they placed charges. According to officials at the mausoleum, the troops then prised their way into the Dowager Empress Cixi's Precious Citadel and, under Sun Dianying's watchful eye, emptied the tombs, placing the contents in a KMT truck:

> First they took the large treasure objects . . . such as jadeite watermelons, grasshoppers and vegetables, jade lotuses and coral. They even grabbed objects found beneath the body and ravaged the corpse itself, taking the Dowager Empress Cixi's Imperial robe; tearing off her underclothing, shoes and socks and taking all the pearls and jewels on the body. They even prised open Cixi's jaws and took the rare pearl from her mouth.[53]

When the ex-Emperor Pu Yi's investigators arrived at the scene, they learned that Sun Dianying had sent the lion's share of the Imperial loot to Nanking. 'Chiang Kai-shek decided not to follow the matter up . . . Sun Dianying sent some of the booty to Chiang Kai-shek's new bride Soong May-ling: the pearls from Cixi's phoenix crown became decorations for Madame Chiang Kai-shek's shoes,' the ex-Emperor Pu Yi wrote bitterly in his memoirs.

Barbara Hutton devoured *Life*'s reports on the meteoric rise of the new Madame Chiang Kai-shek and was intrigued by stories of the thefts. Her own court was now taking shape in New York, San Francisco and Long Island, where at the height of the Depression she partied with Tallulah Bankhead, Fred Astaire, Toscanini and Jimmy Durante. But it was Doris Duke, who had inherited 70 million US dollars at the age of thirteen, who was to become her closest friend, the papers dubbing them the 'Gold Dust Twins'. While Bing Crosby sang 'I Found a Million Dollar Baby (in a Five and Ten Cent Store)', Noël Coward was kinder: 'Poor little rich girl, you're a bewitched girl, better beware! Better take care.' But Barbara lost her virginity at sixteen to her English tennis tutor, lured her bodyguard into bed, dated David Niven and Howard Hughes. She was desperate to be loved.

Her society début was a 60,000 US dollars extravaganza at the Ritz-Carlton on Madison Avenue on 21 December 1930. Attended by more than a thousand guests, star-spangled navy chiffon looping across the ceiling, silver birches and scarlet poinsettias gracing the floor, drifts of artificial snow engulfing the hotel lobby. Ten thousand American Beauty roses and two thousand bottles of champagne adorned the tables despite Prohibition, and at the entrance Maurice Chevalier, dressed as Santa Claus, handed out pocket-sized jewellery cases packed with gems. For Brooke Astor, a rival to Hutton's status as Manhattan's foremost heiress, it was 'to die for'. The New York *Sun* perceived it all as grand folly:

> Even the decks of that great new ocean liner, the *Titanic,* didn't blaze as brilliantly as the French windows of the Hotel Ritz on the occasion of Barbara Hutton's début . . . Let's hope Miss Hutton fares better than the SS *Titanic* on her maiden voyage.[54]

Six months later, dressed in ivory satin embroidered with seed pearls, Barbara was presented to King George V and Queen Mary. At a garden party that followed, she danced with Edward, Prince of Wales, whom she described as 'tipsy' and an unlikely future king, while British newspapers dubbed her 'a spoilt brat', claiming that she planned to 'steal the vaulted throne of the British Empire'.[55] Hutton stomped off to Indonesia where she 'liberated' herself by joining a bare-breasted Balinese dance troupe, before returning to the United States and the serious business of spending her inheritance.

◻

Having been badly injured in a First World War air accident, Victor Sassoon had settled in Shanghai to take full advantage of his legacy, assuming control of the family's business and his father's title. Driving up and down The Bund in a gold Rolls-Royce, Sir Victor earmarked Elias Sassoon's riverside sites for an ultra-modern, luxury hotel that would cost £1 million to build. William Van Alen had recently raised the Chrysler Building in Manhattan, a glass and stone monolith capped with a stainless-steel finial that pierced the New York skyline like King Mindon's Mount Meru. When the Cathay Hotel's doors swung back in 1930 they revealed 'a Ferris wheel of fantasy and reality', the embodiment of a new style that had leapt from the pavilions of the *Exposition des Arts Decoratifs* in Paris in 1925.[56] Art Deco encompassed the spirit of the age. A decorative mania devoid of intellect, it clad the Cathay in sinuous and geometric designs, decorating it with opulence and exoticism, transforming a hotel into a venue for guests filled with the rage to exist.

Sir Victor's 'art deco rocket ship' also cushioned Eastern society from China's 'wars and alarums'.

As Shanghai's elite emerged from the lifts on the eighth floor, Martini laughter floating along the landing from the Horse and Hounds Bar, Chinese footmen led them past back-lit Lalique screens and up the stairs into a fancy-dress world. Old and new aristocracy sipped pink champagne in the Dragon-Phoenix Hall, its lacquered ceilings writhing with sea beasts, its lattice-work windows borrowed from Imperial China. Sometimes they dressed for a shipwreck, one couple who shared a small flannel claiming to have been 'caught in the shower when their liner went down', winning one evening's first prize. Sir Victor hosted, costumed as the Captain, the Ringleader, the Emperor or Le Roi Soleil, sporting a trademark monocle, an affectation from his student days in amateur dramatics, walking awkwardly with the aid of two silver-topped canes, a crowd of beautiful women hanging on his every word. 'I am a wicked man and the last to be accused of virtue,' he boasted as he lured potential lovers with gifts of two dozen pairs of French silk stockings.[57]

So recently liberated from their corsets by designer Paul Poiret, Sir Victor's female guests also revealed their ankles, discarding their large unwieldy hats in favour of Eton crops. Dressed by Chanel, Patou and Schiaparelli, their free-flowing gowns drew on the risqué Oriental costumes of Sergei Diaghilev's Ballets Russes that had stunned Paris in June 1910 with its performance of *Schéhérazade,* a whirling orgy of infidelity, concubine Zobeide's fatal fling with the athletic Golden Slave.[58] Then Léon Bakst's erotic costumes had glittered with slivers of jadeite and now the Stone of Heaven suited the mood. Parisian jewellers Jean Fouquet and Boucheron turned the Dowager Empress Cixi's belt buckles into jadeite corsages, Emperor Qianlong's archer's rings became brooches and pendants, Emperor Xianfeng's jadeite stop beads were fashioned into cabochons. Free to divorce, take lovers, smoke, shimmy and wear blood-red lipstick, the Cathay crowd were accessorised by Cartier, who bought jadeite from Mr Tieh, China's Jade King, and set it into lipstick canisters, cigarette cases and holders and powder compacts. 'The spirit of jade is like a beautiful woman, the godlike rendered viable, the gem of gems, the quintessence of creation,' gushed Spink & Co.[59]

Jadeite illuminated Shanghai, and the Wah Cehn Company of Route St Chevalier in the French Concession supplied the window displays of Bond Street, the Place Vendôme and Fifth Avenue. By 1930 it was a 300,000 US dollars per year business, and the company's pamphlets captured the bewilderment of jadeite's new clients.[60] 'Many foreigners are totally ignorant of the source of jade; some have asked local dealers whether it is grown on trees or artificially made for they have never seen a piece of jade rock or its process of manufacture,' one brochure reveals.[61] Ignorant they may have been, but the Vanderbilts, Astors, Hearsts and Rothschilds parted with hundreds of thousands of dollars to buy into a magical world, spun by George Kunz of Tiffany & Co., who advised his clients: 'When handled, some of the secret virtue of the substance is absorbed into the body.'[62]

The new-found passion for this virtuous stone was immediately seized upon by Chiang Kai-shek. Reviving an ancient Imperial custom, he announced that outstanding citizens would be fêted with the Order of Brilliant Jade. Sir Miles Lampson, British Minister to China, the lynch-pin in negotiations with Western powers, and Patrick Givens, the International Settlement's Special Branch chief, an honourable Irishman who was spear-heading a rigorous anti-narcotics drive, were the first recipients of Chiang Kai-shek's Imperial Green Jade largesse.

The desire for the Stone of Heaven was universal. Cole Porter courted his wife with jadeite. Marlene Dietrich, Merle Oberon and Joan Crawford competed for the largest cabochons. Had they read *Fortune* magazine that month? It advised that the Stone of Heaven was a commodity worth more than pearls or stocks and, 'like the colors of jade, its collectors are legion.' In Henry Luce's 'sober opinion', jadeite's 'value may well double within the next five years'. The KMT was obviously aware. *Fortune* also advertised an unusual sale that was to be the first of many, a single lot of stunning quality that many suggested marked it out as an Imperial funerary treasure. 'Probably the most valuable *Fei Cui* jewel now on the market is a string of 108 matched [Imperial] beads of from six to seven carats each, owned by the Nationalist Chinese government. The string is worth 200,000 US dollars.'[63] In London, such was the clamour to be associated with the Stone of Heaven that there was even a royal indiscretion. Tancred Borenius, editor of *Apollo,* revealed the extent of the British Royal Family's secret collection of looted Imperial jadeite. Illustrated with photographs of a glass cabinet stuffed with belt buckles, ruyi sceptres and brush holders, the once treasured possessions of the Qing, Borenius' article quoted, without irony, from the ancient Chinese *Book of Ritual* that jade was a stone of purity that 'goes from hand to hand unsullied'.[64]

▨

Mr Tieh, the Jade King, now owned the largest outlet for the Stone of Heaven in the world, and in October 1999, after months of searching followed by weeks of delicate negotiations, we finally tracked down his publicity-shy son. Frank Tieh agreed to meet us, but we would have to fly immediately to Taiwan. In a five-star hotel in Taipei, over a *faux* Imperial banquet of tea-smoked fish and duck spring rolls, Frank Tieh cautiously let us into his father's world. He recalled how as a child he had watched the Jade King fight for the best new boulders arriving from the Burmese mines, stones that were named after their colour or the deals struck around them. A Mr Yang purchased the 'Wheelbarrow of Money' after pushing a cartload of cash through the Chinese quarter of Shanghai. An anonymous dealer clinched *lan shui lu,* 'Sea Reflecting a Blue Sky', a stone named after its unique translucent green colour. Frank Tieh's father bought 'Thirty-Three Thousand' and 'Seventy-Four Thousand', the price the Jade King had paid for each in silver taels. As a family of four could live comfortably in Shanghai on 300 taels (150,000 grams) a year, his purchases made headlines throughout China. 'I remember seeing the boulders in my father's warehouse, sliced like a marbled ham,' Frank said, his wife Charlotte, the daughter of a wealthy Manchurian general, nervously fingering her jadeite saddle ring. 'Hong Kong dealers still talk of these boulders today and they were the best to come out of Burma.' The publicity had a price. The Jade King was blackmailed, his cousins and brother kidnapped by an international criminal gang to whom ransoms were eventually paid, his warehouse repeatedly broken into, although the thieves mistook 'Seventy-Four Thousand' for an innocuous lump of stone and left it behind. Then Charlotte intervened. 'Be careful, Frank,' she urged. 'Be careful. You have said enough.'

In 1932, Generalissimo Chiang Kai-shek and his Number One Lady turned their attention to Peking's Imperial warehouse, and it was the Japanese that gave them the excuse they needed to pick the lock. In September 1931 Japan had invaded Mukden and by December the entire province of Manchuria had been occupied. The following month, the Imperial Nippon Navy attacked Shanghai; Japanese marines advancing along North Sichuan Road passed Dr Duncan's discreet clap clinic.[65] Sir Victor Sassoon hobbled out of the Cathay, cine camera at the ready, and was almost shot through the head before retreating to the Horse and Hounds bar, where his guests kept a tally of the corks he popped on magnums of pink champagne.[66] By the time a cease-fire was brokered on 3 March 1932, 12,000 were dead or wounded, 600,000 were refugees and 900 factories and businesses lay in ruins, most of it captured in Sir Victor's home movies. One week later, Japan announced the formation of its puppet state of Manchukuo, hiring the former Emperor Pu Yi as its chief executive. Chiang Kai-shek was berated for failing to counter Japanese aggression, but he had reason. He was busy sending secret telegrams to Peking's Palace Museum.

Chuang Shang-yen, the curator who had found the ex-Emperor Pu Yi's browning apple core inside the abandoned Forbidden City in 1924, was ordered to pack up hundreds of thousands of Imperial treasures, wrapping them in silk, straw and newspaper, supervised by Curio Chang, who conveniently controlled the museum board. On 6 February 1933, the first shipments crept out of the old Imperial capital in unmarked train carriages and by road, accompanied by KMT troops. Over the next three months 13,491 packing cases were removed to Shanghai while Chiang Kai-shek oversaw the construction of a reinforced secret depository on the outskirts of Nanking, behind which was a cave that ran into the bedrock of a mountain in which the most valuable pieces would be hidden.[67] 'To reassure the Chinese people', the Generalissimo briefly displayed the treasures in Shanghai before they vanished into their Nanking cave, some of them never to be seen in public again.[68]

In Europe, Barbara Hutton was also busy, acquiring a title and a crown jewel. On 20 June 1933, wearing lace underwear that had been spun by French nuns, a satin gown by Jean Patou and Marie Antoinette's pearls, Hutton married Prince Alexis Mdivani, a White Russian playboy with a lightweight title, in the fairytale surroundings of Paris' Russian Cathedral. 'Our felicitation and whatever else may be appropriate to Miss Barbara Hutton, who is spending nobody knows how many millions of American nickels and dimes . . . in marriage to a foreigner whose name had slipped from our mind,' sniped the New York *Daily News*.[69] So many presents arrived at the Ritz, including a gold toilet, that a suite was hired to store them. But a gift from Barbara's father, 'a costly jade necklace' of 27 grapesized, flawless emerald green beads, cut from the *lan shui lu* boulder, stole the show. The necklace, valued at 50,000 US dollars, joined a bulging vanity case of green stones that included Catherine the Great's emerald tiara and a suite of emeralds that Napoleon III had given Countess Verasis de Castiglione.

Announcing to the press, 'It's going to be fun being a princess', Barbara Hutton and her Prince set out across Europe in a fleet of Rolls-Royces, squeezing between 70 Louis Vuitton cases, embossed with a dubious coat of arms. She wore her jadeite necklace while tearing down the Grand Canal in Ali Baba, a speed boat gifted to her husband, at the Metropolitan Opera House, and on her twenty-first birthday party on 14 November 1933, when she officially took charge of her vast fortune, now estimated at 50 million US dollars.

Back in China, Hui-lan Koo was entertaining the crowds with her jadeite and Pekinese, having also obtained a title. Tiring of Peking, she had at last moved to Shanghai, where, sporting a new Elizabeth Arden permanent wave and false lashes, she had plunged into the party, dancing the Charleston beside the soda fountains in Jimmy's Kitchen in a cheongsam that she had daringly ripped to the knee. *Vogue* had noticed her antics and named her 'one of the best-dressed ladies in the world':

> My new Shanghai acquaintances imagined me the essence of everything modern and foreign. They were surprised to discover I preferred jade to diamonds. Imperial jade was appreciated only by the elder generation. So when I went about wearing jade bracelets and ornaments, my lack of sparkle actually made me conspicuous.[70]

Renting a suite at the Majestic, Hui-lan raced Sir Victor Sassoon's Rolls-Royce up and down The Bund in her own grey limousine, the famous Crystal Palace. Whether she won, we do not know, but her increasing irritation with the Emperor of the Cathay suggests that the competition was fierce. 'Women are fascinated by Sir Victor, because his wit snaps like a whip,' Hui-lan Koo wrote of a man she described as 'swarthy' and 'crass'. When he publicly propositioned her with two pairs of French silk stockings she spread rumours that he wore callipers and that 'nature had not given him the equipment to be a great lover'. Soon their rivalry spilled into an area in which Hui-lan was certain that she had the upper hand. When her sister visited Shanghai and stayed at the Cathay, much to Hui-lan's chagrin, Sir Victor approached them over dinner and suggested a competition in which he would compare the quality of two of his Imperial jadeite necklaces with the one that Hui-lan's sister was wearing. 'When [she] put hers back on, Sir Victor carefully inspected his two, counting the stones to be sure she hadn't exchanged hers for one of his. He was simply not a gentleman,' Hui-lan Koo wrote.

Madame Koo reserved her respect for warlords. She played dominoes with the Old Marshal of Mukden for 50,000 Chinese dollars stakes and came to the aid of Du Yuesheng when the French attempted to eliminate the Green Gang boss's narcotics business in 1932, canvassing diplomats in Paris to win free passage for his opium ships. She sipped champagne with the Old Marshal's son and introduced him to her dancing partner Edda Ciano, Benito Mussolini's daughter: 'razor-sharp, exaggeratedly slim, with beautiful blue eyes and a severe Eton-cut coiffure'. Edda and the Old Marshal's son scandalised the Whore of the Orient by breaking house rules that stipulated that Oriental men stay out of Occidental beds. But not a word was said about the outcome of another secret tryst. Count Galeazzo, Edda's husband, had used his 'most ardent Latin enthusiasm' to win a young American mistress, Wallis Simpson, who was now scouring the back-streets for a doctor willing to terminate the evidence of her secret romance.[71] How Mrs Simpson extricated herself from the scandal has never been revealed, but soon she would be rushing into the arms of another lover.

Hui-lan's Koo's best friend was the 'delightfully outrageous' Dog

Meat General, whom she christened 'Old Eighty-Six', claiming it was a reference to a 'certain portion of his anatomy'. Only one person remained aloof from the cosmopolitan clique. 'Beautiful and refined', the third Madame Chiang Kai-shek 'made no move to join our silly group which laughed and joked throughout the evening'. Hui-lan wrote enviously of her rival's 'vibrant, beautifully modulated voice and her faultlessly proportioned feet' and secretly eyed up her superior Imperial jadeite jewellery.

In 1934, Princess Barbara Hutton finally docked beside The Bund, Ticki Tocquet, her former governess, and Jimmy Donahue, her nineteen-year-old bisexual cousin, in tow. Before her ship had left San Francisco Barbara had popped into Abe Gump's antique store and paid 50,000 US dollars for a pair of Qianlong jade beakers to celebrate her maiden voyage to the Orient. The city she arrived in was now the sixth largest in the world with a population of 3.3 million, and its department stores pulsed with the finest waves of 'London, Paris and New York; native emporiums [filled] with lacquered ducks and salt eggs, and precious silks and jades'.[72]

Like Shanghai Lily, Princess Barbara Hutton took rooms at the Grand and set out on a marathon shopping campaign in which she scooped up dozens of jadeite bangles, including a unique 'silk melon skin green' wristlet that had once belonged to the Dowager Empress Cixi. She insisted on wearing multiple bangles on each arm, horrifying the Chinese by telling them how she loved their tinkling, unconcerned by the frequency with which they shattered. Cartier's archives reveal how within weeks of buying Cixi's bangle Hutton had sent it back to New York to be mended with a diamond clasp. But she failed to break into the secretive inner circle of Chinese jadeite dealers until she hired a chaperone who persuaded them to reveal what was concealed up their Confucian sleeves. Yu Derling, the Jade Princess, charmed Barbara Hutton with stories of Emperor Qianlong's quest for a Jade Road, his unrequited love for the forlorn Fragrant Consort Xiang Fei, and Cixi's insatiable appetite that filled 3000 Imperial vanity cases. Jadeite stories inspired the five-and-dime heiress to verse, her lines limping along like those of a 200-year-old Qing ruler, fragile rhymes that reveal something of the misery that the poor little rich girl was attempting to conceal:

I bring you my poor dreams
Caught up in a green jade bowl,
Carved untold years ago
Out of a Chinese soul.[73]

Barbara's Asian spree failed to buy her peace, and back in the United States gossip columnist Cholly Knickerbocker invented yet another nickname: 'Age 22 Huttontot has already amassed one of the largest jewellery collections in the world. What better way to spend all those jillions and trillions?' RKO released *The Richest Girl in the World*, a comedy that barely tried to conceal its inspiration, casting Miriam Hopkins as Dorothy Hunter, an orphaned heiress with an addiction to shopping.

There was, however, one Asian treasure that eluded Barbara Hutton, a rumour that pattered through Shanghai about a jewel lost for so long that many believed it to be mythological. Said to blush in the light, it looked as if it would be soft to the touch and around it had been spun an exotic web of perfume and spice. Chinese whispers that started at the Horse and Hounds bar soon tinkled between the champagne flutes at Ciro's until they landed at a party thrown in honour of Lord Willingdon, the recently appointed Viceroy of India.[74] Bored with conversation about Mahatma Gandhi, whom the Viceroy vilified as 'a half-nude gent', Hui-lan Koo railroaded the discussion and suggested a wager.[75] She leaned across the dinner table and collared Sir Victor, betting him that she could find the mysterious Imperial jewel. 'Sir Victor didn't like the idea of risking a thousand dollars, I could tell, but he had no choice when I suggested we each put up the money and Lord Willingdon would hold the stakes. We made a date to meet again,' Hui-lan Koo recorded in her memoirs. They had only one month.[76]

Boarding the Peking Express, accompanied by Princess Yu Der-ling, Hui-lan dashed for the *Tei Yuan Shieng* store, but the Jade King was in a terrible mood. The Mayor of Peking had ordered the demolition of his shop's second floor after complaints from neighbours, who claimed that their single-storey emporiums were being overshadowed. Mr Tieh, 'crawling in his anguish . . . kowtowed and moaned out his problem'. Hui-lan immediately rang up the

Mayor, donning the mantle of *Fu-jen,* but for several weeks her messages remained unanswered. Eventually, with only four days left before the wager was to be adjudicated, a call from the Mayor reached Hui-lan's Peking palace and, now terrified that she would run out of time, she hectored him with a melodrama that would have even raised eyebrows in the Peking Opera. Mr Tieh would be ruined, Hui-lan gushed, his reputation torn down, his family ostracised, his son's future destroyed, their children cast into oblivion by the cruel actions of the municipal wrecking crew. His ears burning, the Mayor relented and Hui-lan immediately summoned Mr Tieh:

> He said I had saved his honour so in appreciation he would tell me a very deep secret: [when] the last emperor of China, Pu Yi, and his wife were forced to flee Peking, they had taken with them, concealed in the belt of the Empress, their most prized possession, the most beautiful piece of jade in the world. Now they were desperate for money and might be willing to sell it.[77]

Insisting that everyone else leave the room, Mr Tieh unravelled a small parcel from the girdle of his gown: 'It was the most beautiful piece of jade I have ever seen. It was like a big emerald and completely translucent.' But the price he mentioned 'made me turn pale':

> All night long I could hardly sleep. Toward morning I dreamed of my father . . . if he had been alive, I'm sure he would have bought it for me. Then I remembered the pin money he had given me over the years . . . It now came to almost a million dollars. When the jeweller returned the next day . . . I gave him the pin money and told him to show it to the Boy Emperor . . . It was Papa's old trick; the sight of money was too tempting for Pu Yi to resist.

Catching the Shanghai Express, Hui-lan raced back to Lord Willingdon's dinner table, arriving with only minutes to spare, but her portly rival was also brimming with excitement. With a magician's flourish Sir Victor and Hui-lan Koo both unravelled silk handkerchiefs and produced almost identical Imperial Green Jade pendants carved into peppers. Emperor Qianlong's gift to his Fragrant Consort Xiang Fei had not been seen for almost 150 years, although it had been glorified in opera, poetry and folklore. But now, before the bemused Lord Willingdon, there appeared to be two.

The Viceroy demanded an inspection and, holding Sir Victor's pepper up to the light, Hui-lan declared that its tip was flecked with 'a definite flaw'. The Emperor would never have commissioned a piece from an imperfect stone, she pronounced, and '[Sir Victor] sucked his breath and gave up the thousand dollars without a murmur. I heard later he had all the dealers searching for a piece comparable to mine, but I doubt if it exists.'

The party for the legendary Persian Pepper lasted into the early hours but was any one of the guests around that dinner table aware that Shanghai was now literally sinking? Inch by inch, year by year, its towers of chrome and glass, weighed down by pride and profligacy, were being sucked back into the mud flats from where they had first emerged.

Nine

As Dead as the Moon

Sir Victor Sassoon was in Bombay at his family's Ballard Estate on Tuesday 8 July 1937, languishing in an incendiary summer, but at least he was still making money. The fourteen cotton mills he had come to inspect were bustling despite the nine million work-days lost every year through strikes inspired by Mahatma Gandhi's homespun militancy. The hundreds of thousands of pounds he had invested in blood-stock was showing a return in England, where one of his race-horses had clinched the One Thousand Guineas. So when a telegram arrived reporting that there had been skirmishes the previous day in China, Japanese and KMT troops firing on each other near the Marco Polo Bridge, south-west of Peking, he dismissed the event as an insignificant tremor.[1]

Within a month the Japanese clashed again with Chiang Kai-shek's troops on the outskirts of the old Imperial capital. For two days they also exchanged fire outside the International Settlement in Shanghai from behind sandbags and bunkers, as 21 Japanese battleships cruised up the Whangpoo towards the Cathay Hotel. But no one seemed to be taking any notice. 'You foreigners are watching . . . as if it were a football game,' a KMT official remarked to Emily Hahn of the *New Yorker*. 'You clap very kindly.'[2]

Hui-lan Koo was busy in Paris, dazzling with her jadeite suite and the Bing Noi diamond, at soirées and night-clubs, dancing, 'disguised by a veil', with young secretaries from the Italian and American embassies. She had arrived in France in 1936 to join her husband who had been posted there, and she was already 'an object of curiosity and gossip'. She lunched with Baron Maurice de Rothschild, dining on truffles flown in from his country estate, on imported 'Devonshire cream', hitching rides in his Rolls Royce that was barely large enough to carry their conceit. Recalling an invitation from the Baron, a 'prolific collector of beautiful women', to attend the opera alongside his mistress, a minor European princess, Hui-lan wrote in her diary that she advised Maurice, 'You are so big and so fat, there will be no room for me between you and the Princess'.[3]

The exotic Hui-lan intrigued Parisian society. 'Eyebrows raised when I appeared wearing the jewels . . . the names of my presumed and generous lovers – some of whom I had never set eyes on – were whispered in social circles,' she told her friends, claiming that Joe Kennedy, the new American ambassador to Britain, had once 'chased me around his desk'.[4] When the Nationalist government bought a mansion on Avenue George V for 30 million francs to house the new Chinese Embassy, Hui-lan decided to transform it into a showcase that would define her status. She chartered an aeroplane to Shanghai, where she planned to shop with the Baron, who was holidaying away from his slender Princess. 'When you go to a Mayor's banquet, you don't take a ham sandwich,' Hui-lan had advised him before he left for the Paris of the East.

Her diary recalls how she left Le Bourget airfield on 10 February 1937 at 9.20 a.m., seen off by 'embassy staff, military and air attachés and wives . . . but not the ambassador my husband', her purse bulging with 100,000 Chinese dollars. She stopped off in Baghdad, a city of 'dirty-hooded women, filthy Muslims, ragged Bedouins, bloody mutton hides, and a bedroom full of flees'. She flew through 'neat and clean' Karachi, into Jodhpur and out of Calcutta before stopping over in 'enchanting' Rangoon for a spot of shopping, snapping up 40 rubies and a silver box. Twenty days after leaving France, Hui-lan landed in China to find the Japanese 'moving on Peking'. She ordered her staff to pack up her palace and ship her Qianlong bed 'hung with lanterns and trimmed with . . . real gold', dining-room furniture and jadeite haul to France. They were also to forward her favourite Pekes, Pao Pei and Ching Ming. Koo would later accuse the Japanese of making *sushi* of her abandoned goldfish, kidnapping the Pekinese litter that she had left behind and looting her Ming dynasty palace.[5]

In Shanghai, she managed a brief visit to her mother, two sons and sister who were staying in an apartment let by Sir Victor's property company, but 'the main object was shopping', and it was 'a task requiring concentration and organisation'. Using 'contacts in the Nationalist government', Hui-lan snapped up a 500-year-old terracotta Buddha 'from an old Temple', bought silks, an Imperial yellow carpet woven with the Emperor's dragon motif, draperies, screens and two 'magnificent and old' jade dragons for her new entrance hall. There was barely time to fill a case with jadeite. The Imperial cargo was loaded onto the liner *Victoria,* along with a delegation of foreign dignitaries sailing for the coronation of King George VI in London. Madame Chiang Kai-shek came aboard on 2 April to wish everyone *bon voyage,* and the precious freight docked 24 days later in France. The following month a triumphal reception for 1300 people filed through the newly decorated Chinese embassy: 'I was gratified to watch the crowd going through . . . not chattering as people usually do at a reception, but looking, touching gently, respectfully, as though they were in a museum.'

Madame Chiang Kai-shek was in Nanking, talking up her pet project, the New Life movement, when the Japanese surprised the Chinese on the Marco Polo Bridge. Wearing a plain dress and no jewellery at all, she roused an audience of women, calling on them to join a moral crusade that would remould China around puritanical Confucian values. Her austerity and regal bearing appealed to the Chinese crowd and also to the manic enclave of the International Settlement, where Emily Hahn noted that Madame Chiang was now compared to 'Joan of Arc, Boadicea, to any military heroine of olden days whose name could be remembered'.[6] Empire-building Madame Chiang had also taken command of China's fledgling air force, whose maverick European and American pilots, some of them veterans of the Great War, fêted her as 'the only man who'll show any action'.[7] When *Forum* interviewed her days after the Marco Polo Bridge incident, she appeared before journalists wearing her finest Imperial jadeite and was described by them as a 'satin-haired Princess' with 'winning black eyes' who pledged to rule China with a powerful combination of political savvy and Christian values.[8] There was no mention of the Generalissimo.

It was not until 14 August, at 4.30 p.m., that the Sino-Japanese spat finally caught the attention of Sir Victor Sassoon and took the polish off Madame Chiang's gleaming new image. As tens of thousands of Chinese refugees fled from the fighting over the Whangpoo, teeming across the river bridges and onto The Bund, war inadvertently came to the lazy oasis of the International Settlement. Lucian Ovadia, Sir Victor's cousin, who had been brought to Shanghai to oversee his Far Eastern operation, was in the third-floor office at the Cathay Hotel when the bombs began to fall. The blast hurled him to the ground and, as the storm of glass and plaster settled, the Cathay's Swiss manager telephoned to report that the hotel's entrance had been hit. Four Chinese warplanes that had been ordered to strafe the Japanese Third Fleet had apparently missed the Whangpoo altogether and accidentally hit Sir Victor's headquarters, the shells ricocheting into the crowded street below.

An 'absolute slaughter' now enveloped those who had applauded Madame Chiang's veterans as they appeared on the horizon. The injured were ferried to hospital in furniture vans. A bus and two trams outside the Cathay were consumed by fire, the charred remains of passengers fixed in a tableau of flailing limbs and silent screams. 'Bodies and bits' were strewn across the street and survivors would later recall how the dead were deposited at the Race Club, 'stacked in piles'.[9] Then another explosive device landed on the roof of the Great World Entertainment Centre, a six-storey building at the intersection of Thibet Road and Avenue Edward VII, a 'hot stream . . . of sing-song girls, magicians and pickpockets' that only days before had become a refugee centre.[10] One thousand died and one thousand more were maimed by the flying shards of glass and twisted steel.[11] 'If I wasn't so terribly busy . . . I think I should just sit down and vomit with the horror of it all,' Dr D. Cater wrote home.[12]

While the blood was being sprayed off The Bund, revellers at the Cathay returned to the bar, throwing back gin-slings, watching a pantomime of white-hot Japanese shells raining down on the Chinese lines, south of the French Concession.[13] Emily Hahn sought a better view, and a letter to her mother, dated 24 August, described the blitzkrieg from her balcony: 'I saw different parts of the native city burning. It was beautiful and horrible, with planes swooping around . . . Nobody can tell if the war will stay here or not.'[14]

By the time Sir Victor Sassoon returned to Shanghai in the autumn of 1937, a quarter of a million Chinese and 40,000 Japanese had died, but the port was still open and his real-estate business was booming. While Hahn's 'native city' had been reduced to rubble, apartments and offices in the International Settlement were much in demand, filled by waves of new refugees from Europe and China.

News of the non-war, the increasingly fierce battles that neither side would admit amounted to an official conflagration, eventually percolated back to Europe, where Hui-lan Koo became 'frantic with worry'. She had neglected to pack up her family in the fury of her Shanghai shopping expedition and now, through her connections with the US fleet and French government, her mother and sister were sent to New York and her sons sailed for France. Koo breathed a sigh of relief and returned to the party where she had just made some new friends.

The Duke and Duchess of Windsor had arrived in Paris after honeymooning in Venice, where Edward had enraged his guests by giving Fascist salutes.[15] One of those who had taken offence was the Duke's former dancing partner Barbara Hutton, who was now Countess von Reventlow, having divorced Alexis Mdivani in 1935 and married an impoverished German aristocrat 24 hours later in Reno at a ceremony witnessed by Princess Yu Derling, the Dowager Empress Cixi's former lady-in-waiting.

Hui-lan Koo found the Windsors 'charming and easy', even though the American ambassador in Paris had refused to shake Wallis Simpson's hand, wary of the British constitutional crisis that her marriage in June had caused. After all, Hui-lan and Wallis had common ground. They both loved Imperial jadeite and had partied together in Shanghai. The Duchess of Windsor even 'remembered a few words of Chinese, notably, "Boy, bring some more champagne."'[16]

But the climate was changing. 'There are no porters at the station,' Hui-lan Koo bemoaned in her diary, and it was the Duke of Windsor who persuaded her that France was no place for children. After sending Wallis to America, he advised Hui-lan, over dinner, to evacuate her sons. The boys were put on a ship bound for New York on which they slept in cots strung across the swimming pool. What was Hui-lan to do? She attended the races at Longchamps with the President of France and was photographed wearing her

Persian Pepper at a party thrown by Douglas Fairbanks Junior and Mary Pickford, who shortly would divorce. She lavished attention on her jewellery, commissioning Cartier to add a 25-carat diamond to Xiang Fei's pendant. 'Louis Cartier was so overwhelmed with the beauty of the pepper that he would not allow anyone in the shop while he was working . . . He told me that it was so unique that no value could be put on it for insurance purposes,' Hui-lan crowed. Behind closed doors, in the mansion on Avenue George V, another undeclared war was being scrutinised in Chinese diplomatic circles. Dr Koo had secretly taken on two mistresses, and finding herself alone one night, Hui-lan melodramatically turned to her diary. 'The lovesick Ambassador sneaked out to see his light-of-love like a thief in the night.'[17] Chinese ambassadors were only paid $600 a month and for seventeen years Hui-lan's jewellery had bankrolled her husband's career. She had glistened at even the most taxing soirées, and now Dr Koo swept her aside as if she were a concubine. 'I was living in an age when Chinese women were struggling to be freed from a long-term yoke of oppression such as Western women have never had to endure,' she complained.[18]

✠

When the Japanese reached Nanking in December 1937 they butchered 30,000 Nationalist soldiers and 12,000 civilians who had surrendered, raped more than 20,000 Chinese women, used prisoners for bayonet practice and buried the injured alive in mass graves. Nanking was bathed in blood, yet the Cathay's bar overflowed with ever-wilder parties attended by Sir Victor Sassoon, the warlords, Emily Hahn and her pet ape Mr Mills, who had been forced into nappies after fellow guests complained about his unsavoury toilet habits. However, some notable Shanghai faces were missing. The Mayor of the Chinese Municipality had jumped ship on 11 November in a chartered plane bound for Hong Kong filled with gold bars and jadeite, only one day after he had assured the local press that he would lay down his life for the city.[19] His last act was to authorise the construction of pontoons to shore up a city that was in reality sinking, concrete rafts that can still be seen today. Du Yuesheng, the Green Gang godfather, had quietly packed up his home in the French Concession and sailed for Hong Kong with a stash of gems.

Booking into Kowloon's Peninsula Hotel, he supervised the escape of Chinese businessmen, for a fee, normally paid in jadeite, many taking with them what they could hide in the dangling sleeves of their silken gowns. Wu Sibao, a former chauffeur, was promoted as the proxy Green Gang leader in Shanghai and extorted so much money, property and jewels from the rich and not-so-rich Chinese that he earned the moniker 'Little Du'.[20] The big boss maintained close contact with Chiang Kai-shek, in 1938 flying to see him in Hankow, a city up the Yangze in east central China to where the KMT leader had fled as the Japanese sacked Nanking. There, W. H. Auden and Christopher Isherwood, on a literary tour of the Chinese non-war, bumped into the 'thin sphinx' whose feet, 'in their silk socks and smart pointed European boots, emerging from beneath the long silken gown', were 'peculiar and inexplicably terrifying'.[21]

Jadeite dealer Curio Chang was already in Hankow when the Marco Polo Bridge incident occurred, but the following autumn he skipped to Hong Kong only weeks before Hankow also fell to the Japanese advance. As Chiang Kai-shek high-tailed it 500 miles further up-river, Curio Chang left China altogether. He headed for Switzerland – his treasure chest preceding him – and then on to Paris, the city of his youth, where he rekindled his friendship with Hui-lan Koo.

Although Chiang Kai-shek refused to declare war, the Imperial legacy was secretly on the move. When fighting had broken out near Shanghai in August 1937, curator Chuang Shang-yen had been ordered to find a new hiding place for the Qing treasure trove. The curator's son recalled the plan in meticulous detail. The best items from the Imperial collection filled 80 cases that were transported to Hunan University in south-east China. Chuan Ling told us:

> As the fighting continued my father ordered the boxes to be moved again and within days of us leaving his decision proved fortuitous. The Japanese bombed Hunan into rubble. But by then we were on the way to Anshun in Kweichow Province. It was an unremarkable town but it had deep caves behind a monastery where my father stored the crates. Whenever there was time he would get the staff to open them up so the antiquities could be aired.

By the time Nanking fell, everything had been spirited into the Chinese interior. 'There was one shipment of 9639 wooden cases that was put on amphibious vessels and trucks, heading for Loshan, in the mountains of Sichuan,' recalled Chuang Ling. 'The third group of treasures was just as well travelled. The boxes were first put on trains and then on trucks, 7229 cases that were taken to Omei in Sichuan. The trucks crashed; they fell off the mountain tracks, toppled into ditches and had to be hauled out. But not one item was broken. Nothing was even creased or torn.'

Few outside China cared. Henry Luce, who was more frightened of Mao Zedong than Japan or the Nazis, promoted Madame Chiang to an apathetic readership as the ravishing face of the war against Communism. Shortly after Nanking fell, she adorned the cover of *Time* that declared her and her husband 'the couple of the year', even though in American diplomatic circles she was being described in more disparaging terms. Washington was warned, she had a 'temperament, which in an earlier epoch would have propelled her to the Dragon Throne'.[22] The 'couple of the year' were barely on speaking terms. Madame Chiang now addressed her husband as 'that man', after finding a woman's shoe under his bed, and concerned American diplomats fired off an official report:

> If the Madame, whose nature is both proud and puritanical, should openly break with her husband, the dynasty would be split and the effects both in China and abroad would be serious.[23]

In Britain, no one rhapsodised China's Number One Lady, although the public was by now familiar with her Generalissimo, courtesy of a BBC Radio comedy that featured a 'Mr Cash-My-Cheque'.[24]

There was, however, some discussion of the hardship faced by Chinese refugees, but the subject of concern was dogs, a theme that Hui-lan Koo would have appreciated. Nanking had been ravaged but *Country Life* was more intrigued by a footnote about an oil painting of a Pekinese reclining on red cushions that hung in the royal kennels at Windsor Castle. A letter written by General J. H. Dunne of the 99th Regiment in 1861 had come to light, and it told the story of how the officer had shipped the Dowager Empress Cixi's Pekinese back to London:

On board the steamer coming home it became a regular matter of contention among the ladies as to who should be allowed to take charge of [Looty], and I was obliged to appoint an American young lady to whom it was alone entrusted. It was a general favourite among the passengers and used to run along the saloon table to escape their caresses.[25]

Country Life revealed that in Queen Victoria's care Looty had survived until 1872 and was in fact one of four Pekinese to have been 'rescued' from the Summer Palace. Admiral Lord John Hay had taken two and the Duchess of Richmond, from whose stock the Goodwood Kennel was founded, had given a home to the remaining animal. *Vanity Fair* joined the debate, noting that the 'Chinese Lion Dog' puppies presented to princesses Elizabeth and Margaret Rose, the daughters of the new King, were descendants of Cixi's looted stock.

Barbara Hutton, also the proud owner of a Pekinese puppy, was now in London, having enraged the American public yet again. This time she had renounced her US citizenship to save 400,000 US dollars in taxes, but spent fifteen times that amount on jewellery in Bond Street and on property in Regent's Park, where she purchased the second largest private residence in town, Lord Rothermere's estate. Here she learned that Europe was heading for war and it was Joe Kennedy who told her. Calling her to his office in Grosvenor Square, Kennedy suggested that Barbara Hutton leave Britain, close down her Regency palace, that she had renamed Winfield House in memory of her grandfather, and become his mistress, an offer that she refused while being 'chased around his desk'. She had already divorced Count von Reventlow, who had earned 1 million US dollars for his troubles and was in the midst of an affair with Queen Victoria's great-great-grandson, Prince Friedrich of Prussia. Her time was short, so she hired Pitt & Scott to make an inventory of her vast collection of French antiques and 'priceless jade collection'. One of the packers remembers:

There were many Oriental objects – intricately carved Chinese panels, jade screens, silk tapestry and so forth . . . I recall the astonishing sight of a huge pile of shoes left in a corner of the main bedroom, all size four, all specially made . . . no less than 300 pairs.[26]

While Pitt & Scott shuttled between Regent's Park and Worcester, where the ex-Countess's Imperial war-time depository was to be based, she bathed off the coast of Capri before heading to Biarritz to pick up her son, Lance Reventlow. Together they travelled on to Milan where Count Galeazzo, Edda Ciano's husband, arranged visas and tickets on the Italian liner *Conte di Savoia* bound for New York. Hutton was heading for the Hotel Pierre on Fifth Avenue and into the arms of yet another lover, Cary Grant.

In the Cathay's Horse and Hounds bar, Sir Victor was confidently predicting that the Japanese 'would bleed to death in China'. But before the war had even been declared he had dined, danced and dealt his way through Mexico, Peru and Chile, establishing secret trusts, before flying on to New York via the West Indies and Florida, where he examined off-shore tax regulations.[27] 'He was seen with so many film stars that it was wrongly thought that he might be planning to buy into Hollywood.'[28] In Shanghai, only W. H. Auden and Christopher Isherwood dared to bust in on the continuing reverie: 'In this city – conquered, yet unoccupied, by its conquerors – the mechanism of the old life is still ticking but seems doomed to stop, like a watch dropped in a desert.'[29]

By the time Sir Victor returned to Shanghai in 1939, the International Settlement was a war shelter, offering protection to Jews fleeing Germany and Poland. Now he secretly sold his two largest Burmese sapphires and a stash of Imperial jadeite necklaces as a contribution towards the purchase of British fighter aircraft.[30]

France fell in June 1940, but since the Nazis were not at war with China, Hui-lan Koo was barely affected – until she began to miss her European friends. In her chauffeur-driven Buick she toured Vichy, only to discover the scale of the deepening crisis. 'There was literally no tea, no coffee, no soap, no salad oil.' But within a matter of weeks the pyjama-party was over and Hui-lan was advised to leave for her mother's apartment in Manhattan's Upper East Side. She slipped out of France, loaded down with trunks that contained the best of her Imperial collection and a menagerie of furs: a chinchilla, a mink and, concealed in a silver-fox cape, her priceless Persian Pepper.

Within months, the great edifice came crashing down. Mussolini had already sided with Hitler in 1939, and in September 1940 the

Japanese followed. The bombing of Pearl Harbor on Sunday 7 December 1941 brought America into the conflagration and the following day, when the Japanese rolled, unopposed, into the International Settlement, Chiang Kai-shek was finally forced to declare war.

The Japanese sequestrated the assets of the Hong Kong and Shanghai Bank, transforming the Cathay Hotel into a holding centre for Allied consular officials and Jardine Matheson's palace of plenty into a military nerve-centre. By December the Long Bar was propping up Japanese Naval Intelligence. Then Shanghailanders started to vanish. Hugh Collar, chairman of the British Residents' Association, watched the creeping terror:

> A few days after Pearl Harbour, about 10 British subjects . . . and a number of Americans were arrested . . . From then on ensued a slow but remorseless series of arrests of 'enemy nationals' who disappeared into the dark portals of Bridge House, the Gendarmerie Headquarters.[31]

Collar sought treatment for those who were released from the former Chinese hotel, their bodies now pockmarked with cigarette burns, striped by a bamboo cane, shoulders dislocated, men made dumb by electric baths, bloated and torn by water torture.

Deep in the Chinese interior, 1400 miles upriver from Shanghai, Chiang Kai-shek was holed up 'on a slice of land shaped like a piece of pie' at the confluence of the Yangze and the Jialing rivers. Chongqing was a joyless place of 'no dancing or light', so cold in winter that its inhabitants stomped around in several layers of sables and quilted jackets, sheepskin boots on their feet. Isolated in the centre of Sichuan province, cursed with 'the weather of depression', a constant battle against driving wind and fog that only cleared for two months of the year, the 'godforsaken hole's' only asset was that the Japanese air force could not see to bomb it. There was 'nothing to do but get drunk and ride funny little ponies up and down the hills', Emily Hahn wrote after waiting there for a year to interview Madame Chiang.[32]

For once in his life Chiang Kai-shek had been pro-active and, foreseeing that China could lose its sea-coast to Japan, had opened up a 715-mile network of tracks that linked Chongqing to Emperor

Qianlong's Jade Road. If the Japanese won control of Shanghai, supplies bound for Chiang Kai-shek could be offloaded in British Rangoon, taken by train north-west to Lashio and then put on trucks that made their way up his 'Burma Road' towards the purple mountains of Yunnan. Dragon Cloud, the Yunnan warlord Lung Yun, who had made his fortune smuggling jadeite and opium, graciously allowed the aid to pass through his territory. When the Japanese learned that Qianlong's Jade Road had been reopened, they calculated that unless it was cut off, the Generalissimo could survive in his bolt-hole for years.

⬧

In the midst of the upheavals, a ship had slipped unnoticed out of Rangoon on 8 August 1940. On board were two Chinese sailors who were unknown to the regular deck-hands. Tan Luan Shung and Tan Su Taung intended to make contact with Mao Zedong through his agents in Shanghai, but they caught the wrong ship and docked in Amoy, a southern port in Fujian Province that was under Japanese control. The sailors were arrested and unmasked as Burmese students. One was Aung San, a 26-year-old from a family of 'freedom fighters', general secretary of the 'Our Burma Association' that was seeking military support for an independence campaign. The other was Mya Hlaing, another student radical, and so in Amoy, Japanese and Burmese aspirations met.

Instead of imprisoning the stowaways, the Japanese put them through military training and smuggled Aung San back into Rangoon in February 1941. Within four months he had recruited 30 comrades, including Shu Maung, a post-office clerk with extreme right-wing views. A womaniser and gambler, who had surprised the nationalists when he asked to join their movement, Shu Maung promptly adopted a pseudonym, Ne Win, 'brilliant like the sun.'

In December 1941, the activists were transported to Bangkok where they formed the Burma Independence Army (BIA) that early the following year secretly re-entered Rangoon accompanied by Japanese troops. Aung San and his men had agreed to assist Japan's operation to shut down Qianlong's Jade Road in exchange for aid in their independence struggle, and the BIA rapidly recruited more than 30,000 volunteers.

America had realised the significance of China and Burma as soon as it entered the war, and in early 1942 dispatched General Joseph Stilwell to Chongqing. A former US military attaché, he was known as Vinegar Joe because of his acerbic disposition. When he arrived he found that there was 'nowhere to live apart from cardboard houses' and the restaurants only served black-skinned chicken. He had been sent to act as Chiang Kai-shek's chief-of-staff, an advisor and motivator to the man who, in January, had been made Supreme Allied Commander of the Chinese theatre of war. But Chiang Kai-shek spoke no English and so Madame Chiang was enlisted as liaison. Snow White, as she was code-named by the Americans, was immortalised in Vinegar Joe's diary, a thumbnail sketch that bore echoes of another century and a yellow curtain:

> A clever, brainy woman. Sees the Western viewpoint. Direct, forceful, energetic, loves power, eats up publicity and flattery, pretty weak on her history. Can turn on charm at will. And knows it. Great influence on Chiang Kai-shek.[33]

Vinegar Joe was assigned a small 'cardboard house' down the road from the Chiangs' imposing stone mansion on the 'slice of pie's' northern shoulder.

Daily, Stilwell was summoned up the hill to the big house, and it was only a matter of months before the Chongqing marriage of convenience was showing signs of strain. At the end of March, Rangoon fell to the Japanese, aided by Aung San's BIA, and KMT troops gave up central Burma with barely a fight. On 29 April Japanese and BIA forces took Lashio, severing Qianlong's Jade Road. Thousands of British soldiers and civilians fled across the hostile razor-back mountains and through the treacherous necropolis of Hukawng, the Kachin valley of death. Staggering in the footsteps of George Bayfield, they limped into Manipur, a princely state in the north-east corner of British India. By July 1942, the Great Golden Land was in Japanese hands.

As the Imperial Nippon Army dug in, over the border cultures clashed. Anxious to penetrate Japanese lines, Vinegar Joe planned an ambitious counter-attack with 30 Chinese divisions, but none of the repeatedly promised troops materialised. As the weeks turned into months, Stilwell warned Washington that the Generalissimo endorsed a system of institutionalised graft that saw his senior officers steal their men's pay and provisions, purchased with American loans. His fears were supported by John Service, political observer for the US State Department in Chongqing, who warned Franklin Roosevelt: 'From his [Chiang Kai-shek] contact with the gangster underworld he learned the usefulness of threats and blackmail. Chiang shows these traits in everything he does.'[34] In his private diary, Stilwell vented his frustration: 'The troubles of a Peanut dictator,' he scribbled on 29 September 1942 as he watched the Jialing River glug by and a sickly fog consume the KMT base. 'It is patently impossible for me to compete with the swarms of parasites and sycophants that surround him.'

Snow White attempted to arbitrate between Stilwell and her husband, emerging from the big house in a sedan chair, bearing gifts of jadeite for Winifred, Stilwell's wife, a cabochon and a Qing pendant, before delivering the Generalissimo's latest excuses. But when she realised that Stilwell's silence could not be bought, Madame Chiang leap-frogged him and launched her own face-saving campaign in Washington.

Snow White's arrival in the United States had been preceded by that of jadeite dealer Curio Chang who, having finally been dislodged from his Parisian air-raid shelter, had set up home in New York. But while he now surrounded himself with a circle of pacifists who persuaded him to sell the Stone of Heaven to fund a campaign for global peace, Madame Chiang waged war. She engineered a highly unusual appearance before Congress in February 1943 wearing a carefully chosen wardrobe that matched the American persona created for her by Henry Luce. *Newsweek* reported that she wore an elegant, long, black dress, 'her skirt split almost to the knee. Her smooth black hair was coiled simply at the nape of her neck. Her jewels were of priceless jade.'

Jewellers in Hong Kong and Shanghai whispered that Madame Chiang's Imperial jadeite saddle ring had once belonged to the Dowager Empress Cixi, her shoes were decorated with pearls that Pu Yi claimed had come from the phoenix crown, and on her wrists were translucent bangles that were also said to have come from the

Imperial tombs. Her speech, if anyone was listening, touched on China's friendship with America, 'unsurpassed in the annals of history', and on Japan's 'sadistic fury'.[35]

One month later, Madame Chiang roused a rally at Madison Square Garden before setting off on a pan-American tour that reached its climax at the Hollywood Bowl at the end of March. Mary Pickford, Rita Hayworth, Marlene Dietrich and Claudette Colbert were among thousands who ogled the Imperial jewellery while listening to a re-enactment of the fall of Nanking, where 'invaders had plundered and stripped the crucified populace of all means of livelihood'. Snow White's evangelical show was stage-managed by David O. Selznick who, four years earlier, had produced *Gone with the Wind,* winning ten Academy Awards. Within six months Madame Chiang had raised 17 million US dollars for the United China War Relief and returned to Washington triumphant. But she had a score to settle, and asked Franklin Roosevelt if Stilwell was effective, questioning the General's understanding of the Chinese. Her queries were filed away.

Oblivious to Snow White's double-dealing, Vinegar Joe's war had taken a turn for the better. Deploying US Army engineers, he had branched out on his own and begun constructing a new 478-mile track that would replace the fallen Jade Road as a supply line between India and Chongqing. It was to pass over 'the Hump', some of the wildest and most uncharted territory in the region, and would link the British railhead at Ledo in Assam with the savage no-man's-land of Upper Burma. Stilwell's road would cut across the tortuous Pet Kai range, an untamed country inhabited by the descendants of the head-hunters who, in 1836, had revealed to Sepoy Singh their secret Kasa Naga Road. Since then they had had little or no contact with the outside world, but Stilwell's men succeeded in cutting a path that roughly traced the ancient route. From the Assam border it passed through the heart of the Hukawng Valley, skirting around the foothills of Loi Lem before coming within a few miles of the jadeite mines and in sight of Kamaing, where Dr Bayfield had almost lost his life, before finally pitching up in Mogaung.

The British would attempt to infiltrate this no-man's-land from India, mounting hit-and-run operations against Japanese supply and communication lines. But the history of the first Anglo-Burma war of 1824, when troops had been forced to abandon a similar plan, must have tolled in their ears. One nineteenth-century account concluded:

> the long distances to be traversed through jangal [sic], swamp and mountain; in country sparsely populated, and yielding no supplies fit for any army of civilised men, presented formidable obstacles to the march of a European force.[36]

Brigadier General Orde Wingate, who hung an alarm clock from the belt of his battle dress and packed a Bible in his knapsack, was charged with the mission. He resurrected a military strategy voiced 180 years earlier by Emperor Qianlong, who had gleaned it from the pages of Sun Tzu's *Art of War*. A specialist in unconventional warfare, Wingate's methods had been honed in Palestine and Africa, and he now sought out Upper Burma's *Ye Jein*, the Kachin.

Although the Burmans, who made up 60 per cent of the country's population, had been galvanised by Aung San and their hatred of the British into supporting the Japanese, the ethnic tribes who lived in the horse-shoe of hills and valleys that made up the border areas bore no allegiance to the general secretary of the Our Burma Association. Relations between the British and the Kachin had come a long way since the days of Captain Adamson. By 1897 the British had given up trying to pacify the wild tribes of the north and instead employed their martial skills, enlisting them into the Upper Burma military police stationed at Bhamo. By the First World War, 349 Kachin had joined the 85th Burma Rifles and the 1/10 Gurkha Rifles.[37] After their success in France and Gallipoli, the Kachin had been allowed to parade through London with their *dahs* slung over their backs, and by 1937, more than 850 had signed up to fight.

Now Wingate recruited the Kachin to guide a brigade of 2800 British soldiers. Known as the Chindits, after the winged *chinthe* icons that had once guarded the Lion Throne, in February 1943 they crossed from North-east India into Burma, fording the Chindwin River before heading for the Irrawaddy. By May, exhausted and malarial, having marched for more than 1000 miles, the Chindits were forced to disperse, having lost a third of their strength and most of their equipment. Although Wingate dubbed the operation a dismal failure, he had radically changed military thinking and vanquished forever the spectre of a hostile jungle that devoured Western soldiers.

The Kachin had proved so useful that another unconventional plan was immediately unfurled. In late 1943, British agents parachuted 'into the guts of the enemy' to recruit hundreds of Kachin into informal levies. These tiny, genial warriors whose survival skills and affinity with the hills had been honed by generations of jungle warfare, as Captain Hannay had noted in his log of 1830, wreaked havoc among the Japanese forces and earned the nickname 'Amiable Assassins'.

By the time Madame Chiang arrived back in Chongqing on 4 July 1943, General Stilwell was barely on speaking terms with the Generalissimo, whose promised troops had still to show up. Chongqing was a 'Chinese cesspool' inhabited by 'a gang of thugs with the one idea of perpetuating themselves and their machine'. Stilwell had privately begun to question the US backing of the KMT: 'We are manoevred into the position of having to support this rotten regime and glorify its figurehead, the all-wise, great patriot and soldier – Peanut. My God.'

For the second time Stilwell struck out on his own and formed a secret unit, Detachment 101, staffed by US military advisors and more than 11,000 Kachin tribesmen, trained by Wingate and commanded by Frank Dow Merrill. 'Merrill's Marauders operated deep in the jungle as individual agents, in small groups, or in battalion strength. They kept the Japanese under surveillance, raided, ambushed and harassed without cause,' Charles Simpson, a 101 veteran recalled. 'The high command in the theatre credited almost 90 per cent of its intelligence to Detachment 101.'[38] Simpson remembered how General Stilwell, obviously unfamiliar with Captain Hannay's report, quizzed one smiling tribesman about the accuracy of his reported kills. The Kachin opened a bamboo tube and dumped a pile of dry ears on the table. 'Divide by two,' he told the General.[39]

The Kachin didn't work for free. The Americans and the British had secretly gone into business with the Dragon Cloud warlord, buying up stocks of opium and jadeite that Lung Yun's men had cleared from the mines before the Japanese occupation. Ian Fellowes-Gordon, a British officer who helped recruit the Kachin levies, recalled how the US Army Air Corps flew in 'large quantities of opium', dropped in 1.28-kilogram packets from Dakotas, distributing them 'with typical efficiency in ample, generous doses'.[40] The British used opium in the northern Kachin villages in exchange for labour and food, but the Americans 'were now paying a number of their guerrillas with it'. When recruitment was running at a low ebb, it was jadeite that was exchanged for Kachin labour, and the stones also bought the Allies shelter and supplies. To raise cash for the British exchequer, the Secret Intelligence Service and Special Operations Executive also traded the Stone of Heaven on the Chinese black market.[41]

Back in Chongqing, Chiang Kai-shek's inaction was threatening his American backing, and the Generalissimo was also aware of the contempt in which Winston Churchill held him. He dispatched Dr Koo to London on a charm offensive. Hui-Lan sailed on the *Queen Elizabeth* from New York and, finding the cabins packed with uniformed men, the deck a squalid mess of soldiers, complained to the captain, who requisitioned a stateroom for her. But she was still unable to sleep. The liner's fog-horn was too close to her room and she pleaded for it to be turned off. The crew asked if Hui-lan had read about the *Titanic*. It was only the echo of the fog-horn bouncing off the icebergs ahead that alerted the captain to their location.

In London she resumed her social whirl. She took tea with Lady Cunard, bumped into Randolph Churchill and 'munched thin buttered bread' with King George VI and Queen Elizabeth at Buckingham Palace. Queen Mary teased Hui-lan over dinner with the prospect of seeing her late husband, King George V's collection of looted jadeite and ceramics that had so indiscreetly been revealed by *Apollo* in 1933. Hui-lan Koo recalled Queen Mary saying: 'I would like you to see my husband's Chinese collection in Buckingham Palace. The room is kept just as he arranged it and will be until I die.'

In Peking, a death on 8 January 1944 threatened to expose the legacy of the Qing to yet another indignity. Edmund Backhouse, one time translator and peripatetic looter, had died in St Michael's Hospital, attended by French nuns. The British government had assumed that he had passed away many years before when he had disappeared into the rabbit warren of *hutongs* wearing a Confucian white silk gown and long, flowing beard. Backhouse was buried at the Catholic cemetery in Chala, where the Jesuits at the Imperial court had been interred, but he left behind an obituary: a typed manuscript encased in a Chinese box. The story told in *Décadence Mandchoue* was explosive. The Oxford drop-out had conducted an extraordinary love affair with the Dowager Empress Cixi, whom he had met in 1902 when he was 29 and she was 67. 'Was I sexually adequate for her majesty's overflowing carnality?' Backhouse asked in his explicit confession. 'ALAS! I doubted it and wondered if I should develop the necessary timely orgasm to meet her unsated lust.' There followed several detailed accounts of the odd couple's bedroom antics:

> Her majesty's bedchamber was blazing with a score of lights . . . Li [Lianying] accompanied me to the Phoenix couch and the Empress exclaimed: 'My bed is cold . . . now exhibit to me your genitals for I know I shall love them.'[42]

Backhouse, who claimed that he used the bizarre relationship to further his collection of Imperial jadeite and antiques, also wrote of visiting Cixi's ravaged tomb in 1928. 'Lying before us,' he wrote, 'her face drawn and ghastly but with familiar features as when I had last seen her 20 years ago ... her mouth wide, extended and set in a horrible grin, eyes partially open and glazed with a yellowish film.'

☒

In the spring of 1944, the combined forces of Wingate's Chindits, Merrill's Marauders, the Amiable Assassins and Chiang Kai-shek's long-awaited army finally moved on Japanese positions in Upper Burma, pushing them back, foxhole by foxhole. Stilwell, delighted to be in the thick of it at last, described the jungle trek in his diary with a humour that had been lacking in Captain Adamson when he marched through the same territory 56 years earlier:

> We eat straight rations or Chinese chow and we live where we have to. And the trails are tough, and we get wet and we get muddy, but we sleep soundly and the food tastes good because we are usually hungry. I expect to see Tarzan any minute now. The jungle is full of his long swinging vines.

After a bloody and prolonged battle, the Chinese and Merrill's Marauders captured Myitkyina airfield on 17 May, and by 26 June the Chindits, led by Brigadier 'Mad Mike' Calvert, had seized Mogaung, their fighting strength reduced by malaria, typhoid and battle from 3500 to just 300 men. But Wingate was not around to see the fruits of his labour, as he had died when his plane ditched over Manipur two months before. By August, Myitkyina was secured by the Chinese, and the Japanese front in Burma was irreparably damaged. Reporters filing copy to America arrived at a novel reason for the performance of Chiang Kai-shek's soldiers. 'Chinese troops in Upper Burma had something more to fight with than their British or American comrades in the Allied recapture of Mogaung,' wrote a correspondent for the *Christian Science Monitor*. 'They had three times a thousand years of legend and devotion centred in the stone that gave Mogaung its nickname, "The City of Jade".'[43]

Madame Chiang, still estranged from her husband, had skipped Chongqing and was in South America. Accompanied by her sister Ai-ling, she had flown to Brazil, where it was rumoured that she was investing her family's ever-growing wealth in oil, minerals, shipping and real estate.[44] What she left behind in China was an increasingly bitter struggle between Stilwell and the Generalissimo. 'The cure for China's trouble is the elimination of Chiang Kai-shek,' fumed Vinegar Joe in his diary.

But it was Stilwell who ultimately lost his grip on power. On 19 October 1944 the poison injected into the White House by Snow White the year before worked its way into the American political system. Stilwell was recalled by Roosevelt. 'Ignored, insulted, double-crossed, delayed, obstructed for three years,' he privately raged. 'Use our air force. Borrow our money. Refuse us men for the equipment we haul.' Even the Chinese people could see what Washington was blind to, Stilwell wrote: '[They] welcome the Reds as being the only visible hope of relief from . . . [Chiang Kai-shek's] Gestapo . . . greed, corruption, favouritism, more taxes, a ruined country, terrible waste of life, callous disregard of all rights of men.'

⬥

The jadeite dealer Curio Chang celebrated the Japanese surrender on 2 September 1945 by opening his apartment windows to listen to the rejoicing in the Manhattan streets below. Having become blind, he had joined an exclusive group of wealthy and sightless jade dealers, Abe Gump being the founder member.

Nationalist celebrations in China were premature. Mao Zedong's troops began rolling down from Manchuria, and Du Yuesheng scurried to Hong Kong. In 1946 Lucien Ovadia, Sir Victor Sassoon's cousin, returned to Shanghai to salvage what he could amid the racketeering, crippling inflation and food shortages. He found the Cathay Hotel fully booked, as refugees converged on the former International Settlement, anxious to see what had become of their businesses and homes. General Albert Coady Wedemeyer, Stilwell's replacement, was occupying Sir Victor's suite and refusing to move out.

In the autumn of 1948 the Jade King also fled south. Frank Tieh recalled how his father took the best of their stones, rough boulders, jewellery and carvings from the vaults of his Langfang store, wrapping them in paper before sealing them in wooden crates that were loaded onto a ship bound for Shanghai. 'But there was a storm,' Frank told us. 'The ship listed badly and then suddenly it sank off the Shandong Peninsula. My father was miraculously rescued but was forced to abandon his treasures.'

While Mr Tieh waited for news of his lost cargo, he sent an emergency telegram to his family in Peking, advising them to stay put. But the telegram operator was careless. 'The telegram said that we should leave immediately,' Frank told us, and his family arrived in Shanghai days later. The Jade King's fury was tempered when he learned that they had boarded the last flight out of Peking. On 31 January 1949 the People's Liberation Army swept into the old Imperial capital and immediately occupied Langfang, raiding Tieh's two-storey shop, confiscating 8000 jades and jadeite items. The news of Langfang's fall reached the International Settlement on the same day that salvage divers appeared with Mr Tieh's lost cargo. The family immediately boarded a ship bound for Taiwan, having used up a lifetime's luck. 'My father started growing a beard during the crossing and until his death he refused to shave it. He called it his 10,000-year beard. It reminded him of what we had lost and also what we had won,' Frank said. 'We still have the receipt from the Chinese government for the jadeite they confiscated. I recently found out that some of it is now displayed in the Forbidden City.'

Lucien Ovadia was frantically busy. He haggled and dealt, selling off a portfolio of property, but only managed to raise a paltry 1.4 million Chinese dollars for Sir Victor Sassoon, who folded his Bombay estates and businesses for 30.9 million rupees. Hui-lan Koo was packing too. Dr Koo had been sent back to Washington to canvass against the Communist advance, and now she wrapped up her jadeite collection, screens, ceramics and bronzes in paper before leaving London for her new home, the former residence of Alexander Graham Bell. When she arrived in the United States she declared herself 'a sensation' and wrote in her diary: 'I had never had this kind of attention before. My jewels and especially my Imperial jades that are the most famous in the world were much discussed. One magazine said in a caption under a picture that I was the most beautiful and bejewelled person in the world.' Her old friend the Duchess of Windsor was also winning column inches in New York. Wallis Simpson had fallen for the charms of Jimmy Donahue, Barbara Hutton's bisexual cousin. 'Jimmy escorts the D&D everywhere and stays up playing cards with the Duchess long after His Royal Highness has retired,' an American columnist sniped. Weeks later the couple were seen holding hands at a fashionable club. 'She's marvellous,' Donahue brayed, playing to the crowd. 'The best cock sucker I've ever known.'[45]

On the West Coast, Barbara Hutton and her baggage train were also on the move. Having married her film star Cary Grant, the couple dubbed by reporters 'Cash 'n' Cary' had spent the war in Buster Keaton's mansion in Beverley Hills. There she idled away much of her time partying with the likes of Marlene Dietrich and Merle Oberon, before celebrating VJ Day with yet another divorce, citing 'grievous mental distress, suffering and anguish'. The ex-Mrs Cary Grant presented Winfield House in Regent's Park to the American government and turned her attention to Paris and Morocco. Barbara Hutton took a 800 US dollars-a-day suite in the Ritz and filled it with the jadeite she had stored in Worcester and a new husband, Prince Igor Troubetzkoy, an amateur cyclist and climber whose heart lay in the Alps while his eyes were firmly fixed on the social summit. In Tangiers, Hutton outbid General Franco to buy Sidi Hosni Palace for 50,000 US dollars and transformed it into an eclectic wonderland. Her new neighbour, the writer Paul Bowles, wryly described Sidi Hosni as her 'Garden of Allah':

> She liked everything around her to show an element of the unreal and took great pains to transform the reality into a continuous fantasy, which seemed to her to be sufficiently charming to be taken seriously.[46]

Chiang Kai-shek was finally facing up to reality. Hundreds of thousands of disaffected Chinese were falling behind Mao Zedong, whose army was pressing towards Nanking and Shanghai. But while the Generalissimo lectured on the collapse of Communism he secretly removed his assets from China. The Imperial treasures were brought down from their Sichuan caves to Shanghai, where the US Navy was on hand to smuggle them to Chiang Kai-shek's new fiefdom of Taiwan, the former island of Formosa that the KMT had pacified, massacring thousands of indigenous inhabitants. Chuang Ling, the palace curator's son, told us how at the age of nine he had accompanied the legacy of the Emperors on its final voyage. 'It all happened so very fast. I remember it was a terrible day. A storm and rain. The American and Chinese navies were standing by as we boarded a ship with the crates. We were on it for five or six days and a terrible typhoon lashed at us. The cabins were packed with sailors and we had to sleep on top of each other. The air below was rancid. I can still taste it now. We arrived in Taiwan on Christmas Day 1948 and as we disembarked the sky cleared.'

A sugar factory was commandeered as a temporary depository for the haul of 242,591 Imperial artefacts, while a hill was hollowed out on the outskirts of Taipei. A memorial was erected to announce that the Imperial palace collection 'has now become the precious cultural property of all Chinese people'.[47]

On the mainland, the advance of the Chinese people had reached critical mass. For two months Mao's People's Liberation Army engaged the Nationalists, culminating in a Communist military victory on 10 January 1949, news of which raced to Washington, where Madame Chiang was once again lobbying for money. But Snow White had lost her lustre and China's First Lady was cold-shouldered by President Harry Truman, who wrote in his memoirs: 'She [Madame Chiang] came to the United States for more hand-outs. I wouldn't let her stay in the White House like Roosevelt did. I don't think she liked it very much, but I didn't care one way or the other about what she liked and what she didn't like.' Truman later publicly accused her family of misappropriating $750 million of American aid and concealing it in South America and the United States.[48]

By the time the Communists finally rolled into Shanghai on 27 May 1949, Chiang Kai-shek was already in Taiwan, having boarded a gunboat that followed in the wake of his Imperial treasures, its hold weighed down with three million ounces of gold. Ai-ling, Madame Chiang's sister, had fled to the States with her husband and brother on diplomatic passports, allegedly taking with them another three million ounces from China's vanishing gold reserves. Sir Victor Sassoon was in New York when the teleprinter regurgitated the news of the fall of the Paris of the East. 'Well, there it is,' he said. 'I gave up India and China gave me up.' Soon the State Enterprise Company, formed by the new People's Republic of China that had been proclaimed by Mao Zedong from Tiananmen Gate, swallowed up the remainder of Sir Victor's property empire, converting the Cathay into the Peace Hotel. The Shanghai Club, Sir Victor was depressed to hear, had become the Seaman's Union, and instead of gin slings the Long Bar now sold 'watery Chinese near-beer'.

More than two million refugees converged on Hong Kong, trans-forming the colony into a haven for jadeite dealers, cutters, jew-ellers and collectors, who set up shop on Kowloon's Canton Road. Men and women with bags of jewellery would turn up unan-nounced at the doors of the wealthy wearing shabby gowns and scuffed slippers, but their haughty demeanour gave them away. Sammy Chow, a Shanghai jeweller before his family ran from China to establish a new gem business in the Peninsula Hotel on the Kowloon waterfront, stocked his shop with refugee treasure. From behind a great expanse of walnut, slices of jadeite at his feet, Chow recalled how business boomed and Barbara Hutton came to the door. 'Barbara stay in Marco Polo suite, upstair, and then she come down to shop. She love bangle. She love their song, love the clink.

When she stay at Marco Polo she order Chinese musician to play at dinner. Sometime she dress in Imperial Dragon robe and wear beautiful jadeite necklace her father give her for wedding number one. All time, even when she go on junk trip in harbour, she wear that necklace.'[49]

Another two million followed in Chiang Kai-shek's wake to join those, like the Tieh family, who had re-established their business in Taipei. Madame Chiang, who was by now commuting from New York State, still estranged from the Generalissimo, celebrated every birthday by sending a chauffeur-driven car to the Tiehs' house to collect the Jade King, who was once again surrounded by a court of wealthy admirers. He was still expected to present *Fu-jen* May-ling with the best jadeite in his shop, from which she would choose a special gift to present to herself.

But Shanghai was now 'as dead as the moon'. Writing about her childhood in the International Settlement, the Chinese author Lynn Pan recalled seeing 'scuffling, staring faces, someone making a spurt, women being herded past a long line of onlookers . . . an excitement breathing over the street'. The round-ups had begun and the 'hot-stream of sing-song girls' was bottled into detention centres:

> When I look back I see myself in a blue boiler-suit, cut one size too big to allow margin for growth . . . I see sartorial greyness . . . I see necklaces unclasped, brooches unpinned, flowers unworn, faces un-made-up, the ballrooms closed, the waltzes and foxtrots un-danced, the neon unlit. And against these an image from an older day, never to be conjured up in Shanghai again: a woman caped in chinchilla, one white-gloved hand resting on a mahogany rail.[50]

Ten

The New Lord of the Mines

Barbara Hutton could barely remember her days in Shanghai. The blur of gin, Coca-Cola and injected sheep cells that an avaricious quack claimed were life-enhancing, made even yesterday difficult to recall.

She had survived several suicide attempts and three disastrous marriages. Her white hair was now dyed a mousy brown, her slender face bloated, her health declining as rapidly as her self-confidence. In 1950, tiring of her White Russian cyclist, she had allotted him a French Chateau, a car and a life-time allowance of 1000 US dollars a month in a settlement that he complained failed to match those of his predecessors. Finding herself alone in Tucson, Arizona, where she was visiting her son Lance at his boarding school, she sought comfort with Michael Wilding, who was soon to marry Elizabeth Taylor. Two years later, the ex-Princess was seduced by husband number five, Zsa Zsa Gabor's boyfriend, Porfirio Rubirosa, a polo champion, diplomat and sexual athlete known as *Toujours Prêt*. Rubi had already entrapped Doris Duke, earning 500,000 US dollars on his wedding day and much more thirteen months later, when he readily agreed to a divorce. And his love affair with the second Gold Dust twin was equally rewarding, a 53-day romance that left him 3.5 million US dollars richer and sent Barbara into the arms of another young suitor, who was then filming *East of Eden*. When she came across James Dean at a Hollywood café he was drunk, so she bought him a burger before they slipped between the sheets. She recalled him leaving in her diary: 'I watched as he climbed on his motor cycle and disappeared around the bend, forever.'[1]

In New York, Curio Chang was confined to a wheelchair, and when he died on 3 September 1950 Chiang Kai-shek held a memorial service for him in Taipei. The following year, Du Yuesheng collapsed in his Hong Kong home, an opium pipe pressed to his lips. In Taipei, Chiang Kai-shek erected a statue commemorating the Green Gang godfather, the words 'loyalty' and 'integrity' inscribed upon it.

In the former Dutch Indies Sukarno, raised to power by the Japanese, had installed himself in the ex-Governor General's place in Jakarta. Now he dismantled the elected parliament and Indonesia's economy plummeted into free-fall, as did sugar baron Oei Tjie Sien's legacy, that was nationalised. 'I was becoming aware that my personal fortune would not last forever,' Hui-lan Koo privately admitted in her diary. These were difficult times for the 'heiress-of-the-moment', compounded by news that her mother's house in Paris had been taken over by squatters and that the Japanese had stolen jewellery from a bank vault in Tientsin. Hui-lan secretly pawned her Cartier tiara and the Bing Noi diamond. But she would never, voluntarily, part with her famous jadeite collection.

Neither would China's former Emperor, Henry Pu Yi, who had been pushed out of another job as Chief Executive of Manchukuo on 9 August 1945. Elizabeth, his wife, who had become a hopeless opium addict, fled to Kirin in Japan, where she died the following year, but Henry flew to Shenyang, a bulging suitcase in hand, only to be arrested by Soviet troops. The ex-Chief Executive was taken to a Russian prison camp in Chita, a spartan city near the Mongolia border. 'I had brought with me enough jewellery to last me for the rest of my life,' Pu Yi confided in his diary. But he was unprepared for prison life and, becoming fearful of his guards, foisted upon them handfuls of jadeite 'as a contribution to the Soviet Union's post-war reconstruction'. What was left was stashed beneath the false bottom of his suitcase, inside soap bars, behind radiators and under bushes in the prison garden.

Pu Yi remained oblivious to events in China until 31 July 1950, when he was recalled for re-education to Fushun, a miserable town on the outskirts of Shenyang, where he was force-fed the political texts on which the People's Republic of China had been founded. Separated from his servants and family, unable to even tie his shoelaces, Pu Yi became a fetid mess. From Fushun, the crumpled ex-Emperor and his suitcase were transferred to Harbin, north-east China's second largest city, where he was incarcerated in a former Japanese prison. Again he tried to win favour, offering a special gift to the People's Republic, a set of exquisitely carved Qianlong seals that he pushed across his captor's desk. The camp commandant sat stiffly for an eternity before advising Pu Yi that his gift would be added to the collection of artefacts that had been found behind radiators and under bushes in Chita, along with the jadeite presents he had given to his Russian guards. Nothing would part Pu Yi from a legacy that was fast becoming a body of evidence, in an investigation into his role as a Japanese collaborator and an Imperial cat burglar. There were still 468 items hidden beneath the false bottom of his battered trunk and Pu Yi, anxious to be distanced from his former self, now handed them all to the commandant.

The cultural relics were sent back to Beijing, China's resurrected capital, where they were given to Yang Boda, a bored young curator at the virtually empty ex-Forbidden City. It would be reopened in 1954 as the Imperial Palace Museum, a sign posted outside advising the public to 'value the cultural heritage of our ancestors, shoulder the historic mission of conserving their relics'. Professor Boda, who later became director of the museum, had retired by the time we met him in his tiny apartment in Beijing, beyond the walls of the ancient Tartar City that had been demolished in the 1950s to make way for a ring road. 'Pu Yi's relics? Yes I remember them,' he mumbled. 'There was nothing in that suitcase I was interested in.' He sat in silence in the stifling living room, its white-hot radiators centrally controlled, listening to the caged song-birds that chimed on a neighbour's balcony. 'Yes, there was jadeite, nephrite and diamonds,' he eventually explained. 'But what I thought about when I looked into that case was all of China's stolen cultural relics, and I was furious.' He swept a wisp of hair from his face and stomped into his study.

However, Professor Boda didn't mention the curious fund-raising programme initiated by the People's Republic. It was the Stone of Heaven that paid for the eves and lintels to be rebuilt, for the glaziers who replaced the shattered panes, for the carpenters who shored up the derelict pavilions and for historians like him to study what Chiang Kai-shek had cast aside. Jadeite, denigrated by Professor Boda and his government as a brash Qing novelty, transformed the dilapidated remains of fifteenth-century Ming Emperor Yongle's Imperial vision into a World Heritage site.

On a biting cold afternoon in New York in February 1999, a Chinese footman ushered us into a 13,667-square-foot apartment on Fifth Avenue, carpeted with Qianlong's dragon rugs, its shelves laden with ancient Chinese ceramics and calligraphy, to meet the only foreigner on China's Cultural Relics Committee. Robert H. Ellsworth, the son of La Ferne Hatfield, a Metropolitan Opera House singer famed for appearing on stage 'dressed in nothing but her pearls', began buying Imperial pieces in Beijing in 1949 and re-called how the Chinese government whetted his appetite. 'The best pieces of jadeite I saw that belonged to the Palace Museum were sold by them for restoration. Better they sell the green pebbles than something aesthetically important. The stone's not art, it's money. But a lot has been sold. There's no doubt about it,' he drawled.

Knocking back a triple bourbon from a silver chalice, 'dating to the crusades, not another piece like it', his leather waistcoat flapping, his arms a whirl, Ellsworth told us how he made a fortune trading Chinese art as his footman, powdered and perfumed, padded reverently around his Manhattan palace. The story of how Claudette Colbert had been his house-guest for 30 years filled a moment's silence, until the golf-ball cabochon that weighed down his little finger caught our eye. 'You like my rock?' Sucking the jadeite ball off an arthritic joint, he rolled 6 million US dollars across the table. 'I swapped it with a Hong Kong jeweller for 27 of the most important archaic jades in the world. It was one third of a large stop bead from one of Cixi's court necklaces that the jeweller had bought from the Chinese government in 1956.' A fresh cup of bourbon on a silver salver. A new packet of 555s. Ellsworth's Labrador dragged its bottom along Qianlong's dragon rug. 'The piece on my finger says I'm the biggest dealer in the world. It's my shop sign. I wear it when I'm gardening and when I go drinking. It's a question of face. I'm more a Chinese than the Chinese, according to the Chinese.'

On 4 December 1959, the man accused of betraying the Chinese received a surprising telegram. The Supreme People's Court announced that the 'Manchukuo war criminal Aisin-Gioro Pu Yi, aged 54, who has now served 10 years' detention' was pardoned. Five days later Citizen Pu Yi embarked on a tour of a city that he barely recognised. For the first time he saw Beijing's Tiananmen Square that had been concreted over in 1958. Citizen Pu Yi saw the Great Hall of the People, built to its west, and the Revolutionary Museum, built to its east. He made his way to the Imperial Palace Museum and patiently queued alongside thousands of others to press his face up against the fogged glass. 'Very little of the palace collection of jade, porcelain and calligraphy had been left,' Pu Yi noted forgetfully. But then he caught sight of a painting of the Spring Festival that reminded him of his brother, Pu Chieh, who had cut it down and smuggled it to Tientsin. 'How had it got back?' he pondered as he cycled beneath the great Meridian Gate.

Days later, Citizen Pu Yi received notice that he had been as-signed a new life. The ex-Emperor was now a handyman in Beijing's botanical gardens, where he would remain until his anony-mous death from cancer on 17 October 1967. By then the Cultural Revolution had pitched China into its second year of convulsions and the Red Guard confiscated the last Emperor's corpse. His ashes were consigned to a locked vault in the People's Cemetery in Bei-jing, despite Citizen Pu Yi's dying wish to be interred beside his adopted father, Emperor Guangxu, who had been buried in Xi Ling, the Western Necropolis.

⬚

Burma too was now a turbulent state. The Second World War had launched the Great Golden Land on a path to independence, but it had also aggravated centuries-old tensions between the Burman people and country's insular minority tribes.

In 1946, the 31-year-old nationalist leader Aung San had strug-gled to get Clement Attlee, the British Prime Minister, to the nego-tiating table, while the country's disparate ethnic groups accused him and the Burmans of being Japanese collaborators, although 11,480 guerrillas from the Burma Independence Army had switched sides to help the British storm Rangoon in May 1945. Aung San was painfully aware of the Great Golden Land's chaotic history. An ill-defined country with porous borders, Burma had al-ways been in a state of flux. Waves of migrants had trekked into the land lying in the folds of the Himalayas from China, Mongolia, Tibet and India, fighting over territory, forming disparate princely states that rose and fell amid such bloodshed and with such speed that few contemporary records survive. Today the landscape is dotted with the ruins of dynastic capitals, but often only words inscribed on pagoda foundation stones or onto monastic bells provide clues as to who had lived there, where they had come from and by whom they had been put to the sword or torch.

Only a union of states would keep intact the fragile cobweb of fiefdoms, and a British-backed investigation was launched to consider how to entice the tribes into Aung San's vision. It was a monumental task, made harder by the isolation of some, including the black-turbaned Wa head-hunters from Shan State, who failed to even understand the questions:

Q. What do you want the future to be of the Wa States?
A. We have not thought about that because we are wild people. We have never thought of the administrative future. We only think about ourselves.
Q. Don't you want education, clothing, good food, good houses, hospitals, etc.?
A. We are very wild people and we do not appreciate all these things.[2]

On 27 January 1947 Aung San flew to London and at last obtained Attlee's signature on an independence charter. Three months later the British 'Frontier Areas Committee of Inquiry' reported:

the hill tracts have three main sources of wealth and . . . it is going to be essential that these resources be developed in the full. Agriculture, Forests and Minerals have in the past provided Burma's wealth yet these great resources have invariably been left in the hands of inadequate government departments.[3]

Here was a remarkable admission by the British. Since the capture of the Lord of the Mines and his Great Golden Land in 1885 the Empire had been unable to find, chart or utilise the country's natural resources, particularly those hidden in the Kachin Hills. 'For a country possessing Burma's mineral wealth', the Mines Department established by the British 'was lamentable', the retreating Empire concluded.

umerous members
f the foreign
gations looted
hina of its Imperial
eritage in the weeks
llowing the Relief of Peking: (Clockwise
om top left) Sir Claude MacDonald, the
ritish minister, staged auctions in his gar-
en; Polly Smith, an American heiress, was
owered with looted gifts by admirers
cluding George Morrison, *The Times* cor-
spondent, who confided to his diary
efts that he never deigned to mention in
s dispatches; Edmund Backhouse, the
iled Oxford scholar, who donated his
oted collection to the Bodleian Library in
attempt to win a professorship.

Above: Two-year-old Pu Yi, swamped by his Imperial Dragon Robes, shortly before his coronation in 1908.

Above left: Reginald Johnston, tutor to the Last Emperor of China, adopted the sable robes of a First Rank Mandarin and was presented with an Imperial Green Jade ring by his grateful student.

Henry Pu Yi, the Last Emperor of China, with his wife Elizabeth Wan Jung, having rejected Imperial robes for Western fashions while imprisoned in the Forbidden City.

With his eyes of 'the true cat green', secret society boss Du Yuesheng, seen here on the right, controlled 1930s Shanghai and titillated the European cocktail circuit with his resemblance to Dr Fu Manchu and his reputation as 'killer of a thousand men'.

'Poor, little rich girl', Barbara Hutton, the Woolworth heiress, wearing her legendary jadeite wedding necklace to the Metropolitan Opera House in 1933, shortly before she left for Shanghai.

Heiress Madame Wellington Koo, voted the best dressed lady in China by Vogue, chats with another doyenne of the Shanghai party circuit, her best friend Edda Ciano, Benito Mussolini's daughter.

Madame Koo 'munched thin buttered bread' with the future Queen Mother, at a tea party at Buckingham Palace during World War Two. Edwina Mountbatten looks on.

Chiang Kai-shek with his second wife Jennie Ch'en shortly before he asked her to temporarily 'step aside' so he could marry May-ling Soong.

The Generalissimo and the third Madame Chiang Kai-shek sharing a rare joke with General 'Vinegar Joe' Stilwell, who would soon damn them both as thieves and parasites.

Madames Chiang Kai-shek and Wellington Koo, rivals for the title of China's fu-jen, Number One Lady, resplendent in jade at a US fundraiser for China relief.

Sir Victor Sassoon, the Emperor of Shanghai's Cathay Hotel, and the 'Southern hill-billy' he married after she nursed him back to health, at the races.

Opposite:
The generals' Jadeland: a church teeters as a mountain of jade is whittled away beneath it; an overseer checks names against her human inventory as miners climb out of a cauldron in Hpakant Kyi; exhausted girls heave bamboo panniers of rough jade into a waiting tipper truck.

Pictures that the Burmese junta did not want the world to see: an emaciated and dying miner, infected with HIV, photographed by a government doctor for a report that was suppressed and smuggled to Thailand.

Tutu, the 105-year-old grand-daughter of the Last King of Burma, who now lives on a rubbish tip in Ratnagiri, on the West coast of India.

A former miner from Hpakant, crippled by HIV that he con-tracted from a dirty needle in a government-controlled shooting gallery, lies under the border fence at Ruili, too weak too pull himself into China or crawl back into Burma.

But that was history. Within months Aung San peacefully achieved what the Burmese monarchs had only ever managed through bloodshed. All but one of the country's ethnic groups, including the wild Wa, agreed to put up candidates for a committee that would draft a new constitution for the Union of Burma. On the morning of 19 July 1947 Aung San kissed goodbye to his wife and three children at the family's Victorian villa overlooking Kandawgyi Lake, a shaded oasis in the fraught post-war days, a wild rockery and tangle of palms and jasmine that screened them from the hubbub of Rangoon. To the right of the hall was his study, its bookshelves packed with leather-bound biographies: Oliver Cromwell, William Gladstone, Mahatma Gandhi. Above was the sparse nursery with three wooden cots for his two boys Lin and Oo and his two-year-old daughter Suu Kyi, her coverlet scattered with hairless plastic dolls and a battered tin kaleidoscope.[4] Aung San drove off towards the Rangoon Secretariat to lead the Union into a new era. At 10.37 a.m., as he and his cabinet sat in his second-floor office, unexpected visitors burst through the door and sprayed the room with bullets. It was an epiphany for the Golden Land. U Saw, a right-wing opponent of Aung San, was found guilty and quickly hanged, but it was later revealed that his arrest warrant had been issued an hour and a half before the shootings. It would also be claimed that the real culprit was Ne Win, the former post office clerk, who had fallen out with Aung San during the Japanese occupation of Burma because of his continual womanising and drinking. Ne Win's 30-second act of vengeance claimed seven of Burma's most articulate leaders and killed all hopes of a peaceful transition to democratic union.

U Nu, Aung San's deputy, a student activist who had been president of Rangoon University Union before the war, stepped into the breach. Burma became an independent republic at 4.20 a.m. on 4 January 1948, but the country was still immersed in grief. Prime Minister U Nu recalled the 'dim and distant days in the mists of antiquity' when the ethnic groups 'born of the same mother' had lived with the Burmans 'in loving friendship', but was there anyone now listening? Aung San's bond of trust lay in shreds in his Secretariat office and, as U Nu ushered in the Union of the Republic of Burma, the ethnic tribes began to arm themselves. The Karen of the south-east had broken away even before the assassinations and now their neighbours the Karenni also took up arms. In October the Arakanese, who lived to the west, split with Rangoon. When the 1st Kachin Rifles, who still referred to their service with the Allies as a 'time of big honour', were ordered by the government to attack their Karen compatriots, they too mutinied. Burma was once again at war with itself.

It fell to Ne Win to deploy the country's small army. Within a year he had reduced a civil war to a simmering insurgency, rallied by Britain and the Commonwealth, who provided the army with new weapons and his officers with military training. Within two years Ne Win's model army could deploy more than 40,000 soldiers and by 1957, he had emerged as the commander of a military machine that was threatening to eclipse the civilian government.

In another country, another dynasty had become enfeebled. A series of heart attacks had left Sir Victor Sassoon in a wheelchair and propelled him into the arms of Evelyn Barnes, a young nurse from Dallas, Texas, who described herself as a 'southern hill-billy'. In 1959 Evelyn married her 77-year-old employer in the Bahamas, given away by her brother, a building contractor from the Lone Star State, while the groom quipped to his friends: 'After all, 77 years of bachelordom are essential to acquire enough judgement to choose the right wife.' However, by August 1961 Sir Victor was living in an oxygen tent and on 12 August, after refusing a shot of painkillers from Evelyn, he was dead.[5]

He left behind a will that mystified everybody apart from those who knew him well. Lucien Ovadia had channelled Sir Victor's millions into a network of off-shore trusts, and the total value of his British estate was a meagre £12,602. Almost all of his assets, including his British stud, its shares valued at £1 million, were now controlled by companies registered in the Bahamas. The vast majority of the Sassoon legacy, his personal papers, jadeite and nephrite went to the southern hill-billy who was also left a trust that contained £214,000. But without an heir, Sir Victor's death brought to an end his baronetcy, consigning to obscurity a mighty dynasty that had once claimed King David's pedigree, that rode 'in gold tissue' to the palace of the Pasha, that sailed in scrambling dragons to the mud flats of Shanghai.

Seven months later, on 2 March, 1962 Burmese radios crackled into life at 8.50 a.m. to announce that a new order had seized control. Ne Win's troops had arrested Prime Minister U Nu and the armed forces had 'taken over responsibility and the task of keeping the country's safety'. Within months, General Ne Win's military and its manifesto, *The Burmese Road to Socialism,* had usurped parliament and the Burmese constitution. He hijacked the country's financial institutions and transformed Burma into an economic desert.

It was the students of Rangoon University who were the first to test the General's resolve, gathering on 7 July for a day of peaceful demonstration. Ne Win's response was emphatic. According to the junta, no more than fifteen students died, but diplomats put the fatalities in the hundreds. The university, they said, was 'a slaughterhouse', and the next morning its union building, where Aung San and U Nu had forged their debating skills, was blown to pieces.

Unlike most, the Kachin had been prepared for the assault on democracy. A group of World War Two veterans, led by Zau Seng, who had fought with Merrill's Marauders, had met secretly in Rangoon to plan an insurrection. Called Seven Stars, a name that referred to the constellation of Orion that was clearly visible during their night-time liaisons, they had formed the Kachin Independence Army on 5 February 1961.[6] But between them, the fledgling guerrillas of the KIA could only muster a clutch of blunt *dahs,* 30 World War Two rifles and a few rounds of ammunition.

In 1998 we travelled along the Sino-Burmese border, wobbling on borrowed bikes across the narrow paths that divided the paddy, hopping from village to village in search of Kachin veterans. Eventually we found one of the Seven Stars, dressed in a tweed jacket and tie, his silver hair freshly lacquered. 'We were well trained by the British and Americans but we had absolutely no money and the few guns we owned were not usable. So the first thing we did was to confiscate the Burmese bank in Lashio,' the veteran told us.

What exactly did he mean? Sitting in a curtained-off back room of an upmarket Chinese restaurant, our simple question hung in the air as our food congealed. Eventually he answered: 'We robbed it. It was early. No one there was really alert. They were eating breakfast in fact. We went in, you know, and then we ran out with

90,000 kyat. That's how it all began. But we needed more guns –
and more money. We needed to look at the bigger picture.'

In January 1950 the tattered remnants of the Chinese Nationalist forces, pinned down in Yunnan, had retreated across the Burma
border and established a secret base, deep in the jungles of Shan
State. From the safety of Taiwan, Chiang Kai-shek ordered his isolated units to strike at the People's Republic of China, and the US
Central Intelligence Agency supplied them with guns. But after
years of living rough in the malarial jungle, a better offer emerged
from the undergrowth. The KIA officer was now in his stride: 'We
approached the KMT forces and established a base near them, taking sacks of rough jadeite that we bartered for guns and munitions.
The KMT troops were more than happy to exchange their CIA
weapons for the Stone of Heaven.'

The KIA needed a regular supply of jadeite to fund its expansion,
but the Dragon Cloud warlord Lung Yun had flooded the mine
workings before the Japanese occupation. So the Kachin scoured
the jungle for new seams, digging shafts into the baked earth, following the path of the Uru River. They knew that there was a fortune wedged beneath their feet, but there was no one to extract it.
More than 10,000 Chinese labourers had once sluiced the pits, but
all of them had fled the Japanese and were now prevented from returning by the Communists.

Our journey through Yunnan began every day with a dawn
breakfast. One morning, as we sat dunking Chinese doughnuts into
bowls of condensed milk, waiting for pork buns to whistle with
steam from their bamboo tower, a 40-year-old Kachin trader pulled
up a chair. A jade seam clung to a gold band on his finger, a crisp
polo shirt stretched across his taut shoulders and his Cuban heels
were a mosaic of mock crocodile. After wolfing down our tray of
buns, soaked in crab-apple vinegar, the trader, whose father had
been a schoolteacher before joining the KIA in the 1960s, revealed
that he had been looking for us. Did we want to know how the
Kachin realised their fortune? 'OK. We found new jade but no one
want to break their back in pit. We soldiers busy fighting Burman.
Could not be miners as well as fighters. We sitting on fortune but no
one want to dig it. It was *Yu Li Ku* that help us in end.'

We looked perplexed and he struggled to explain. 'How you say?

Rats. Everywhere. Ate everything. Ran everywhere. Destroyed Kachin field and drove families to mine. This was beginning for us.' He had finished his story and our pork buns and left us as he had found us, waiting for our breakfast, mulling over the rodents who had helped resurrect the jungle revolution.

The Kachin Hills once again rang with wild incantations, the forest smogged by campfires. The KIA now bought truckloads of weapons from the KMT, who acquired a mountain of jadeite that they sold on to the refugee dealers and cutters of Kowloon's Canton Road. One russet-skinned boulder that was bartered by the Kachin, weighing 28.8 kilos, was sold by the KMT for 88,888,000 taels of silver (about 11 million US dollars). In 1997, one small suite of jewellery carved from this stone (named '8888' because of its price) sold for more than 300,000 US dollars.[7]

Chiang Kai-shek stockpiled boulders, selling them off to build his kingdom-in-exile, where the legacy of the Emperors was at last unveiled to an invited audience of dignitaries that included Madame Chiang, who had flown in from New York for the première. She had given up on her unfaithful husband, buying a spacious apartment on Gracie Square in Manhattan's Upper East Side, from where she peered down on the mayor's villa. There she lived in a bubble of Chinese republicanism set among the brawl of tenements that overlooked the East River. But now, her shoulders draped in fur, curious to see what had risen in a northern suburb of Taipei in 1965, she entered the National Palace Museum. It was a miniature Forbidden City emerging from the folds of the wooded hills. Dragons and phoenixes coiled around stone pillars, roofs picked out in Imperial yellow, its walled gardens laid out like a Song Dynasty water park, its tea room a replica of Qianlong's private study. There were so many Chinese treasures stored in the deep cellars beneath the palace that Chuang Shang-yen, now chief curator, was forced to rotate exhibitions. It was to the jadeite rooms that the crowds rushed, and there in glass cabinets were many pieces that were identical to those that had been stored in the Qing tombs, including a carved cabbage from whose leaves emerged a crystalline cricket that is still on display today.

Chiang Kai-shek basked in the legitimacy that his National Palace Museum lent him, but he didn't have long to enjoy it. Jennie

Ch'en, his second wife, had returned to China in 1932 where she lived in penury, a forgotten woman. Until now. Out of desperation, she decided to publish her memoirs, which threatened to reveal Chiang Kai-shek's seamier side. He had tried to rape her when she was thirteen years old and had cast her aside for a marriage that was in fact technically bigamous, as they had never officially divorced. So explosive was the manuscript that Ai-ling, May-ling's sister, threatened to sue. Jennie's agent was beaten up in a New York hotel and several attempts were made to steal the memoirs. Eventually, a lawyer acting for the Chiang family paid Jennie 170,000 US dollars for two copies. When she died in 1971, buried in Hong Kong with little ceremony, requesting that her death be registered in her maiden name, Chiang Kai-shek must have breathed a sigh of relief. But what he didn't know was that Jennie's agent still had notes taken from the original manuscript. On 5 April 1975 the 87-year-old KMT leader died, a hero to his nation. But in 1993, Jennie's long-lost story finally emerged, revealing to all the illegitimacy of China's *Fu-jen*.[8]

⌗

Hui-lan Koo was now reliant on the comfort of strangers. The former wife of China's ambassador to the US had in 1970 moved into a one-bedroom apartment in Sutton Place, overlooking Manhattan's East River, carpeted with Imperial rugs that had once graced her Peking palace. Cast aside by Wellington, who had taken another wife, impoverished by Sukarno, who had swallowed up her Indonesian legacy, the ex-Madame Koo had been left to fend for herself:

> I didn't know how to light a stove let alone boil an egg . . . my two amahs left me and . . . my Chinese chef had already opened a restaurant. I used to stand out in my garden and sniff the cooking of the two young bachelors who lived next to me. I would cry out, 'How delicious everything smells!'[9]

In her neighbourhood she was the lonely and dishevelled old Chinese woman who shuffled around the park with her dogs. At night she would return home to scour the photographs of her former lives and watch old cine films of the social events that once she had attended in her jadeite finery. Only her memories kept her alive and in 1972 they too were taken. As the ex-Madame Koo returned to her apartment, she was attacked and wrapped up in her own sheets 'like a Chinese spring roll'. She watched helplessly as her assailants forced open a drawer and 'scooped out irreplaceable heirlooms given to me by my mother'. Her life was now filled with uncertainty. 'I meet people who know when they are going to die. I don't – and I am glad. I would like my sons to take my ashes to a high mountain and scatter them on the breeze. I wonder if I will be around to see it?' she pondered morbidly in her diary.

Not everything was taken from the ex-Madame Koo on the day of the robbery. Robert H. Ellsworth had told us how he had befriended the heiress and advised her to place her most treasured possessions in a bank vault. So the famed Persian Pepper and her jadeite necklaces, including the wedding gift from her father, were locked away when the robbers called but after the break-in Hui-lan could no longer bear to wear them. She sold the jadeite wedding necklace to her sister and her old Shanghai rival Madame Chiang Kai-shek received 'a second good string'. Only the Persian Pepper remained: a memento of how she had fleetingly eclipsed the richest man in Shanghai with the finest Imperial piece in the world. Robert H. Ellsworth had filled his silver chalice with bourbon before recalling the ex-Madame Koo's demise, his splayed consonants stumbling into his softened vowels. 'The last time I took her to lunch she wore a broad-tail jacket so worn, she looked as if she was homeless,' he had told us.

⬚

In the jungles of Kachin State a jadeite robbery had shaken the KIA rank and file. In 1975 a radio message crackled through the hills. Three of the most senior KIA officers had been removed from duty, among them General Zau Seng. A military court of inquiry alleged that they had siphoned the proceeds of the jadeite sold to the KMT into their personal bank accounts in Bangkok. On 6 August they were executed.[10] The KIA was forced to reorganise its hierarchy and its jadeite business.

The jungle trial revealed the corruption within, but it also uncovered the vast jadeite profits being realised by the KMT. So, when

China eased its border restrictions with Burma, the KIA decided to cut out the middle-men by moving closer to Yunnan and reopening Qianlong's Jade Road. The stones that passed through a newly constructed border gate on the outskirts of a run-down Chinese village called Ruili earned the Kachin more money than they had ever seen. Forming a jadeite company called Bu Ga, they used the profits to recruit and arm yet more guerrillas to combat Ne Win's ever-growing army, to construct schools for 30,000 pupils and to build modern field hospitals that were even equipped with operating theatres. Soon the KIA had secured 40,000 square kilometres of territory and governed over 300,000 people.[11]

Our journey through Yunnan eventually led us to a KIA major, who listed like a bloated Buddha, his teeth masked by betel nut that he hawked in crimson jets onto the floor at the very mention of Ne Win's name. The major regaled us with stories of how the Kachin made their fortunes from mines that were now known as Hpakant: 'We sold claim to Chinese mine operator and tax stone that worker dug. It was time of KIA control. We keep best pits for ourselves and vet everyone in area. Kachinland now family affair.'

The Kachin built palaces in the remote jungle equipped with satellite TV, the major said, reclining on an imported leather sofa beneath a picture of a naked Chinese dancer, who jiggled dice in her manicured hands. It seemed that he too had profited from the insurgency – his stone-clad bungalow had double-glazing and five bedrooms. We sipped fresh juice squeezed from grapefruits grown on his fruit farm before he took us on a brief tour of his assets, a strong-room that held more than a dozen uncut jadeite boulders scored with their weight and value. Returning to the living-room, the major reclined into his memories, recalling how Hpakant became a Klondike in the jungle. 'Suddenly black market arrive in Kachinland. Trader sell anything you want. Chocolate. Cigarette. American and British. Tinned cheese and ham, pork and duck, roast beef if you want. We drank French cognac, Chinese champagne. Real thing too if you had money. People say Hong Kong best market but Kachin mine had everything. People made fortune and lost fortune. It was time of big gamble.'

But the KIA wanted to up the stakes. They struck a deal with a Shan warlord who agreed to guide their jade caravans to the free market in Thailand in exchange for stones. The suave Khun Sa, a reclusive entrepreneur as comfortable in a blazer as in his olive fatigues, ruled the Shan State with his Shan United Army, 'iron-legged soldiers', who kept Ne Win's troops at arm's length and also happened to police one of the largest heroin cartels in the world.

Quartered in Ban Hin Taek on the Thai border, the few outsiders who were invited in reported that his jungle lair was a narco-boomtown filled with bars, restaurants, dance halls and temples. The international trafficker had made millions from a business he claimed to have learned from the Allies in World War Two. The self-styled Prince of Darkness, who bragged that he smoked sixty 555 cigarettes a day and had a penchant for French cognac, now established Saha Charoenmit, a jadeite brokerage in Chiang Mai. The man in charge was Charlie Win, a.k.a. 'Agent Thunder', Khun Sa's chief of staff, who had won his leader's respect after springing him from Mandalay jail in 1974, where he had languished for five years, found guilty of waging war against Ne Win. Saha Charoenmit was also, according to the United States Drug Enforcement Administration (DEA), a cover for Khun Sa's narcotics empire, whose poppy fields and jungle laboratories along the Burma-Thai border now fed Western habits.

The KIA's deal with the Shan heroin warlord bought it even greater wealth, but another of the world's great jadeite fortunes was being whittled away, its beneficiary having slumped into a morphine stupor. Having been a princess and a countess, Barbara Hutton became a baroness in 1955, eloping with Baron Gottfried von Cramm, a professional tennis player to whom she gifted a 2 million US dollars dowry while rewarding herself with a face-lift. While he cavorted around Europe with a string of boyfriends, Barbara sat in her hotel room alone, tan foundation smeared unevenly over her swollen cheeks, a blot of eye-liner colouring her thinning eyebrows. It was only a matter of time before they were divorced, Barbara losing 600,000 US dollars in the process. In 1964, the ex-Baroness was wooed by another suitor, Raymond Doan, a handsome Franco-Vietnamese chemist, who set eyes on her in Marrakech and jettisoned his wife for the five-and-dime fortune. Doan scored 1.5 million US dollars on the couple's wedding in April as well as pocketing a 10,000 US dollars-a-month allowance and a title. But only aristocrats could share her fantasy and so Barbara strolled into the Laotian Embassy in Rabat, where she was on holiday, and offered an ageing clerk 50,000 US dollars to sell his antecedence. The chemist became Prince Raymond Doan vinh na Champassak and Barbara became Princess vinh na Champassak, the heirs to a defunct kingdom that centuries before had been subsumed by Thailand. But the Prince was out by 1971, 2 million US dollars richer, paid off with Catherine the Great's tiara, and Barbara Hutton was so anaesthetised that she not only immediately forgot her Prince but left 5 million US dollars of jewels in a hotel suite in Rome. Gone were Marie Antoinette's pearls that she had worn to her first wedding and a ruby tiara once owned by Empress Eugénie. One year later Hutton lost her son Lance, who had followed her down the path to addiction. In July 1972, the 37-year-old heir had taken off in a Cessna 206 to show off some real estate he planned to buy. But his plane crashed into a mountain in Aspen, decapitating him and killing his three friends. In that wreckage of twisted metal lay all that remained of the Woolworth lineage.

Seven years later, on 26 March 1979 Barbara Hutton was admitted to the Cedars-Sinai Hospital, carried from her suite at the Beverley Wilshire, a rag doll in the burly arms of Colin Frazer, her bodyguard. Her medical files reveal that she now only weighed 80 pounds, 'her bones were like chalk', her legs a tapestry of bedsores.[12] When she was discharged, it was back into the arms of Frazer, and a slew of demands from jewellers for unpaid bills. Tiffany claimed 40,000 US dollars, Harry Winston demanded 30,000 US dollars, and a law-suit filed in Los Angeles from a gem dealer asked for 660,000 US dollars. Back in her darkened tenth-floor suite, surrounded by half empty glasses of Coca-Cola, pyramids of tranquillisers piled high on her bed-side table, Barbara slipped into a netherworld, setting her Dior dressing-gown alight, calling staff to hose her down. Her jewellery now lay locked inside three cases by her bed, and not even the occasional letters from Cary Grant raised her from her self-induced coma.

Kathleen Murphy, her nurse, told Hutton's biographer that on 11 May 1979, her 66-year-old employer beckoned her over and exhaled a sigh of relief. Her 'continuous fantasy' was at last over. But within 24 hours of her death, her hotel suite in LA was mysteriously picked clean and her corpse stripped of its jewellery, according to Murphy and Frazer. Barbara's funeral was held on 25 May at Woodlawn Memorial Cemetery in the Bronx, but neither her friends, nor her seven husbands, nor the press that had once grazed over the minutiae of her life witnessed her departure. When her will was validated six months later, the poor little rich girl's only asset appeared to be a 3500 US dollars bank deposit. All of the jewels and Imperial antiques that had illuminated her world and that she had bequeathed to her staff, friends and institutions had vanished.[13]

Within months Barbara's possessions began to reappear on the open market. In 1979 Sotheby's auctioned a necklace, ring and jadeite ear-rings, and the following March sold her snuffboxes in their London sale-room for 350,000 US dollars.[14] Jadeite was becoming a bankable commodity. Five years later the auction house announced its entrance into the Imperial Green Jade business with its first sale dedicated to the Stone of Heaven, its star lot being a 108-bead court necklace that had once belonged to the Dowager Empress Cixi. It made 330,000 US dollars and Lisa Hubbard, of Sotheby's New York, was immediately sent to Hong Kong to capitalise on the re-emerging Stone of Heaven. We met her at a beach-front restaurant in Santa Monica, all sun-tan, pearl teeth and tucked, a rosy advertisement for the West Coast life. 'I realised that the market for the best quality jadeite would never be satisfied. There would never be enough, the stone is truly, truly rare,' Lisa said. 'It is like cash in your pocket. It's the refugee mentality – take your jewels with you. After all, China is just one long haul.'

A plate of stone crab claws turned into a five-hour journey through the living-rooms of jadeite connoisseurs: a herbalist who used it to launder his black money, the porn star who bought into the Stone of Heaven, the granddaughter of a Manchu bannerman who loved it so much that she named her daughter Jade. Warlords, republican ladies, heiresses: 'The Chiang Kai-shek generation was getting old and dying and I was walking around the history pages of China. The Young Marshal, who was now not so young, cooked me dumplings and talked about Madame Hui-lan Koo and Edda Ciano. Famous pieces, including a Hutton bracelet that had once belonged to Cixi, were turning up everywhere. One of her pieces came to me via Honolulu, of all places. I was amazed when I sold it for 1 million US dollars,' Lisa said.

※

A long-lost manuscript from China had also now turned up, at Basel Airport, in the hands of a Swiss doctor, Reinhard Hoeppli. He had ministered to the reclusive Edmund Backhouse in the last years of his life and had been given *Décadence Mandchoue,* the extraordinary story of Cixi's torrid and secret affair. For 30 years Hoeppli had hidden it away, unsure of what to do with the scandalous document, and now he gave it to a former British intelligence officer and Oxford historian, Hugh Trevor-Roper. Hoeppli asked him to assess its veracity with a view to it being deposited in the Bodleian Library alongside the 27,000 looted Chinese volumes that Backhouse had donated to the University. But in 1976, Trevor-Roper revealed that the manuscript was nothing more than a tissue of lies: Backhouse had never met the Dowager Empress let alone slept with her. He had lived a sad and lonely continuous fantasy during his decades in Peking. It didn't matter. Extracts from *Décadence Mandchoue* were now in the public domain, titillating a new generation of would-be Orientalists who were also buying into the mysterious mine of the East.[15]

In Burma, the ageing Ne Win was increasingly seduced by fantasy, wrapping himself in the millenniums of superstition that had been woven around the Great Golden Land. The General consulted astrologers before forging economic policy and in September 1987 he executed a bank robbery of his own, removing from circulation all 25, 35 and 75 kyat bank notes, numbers that he believed to be unlucky. Overnight, the Burmese were left with bags of worthless cash.

In March 1988, thousands of demonstrators took to Rangoon's streets waving their useless bank notes in the air, and the General retreated to his guarded *dacha* on the shores of Inya Lake, warning all that 'If the army shoots it hits.' His threats were met by a general strike on the lucky eighth day of the eighth month in 1988. Hundreds of thousands took to the streets waving photographs of Aung San, ranging around the capital until 11 p.m., when the tanks rolled out. What followed was flashed around the world, triggering unanimous condemnation. Unarmed protestors carrying banners that pleaded, 'Pull us out from hell', students who kissed the boots of the soldiers, were mown down in lines, in five days of blood-letting. 'Four separate eyewitness accounts . . . describe how soldiers knelt in formation and fired repeatedly,' reported the American Embassy. 'Deaths probably numbered over two thousands but the actual numbers can never be known. In many cases as soon as they finished firing troops carted off victims for surreptitious mass disposal in order to mask the extent of the carnage.'[16] There were echoes of the Mandalay massacre that had brought King Thibaw to the Lion Throne.

Shuttered away in a villa on Inya Lake with its wild garden of casuarinas and red roses, Aung San's only daughter Suu Kyi listened to the cackle of gunfire at the end of University Avenue, but her mother was dying and she was unable to leave her side. She had slipped back into the country in March after an absence of almost 30 years, having left Burma to be schooled in India before going up to St Hughes College, Oxford, where she had fallen in love with Michael Aris. Their courtship had been literary and in the eight months before they married in 1972 she had sent him 187 letters, many of them prescient. 'Sometimes I am beset by fears that circumstances and national considerations might tear us apart just when we are so happy in each other that separation would be a torment,' she had written.[17] Now as the Burmese summer of 1988 drew to a close, ringing with gunshots, Aung San's daughter was prompted to act.

On 26 August, as hundreds of thousands gathered outside Shwe Dagon Pagoda, an ancient epicentre of the Buddhist faith, a genteel figure walked onto the platform, her mahogany hair pulled back into a chignon laced with flowers. Suu Kyi, her husband and two sons at her side, appeared before a hushed crowd. It was as if Aung San had returned to save his people. Aware of how his old enemy would attempt to undermine her marriage to a foreigner, she used her maiden speech to pre-empt Ne Win's bile. 'People have been saying that I know nothing of Burmese politics,' she said. 'The trouble is I know too much. My family knows better than any how devious Burmese politics can be and how much my father had to suffer on this account.' For many, her presence conjured the second-floor committee room smoked by cordite, and they tearfully rose to her side.

The junta responded by renaming itself the State Law and Order Restoration Council (SLORC), rechristening Burma as Myanmar, and returning to the old ways. On 18 September, as Rangoon was once again awash with demonstrators, buoyed by Suu Kyi's stand, armoured cars and troop-trucks rolled out of their barracks. More than 1000 people were killed, although the junta would later claim that the number was just over a dozen. America, Britain, Australia, Germany and Japan cut off financial aid, while Suu Kyi attempted to reach out by forming the National League for Democracy (NLD). One of her deputies was drawn from the ranks of Ne Win's army and another was the dictator's former defence minister.

On 20 July 1989, having been subjected to a torrent of abuse from the state-controlled media, Suu Kyi was placed under house arrest in her mother's villa. But to the consternation of the military government, the NLD scored a resounding victory in the elections of May 1990, her party winning 392 out of 485 seats.

The SLORC regrouped. It refused to honour the results. In August, Burmese monks, their alms bowls upturned, took to the streets of Mandalay, only to be cut down. By the time Aung San Suu Kyi was awarded, in absentia, the Nobel Peace Prize on 14 October 1991, the NLD's party structure was decimated and opposition to the SLORC had been forced underground.

※

In Geneva, the talk was of a brilliant string of beads carved from a legendary boulder, *lan shui lu*. At a Christie's sale there, Barbara Hutton's jadeite wedding necklace had somehow slipped among the lots offered as part of the estate of Nina Mdivani, Hutton's former in-law. It sold for 2 million US dollars, a world record for jadeite jewellery.[18]

In Burma, where an economic embargo had begun to bite, news of the record jadeite sale was registered by the impoverished generals who immediately dispatched 200,000 soldiers into the Kachin Hills. But despite driving the KIA out of its jungle base and blockading the jade road to Chiang Mai, the Burmese army was unable to flush the Kachin out of the mines of Hpakant. Ne Win now embraced the *Art of War*. Hearing that two of the Kachin's ethnic allies and neighbours had broken from the jungle alliance, he secretly dispatched an intermediary to woo them. The duty fell to Luo Xinghan, an opium warlord and former ally of Khun Sa, who had escaped a death sentence for drug trafficking by striking a deal with the SLORC. In exchange for millions of kyat that he would be permitted to invest in opium plantations, Luo had pledged to assist the junta in undermining the ethnic insurgencies. Now the turn-coat carried a lucrative offer north, to the disaffected Wa and Kokang tribes: 10 million kyat to join Rangoon. Both groups accepted the money, re-arming their militias, turning their guns against the Kachin and their one remaining ally, Khun Sa.

Then China closed the KIA's last route out of Burma, shutting down the border point at Ruili. The Kachin were encircled in a jungle that for centuries they had ruled, and entered into secret peace talks with the SLORC. The insurgents demanded the return of their jungle headquarters, amnesties for all and a guarantee that the jadeite mines of Hpakant would remain in Kachin hands in exchange for putting down their weapons. The SLORC readily agreed and counter-signed the cease-fire on 24 February 1994.

Two months later Christie's sold an 'extraordinary necklace' that had once belonged to a woman who had lived a 'real-life fairytale'. 'Her sumptuous jewellery, she believed, could only add to her country's image and to that end she wore . . . jade, the magical jewel of the East,' wrote Edmond Chin, a former Singaporian banker who was now Christie's resident jadeite expert.[19] Here, in the pages of the catalogue, he conjured up a story of 'elegant mansions', 'fancy cars', 'the finest cuisine' and 'furs and jewels'. Steeped in stories, Hui-lan Koo's wedding necklace fetched 1 million US dollars.

Six months later, Barbara Hutton's jadeite wedding necklace was back on the market. In a Christie's catalogue, whose expansive introduction by Edmond Chin featured photographs of the Dowager Empress Cixi and Madame Chiang Kai-shek, that quoted from Confucius and Heber Bishop, the prize lot was described as 'a natural phenomenon'. Illustrated with a photograph of Barbara Hutton wearing it to the Metropolitan Opera House in 1933, Edmond Chin described her as having 'the world at her finger-tips', indulging her 'passion for jewels that was endless', living 'a life of splendour and magnificence that is usually the purview of royalty'. The hammer fell on a staggering 33 million Hong Kong dollars (4.3 million US dollars). The anonymous buyer was Barbara's former jeweller.

When we met him at his shop in the Peninsula Hotel in Kowloon, Sammy Chow revealed that Madame Chiang Kai-shek had also asked to see the beads, intending to buy them for herself as a one hundredth birthday present. 'Local people say I pay crazy price to make my name. But this necklace best world ever seen,' Chow said. 'I can sell now for 20 million Hong Kong dollar profit.' François Curiel, Christie's International Jewellery Director, was delighted to reveal that the entire sale had netted 9.6 million US dollars. 'More than 1000 people a day attended the viewing' of the Hutton necklace, considerably more than had turned out for her funeral. Edmond Chin had rejuvenated the jadeite trade and, the following year, introduced his clients to a saddle ring carved from the Jade King's '74,000', a boulder that had escaped the warehouse robbers, the kidnappers, the sinking of Mr Tieh's ship bound for Shanghai and his flight to Taiwan.

Three months earlier, on 10 July 1995, Aung San Suu Kyi emerged from six years of house arrest into a country that she barely recognised. Her ability to endure had transformed her into a talisman, her image hidden inside amulets and behind picture frames. To capitalise on its goodwill gesture, the SLORC issued a triumphal statement. A country accused by Western intelligence agencies of having become a narco-dictatorship announced that it had destroyed one of the largest heroin syndicates in the world.

In January 1996 Burmese and Thai journalists were flown to a secret jungle camp above which fluttered a fountain pen crossed with an assault rifle, the insignia of Khun Sa. The Prince of Darkness had been indicted by an American Grand Jury in 1989 for drug smuggling and a 2 million US dollars reward had been offered for his capture. Now, before the cameras, 10,000 of Khun Sa's 'iron-legged soldiers' laid down their shoulder-launched missiles. The warlord had apparently surrendered and was to be transported to Rangoon's Insein Jail.

Three months later, Christie's sold a translucent jadeite hairpin on which a dragon coiled around clouds, ruby-red flames flickering from its nostrils. Edmond Chin announced that it was 'plausible to assume' that the Empress Dowager Cixi 'may have once been the owner'. Its 'pair', he stated, was displayed in the Shenyang Palace Museum where the director claimed it was part of 'a cache of treasures brought by the last Emperor Pu Yi to Manchuria'.[20] His catalogues now bubbled with a cocktail of jadeite celebrities: a wristlet once owned by Yuan Shikai, a pair of jadeite bangles that had been bought by the Dragon Cloud warlord Lung Yun, and the collection of the late Audrey Meadows, an American television actress. Meadows' sister Jayne appealed breathlessly to Christie's clients: 'I hope you will be a successful bidder in this auction and that these jewels will bring you the same good fortune that they brought my dear Audrey. May the honeymoon never end for you either.' The glamour of Hollywood was once again draped around the legacy of the Emperors. Chinese folklore intermingled with the allure of the silver screen.[21] 'Jade,' proclaimed Christie's, 'is a possession to be cherished by anyone who can find it or buy it or steal it.'[22]

In Burma, Ne Win ordered his troops back into the Kachin Hills. Within nineteen months of procuring a cease-fire from the KIA, the SLORC overran its territory, transforming Myitkyina, Kamaing, Mogaung and Bhamo into garrison towns for tens of thousands of troops, trampling on the terms of the 1994 cease-fire. The generals in Rangoon were clearly intent on becoming Burma's new Lords of the Mines.

On the regime's tourist map of Burma, the Kachin Hills were now covered by a big, black blot. The mines of Hpakant, it was rumoured, were encircled by thousands of soldiers, locked into a high-security zone, where troops had been issued orders to shoot on sight.

In Hong Kong, on 27 April 1997 Christie's unveiled its 'Imperial Delight – the collections of the Qianlong Emperor, the Emperor Supreme'. Among the lots was a jade grotto stolen from the Summer Palace by Charles Gordon in 1860 and a cinnabar treasure box painstakingly carved with carp and cherry blossoms that swirled in the ripples of a pool. For 43 years Qianlong had cherished this box, filling it with seven archer's rings, smooth bands on which he had inscribed his most intimate thoughts, including one of bright green jadeite that in 1785 he had described as his 'treasure among treasures'. Seized by a French cavalry officer from the Summer Palace in 1860, the treasure box and its contents had been spirited away to Paris, where it had remained until the chevalier's descendants cashed it in to buy a new apartment.

Pierre Chen, president and CEO of the Yageo Corporation in Taipei, had spent the last decade building his fortune by manufacturing passive resistors. Now he paid 500,000 US dollars for the Emperor's cinnabar treasure box and its 7 rings that returned to the East after an absence of 137 years. Mr Chen locked it away in a safe, inside an office protected by armed guards and security shutters, triggered by fingerprint recognition.

Eleven

Welcome to Jadeland

Edmond Chin has a favourite story. 'A bad-tempered master carver from Mandalay used to stride into his workshop every morning, bellowing at his apprentices before stubbing his toe, without fail, on a grimy rock that had for years served as a doorstop,' he told us. One day, after cursing the block of stone, 'he hurled it out of the window'. Seeing it lying in the mud, one of his apprentices retrieved the boulder and used it to practise his polishing skills. 'He covered it with a film of Carborundum before pressing it against the face of a circular grinder,' Edmond Chin said. 'Clouds of crystal-dust flew through the air and then an emerald-green streak began to emerge.' The apprentice bellowed for the master carver, who sent for the rock's owner, who contacted the city's dealers, who refused to believe that the worthless doorstop concealed the Stone of Heaven.

'The rock was split like a ripe melon. Then the jeering stopped,' Edmond Chin recalled. 'At its heart lay peerless veins of jadeite that, when extracted, weighed more than a kilogram.' The master carver would soon create a 27-bead necklace in the image of the grape-sized beads that once graced Barbara Hutton's jewellery box. What remained of the boulder made the rock's owner a kyat millionaire, but he kept the necklace and christened it *Shaung Cai* or 'Doubly Fortunate', a souvenir of the greatest find of his life that was nearly thrown away.

Shaung Cai would have remained locked in the family's vault if Edmond Chin had not spotted it while on a trip to Mandalay in 1997. He persuaded the owner to place Doubly Fortunate in Christie's 1997 winter auction. The *South China Morning Post* reported how that sale transformed jadeite, overnight, into a gem that was more precious than diamonds:

> An Asian buyer yesterday paid 72.62 million Hong Kong dollars [£5.8 million] for a jadeite necklace in a Hong Kong auction, the most paid in Asia for a piece of jewellery or art. The 27-bead jadeite necklace, described as flawless by experts, was bought by a private collector at around 3.30 p.m. after seven minutes of frantic bidding.[1]

Anthony Lin, Christie's Hong Kong managing director, was ecstatic. 'Burma jade is probably the rarest gem in the world. At its highest quality it is harder to find and rarer than a perfect diamond and this sale demonstrates that collectors value it even more highly,' he crowed. 'Our target market now is those with a passion for jadeite; they must appreciate good jadeite. They must know. For us the sky is now the limit.'

Gem dealers and auctioneers raced to capitalise on the Doubly Fortunate sale. Sotheby's invited Chanel to design a piece of jadeite jewellery, a flowering camellia that the sale catalogue described as a 'subtle blending of two cultures'. Jadeite was 'a stone symbolising eternity' and it was 'imbued with wondrous powers, protecting its wearer from evil, from sickness, with curative powers and to bring good luck'. Qianlong's kingfisher gem was 'a jewel of the moment as well as for all time'. Quek Chin Yeow, Sotheby's jadeite director, told us 'it was to die for'.

Within months, Van Cleef & Arpels, the international jewellery house that had once claimed the Duchess of Windsor and Daisy Fellowes as clients, announced the launch of a new fragrance with a cascade of publicity. H. Rider Haggard had conjured up 'a quest for a legendary hoard that for three centuries had tormented men's dreams', and Van Cleef & Arpels gushed about 'a melody reminiscent of exotic distant lands'. 'Birmanie' was not simply a perfume but 'a hymn to the bewitching mystery and rarity naturally associated with precious stones'. It was 'an oasis of beauty where dreams and emotions can freely be expressed like a Princess'. It was 'evocative of a journey to the very heart of a mysterious country', and for £54, 100 millilitres of the 'Birmanie' elixir would transport the wearer to a 'secret valley said to be guarded by tigers and eagles' in which lay 'incredible treasure'.

Now the generals in Rangoon hired Jackson Bain, a former NBC White House correspondent, for 252,000 US dollars, and Ann Wrobleski, a former US Assistant Secretary of State, the architect of Nancy Reagan's 'Just Say No' anti-drugs campaign, on a 400,000 US dollars retainer, to reposition the junta in the international market-place.[2] On 15 November 1997, two weeks after Christie's record sale, the curtain was pulled back on the smooth-sounding State Peace and Development Council (SPDC). Gone was the SLORC, the guttural 'law and order' and the baffling sentiments of 'restoration' dreamed up by old men in braid who had failed to honour the country's general election. Senior General Than Shwe, now the chairman of the SPDC, and his baby-faced vice chairman, army commander General Maung Aye, welcomed visitors through a new portal. With virtual flags fluttering, 'www.myanmar.com' introduced 'one of the most pleasant places created by Mother Nature'. It noted in passing how Burma had once 'been a place of violent historical events with their ups and downs', but it was now enjoying 'peace, stability and economic progress as never before in national history'. Its 'treasures from the gem mines of Myanmar, famous since the days of the ancient kings', were waiting to be explored.

Rangoon too was covered in a new patina. Its grand old colonial hotel, Sarkies' The Strand, on the banks of the Irrawaddy, heralded in a 1912 Thomas Cook Guide as the 'premier hotel of Burma – with electric lights, bells and fans', was re-opened. Its stationery was embossed with the words of Kipling: 'This is Burma, and it will be quite unlike any land you know about.' Gilding the country's empire days, Eastern and Oriental Express now offered tours to 'discover the mysteries of the ancient and breath-taking cities along the shores of the Ayeyarwady [sic]', aboard the recently refitted and renamed *Road to Mandalay* cruiser.

But it would take more than Kipling to preserve the satin sheen of the SPDC's professionally honed respectability. Soon Burma was again troubled by some 'ups and downs'. Amid reports of nine tonnes of gold bars found stashed in a government minister's house, three SPDC generals were arrested. In January 1998, the family of one general deserted him and fled to Singapore, where they were said to have hidden millions of dollars. In February, another who had taken a shine to the gold bullion was admitted to Rangoon General Hospital. A picture display of the SPDC's military commanders mounted on a wall at the Defence Services Museum was now missing more than half of its photographs. That month, a revealing footnote on the cannibalistic regime was carried by the state's maudlin newspaper, the *New Light of Myanmar* (motto: 'To have immensity of knowledge, this is the way to auspiciousness'). Khin Nyunt, Secretary No 1 of the SPDC, the country's secret police chief, the man regarded by Ne Win as his heir apparent, had placed a curious advert. 'Dr Ye Naing Win is disowned by the parents for his inexcusable deed.' People were requested 'not to inquire the parents about the matter'.

In fact, the spy-master's son had married a Singaporean airhostess and ensnared his father in a trap set for Aung San Suu Kyi. Khin Nyunt's legislation stipulated that no Burmese citizen with foreign relatives could participate in government. Did Bain and Wrobleswki appreciate how hard they would have to work for their money?

The collision of publicity from Paris, Washington and Rangoon, news of the Doubly Fortunate record sale, coincided with a trip we were about to make into Burma, lured by equally unbelievable stories that were creeping out of the Kachin Hills. For a year and a half we had been filing to *The Sunday Times* from inside the country, where rumours of a tragedy in Upper Burma were now on everyone's lips. Foreign journalists are banned by the junta and any travel outside the capital is heavily restricted, so we had spent months being smuggled across the porous Thai border by insurgents still fighting the regime. Former students, farmers and refugees from the massacres of 1988 relied on their intimate knowledge of the country's sprawling network of tracks to evade and hamper the *Tatmadaw,* the SPDC's forces whom they ambushed from the tree-tops. For weeks at a time they survived in the harsh interior, combing banks and thicket for herbs and vegetables, striking and feinting against the urban government forces. The Karen, Kachin, Shan and Wa found extra food for us to share. As they charged ahead with packs so heavy that their flip-flops were pressed paper-thin, we lagged behind, the last to reach the camp-fire, often dehydrated, sometimes blistered, but they never complained.

Sleeping on bamboo matting while they crowded around a short-wave radio to listen to the BBC's Burma service, it was all too easy for us to forget the war: silent nights, exhausted after a day's march, the generous hospitality of people we barely knew, our full stomachs and their good humour. On one journey in long-tail boats that navigated the fast-flowing Tenasserim River, we cut through curtains of uncharted rainforest, squashed between men and women in tattered olive fatigues, our cameras and bags rammed inside their coils of ammunition. Our imaginations panning the jungle while they scouted for boot-prints in the silt banks. We day-dreamed of sailing towards a country's hidden treasures while they strained to disentangle the sounds of the jungle.

Occasionally we caught a glimmer of the life they once had lived. News of an urgent engagement tumbled us out of our cotton bags one morning to find that the Karen politicians were slated to play the Karen army in the insurgent league's annual football final. It was National Day and the jungle was transformed into a village fête, trestle tables hauled out of boats and bunting strung in the canopy. The military accused the civilians of playing dirty but the politicians held on to the trophy and the 2–0 score-line.

In early 1998, after walking for six hours through the jungle, we had arrived at a gathering of stilt huts where guests were waiting excitedly for a bride and groom to pass a Polo mint between their mouths in a jungle rendition of matrimonial vows. We had come to the wedding of a local insurgent commander, but there were two couples sitting cross-legged on the floor. The second ceremony was a spontaneous affair; the bride had only appeared that morning. 'I knew that I would be arrested if I stayed in Rangoon any longer, so I walked through the jungle,' the 22-year-old student told us, as if describing a stroll to the shops. 'When I arrived I found my boyfriend, who I thought was dead. I decided, there and then, that we should also get married. Thank you so much for coming.' We were still recovering from the trek, streaked with sweat and dust, as she sat composed and ecstatic, dressed in her freshly pressed fuchsia longyi and blouse, her hair combed into a sleek chignon.

But this was a costly war of attrition. A dogged human-rights worker whom we met in a Bangkok shopping mall had survived for months behind Burmese lines and brought with him a backpack crammed with reports and photographs, the paper trail for a concealed conflict that we examined in a quiet corner of Dunkin' Donuts. 'Burma is the dirty place behind the stove you never clean,' he said as he showed us photographs of villagers accused of collaborating with insurgents – ethnic chiefs, their heads on stakes, their homes put to the torch by the government. A knot of bodies snagged by driftwood somewhere down the Tenasserim. A woman mesmerised by her ragged ankles moments after stepping on a mine. Eventually we saw it for ourselves.

A fragment of torn clothing snagged in the reeds, the acrid smell of a fire, a distant cry or the footfalls of a Burmese battalion crashing through the undergrowth were often the only clues that the peaceful jungle was in fact the cockpit of a war. One day we disembarked at a defile in the river where towering rocks rose like giant knuckles from the shingle, and followed a trail of mismatched flip-flops speckled with blood. They led us to a clearing where a bundle of corpses lay; 27 men and women, their hands tied behind their backs, the broken wheels and yokes of ox-carts that had been packed ready to flee, lying around the pyre like pieces of a child's dismantled puzzle. A *Tatmadaw* notice pinned to a wooden pillar told how the villagers had been ordered to a relocation centre. Invariably the government camps were erected in barren valleys, and these people who were to become forced labour must have crept back to their homes, packing their carts with rice and chickens – only to be caught by Burmese soldiers who exacted their revenge. That evening, after a scout had plundered the riverbank for ferns and weeds, we sat down to a candle-lit feast, dwelling on a day spent counting corpses in the clearing. A young captain prepared his troops for the months ahead, while we re-enacted in our heads a cruel pursuit and the execution. He debated tactics and supply while we mulled over deadlines and copy. Was it only curiosity that had brought us here and would our stories make any difference? Filling our mugs with rice whisky, the captain reached into a dusty old box, produced a Casio keyboard and his men began to sing, drawing us out of a morbid torpor. 'Take me home country road, to the land where I belong . . .' It wasn't the first time that Jimmy Cliff had filled the Burmese jungle or that we would face a ten-hour trek with thick heads.

Everywhere we went, we moved against a tide of refugees, tens of thousands fleeing their villages in the wake of the government's pacification programme. And among the almost routine stories of pillage and torture we at last began to hear strange accounts from a state further north, where no reporters had been. As we moved further into the bush, we came across scores of people who told tales of a secret government project in the Kachin Hills that was said to hold captive a population of more than a million people. It was rumoured that a city had grown out of the wilderness, spreading like a cancer, multiplying in the valleys, consuming the jungle. Some claimed that it was ringed by trigger-happy troops with orders to shoot on sight. It rumbled like a freight train in the day and through the night it glowed as if lit by a million candles, they said, a beacon in the blackness that could be seen from miles around. Above it hung a sickly cloud of dust that smothered the Kachin Hills. Every day a long line of trucks drove in, carrying people stacked like freight, and left in the evening loaded down with bundles of discarded longyis, sandals, shorts and hats, all wrapped up in oil-skin and twine. But these were no more than rumours.

It was to one of the thirteen refugee camps that sprawl along the Thai border, to where more than 90,000 Burmese have fled, that we went in search of information, and found a doctor from Myitkyina, the capital of Kachin State. Although frantically worried about the colleagues he had left behind, he showed us a report that had been smuggled out of Burma. Health workers had visited the region on the orders of the SPDC. But according to the doctor, their findings had been suppressed and they had been sacked. A map drawn by them suggested that they had been to the jadeite mines of Hpakant. The area was encircled by arrows, dotted lines and hatched boxes that, according to the legend, were heroin refineries, opium routes and poppy fields. The document was a poor copy, sections of text illegible, several pages missing, but the introduction was intact and it began with a warning. The region was infected by something the locals called Jade Disease, a condition that provincial hospitals could not diagnose or treat:

> In the years gone by, the Kachin people suffered only from such fatal diseases as malaria, venereal disease etc. Recently a new fatal disease has raised its ugly and deadly head. The younger generation in partic-

ular is in danger of near extermination if something is not done to control this disease, which seems to be directly linked to the notorious drug heroin that is now available in every single village in Kachin State, often sold by government soldiers, policemen and local officials.

There were repeated references to the mines of Hpakant as the focus of an epidemic, but that critical section of the report was missing. All that remained was a single, dislocated paragraph:

> The place is always full of people and cars. As there is a cease-fire at present there are all kinds of people and all kinds of habits. Everyone is trying their luck here and all kinds of methods are adopted. Nearly everyone is sick and people lie dead on the roadside.

Several photographs had, however, survived the journey out of Burma. In the first, two men toke greedily, their thin faces boosted by a lungful of weed. In another it is impossible to distinguish the rubbish piled up on a spoil tip from the stiffened limbs that lie beneath it. The third: men and women with hollow cheeks, their arms and legs like bamboo poles, appear tethered to iron bedsteads, consumed by a wasting disease. There were pictures of skeletal boys squatting on their haunches, jabbing each other with blackened needles, oblivious to the flash of the camera. Captured here in these intrusive and confusing images – unconscious men with matted hair who looked blindly into the lens – were the undignified moments of people too weak to care. And in the last photograph, a naked boy staring defiantly, as if to ask us if we were enjoying what we saw. We were conscious of that terrible voyeurism that overtakes all of us when confronted with images of disease and disaster, a macabre curiosity with the pornography of death, a guilty fascination with the hilarity of jumbled limbs and bloated torsos, the dislocated components of a disaster presented without context or explanation. Who doesn't want to see what it looks like without having to experience it for themselves, to confront sordid and unsavoury realities that have all but been scrubbed away from our disinfected lives? We slid the photographs back into their envelope and took them to a copy-shop, hoping the teenage girl, chatting behind the counter, wouldn't look too closely. But of course she did. At every one. 'Burma,' she said without hesitation.

Inside that brown paper envelope was a glimpse of an irresistible and horrific story, but we had no idea how to get to the mines of Hpakant. We took off for a village three hours beyond Chiang Mai. There, marooned in a paddy field, was a bungalow that served as the intelligence headquarters for one of Burma's most successful insurgent groups. Inside, where dozens of young men watched Premier League football on a Thai cable channel, a normally encouraging battle-hardened student glanced at the photos and handed them straight back. 'It's impossible,' he said. 'You will never get to Hpakant. It's dangerous for you to try. Sorry we can't help you. I'm not sure that anyone can.'

Instead he pulled back a curtain to reveal stacks of colour-coded files and piles of old newspapers, official government reports that had been spirited out of Rangoon. Inside, he said, was another part of the story, a library of dusty information, of arid SPDC memoranda and circulars and, thankfully, a gangly librarian who would guide us through it. So we began to root through the archive, and a story emerged of how the Kachin were betrayed by Ne Win, who had set his eyes on the mines of Hpakant long before Lisa Hubbard and Edmond Chin had even spotted the market for the Stone of Heaven.

A compendium of laws revealed how in 1976 Ne Win had established the Myanma Gems Corporation under the control of the Ministry of Mines, desperate for money and mindful of the country's natural resources. No doubt Ne Win had read the Frontier Areas Inquiry report and had no intention of repeating the mistakes made by the British Empire. But the KIA was making its fortune out of jadeite and the Burmese, kept at a distance by their fear of a jungle stacked with rifles, only secured 9000 kilograms of the stone that year.

By 1991, the SLORC had re-armed, courtesy of China, that had transported tanks and guns to Rangoon along Qianlong's Jade Road. Now the junta began to crack down on the KIA and laid the foundations for a Gems Emporium in Rangoon, overlooking Suu Kyi's home on Inya Lake. It was intended to house an annual sale of jadeite and rubies that the regime secretly intended to mine in Upper Burma. But they needed a wealthy partner to oust the Kachin, upgrade the mines' infrastructure and invest in diesel-powered diggers, and, of course, they also needed a market. The Chinese government agreed to close down the border, suffocating the KIA, in return for a stake in the mines of Hpakant.

The Gems Emporium was completed in 1994, shortly before the KIA signed a cease-fire with the junta, and five months later the Chinese opened a consular office in Mandalay, inviting Lieutenant General Khin Nyunt to Beijing. In 1995, the year that China officially endorsed the SLORC, Premier Li Peng visited Rangoon, and the Myanma Gems Emporium attracted buyers representing 240 firms from 70 countries, ringing in a profit for the SLORC of 18 million US dollars. In September 1995, after the junta removed the state monopoly on exporting jadeite, the Chinese imported over 46 million US dollars worth of gems, representing one third of Burma's total exports to Beijing.[3]

The insurgents' archivist was also an accountant, and he interpreted dense SLORC spread-sheets that showed how by October 1995 Myanma Gems Enterprise, a military-run company, had won complete control of Hpakant and, by 1997, had leased out 1843 new jadeite pits to Chinese contractors. It was a profitable arrangement for the SLORC, as the operators were taxed on everything they extracted and were charged up to 500,000 US dollars per year per lease. The military reserved the best seams for themselves. Now the most productive company in the Kachin Hills was 'U Pine', a name that in translation meant 'First One Captured', a jadeite mine taken from the Kachin and operated by the son-in-law of General Maung Aye, the vice chairman of the SPDC, whose official income was less than 20 US dollars a month.[4]

Most revealing of all were the production figures that showed how, within a few years of having ambushed the Kachin, the government had transformed Hpakant into a money-spinning machine. By 1997, 4.4 million kilograms of jadeite were being chiselled out of the hills.[5] Chinese companies owned 70 per cent of the haul. The generals in Rangoon owned 20 per cent. The Kachin only retained 5 per cent and had to pay tax to the government. The SLORC celebrated the record increase in jadeite production, the refilling of its barren treasury and its hoodwinking of the KIA by building a Jade Garden Amusement Park in Rangoon. Its centrepiece was a 33-tonne jadeite boulder that had been confiscated from the Kachin and airlifted to the capital where it was declared a national treasure.

The figures were daunting. The Burmese project was clearly growing by the day, but how would we ever reach it? The maps drawn by the British survey teams had been stripped out of the New Delhi archive files by an Indian government paranoid about borders. The only landmarks on the health workers' map were heroin refineries and opium fields. All that we were left with was Captain Adamson's confused ramblings. It placed Hpakant somewhere between the 'breasts of Sheba', the twin peaks of Loi Lem and Loi Law, past the defile on the Irrawaddy and the whirlpool of Pashio, with its schools of 'tame catfish', down the Kasa Naga Road, once navigated by Sepoy Singh, all of which was eclipsed by the ominous shadow of Hukawng, the Kachin's valley of death. Hardly a route-planner.

But there was a more pressing problem. Burma was in the midst of a security crack-down. In January, a Japanese journalist posing as a tourist had been arrested and interrogated for fifteen hours before being deported. In February, a Reuters correspondent was attacked in his Rangoon hotel room by nine members of Khin Nyunt's secret police. In the same month an American woman who had been allowed to visit Suu Kyi had been thrown by Military Intelligence (MI) officers into the path of a speeding car. The elderly parents of Steven Tissamy, a 48-year-old tourist, were still scouring the streets of Mandalay for their son, who had disappeared the previous year, his clothes and passport abandoned in his hotel room.

More pressing was the revelation that the junta already knew who we were. While researching in the insurgents' library we came across an article about ourselves in the *New Light of Myanmar*. The full-page feature, headlined 'Truth and Ethics', by Mya Thinn referred to a previous trip we had made and accused us, among other things, of having 'entered Myanmar illegally and flirting with illegal insurgent groups'. We had written 'a whole bag full of lies'. Apparently a ministry we had once visited under cover was 'not at the end of a long tree-lined road but just off the main road and down a short lane'. There were 'no undemocratic practices' in Burma and the government pledged to 'plod along regardless of support or no support and the likes of Levy and Scott-Clark trying to upset our plans'. It was 'against the ideals and principles of the UN Charter to victimise a sovereign state that is a fully fledged member of the international previleges [*sic*]'. There was no attempt to deny the routine use of torture, the slaughter of the Karen or the destruction of villages, that had been the subject of our articles in 1997.

Our names were now on an immigration blacklist pinned up in Khin Nyunt's intelligence headquarters, as were our photographs. In Rangoon we had interviewed Aung San Suu Kyi, passing through the check-points and security cordon that surrounded her home on University Avenue, only to be intercepted at Mingaladon Airport, minutes before our flights home. We recalled the sinking feeling of being stopped by a woman wearing black popsocks and stilettos. Pushed into cubicles, we were stripped and searched, but the films and tapes that they were looking for had already gone on ahead. So, frustrated by their lack of success, the MI assigned a suave state photographer, thinly disguised behind his sunglasses and expensive black leather jacket, who recorded our passage through the departure hall. Darting between pillars, he snapped us at the check-in desk, shot us in the immigration hall, hosed us down at the customs counter. He got us again in the departure lounge, stalked us across the tarmac and bashed off a couple of frames as we scaled the steps to board the plane. Even as the Thai Airways jet took off, he continued to snap until all he could have possibly seen was a dot on the horizon. Then we had found it all quite droll, assuming that we would never return.

Now our only chance of getting into Burma and out of the airport was by reinventing ourselves. In Thailand, the land of false smiles and alibis, it took less than a week to acquire new sets of identity documents, credentials, business cards and letters of recommendation. We could now be variously described as British gemologists, legal representatives for an Australian mining company or university lecturers. Dyed and cut, we booked separate flights to Rangoon. Memorising a list of hotels, we agreed to meet at a fixed place and time, but if only one of us made it to the rendezvous, then he or she would have to attempt the trip to the mines alone.

The fear began at Don Muang Airport on the outskirts of Bangkok. They call it Burma Head, that creeping state of paranoia that begins with the balling up of your stomach and evolves into irrational and obsessive behaviour. Not to walk down the same street twice. To move hotel rooms every two days. To keep a chair pressed against the door. Not to make phone calls. To presume that everyone knows who you are. And of course paranoia drifts into delusion: chance conversations becoming an interrogation, the smiling face an attempt to prise open your cover. So the check-in at the airport, the line of suited businessmen, became a queue of returning MI officers and informers. The self-conscious attempt to appear ordinary, the desire to become anonymous makes you grip your passport a little too hard, smile a little too broadly and laugh a little too loudly.

Our flights circled Rangoon several times before skittering over the tarmac at Mingaladon Airport. Our tactics were similar, to be absorbed by a boisterous crowd of backpackers and hurtle with them towards the immigration desks. On those two separate journeys, both of us jockeyed to get our passports stamped, but still felt no relief. Landing at the airport is not difficult. Leaving it is. The MI casually slouch in checked longyis, forming a cordon in the arrivals hall, like Graham Greene's brooding Tontons Macoute, seething behind their aviator shades, men more evil than the generals they follow.

Then came the jubilant taxi-ride into the city past the Gems Emporium, beside Inya Lake, past the ministry ('not at the end of a long tree-lined road but just off the main road and down a short lane') and past the turning into University Avenue, where a government bill-board proclaimed 'The People's Desire':

- Oppose those relying on external elements, acting as stooges, holding negative views.
- Oppose those trying to jeopardise stability of the state and progress of the nation.
- Oppose foreign nations interfering in internal affairs of the state.
- Crush all internal and external destructive elements as the common enemy.

Goonish Post-it notes stuck up by the regime and ignored by everyone who cycles past. Beyond lay that famous villa smothered by green moss and fronds of peeling plaster, decorated with red pennants, which fluttered like balloons inviting guests to a child's birthday party. 'That's where Aung San Suu Kyi lives,' the taxi driver remarked, looking for a reaction in his rear-view mirror. 'I'm not just a taxi driver, you know. I used to be Professor of Dentistry until they closed down my department. Seven years at university. Twenty years in practice.' The conversation petered out into a guilty silence. A draught through a half-open window blew a newspaper off the front passenger seat to reveal a pair of aviator shades.

Rangoon is a suffocating haze of shattered pavements, a place where to catch a stranger's eye is to acknowledge the fear that rules the country, where the oppression is so deeply rooted that the Burmese have learned to live alongside it. They picnic in People's Park while soldiers loom in the bushes with cocked guns. They sip tea and deconstruct the junta around Sule Pagoda, while tanks brood in the compound opposite. And for those Western tourists who choose to visit, it is possible to tour the capital and see absolutely nothing beyond the markets and pagodas, the temples and museums, to be seduced by the sultry pace of an exotic garden city lined with palms, whose roofs are rubbed with gold, to absorb nothing more than the ghost of Kipling. But Burma is a kaleidoscope. It appears to shine brilliantly with its fields of oil, forests of teak, pearl-filled straits and valleys of jade, but beyond the iridescence lie malarial slums, the universities' locked gates, the crumbling roads and railways and the chain-gangs conscripted to repair them.

It was Day Five before we collided in the upstairs corridor of a family-run hotel, and it was hard not to raise a cheer or run grinning down the hall. Instead, we vanished behind a locked door and, while the taps and shower pelted, poured glasses of cold Mandalay beer and swapped stories in whispers. We had both seen the man on a black Chinese bicycle doing relays up and down Bogyoke Aung San Road, spotted the red mini that curb-crawled Pyay Road and stumbled over the men who tumbled out of bushes, clutching notebooks like over-eager reporters.

But now there was no more time to kill. We had used up a week of the 28-day visa. We would have to find a quick way of reaching Upper Burma. As the regime continually changes its mind, often the straightforward approach is worth a try. Areas that for decades have been off-limits are overnight re-designated as tourist attractions, depending on the success of the SPDC's pacification programme and the speed with which it mops up the evidence of in-surrection. So on Day Eight we went to the State Tourist Office, squatting in an airless colonial hall, staffed by picture-book Bur-mese girls, who leapt from their chairs when we tumbled through the towering double doors.

'Please to come in. Please to come in. Water? We can help you,' beamed one of them.

'We wanted to go to Hpakant,' we said, getting straight to the point.

'Pagan is very beautiful. The temples are very beautiful. The people are very beautiful.'

'No, Hpakant. The jade mines. Hpakant,' we said, again and again.

'Buy jade? Yes, the Gems Emporium. Very beautiful. Only ten minute by taxi.'

Riled by her wilful deafness, we pointed to the Kachin Hills on a map we had bought in London. She blanched and giggled before vanishing into a back room. Fifteen minutes later, after whispered conversation behind a curtain, a stern-faced manager emerged, holding aloft a leaflet that stated: 'All out efforts are being made un-der the Ministry of Hotels and Tourism to facilitate tours of foreign visitors in Myanmar.' But her stubby finger ran down the page un-til it tapped on a small paragraph at the bottom: 'Hpakant is not al-lowed to foreign travellers.'

What of the 'treasures from the gem mines . . . famous since the days of the ancient kings'? She unrolled an official map of Burma and banged it down on the desk. Wherever it was hatched and high-lighted was a high-security zone where foreigners could not go. Vast regions of Burma were blotted out, smothered by the censor's marker pen. But we were mining consultants or perhaps even gemologists; our Bangkok credentials spilled out of our pockets. Her eyes narrowed and she picked up a phone, gabbling into the handset before tearing a strip off an insignificant corner of Burma, on which she wrote a name. 'Myanmar Economic Holdings, ex-pecting you this afternoon. Go to office and report. Bye bye,' she said, helping us out of her office, foisting into our hands a copy of *Myanmar Today* that commemorated the golden jubilee of inde-pendence. Pages of portraits of unsmiling generals and their cohorts were followed by lists of the junta's commanders and ministries. A double-page spread was devoted to the 'Narcotic Drugs and Psychotropic Substances Law 1993' and another detailed the alleged success of the country's drug destruction programmes in kilograms, litres, ampoules and tablets. At the back were the lyrics to a song that would have made Aung San wince:

Free like the flapping wings of birds
Brilliant freedom already completed 50 years
Independence cannot be gained by sitting down and saying the magic
   word,
National Brethren made equal sacrifices for the whole country to be
   free and happy
The buds of independence now in full bloom.
Patriotic mind and patriotic blood most important . . .
In building a modern glorious nation like purified gold.

We had been thrust into a meeting with the military. The last place we wanted to be. Myanmar Economic Holdings was an army-run company that oversaw the country's natural resources, but we could not fail to show up. Things were now moving far too quickly. We still had cover stories to inflate. Once before we had almost been caught out in the ministry that-wasn't-at-the-end-of-the-long-lane. Then, we had announced ourselves as environmental scientists, only to be confronted by photographs of rare tubers and plants that were seemingly produced by way of small talk but, more than likely, were also a test of our credentials. Then we only survived by diverting the conversation, but how would we cope against a Burmese geologist eager to sound out our expertise on carboniferous clay?

It became apparent, almost instantaneously, that the man we faced that afternoon was a career soldier who obviously knew a lot about pacification and little about the rock-face. Sitting in his shuttered office beneath nineteen framed photographs of the SPDC, military men bedecked in medals and funereal ties, he introduced himself as Colonel Maunt Maunt Aye as we gabbled about jadeite and the mines of Hpakant. We talked too much and nervously rattled our cups of green tea until the uniformed Colonel held up his hands.

Why hadn't we given him some warning? What company did we represent? What exactly did we do? Why were we here on a tourist visa if we were not intent on sightseeing? His English was too good for us to side-step, but thankfully he left us no time to answer. It was all very difficult, he said. We understood. It would be extraordinary, he said. We agreed. But there was an outside possibility, if we could contribute to the cost of arranging such a difficult journey. A silence crowded his tiny office. Was the Colonel asking us for money? 'About . . . 1200 US dollars in theory . . . my administrative costs . . . your difficult journey,' he stuttered into his tea.

The price was the equivalent of ten years' salary for a man of his rank, and we all sat in silence, weighing up the consequences of what had just been half-said. The Colonel rummaged through a drawer. We smiled and listened to the murmur of the ceiling fan. Then at last he gathered himself. 'Even if I help you it's all going to be terribly difficult,' he said. Our request would have to be forwarded to his superiors and several other ministries. Of course, the cost of a military escort to the mines was exorbitant. 'Do you know how difficult this is going to be? I am a busy man and don't have time.' Was he now back-tracking? 'It's entirely up to you, but if half the money is at the gate, maybe tomorrow, then it could help bring things to a happy conclusion.' The Colonel straightened his cuffs. 'Let us say one week. Yes, one week. Well, maybe more . . . if it happens. You will have to be in Myitkyina, ready to go. I don't need to see you ever again. See my officers on the gate. Maybe tomorrow. Half tomorrow – put it in a sealed envelope. My name on the front. Don't need to say anything. Pay the remainder on completion.' He stood up and we all shook hands, accomplices in an unstated agreement, and left without speaking another word.

We raced back to the hotel room, and through the din of the blasting shower debated our next move. If we gave the Colonel money would we ever hear from him again? It was not as if we could call the police. Would we be arrested for trying to bribe the SPDC? How would it look if it became known that we had paid the junta for a story? No one likes to pay for the truth by the yard, but there was no other way of getting into Burma's most heavily guarded project. And with the photographs from Hpakant in our minds, we headed for the bank.

※

The military had requisitioned the majority of seats on the Myanma Airways plane, forcing paying civilians to squat in the aisles. We had to fight, shoulder-to-shoulder, with colonels and captains, but then we seemed to be the only passengers who actually wanted a window seat. It was Day 10 and our ancient Fokker F-28 pitched and yawed along the great Irrawaddy. A Victorian traveller had described it as 'an artery of the world . . . that flows for a thousand miles from its mysterious birthplace in the Himalayas . . . to the sea into which it pours through a hundred mouths.'[6] Now we fluttered above the waters that were once 'the life of the common people with its passing joys and sorrows'. Plunging out of the clouds, our Fokker skimmed over the bones of mad King Sagaing Min's Ava, only the crumbling remains of a watch-tower visible, and we thought of Major Burney who had glimpsed it in 1829 as he had sailed towards the 'city of gems'. We hopped over an islet in the Irrawaddy where King Bodawpaya had imprisoned Michael Symes in 1795 and recalled how the Empire's ambassadors had steadfastly refused to unslipper. Off to the right was Amarapura, the 'city of immortals . . . lasting as the firmament', but it was now a pile of abandoned joss houses and hoary tamarind trees.[7] We refuelled in Mandalay, King Mindon's mythological escarpment. The axle around which the world had once rotated had been whitewashed by the SPDC and chain-gangs had re-cut its moat. The F-28 hurtled over the upper defile, the silver thread of the river below, and we thought of Bayfield and Griffith racing back to the British residency through the restless waters of the Elephant and Cow gorge. When we landed in baking Myitkyina, a once-feared outpost on 'the borders of savagery', we tried not to stare at the manacled prisoners who mended pot-holes in the broken runway.[8] To the right, plains petered into jungle that now obscured Qianlong's Jade Road. Before us, fading into 'the blue distance', were the great peaks of Loi Lem and Loi Law and on the horizon, at last we saw the purple mountains of Yunnan.

The desiccated capital of Kachin State was covered in a sickly layer of fine yellow dust that coated skin, hair and bags. We had hoped to disappear in the crowds, to pass our time unobtrusively, waiting for the Colonel's messenger, but in a frontier town black with government troops, it was obviously a stupid plan. We were the main attraction in a place short of side-shows, lines of children chasing us into the stifling morning market, chattering and grabbing at our clothes. There were old women hacking up chickens with *dahs,* who peered at us from under their conical hats. Apothecaries selling sticky pellets of opium broke off from the barter to gape slack-jawed at the strangers. We could only hope that the Colonel's greed would deliver us a permit – before we ran out of time.

Myitkyina's crumbling colonial trading houses were now Indian-run general stores that sold plastic buckets and water-pistols that had been manufactured in the Chinese hinterland. The only map permitted by the government was a faceless grid of streets without names. But here was the Hsu Taung Pyi Zeditaw pagoda, where the faithful prayed at dusk. We found the Islam Nawku Htingnu mosque and the pungent curry house next door with its pyramids of samosas. We visited Christ the King with its nostalgic Home Counties spire and high-arched windows. And we shaded ourselves beneath a banyan tree, scoured the morning and afternoon markets, touched a stone that had been blessed by Buddha. All of which took only one baking afternoon.

We visited the famed confluence, where the N'mai Hka and the Mali Hka Rivers writhed together to form the Irrawaddy, the only place outside Myitkyina to which we were permitted to travel. We spent an afternoon in the graveyard of the Church of our Lady Queen of Heaven, wandering between loving epitaphs for English mothers and daughters who 'had fallen asleep in Jesus'. Buddhist nuns, swathed like Tantric gurus in white cotton and crimson, their heads shaven and their eyebrows plucked, waddled along the banks of the river as we skimmed water-worn stones before setting off back to town.

In the rush to pack we had brought with us only one book each, that we had greedily devoured by Day 11 and then read again and again until we grew to hate Jeanette Winterson and William Dalrymple. The only other English-language books in town were bibles, the legacy of American missionaries who had flooded the Kachin Hills at the turn of the twentieth century, so there was nothing to do but play word-games and eat. The town was awash with restaurants, and we made balls from fermented fish paste and glutinous rice at the Happy Garden, that also broadcast state TV. Humourless presenters read pointed advice in English and Burmese on how to avoid snakes in the grass, while a choir of tame ethnic women, who had 'returned to the legal fold', sang a hymn to the SPDC every hour after the news. There were a dozen dusty roadside canteens that served 'Chini', 'Biriany' and 'Europe' food, and in each we ate the same curry and rice that clung to our palates like second-hand gum. But we lingered over every grain, savoured the grain and de-seeded the chillies while babbling diners made notes. Soon the friendly guest-house manager was asking when we were moving on, as every day he was required to fill in 21 police reports that recorded our every movement and motion, our meals and even the timing of our showers.

Interminable days beside the river, watching long-tail boats loading and unloading guns bound for some government garrison. Again and again two boys carrying baskets of jujubes who tossed us words of broken English. 'Mr America,' the taller one cried. 'See you last week.' And his short companion slapped him on the back, pleased to have such a friend who could converse with the foreigner. Time was ticking away and all the while a queue of English-speaking Kachin missionaries ground us down with their inquisition. They waited outside the guest-house. They followed us to the market. They trailed us along the river-bank, their woven bags filled with little green books published in Florida by Bill Bright of the Campus Crusade for Christ Inc. 'Dear Friend, yes, you can know God personally, as presumptuous as that may sound. God is so eager to establish a personal, loving relationship with you that He has already made the arrangements.' Inside was a diagram of a train drawn by the 'engine of fact' that chugged along the lines of feeling, pulling behind it two carriages loaded down with 'faith'. We were too hot to run away.

Day 14. No word from the Colonel. We struck out on our own. Driven by boredom and anxiety, we tried for a lift to Hpakant. A taxi driver laughed in our faces and then quickly reversed down the street, as did the driver of an empty tipper truck and a restaurant manager in a buckled Morris Oxford. Although we were supposedly only 60 miles away from the mines, we might as well have been sitting in London.

Day 20. Six days had slipped by, our hopes were fading. We rose at dawn, unable to sleep, and strolled down to the market, where we saw lines of Chinese trucks loading up with people who looked like the Karen from the south. They seemed out of place, and so we walked over, tracked by an ever-present missionary. The people in the trucks were gabbling excitedly about the journey ahead, he said. They were talking about green stones that would change their lives. An old woman was planning to open a shop, a young boy wanted a ticket to America, a teenage girl was planning to buy a wardrobe full of shoes. The trucks were bound for Hpakant and, according to one of the drivers, those returning from the mines would reach Myitkyina later that night.

The town's electricity ran out by 7 p.m., when Myitkyina was plunged into a half-light stalked by nervous soldiers. Candles and paraffin lamps transformed it into a shadowy fairground for the gold-rush rich. Small groups of Chinese merchants and men who would be jadeite kings squatted on their haunches and shone torches on green stones the size of rice grains. Drunken peasants in shiny trousers so new that they hadn't had time to turn them up spilled out of karaoke clubs and private bars, the only buildings that were powered by generators, apart from the home of the local *Tatmadaw* commander. In his compound there was plenty of light and music and girls. His outhouse had been transformed into a brothel, its entrance draped with fairy lights like Santa's grotto. A sergeant sitting on a garden chair had been detailed on pimping duty. The commander's corpulent wife, wrists weighed down by jadeite bangles, was the raucous madam who kept everyone in check, cuffing errant customers, screeching at disobedient girls and for us to go away.

We stopped in a bar overlooking the Irrawaddy, to pass a few hours sipping beer, until the owner insisted that we leave. The shadows of boats were moving towards us, low in the water, their decks weighed down with a mysterious cargo, guarded by soldiers with raised guns. 'You shouldn't be here. It's not good to see this,' the barman warned as he showed us the door. It was barely 10 p.m., but Myitkyina was already dead as the moon, silent except for a distant rumble that came from beyond the airport road. Hiding in the doorway of a trading house that still bore the legends of enterprise from a century before, 'quality and cheapness in woollen cotton', 'fancy goods, building and road contractor', we watched as trucks rolled into town. They tipped a shamble of men and women, mud-covered and exhausted, onto the darkened streets, most of whom quickly shuffled away. We asked our ecclesiastical shadow, his Florida booklets in hand, to talk to one woman who remained, sitting dazed on the steps of a store. She had come from Hpakant, she whispered, her age masked by dirt. 'I had to work for three months just to raise the money to get out of there, and I'm never going back.'

We followed her down a dusty buffalo track that led to a crumbling hall. Inside ceiling fans stirred soupy air. Motionless men and women lay in rows of rusting iron beds, like the casualties of war. We asked a solitary young doctor what was wrong with his patients, and he said they were miners from Hpakant. He was clearly uncomfortable talking to us, but he opened a medicine cabinet and inside were rolls of gauze and antiseptic fluid. No needles or syringes as they were banned by the SPDC, he told us. In a country that was one of the largest producer of opium in the world, there were no drugs, not even morphine. Outside, away from prying ears, the doctor flopped to the ground. 'Every day they come here in a terrible state. Hundreds and hundreds. Back from the mines. I don't know what is going on there. We are not allowed to see,' the doctor said with his head in his hands. 'We are not supposed to talk about this, about what is happening. It's a crisis that no one wants to deal with. The foreign doctors have come here and tried to help us. But the government prevented them from even leaving this town. They wanted to go to Hpakant but it was forbidden. They told us that this is AIDS and it is a human disaster on a biblical scale. I'm not equipped to deal with this. All I have is gauze.' He scrambled to his feet and retreated into the clinic, leaving us in the darkened garden to listen to the rising tremble of cicadas.

Day 21. We woke early. Our time was up. The Colonel had taken the money and run. The guest-house owner needed our room. Our presence in the town was causing difficulties. All we had were the scattered fragments of a story, a glimpse into the regime's secret project and a few photographs that were not our own. The dust-cloud that loomed above us was now a constant reminder of our failure, and bitter and protracted silences made living in our cramped flop-house unbearable. We secretly blamed each other, snapping at the slightest provocation, and when one of us suggested that we pack, we threw all our possessions into bags in less than five minutes, abandoning Winterson and Dalrymple to the missionaries. There was a flight at 12 with two seats available, and so we sat down to one last, tense breakfast, staring blankly at a slogan painted on the wall. 'Natural Resources are Limited. Creativity is Limitless.' Our coffee undrunk, the doughnuts wilting, we walked out of the gate as a rickshaw drew up. Wiping the dust from his new nylon sports jacket, his perfect plumped quiff arriving before him, a small satchel strung over his back, here was the new guest who would take over our room. We scowled as we hopped into his rickshaw and told the driver to head for the airport. We had hours to kill before the flight, but we could no longer bear to sit on the edge of a story. The rickshaw driver was standing up on his pedals, straining to get his heavy load moving, when a voice came from nowhere. 'Where is Levy?' We shot a look towards the courtyard. The rickshaw back-pedalled and our eyes met with an expensive pair of sunglasses. 'Levy and Clark,' he purred, drawing a pink plastic comb through his hair. 'I am Corporal Aung Nye.'

The Corporal sat down, uninvited, and helped himself to a cup of green tea before cramming our doughnuts into his mouth. 'I am Corporal Aung Nye. I have studied English for six years. I have read many interesting books. I have travelled all over my country and have spent days trying to get here. You are very, very lucky I have come.' He sent a boy scurrying for a thermos of hot water with a flick of his wrist and shouted at the guest-house manager to bring him some towels. He ordered us to sit down and pay atten-tion, and lifted up his aviators. 'I have been told to take you to Hpakant,' he said, his black eyes gathering like a storm. 'I don't know how you got permission. I don't want to know. It's going to cost you a lot of dollars but I will do my duty and you will pay me. You will pay the Colonel. You will pay the General and you will pay the check-point guards. You will listen to everything I tell you, carefully. Is all of this clear like the crystals?'

Before we could say a word, he pulled a piece of paper out of his satchel. Here was a scribbled picture of a mountain range, two triangles with ruffles of snow, a river with fish jumping out of the water and a lake on which sailed a floating pagoda. The Colonel had obviously spent hours drawing our route. A path and a place that he had designated as a picnic site were marked with a black line and badly drawn cutlery. And a sparkling gem located the mines of Hpakant. Across the top of the page, one of Rangoon's most decorated officers had written in different coloured pens, 'Welcome to Jadeland', and in the corner, 'Copyright – Myanmar Economic Holdings.'

We thought Burma had run out of surprises. But here was a government soldier assigned to take us to the mines of Hpakant. Then he whipped out another piece of paper that was apparently a permit that had been counter-signed by the Managing Director of Myanmar Economic Holdings, General Than Oo. We would start before dawn. The journey would be long. It was a dirty and sordid place and he couldn't think why we wanted to go. But no, no, he would help us, he would find us a driver and a vehicle. We watched as he swaggered out of the courtyard, and we realised that we had not spoken a single word. 'Don't be late,' he shouted over his shoulder before hijacking a passing car and, despite the perplexed Kachin driver's protestations, the Corporal ordered him onwards, down the broken back streets, into a cloud of billowing dust.

Racing back into the guest-house, we pleaded for a room for one last night and then sat down to study the permit. But, of course, it was written in Burmese. What did it really say? Was it even a permit? How could we rely on a soldier so full of contempt, his impatient fingers drumming on the table in time with his orders? There were no telephones in Myitkyina that worked. There was no way of letting anyone know what we were about to do. There was also no way of checking his story. One suspicion that we each tried to quash was that we had been uncovered and that this time there would be no printed denouncement. Instead, would we be led to a remote place and then vanish as had so many others? Zaw Tun, Myo Myint Nyein, Aung Myo Tint and six more, accused of opposing the SPDC, had been caged in dog kennels in Rangoon's Insein Jail. U Thein Tin, an NLD leader, had been summarily tried in a prison compound, hooded and beaten, before dying from his injuries only a few days before we had entered the country. In Burma, small crimes have extreme consequences: the illegal possession of a modem or a fax machine that had resulted in the jailing of Leo Nichols. The 65-year-old was godfather to Aung San Suu Kyi and was imprisoned in April 1996, only to die less than two months later in Insein's hospital block. As the evening wore on, our concerns seemed self-indulgent, but Burma sometimes does that to you.

We were ready at 3 a.m. The Corporal called at 4 a.m. in a battered family saloon. He sat up front next to a teenager driver who was propped up on piles of cushions. We squeezed behind with a Kachin translator, who quietly revealed that he suffered from travel sickness as we drove to where the trucks were loading up with their human cargo. Together we roared out of Myitkyina, kicking up a stream of yellow dust, and like a Panzer division storming the desert, the convoy rumbled through town, shooting past the airport and into a militarised zone, the headquarters of the *Tatmadaw*'s Northern Command. Legions of troops marched on the roadside, their boots and tunics caked in dirt, churned up by armoured cars that hurtled across the scorched ground. Beneath us the earth trembled as the Burmese military machine awoke. Endless lines flew past the car windows, barricades and barbed wire stretched to the horizon, trenches and gun emplacements on every bend, pointing towards the twin peaks of Loi Lem and Loi Law. Amid the ordered chaos of the army's mobilisation, heads spun around to catch a glimpse, whispers passed down the lines, a rumour slowly spreading like mustard gas through the battalions of infantry: *kullas* were on the road to Hpakant.

Then a soldier with an assault rifle leapt out into the road, screaming at the car to halt, forcing us out and onto the bonnet, kicking our legs apart. Now we would find out whether our permit was valid and the Corporal was capable. He intoned calmly to the sentry who slowly backed off, all the while keeping his aim. We were pushed back into the car while the Corporal jogged over to the guard-house. We saw flailing hands and heard raised voices, but a few minutes later he emerged, his face fixed in a victorious sneer. 'Move on,' he shouted at the driver, licking his thin lips. 'I want my breakfast.'

The metalled road took us as far as Mogaung, which George Bayfield had found surrounded by a timber stockade. Now barricades and roadblocks fenced everyone in. Bayfield and William Griffith had stopped to take on supplies in a tense and miserable settlement guarded by 2000 bare-breasted soldiers. The ugly, tiled tenements and half-finished brick homes that fought for space along the narrow lines still crawled with soldiers, only now they bristled with Chinese assault rifles.

The driver was directed to a restaurant overlooking the Mogaung River, but the Kachin translator refused to get out. He sunk into the back seat while we accompanied the Corporal inside and perched on tiny stools. A teenage girl brought bowls of eggs and glasses of sludgy coffee as a Burmese rock group, thrashing on TV, welcomed everyone to 'otel California'. It was only then that we noticed that our fellow diners all squinted through aviator shades. 'This is the MI canteen, the food is always good here,' the Corporal chuckled, as he cracked open an egg and sucked out the raw yolk. The letters of Captain S. F. Hannay came flooding back, how he had been kept hostage for a month in Mogaung to prevent him reaching the jade mines, and we too cracked open our eggs and gulped down the viscous albumen.

Sepoy Singh had left Mogaung heading north along the secret Kasa Naga Road before skirting around the Great Golden Mountain to set out for the Assam border. We would have to bear northwest and head towards Kamaing along the Mogaung Valley. Now there was no road but a rutted track that raced through an arid landscape of scrub and elephant grass. Midway through a desolate valley, two soldiers sat on chairs beneath an umbrella. They were miles from the nearest village. They looked like they should be selling raffle tickets, but leapt to their feet when they saw us approach. Two packs of 555s, two dollar bills and a handful of sweets. The Corporal threw them out of the window, ordering the driver on.

The Corolla threw up a dragon's tail as we sped into Kamaing, once a 'mean and paltry town' of two stockades that ringed a hill and a fort, and now the last fresh food stop before the mines of Hpakant. The Corporal screamed at the driver to accelerate, scattering grapefruits, long-beans and children. He bellowed out of the window at Kachin traders in woollen top-hats embroidered with pink and purple pom-poms, their vests shimmering with discs of milk-bottle-top silver. 'I want oranges,' he screamed. 'Officer passing through. I want oranges.' He spied a stall and made the woman fill up a bag, throwing a wad of kyat out of the window, shouting at the car while pointing at the hills.

Bayfield and Griffith had left Kamaing on a 'tedious march', for four days climbing to 2799 feet through a 'heavy and wet' landscape 'with large leafed tea plants' into a 'jungly and evil place'. But within a day they had seen evidence of the mines, giant boulders 'carried by four or five men on bamboos', smaller stones born on 'ingenious frames that rest on the coolie's neck'. Our road out of Kamaing wound its way up into the hills and dissolved into trenches of mud, the Corolla skating on a churning track that regularly swallowed up trucks. The towering conifers and broad-leafed teak trees were now no more than spindly saplings. Vast areas of the jungle had been logged, and without the canopy there was no shade from the sun that beat down relentlessly onto the car's roof. We tried winding up the windows to keep out the dust, but stewed in the suffocating heat. We opened them up again as the car joined the jungle jam of lorries that overflowed with rice-sacks and people, only to be covered in the Corporal's orange spittle.

Everything ground to a halt as we approached the first fortified check-point. Every authority had its own bunker and barrier, the military intelligence and strategic command, the police and immigration, a criminal inquiries unit, pharmaceutical and municipal inspectors. Flies buzzed our ears and sat in our eyes, sweat mingling with the yellow dust to stain our clothes, and above us towered a stockade, ringed with razor wire, its slopes punctured with Burma spikes on top of which sat two men astride a pair of machine-guns. Illiterate soldiers demanded written proof of ID and copies of permits that they could not read. The jungle was seething with insects and men with clipboards. The Corporal argued with them all, waving his papers before slowly climbing the hill of spikes towards the summit. He slid back down 20 minutes later, carried by a stream of mud and effluvia from the camp toilets that were regularly discharged from the crow's nest. 'Dollars, cigarettes and sweets,' the

Corporal muttered as he clambered back into the car, ringing out his spattered longyi. 'Dollars, cigarettes, sweets, or they'll turn us back to Myitkyina.'

He made sure that we only gave the prescribed amount, two dollars, two packets of 555s and a handful of toffees to each, cast out of the window and into the mud, as regulations demanded. If we ever got to the end of this road there had to be enough left for the Corporal.

It took eight hours to clear the 26 check-points that perforated the jungle, and every one of them was the same. Angry soldiers charging at the car, demanding to know why *kullas* were on the road, staring in disbelief at the permits issued by Rangoon, banging their Chinese field sets against the bonnet in futile attempts to contact their commanders. Like Mayouk Teza Naratta, the backwatching governor of Mogaung, no one wanted to take responsibility for allowing strangers into the SPDC's pet project. It was now that our Kachin translator, who endured it all with increasing bad grace, chose to reveal himself by producing small green leaflets from Florida. 'God have mercy on our souls,' he wailed as we ground to a halt. 'If the dust doesn't kill us the soldiers will.' He turned to Bill Bright for salvation.

By the time the hills flew down into a valley, the translator and the Corporal were asleep, exhausted by hours of praying and haggling. They didn't see the broad strip of mud along which restaurants had been built or the warning signs that were strung out along the jungle service station. Small wooden placards, all of them written in English, proclaimed: 'AIDS is a national concern; Anti Narcotics Suppression Association is here.' They were decorated with pictures of wilting poppies and matchstick men stuck with giant syringes that made them all look like voodoo dolls. Then the Corolla dragged itself to the summit of a razor-back ridge and shuddered to a halt. Below us was a steep incline that swept into a shimmering desert obscured by a billowing yellow cloud. The Corporal woke up, wound down the window, cocked his head towards the vista and snorted. 'Welcome to Jadeland.'

Here was the British explorers' 'Lat 25° to 26° North, Long 96° to 97° East', the legendary hills of jadeite, but not as Captain Adamson would have seen them. Before us was a brutalised landscape, the mountains reduced to rubble, the valleys sunk into dark chasms as far as the eye could see. It was impossible not to be awed by the magnitude of the SPDC's project. The sheer scale of the enterprise and their ambition, a termite mound seething with hundreds of thousands of scurrying figures, everything being stripped and sorted, broken down and carted away. And through it all snaked a viscous orange ribbon. Adamson had described the Uru as 'clear as crystal and so alive with fish that they rose to the surface in the evening like trout in an English stream'. But could anything now be living in its poisoned waters?

Twelve

The Valley of Death

We careered into Jadeland on a mudslide, the boy driver whooping with delight until we all spotted the gaping shaft ahead. Grappling with the handbrake, slamming the car into reverse, both feet pinned to the brake pedal, he spun us into a bank of shale. The Kachin translator was praying, the Corporal was cursing and we were in the brace position when a jet of brown water spurted out of the crack in the earth like the blower from a surfacing whale. It poured through the windows, dampening Bill Bright's sermons, covering us all in a film of slurry. The Corporal was caught open-mouthed and scrambled out of the car spluttering, screaming at the miners who bobbed out of the flooded pit. The exchange was in Burmese, but when the half-naked men dived back into the water his meaning became clear. 'They were following a seam,' he raged, ringing out his dripping longyi again. 'They dug up the bloody road. Fucking stupid miners. I can't believe I agreed to do this.'

The driver disentangled himself from the steering column, restarted the car and followed the gusher into town, the wheel arches dragging on the tyres, the exhaust knocking against the chassis. The fountain of water was surging towards the shops and houses that tumbled before us, and we dived into a steaming city, recycled from salvaged wooden planks, bamboo poles and iron sheets, tied together with barbed wire and cane.

The road ahead suddenly split six ways, but the Corporal ordered us on without stopping. 'It's all new,' he said as the car banked to the right. 'There was only one road last time I was here.' The car banked to the left. We scattered the crowds that had begun to emerge as news of our arrival flew through Hpakant. The

Corolla hurled us from side to side, our heads crashing against the roof, veering into dumb-struck shoppers and children, idling by the roadside. They jumped to their feet and ran behind us as we slewed like a rogue waltzer along a track that was abruptly intersected by a newly built wall. But the Corporal screamed 'faster', and the car pin-balled down an open sewer. Bumping over the debris of Hpakant, we were spat out onto a dry river-bed and clung to the seats in front, choking dust rising through the fractured chassis beneath our feet. 'You're in safe hands with me,' the Corporal beamed, oblivious to the detritus that now caked the windows and the oil that slowly seeped from beneath the hood. Had there been an aerial bombardment, had snipers strafed the houses and tracks, had shells removed the fascias of the buildings, had anti-tank mines clawed the ground? 'No,' the Corporal waved his hands furiously. 'No, no, no. The jadeite mines have returned to the legal fold. It's always looked like this.'

Hpakant was constantly re-inventing itself, a work in progress, and in the exhausting rush to follow the veins of jadeite into the valley, through the city and out the other side, houses were flattened, streams became roads and roads became mines. The only permanent structure in the midst of the chaos was a 50-foot-high cement bayonet. 'The symbol of democracy,' the Corporal boasted, pointing to the statue, around which a pack of hang-dog men sprawled. Behind it was a colosseum built from corrugated sheets and tank-tracking, its slit of a door guarded by a soldier with an assault rifle. 'Fresh food,' he explained. Behind the tin-pot towering walls were crates of bananas, beans and pork bellies, imported by truck from Myitkyina, that men in spanking new jeans and khaki were loading into Burmese army jeeps emblazoned with the insignia of the local battalion commander.

The town was a free festival of frantic workers, touts and chancers, from every corner of Burma, a multitude of faces and costumes, but everyone wore the same dazed expression. Until we drove into town that day, they probably thought they had seen it all. Then the car juddered, the driver squeaked and the Corporal ordered us out of the Corolla that had finally ground to a halt. We would have to join the sweating log-jam on foot. The crowd pressed forwards to touch: tattooed men from Nagaland, their severe bangs framing their faces, flesh-tunnels bored through their ear-lobes; sinewy men from the hills of Shan State in their Ho Chih Minh canvas caps and indigo flares; bedraggled Kachin, wrapped in crimson blankets, their embroidered bags slung under one arm and a sheathed *dah* thrown across their backs. Men with legs bound in rough black sacking patted our faces. Women, their gaping mouths a slash of betel-red, stroked the sun-bleached hair on our arms. Country and Western would-be guerrillas, strapped into empty ammo pouches and pristine commando slacks, played ball with a boy sporting a 'Bad to the Bone' T-shirt. A middle-aged peddler ran beside us pointing to his incongruous vest that declared in large red letters: 'Kill All Hippies'. Waves of hands pushed and pulled, tugged and yanked at our shirts, and behind them we could just make out gangs of boys and young men who hung in doorways, skinny and listless.

Soldiers grabbed for their guns before seeing the Corporal who screamed in Burmese, waving our permits above his head. And all the time there were questions in a cacophony of ten different languages. Everyone wanted to know who we were, and at last the crowd pushed forward a crook-legged merchant from Yunnan. He sidled up, chewing on a wad of tobacco, and spat out a few words of something. 'Mercia, Franc, Ingleesh?' he enquired. 'What you do? Name? Michael Jackson, Lady Diana? Why you here? Manchester United?' The delighted crowd applauded until the Corporal lashed out with his boot, kicking the merchant's crippled leg from under him, sending him flying into the wall of faces with a splutter of Burmese expletives.

We pressed on through the treacly heat and into a beggar's bazaar, past alchemists, magicians, faith-healers, quack doctors and 'head surgeons'. Their stalls were crowded with wan patients slumped beneath Sanskrit, Chinese and English signs that announced miracle cures for cancer, foot rot, tooth-ache, 'women's weakness' and Jade Disease. 'Feet and teeth expert', 'Cancer Glue sold here', they proclaimed. 'If you have feeling weak. We can make you strong.' Limp pyramids of Toblerone toppled onto Marlboro cartons stacked like targets at a fair-ground shooting gallery. Chinese champagne bottles lay on top of crates of Johnnie Walker besides rolls of gauze and sterilised bandages. Tinned cheese and potted shrimps, Danish ham and luncheon meat, antiseptic lotion and thousands upon thousands of bottles of Tylenol, enough to ease a hang-over the size of Manhattan.

We squeezed between wooden carts of pills and potions, packets of teak shavings, wrapped in their English instructions, 'to be boiled and swallowed three times a day', for all known diseases but particularly 'in the heart and trousers'. Cloven hooves and tiger's penis. Bell jars of floating foetuses. Star-fish and sea-horses, snakes and lizards. Then two large taloned shadows fell across the path, cast by a pair of giant paws that clung to the rim of a large box. We hesitated, the crowd giggled and the trader slowly tipped the cardboard box forward, but inside there was no body. 'Soup, soup,' the Corporal slurped theatrically, lifting an imaginary ladle to his lips. 'Very good. Bear paw soup.' A pile of rubbish wilting in the sun behind us began to rustle, and out of it crawled a marmoset, chained to a stake in the ground, pursing its blistered lips. Was there anything on it left to eat?

Before us the road fell into another deep shaft that had momentarily displaced the market. An animal trader claimed to have found gold in the dust, and now his rumour was being excavated. More than 100 men and women feverishly panned around the rim, using liquid mercury that they had been told would separate gold dust from mud. But there was no gold and the metallic poison ran over their feet and hands.

The market ended where the evil-smelling Uru River ran through town, bobbing with empty penicillin bottles, the razor-sharp remains of severed Coca-Cola cans nestling in a log-jam of charred silver foil. The orange ribbon of sewage, in which women beat their clothes against boulders, had been re-routed on the orders of armed forces chief, General Maung Aye's, son-in-law to expose a jadeite vein, the Corporal said, and before us was all that remained of the Kachin Hills. The once verdant peaks and tangled slopes had been sculpted into thin chimneys of rock and earth, whittled away by years of hard labour. Below, the valley floor plunged into an amber chasm that appeared to engulf everything in its path. Its walls, like a Roman amphitheatre, dropped hundreds of feet into the dark, where only the fluttering shadows of miners could be seen amid the dust. As we drew nearer we could make out thousands of nearly naked men and women cloaked in mud and bamboo hats, hauling boulders and earth in cane baskets. Others plunged eight-foot steel staves into the hillside, breaking away crumbs of rock and soil. To the left, men and women washed themselves in the slurry, pouring it over their hair and limbs. To the right, skeletal wooden ladders rose out of the crater and ran up rock chimneys. The miners who scaled them, those who scrambled along the sharply winding hairpin paths, the distant figures chipping away in the chasm and on top of the hills, the cantilevered gantries that whirred as they hauled rocks up to the surface, all moved in unison like the workings of a giant glass-backed watch, with its springs and balances, spinning-cogs and wheels driven in precision by jewels.

The heat forced us back, and we squatted in the shade of a tipper truck until a flood of people overflowed from the lip of the cauldron, spilling past us with down-turned faces, all registered by a young woman who checked their names against a human inventory. Saturated with sweat, blistered and panting, they threw their loads into the waiting trucks, oblivious to everything, conscious only of the long climb back down into the fiery pit.

All we had with us was a small instant camera, afraid that anything more sophisticated would not pass for the tools of a mining consultant interested in the process of extraction rather than the human by-product. For the first time we attempted to grab some pictures and forced our way to the edge of the pit. The people straining under the weight of their soil-packed panniers parted without losing a stride. There was no talk of Manchester United, no curious smiles or outstretched arms, only a dogged determination to reach the trucks and the end of the shift.

Of course, the Corporal saw us with our camera and charged over. We thought of trying to cover it with our shirts but he was on us in seconds. 'You'll get a better view of it all if you come round here,' he said and, to our amazement, took us behind a gantry. 'You want to take a closer look, to see how we do it?' He dodged between the ascending miners and we followed him down, gasping for air, the dust choking our throats and eyes, until we reached the very bottom, coated in a moist yellow film that was glazed by the incendiary air. Hundreds of diggers and carriers, all lacquered with mud, turned to look at us, their heads raised by our alien consonants, while we pondered how little must have changed since the days when King Bodawpaya's Manipuri conscripts worked the pits. 'Dig, dig. They want to see you. Dig for the foreigners,' the Corporal shrieked. 'Harder. Do you want them to think you're useless?' We wanted to shout him down, to tell those people who looked at us with contempt that we were not clients of the State Peace and Development Council (SPDC), but instead we dutifully snapped away as the Corporal played the role of overseer. Suddenly a miner dropped to his knees, his bruised arms scooping a stone out of the dirt, but the Corporal was there before him. 'Green, green. I saw it first,' he yelled, knocking the teenage digger aside, snatching his splinter of jadeite. The boy fell to the ground, his longyi riding up, his spindly legs and arms a jumble of bamboo poles. 'A present from Hpakant,' the Corporal said, presenting us with the nugget. We were too ashamed to look at the miner who had lost his shard of jadeite and walked away, crawling up the hairpins and out of the chasm. We had had enough of the Corporal for one day, but he lagged behind us, eyes trained on the spoil. He appeared to find it hard to leave the money pit that intoxicated everybody who climbed into it. 'Jade eyes,' he said, catching us up, gasping for air. 'I have jade eyes.'

We all struck out towards a white-and-green wedding cake that teetered up on the hillside, its walls wrapped in ribbons of poor jadeite, its rough concrete base still wet to touch, and embedded in the top was a plastic sign announcing the 'luxury standard Jade City Hotel'. A Chinese contractor plying for trade among Burmese government officials and dignitaries had apparently just opened its doors. The unlit foyer was a vast expanse of marble, staffed by a saturnine receptionist who demanded to know why we had been brought to the generals' accommodation. The Corporal turned his back on her. 'Stay here,' he ordered, 'do not move until I come back. Then we'll go for dinner.'

Rattling a coat-hanger full of keys, our sulking hostess stomped up a cancerous concrete staircase. We came to a halt on the second floor where labourers on their knees were laminating everything in green lino. She unlocked our room and scuttled away without uttering a word. Inside was a king-size bed draped in Chinese fun-fur blankets that were still in their wrapping. A bulbous television squatted on a veneer plinth, encased in its polystyrene and plastic packaging. There was even an air-conditioning unit, a satellite receiver and an en-suite bathroom, and we contemplated a long soak, a cold beer and a snatch of MTV before a middle-aged man unlocked our door with his key. 'Use mini bar,' said the Burmese hotel manager, flustered by his first-ever customers. 'Use all facility. Have great time. Welcome to Jade City.' But inside the fridge were pale-green towels, a toothbrush, a comb and a small green bottle of shampoo labelled 'Happy Hair'. The taps exuded a trickle of sludge that slipped into a nicotine-yellow bathtub. There was no electricity to power anything in any of the twenty rooms, but then again there were no guests to complain. Like von Sternberg's papier-mâché Shanghai, the Jade City Hotel was simply a card and cloth illusion.

In the absence of gushing taps, we sat in the dark and discussed our plans via written notes. Almost certainly the Corporal was now announcing our arrival to all of Hpakant's governing agencies, the MI and the *Tatmadaw*. Our chaperones would undoubtedly want us to spend time visiting pits, discussing the costs of the new bulldozers, recording the views of Burmese mineralogists and Chinese contractors. They would not want us to stray from their sides. On our whistle-stop tour we had so far only seen symptoms of the stories that had escaped through the Burmese jungle. Somehow we would have to lose our minders. But if we struck out on our own, how would we make ourselves understood? If we used our Kachin translator he would be dangerously exposed by anything we wrote. We would have to find another way.

We smelt the after-shave and whisky seconds before the spirit of Graceland came through our door. The Corporal had obviously showered elsewhere and was ready for a night on the town. 'Let's go for a Chinese,' he announced, skipping down the fractured staircase to where our patched-up Corolla was waiting. 'Get in. No walking at night. You never know what you'll bump into,' he giggled as we tore off down the lanes in a blur of neon and fairy lights. We drew up at a gleaming new restaurant in a long terrace of faceless ply-board dwellings and stepped inside, passing over discarded bones and knots of noodles. A plastic curtain was whipped around us and we sat in silence in our fortune-teller's booth staring at the

Burmese menu. 'Whisky,' the Corporal bellowed at no one in particular, and a half-empty bottle of 'Johnnie Black' was pushed through the curtain. He troughed the heaving plates of chicken, pork and rice that followed, smearing it all in fish paste, eased down with gulps of whisky, and the more he swigged the clearer it became. We ordered a second bottle of 'Johnnie Black' and soon all of our glasses were overflowing with *bonhomie*. We sipped while he glugged, listening while he gabbled, narrating the story of his life: school; army; conquests; a girlfriend in Rangoon and a wedding he had pencilled in for the following September. Finally, at 9 p.m., he called for the bill and we weaved back to the Jade City Hotel. 'I'm next door,' he slurped. 'Sleep well. We'll start at 6 a.m., when the new shift begins.'

We sat on the fun-fur blankets, waiting to hear the heavy breathing begin, contemplating whether he was a light sleeper, if a watchman guarded the hotel, whether the army patrols that we had seen sweeping through Hpakant by day worked through the night. It had been difficult enough disappearing in the Burmese jungle, and here it was impossible to tell enemies from friends. But when we thought we could at last hear the rumble of congested airways through the paper-thin walls, we disguised ourselves as best we could. Slipping into long-sleeved dark shirts, baseball hats pulled down over our heads, Burmese sandals on our feet, we pushed open our door. We needed some air. We were feeling sick. We were looking for a cup of coffee: all and any of the flummery of excuses that come to mind in anticipation of being caught.

We spent much of that first night searching for a man whose name we had been given in the weeks before we flew to Upper Burma. He didn't know that we were coming. We entered his dimly lit home, unsure of whether it was the right house or even whether he was the right man, but when our story tumbled out, he fell to his knees. 'It's a miracle,' he whispered. 'How could foreigners have got into the mines? You have risked and I will risk. I will show you Hpakant.' He gave us dark longyis in exchange for our filthy jeans, and together we walked out into the city of lights.

Hpakant's steaming lanes of timber-frame houses throbbed with laughter and drinking, their upper windows 'bulging with glass like dirty soap bubbles, yellowing at the edges'.[1] Like 1930s Shanghai,

Hpakant was an insolent town, a 'panoramic mural of the best and worst of the Orient . . . bawdy and gaudy . . . a contradiction of manners and morals'. Revellers in satin suits dined on rice and roast meat, smoking American cigarettes in the hundreds of tiny bars that peeked out from behind the plywood doors that in the daytime had been bolted shut. Off-duty soldiers, their twill shirts opened to the waist, their wide-brimmed hats tilted, staggered hand in hand through the mud and dust, bottles of beer and rice whisky passing along their lines. Girls pattered in high heels, their hair entwined with night queen, their mouths picked out in crimson-lake, arm in arm as if they were pacing The Bund. The mournful whine of karaoke stars echoed across the Uru River, the top notes of the mining town underscored by the percussive rumble of Hpakant-kyi, the largest pit of all. The empty orchestra thundered on through the night, thumping and grinding as a constant reminder, to those who had already clocked off, of the next shift to come. With its terracotta glow, the dust sparkling in the moonlight, Hpakant assumed a magical air. It was not too hard to imagine how the ancient legends of a sparkling lost valley in Old Cathay had mesmerised those early Western explorers. But with its arcades and boardwalk cheer, Hpakant was now more like Coney Island. Promiscuous couples promenaded in a feverish climate, a clinch in a darkened doorway, the tension and fever of a gambling town with its promise of fortune and threat of ruin. And as in those 1930s Shanghai romances, the city was a 'symphony of lust', waltzing to the 'rhythm of abandon', and evenings that began in Love Lane always ended up in Blood Alley.

Our friend urged us on, past a terrace of compounds around the rim of Hpakant-kyi, through the bamboo lock-ups that the Corporal had told us were storerooms. Now, outside them all were sentries who whistled at passers-by. 'Hurry, hurry, keep your head down,' our friend insisted. 'Turn left, through the door and keep on going.' The angular shadow of a bony young miner slipped past, tying his open longyi into a knot as we entered the yard of a two-storey building whose windows were nailed shut. Inside was a spartan waiting area with a few broken-backed chairs, and beyond were half a dozen stifling rooms that all seemed empty. We could hear voices on the other side of a door but were steered into a cubicle. Inside, there was a single bed pressed against the wall, its stained sheets still warm. A dripping candle illuminating soft-focus posters of Burmese beauties that had been ripped from an out-of-date calendar. In a corner was a small wooden locker decorated with cut-outs of Burmese pop groups, 'Emperor' and 'Iron Cross'. And photographs: a smiling girl in a new pinafore dress standing before Shwe Dagon Pagoda; a laughing wedding party beside a river, toasting each other with thermoses of tea. A plastic comb, toilet paper, a sliver of soap, a single longyi neatly folded. Then a girl tumbled into the room, pushed from behind by an unseen hand. There was barely space for us all, so we sat in a line along her unmade bed as her friend reassured her.

Her hair was cut into a ragged bob, her cheeks smeared with circles of *thanaka,* and she could have been any one of the women we had met along the banks of the Tenasserim. Her hand cupped over her mouth, she whispered that she was 25 years old, had come from Taungoo in Shan State where her three sisters still lived, and couldn't remember how long she had been in Hpakant. Four months after her father had died of malaria – leaving the family with debts of 40,000 kyat (£133) – she had left home. 'I came here looking for work with my only brother,' she told us. 'He wanted to go to university.'

We waited. She kicked her feet. 'He needed money. My mother needed money. We had to clear our debts. We heard that money is made here and we saved to get a truck ride to the mines.'

She fiddled with a splinter of bamboo. 'We both worked in the mines but my brother changed. Within a month. He didn't want to talk to me. He was tired all the time. He said he was moving in with friends but I never saw them. Then he vanished and I was left on my own. I was exhausted. I worked for fifteen hours at a time. The night shifts were a little bit better because it was cooler. One day I met a woman in the market who told me she would be my aunt. She would buy me clothes and could help me earn a lot of money. She brought me here. She said it was a business but I didn't know what she meant.'

The girl shrank back further into the corner. 'They locked me in this room and then men came in and wanted sex. Six or sometimes ten men came every night. I have been here for weeks but I still cry when they come in. I'm afraid of having sex with them. It hurts. Some are very violent.'

The shuddering of the partition wall, urgent male voices, the sounds of drunken laughter like broken crockery coming from the room next door. We pressed her on. She said that the brothel owner charged 600 kyat (£2) for sex, and from that money she paid for her food, her locker and her room. The brothel owner took 10 per cent of her earnings to give to the army, which licensed all the working girls in town. He took 50 per cent of the remainder for himself, and we calculated that for every man she slept with she earned less than 25 pence. Did she use condoms? Had she ever heard of AIDS?

'The brothel owner said he could sell me condoms but I didn't know what to do with them and couldn't afford the price. The men laughed at me when I asked them what they were for. So, I wash all the time, every day, after each man, out in the yard, but we also have to pay for the soap and toilet paper, so often I just use cold water. Is that safe? Is that OK? What should I do? Other girls here have disappeared. I hear the older girls talking of a Jade Disease. I never leave the compound. Can you help me find my brother and bring him here? All I want to do is go home and cut paddy with my mother.' She stared at her fading photographs pinned to the door of the wooden locker.

How could we find her brother in a rabbit warren of more than one million people? We gave her whatever money we had on us, a sachet of Happy Hair and two oranges, before leaving her alone with her paltry photographs and our hopeless gifts. As we walked back into the waiting area, the brothel owner screamed for his twenty girls to parade before new clients. Two miners with wads of notes clipped to their longyis were impatient for their turn. 'Get out,' the brothel owner hollered at our friend. 'Get out or I'll call the police.' And we crept out into the lanes, noticing for the first time how they were all lined with fenced compounds, their windows nailed-down, their doors guarded by whistling sentries.

Alongside the pits, besides the bars, behind the Jade City Hotel, over the bridge that spanned the Uru and into the adjoining township were similar enclosures packed with girls who had travelled to Hpakant from all over Burma. We waited on a darkened street corner while our friend went on ahead. 'I'll bring someone back to talk to you. Don't show your faces,' he implored before disappearing into the crowds. Ten minutes later two figures scurried towards us: a girl in a red woven longyi with a small bundle under her arm, accompanied by our friend. 'Round the corner, somewhere quiet and dark. She is not supposed to be out,' he said, and pushed us all through an alley onto a triangle of wasteland. 'She is very frightened but I told her that you were more scared. I told her that you had come a long way just to hear her story. But don't ask her about sensitive things. If she wants to talk, she will.' We were conscious of having been too insistent in our previous interview, of having pushed a little too hard to get the story, but who knew how long it would be before we were all suddenly cornered in a darkened alley?

The girl before us trembled on her spoil perch. The heavy *thanaka* she had smeared over her face barely disguised the scars and bruises on her rice-paper thin skin. She told us that she had been brought up in Mandalay in a house with a wild garden of bougainvillaea. Her father had been a teacher and she had been a good student too. She had enrolled in university to study history, but two years ago her brothers had fled the city for the jungle. Then the *Tatmadaw* had accused the family of supporting the insurgents. 'They broke everything and said we would suffer if my brothers didn't come home.' One month later the soldiers returned and arrested her father and mother. 'I was taken to an army camp and raped. I was there for a week. I don't know where it was, but not too far from my home. Then they put me in an army truck with other girls from Mandalay and Rangoon. For days we travelled but could not see where we were going. I have been here for eight months and I have hardly left the brothel. When the other girls began to get sick they injected us all with penicillin and told us it would protect us against everything. But I know that's not true. Penicillin cannot cure many things. Some of the girls I arrived with have already disappeared. Others are very thin and weak. Some say it's malaria but I know it isn't. The symptoms are very different. It is something I have never seen before. I am sure the miners have it too. Have you noticed yet how everyone in Hpakant has the same look?'

Before we could answer she brought up the subject that we had tiptoed around. 'I do know what condoms are. But the men beat us when we insist they use them and then the brothel owner beats us for making his paying guests angry. A circle of beatings,' she laughed, 'and anyhow it's all too late. Do you think the soldiers who took me used condoms? Now do something for me. I have written a letter to my brothers. By now they might be in Thailand. Other girls have written notes too. Will you take them with you?' She thrust the bundle into our hands, scraps of paper with a few scribbled lines of Burmese, scrawled pictures of stick-girls with smiling faces, a large heart pierced by an arrow. 'Thank you,' she said in English, her hands cupping ours. 'Thank you for coming to see us here and for taking our messages.'

We had been missing from our room for three hours and needed to go back, but our friend insisted that we see one more girl who, he said, had come for help earlier that day. We hurtled along the crowded lanes, past pyramids of spoil banked up against the rim of Hpakant-kyi, noticing for the first time the insipid silhouettes of men and women scuttling like mud crabs over the clods and shale that had been discarded by the day shifts. With broken knives and bare hands they scavenged, hopelessly searching for a blade of green. Some already lay exhausted while others picked at the soil around them. 'They were miners once,' our friend said.

She was sitting alone by a fire; her hair neatly bunched with green ribbon, a golden pendant hanging around her neck. She said she was nineteen but looked much younger, and told how she had come to Hpakant with her sister the previous year. Our friend held her hand as she talked about the gaping mines, and the pencil-thin women who worked at the bottom, and how she had been frightened of it all when they first arrived in town. How both of them had decided to leave Hpakant. They had started to save money for the truck ride back to Kengtung. Her hands shook as she polished the locket. 'Open it up and show them,' our friend gently whispered, and she prised open the locket and tipped it towards us. Inside was a photograph of a teenage girl in a print dress, her hair in a bun, her hand covering her laughing face. 'My sister,' she said, snapping the locket shut. 'She died yesterday. Only seventeen.'

Without a word the girl stood up and scrambled across a scree slope, leading us down into the scrub that concealed a flooded shaft. Kneeling down at its edge she said: 'My sister was very sick and couldn't work in the mines any more. She could barely lift her basket. She had worked very hard. We both had. She said she was going to work somewhere else for a few weeks. I saw her walking with strangers in the market wearing lipstick and flowers. Then a few days ago she found me again. She said she was sick. We gave her some hot water and sugar, but we did not know what was wrong with her or what to do . . . who to tell. Maybe it was malaria. But she started coughing. All night she coughed. She had a fever. Then she died. They came in the night and took her body. They said no one must know that people are dying here. It is bad for business. But I followed them. They tied her down with stones and threw her into this pit. When they had gone I found these hidden under some branches.' The girl reached into her woven Shan bag and pulled out a pair of green *panat*. 'These were my sister's favourite slippers. There is nothing else left.'

She ran off into the dark, and we listened until we could no longer hear her *panat* slapping against the scree and turned to her friend, who sat brooding next to the flooded shaft. He wanted to confront the brothel owner who had employed the girl's sister. He wanted to hear him explain and although we could not afford to get involved, we jogged behind him, zig-zagging back into the alleys, angry, breathless and fearful of what was about to happen. Our friend seemed to know exactly where to go, and we rounded a corner, and there before us sat a slope-shouldered man sharing a bottle of Mandalay beer with some friends, a cigarette burning between his fingers, forced into a slap by his gold and jadeite rings. A Buddha amulet hung around his neck. He refused to let us inside. Why should he? Anyhow, we were not supposed to be here. He would call the police, he screeched in English, as he grabbed at our friend's shirt and threw him to the ground. He spat at us, but we stood motionless and slowly described the scene: the flooded shaft, the pair of slippers, the photograph concealed in the golden locket.

The brothel owner flicked his cigarette stub into the dark. Without saying a word he led us to a rubbish heap. Squatting on a discarded tractor tyre, his T-shirt soaked with sweat, he launched into a story weighed down with melodrama and self-pity. He claimed to have hired twenty women to work in his brothel, but three of them had died. As soon as his remaining girls had brought in sufficient profits he intended to replace the dead girls with new recruits supplied by the *Tatmadaw*. 'What am I supposed to do? If you close me down there would be a hundred men to take my place. If I don't run this business, then someone far worse will,' he said, taking out a bloated wallet from which he produced a set of photographs. 'I have a family too, you know,' he said, fanning them into a poker hand. 'What will they live on if I go bust?'

Did he provide condoms? Was he worried about AIDS? 'Sure,' he said obliquely. 'But if I made the clients wear condoms they would stop coming to me. They would go elsewhere. AIDS is a foreign disease. You cannot get it here. I have seen announcements about it. The government has done surveys and they have not found a single case in Myanmar.' We said: 'So were all his girls healthy? What about the body in the flooded shaft?' He said: 'People don't want to sleep with sick girls. I don't know what's wrong with them. Staying healthy is their problem. They must wash properly; we provide soap and towels for less than the market charges. Look, I have to pay money to everyone to keep my place open. I pay 2000 kyat [£6.50] a week to the army and also to the local government. I pay everyone not to have to answer stupid questions like these.' He was bored, angry, emboldened by the talk of protection money. 'I have work to do.' And with that he was gone, a small photo of his young boy carelessly abandoned by the tyre.

We crept alone back to the Jade City Hotel and slunk up the bowed concrete staircase, loose grains of cement cracking beneath our feet, anticipating a room full of questions. The empty, unlit corridor stretched ahead dimly. We pressed our ears against the Corporal's window but there was no sound from his room. As we gently pushed the key into the lock the door fell open. We remembered the Reuters correspondent in his Rangoon hotel. We were certain we had left our door locked. We shone a torch around the concrete bunker. Our bed had been made. There were now towels in the dismal bathroom. Our bags that had been thrown into a cheap Chinese wardrobe, lay open. There was no one waiting for us, but someone had come into our room. We lay awake dramatising our capture until the Corporal burst in. 'Sleep well?' he asked. And how should we respond? We descended heavy-eyed into the lobby, looking for the receptionist, for the manager, for the staff who inevitably spied for the MI, but no one was waiting apart from our boy driver.

Uncertain of what had been seen or said, of how much anyone knew, we decided to carry on. All our evenings were measured in whisky and we spent our days impatiently touring pits, talking jadeite, listening to the Corporal's bottomless stories, watching him drain our spirits. Nothing had prepared us for what Hpakant would look like. Hpakant-kyi, which covered a square mile, was only the beginning. Over the river was its sister pit which, although slightly smaller, could still have held within it several football pitches. Behind the tomb-stone hills, beyond the chimneys of red rock, was a parallel valley whose length and breadth was being cut away, and beyond that yet more scarred valleys and chimneys as far as the eye could see. Up high, on a perilous ridge, teetered a wooden church, clinging on as the soil beneath its foundations was sorted, sieved and taken away. 'That was a hill last time I was here, and the church sat on the crest,' the Corporal said, visibly surprised by the government's enterprise. 'Look at them work. The speed of it all.' He whirled us around and pointed to a virgin peak. 'See that,' he said. 'It's next. The military own it and will begin mining there very soon.'

We asked to see the cutters and carvers, and crossed the Uru into the village of Seng Tong (whose name meant 'Big Lump of Jade'). Its grid of narrow, unmade streets was packed with covered stalls selling slivers of polished stone, small piles of cloudy cabochons, bangles and necklaces that would never make a Christie's catalogue. Behind were the groaning cutters' shacks where rows of men crouched over abrasive water-wheels, slicing and polishing, grinding and shaping grey slabs of cheap jadeite, and beyond these lay a labyrinth of alleys, fenced with plaited bamboo, along which stretched terraces with patched-tin doors that were bolted shut. 'Gone bust,' the Corporal muttered with a dismissive shrug, before moving on to a stall where he fingered the stones, lifting them all up to the light. 'I'm buying an engagement ring for my girlfriend. She doesn't know we are getting married but the jade will convince her.'

The Corporal slouched off, leaving us with a surly Chinese dealer who engaged us in a conversation about gambling. The week before, he had bought a boulder of jadeite, having shone his torch through its window and brokered a deal with the mine owner, their fingers blindly entwined beneath a piece of sacking. 'Look, look,' he said, producing it from a bag on the ground. 'I spent 20,000 US dollars on rock. I was sure about it and took it back to workshop for cutting. But inside, nothing. Nothing at all. Even Chinese make mistake. You foreigner will not have heard of Doubly Fortunate. But people here talk of great priceless stone. I am doubly unfortunate and tomorrow I walk back to Hong Kong.' He wobbled away, down the lanes, cursing under his breath.

That evening we returned to Seng Tong's plaited-bamboo alleys and found that they had come alive. The maze of stifling wooden huts, strung out like upturned coffins, was home to thousands of exhausted miners who had completed another fifteen-hour shift. There were no showers or toilets but buckets of water dragged from the Uru; no fans to cool the cramped and strained bodies and no one seemed to bother with food. Inside, dozens of sweating miners were packed together in mosquito-ridden cells, a jumble of limbs, of clammy skin, of pin-prick pupils and ripped longyis all enveloped in a cloying stench of vomit and ammonia. Our friend introduced us to Hpakant's itinerant community, and inside one hut we found a miner chain-smoking cheroots. He puffed away, still covered in the day's grime, too tired to do anything about it.

Zaw Min, who spoke fluent English, was 32 years old and had been a first-year student at Rangoon University when the city had erupted in 1988. 'We were optimistic then. I was charging around Sule Pagoda, chanting and shouting. Then the shooting started and friends fell to the ground. We couldn't believe that our army was firing on us. Burmese soldiers killing Burmese people.' Zaw Min stubbed out his cigar and stuffed the butt into the knot of his longyi, sipping from a metal beaker of clear spirit. 'I hid for a while. The University was closed. I dreamed of getting my science degree and then studying for a PhD. But we had no money and no time. The funny thing is that even if I had completed my studies, I would still have only earned 10 US dollars a month in Burma. So I decided to gamble for a living and when I first arrived here it was exhilarating. I told myself that every piece of stone I dug out of the pit was something special: a motorbike, a home, a priceless bead necklace. But I never found any stones of value and I'm still here, like a fool.'

The bundle of soiled clothes lying next to Zaw Min twitched. A dark-skinned face emerged from the heap: Lui Vang, a 28-year-old farmer from Chin State, forced into friendship with Zaw Min by circumstance. Propping his head up on a folded Chinese backpack, Lui Vang said the *Tatmadaw* had occupied his village six months before and taken his family's store of rice. His wife and children had fled into the jungle but he and twenty friends had clubbed together to pay for a six-day truck ride to the mines.

Coming from a remote region that bordered India, how had he heard of Hpakant? The farmer laughed. 'What do you think? Everyone has heard about the jade. Burma is a poor country and everybody dreams of making money. Twenty of us came here but now only three of my friends are still working. The SPDC has a price on our heads.' Lui Vang's voice trailed off and he curled up on the board that was his bed. 'I'm tired now,' he said. 'Go away. I want to sleep.' But Zaw Min spoke up. 'I'll tell you what happened to his friends. Twelve of them are dead. Four of them have disappeared. One is alive, kind of. What do you think happens here?'

Lui Vang rolled over and eased himself into a pair of jeans, wincing as he bent his swollen knees. 'You want to see what happens to us? We all wanted new lives but this isn't living. I want to get out and go home to my wife and two children, but it's too late. I dream of her cooking chicken, spending hours eating at our table. But these are all stupid dreams and they cannot keep me alive. If you want to know what Hpakant is, then come with me now.' We got up to leave and Zaw Min called after us. 'If you see a guy called Myint Thein, a fancy guy wearing a red Coca-Cola T-shirt, tell him I have been looking for him for three weeks.'

Of course we saw the sores covering Lui Vang's bruised arms and legs, and we tried not to stare as he stumbled along with his bamboo stick. Together we shuffled to a neighbouring alley, filled with expectation as Lui Vang cleared the path before him, the broad swipes of his cane beating back the wild dogs that sniffed at his legs. We reached a Chinese general store and uneasily followed Lui Vang inside, unsure of what to do or where to go, uncomfortable with the staring faces, waiting for questions to be asked. So we found the darkest corner and squatted in silence among the mosquitoes. Gate-crashers at a private party, we smiled with exaggerated grins. And then we pulled our shirts up over our faces to block out the stench of stale urine and sweat that no one else seemed to smell and watch the story of Hpakant unfold.

Two figures knelt on rush mats around a fire pit. An older man dissolved white powder in a solution and then examined the younger man's identity card. The older man scribbled in a notebook and then whispered in the younger man's ear. He seemed familiar with the drill and rolled up his denim sleeve. The older man picked up a rubber hose attached to a blackened needle and jabbed it into the younger man's vein. He sucked hard until the tube was full of blood and poured in the heroin solution. He then took a deep breath before blowing into the pipe. The mixture of blood and heroin surged into the younger man's blood-stream and a smile flew across his face. 'Go now, see you tomorrow,' the shooting gallery owner urged, wiping blood from the needle on his longyi. The younger man floated out of the hut, breathing in short, shallow gasps. The older man put the open end of the perished tube back into his mouth and blew it clear. Now he called for Lui Vang who popped up, his sleeve already rolled. The older man checked his identity card before the drill was repeated. New heroin solution. Same needle.

It was a macabre peep-show and we felt ashamed as Lui Vang showed us how he bought peace with a needle that would probably kill him. Grimacing as his arm was hooked up, he jerked and gasped as the solution mingled with his blood. He turned to us, his pupils contracting, his knotted shoulders falling back, euphoria bleeding from his arm. 'Want some?' he stammered, pushing the perished tube towards us. 'Feel Hpakant. Take the tube.' We recog-nised that heavy-headed expression. That stoned-Sunday blur. But he saw the fear on our faces. Our friend jumped up and grappled with the pipe. Both men talked in urgent tones. They spat words around the room, waggling and waving in a vicious semaphore whose meaning was abundantly clear.

It was rumours and pictures that had drawn us to Hpakant; hazy images of lives-in-limbo, limbs and longyis captured by an unknown photographer. But having travelled thousands of miles to see it all for ourselves, sitting in this greasy hut, gathering scenes and quotes, we found that we were still passive spectators on the sidelines of other people's lives. Until Lui Vang had asked us to join him.

It's so easy to reassure yourself that the painful images you are gathering will act as a wake-up call for people living thousands of miles away. And suddenly there is a semblance of order amid the disorder of shipwrecked lives, a reason for filing copy while watching others throw away their last chance. But when the story starts, real life doesn't stop, and by asking us to participate in his story Lui Vang had demolished the dogma of journalism school. And we just sat there and said nothing.

Now he lurched into the corner of the hut muttering, 'This is how we forget', while a hut-full of paranoid eyes popped like flash-bulbs, finding our misfit faces in the gloom. Hands pushed us up onto our feet. The older man sucked on the perished tube. Our friend pulled on our shirts. 'People are afraid of you. We must go. Later we will talk some more. Talk to the gallery owners. Not here. Get out. Now.' The decision had been taken for us and we found ourselves racing out of the door. When we turned to find Lui Vang he was already somewhere else, another Hpakant refugee, slumped in the corner, gazing at a gecko that was stalking a mosquito, his purchased smile slack across his face.

Outside the lanes of framed houses still throbbed with laughter and drinking, but now beneath the bulging bubble windows we saw the trail of men and boys who slept as they walked and tripped and fell. For the foreigners who lived there, Shanghai had been a thin strip of affluence and romance, and here also, behind the fairy lights and neon signs were the countless shadows of the opiated, who fixed everyone with insipid stares. This was a panoramic mural populated by swaggering dandies in satin suits; women still fluttered hand in hand like brilliant butterflies. But now we noticed how they all side-stepped the prone bodies in the lanes, how they sashayed past the lifeless faces, how they clinched in darkened corners where others had spilled their guts. How the night queen and French after-shave barely masked the smell of vomit. How the people had grown to resemble the stickmen in the posters and how they all slipped between the warm sheets of their addiction, stretching out beyond the mournful whine of the karaoke stars, snuggling up to the rumble of Hpakant-kyi. The lost valley that explorers had once dreamed of reaching, was, after all, inhabited by a poisonous predator.

Hpakant had over time found a myriad of ways to mesmerise its labourers. The downward spiral that began with eating opium graduated to chasing dragons around severed Coca-Cola tins. The heroin blowpipes were then taken by those more committed to losing themselves. But there were halls and huts around every pit, beside very bar and brothel, each of them offering variations on the same addictive theme. When the paranoia of shooting in public set in, many chose a more anonymous boost to their morale, thrusting their arms through holes cut into a wooden partition, offering their identity cards in return for a fix from an unseen hand. If anyone needed more, then there were even self-service plastic bags filled with heroin solution that dangled from the rafters to which customers hooked themselves up, absorbing a few drops before passing the tube to the next in line. And then, when veins clotted or collapsed, when it became too difficult to find a vessel, when your arms, legs, feet and groin could no longer bear another puncture, quacks were waiting in the bazaar with blunt razor-blades, to slit open your scalp and sprinkle heroin powder into the wound.

Only dawn exposed the debris of Hpakant, lying face down in the alleys and on the waste-land, waiting to be thrown into the flooded shafts, to be sunk in jungle graves or burned like rubbish. For those who survived the night, the rich and the poor, the prone and the able-bodied, it was to the pits that they returned, side by side, knee-deep in mud, manhandling steel staves that we could barely lift. And as they walked past the human detritus from the night before, it seemed incredible that none of them were wise to the great jade lie.

One morning the Corporal introduced us to a Chinese mine operator, and we sat with him overlooking his pit near Seng Tong on plastic garden furniture, shielded from the sun by golfing umbrellas. Sipping Coca-Cola, he calmly discussed the economics of Hpakant, smoothing down his Ralph Lauren shirt, admiring the translucency of his jadeite signet ring that glowed like a green jelly-baby. The mine owner pointed to his employees toiling at the bottom of the pit, his little finger extravagantly cocked. 'They come to the mines with ideas of making fortunes and, of course, we pay them according to how much jadeite they find. But it's a three-way split. These agents tax us 10 per cent. I take 40 per cent, and by the time you have split the remainder between a team of 50 miners, each man or woman is left with only a small bundle of kyat. I never promise anything else.'

He swatted away a gentle question about drugs with a defensive monologue. 'Look. These people come with high hopes. They are all jade kings until they appreciate the harsh realities of mining in this town. We can't all be winners and I don't apologise for that. All it takes to keep the myth going is for one man to find his fortune, and then a hundred more will come to me asking for jobs.' So did his money only come from mining jadeite? 'I am a good businessman,' he laughed into his can of Coca-Cola. 'Thank you for coming to see me.' The meeting was over.

But that evening the owner of a shooting gallery put a different spin on the same story. Sitting behind his thriving premises, he described the stages of addiction. Hpakant was thick with cerebral malaria, the days and nights were long and exhausting, and hunger and pain were constant factors. Opium plantations and heroin refineries surrounded the mines. For centuries the Kachin had used opium paste to stave off hunger and counteract diarrhoea, and many in the mines followed their example. When the realisation dawned that even raising the ticket money home would be a struggle, the mine operators proffered a solution. They offered their crews pure heroin in lieu of their wages, the value of the powder set against any future jadeite they might find. 'Hpakant is a miserable place and heroin stops the pain. Heroin makes memories distant,' the shooting gallery owner counselled. 'It is better for the mine owners this way. Their workers are very passive. They are addicted to Hpakant.'

But how was he able to keep his business concealed in a town squatted by the *Tatmadaw* and encircled by military check-points? 'I don't.' He seemed surprised. 'The government licenses my business. The soldiers deliver the drugs here or they pay truck drivers to bring it in. Some of the heroin I provide has been pre-paid by the Chinese mine owners who arrange for us to give free daily fixes to employees who show me their identity card. The rest we buy from dealers approved by the army. If a miner needs more than his daily quota he can buy 15 grams for 2500 kyat [£8]. The heroin is always pure; this is Burma, after all. My only problem is needles. Needles are hard to come by, and so we have to make them last. Eight hundred customers per needle, I reckon. Sometimes fewer if they break.'

We crawled back towards the Jade City Hotel, weighed down by disjointed vignettes of Hpakant, from which seemed to be emerging a grim picture of a regime that encouraged and administered a cycle of destruction. The prostitutes, the miners, the shooting gallery owner and the miner operator had all described the nuts and bolts of death, and it was only the sight of a red Coca-Cola T-shirt wrapped around a fallen body that brought us back down to earth. Was it Myint Thein, the 'fancy guy' whom we had been asked to look out for? We knelt beside him and shouted in his ear. But nothing could clear his narcotic fug and he just lay there, his eyes staring madly, saliva frothing at his lips. We went to Zaw Min's hut and gabbled about finding his long-lost friend. But the science student, who was writing a letter, had already forgotten our conversation. We noticed the raised needle tracks that ran down both of his arms. Was there anyone in Hpakant who was free from addiction or infection? After a long silence Zaw Min spoke. 'Send this letter to my parents, please. I've told them I'm doing fine.' He slumped back on to his bed. 'Don't think that I am weak. Everyone takes it. Some of us get it instead of our split of jadeite. For a long time I tried not to take any, but then I realised that the mine owners were ripping us off. Whatever the size of the boulder or the quality, we never seemed to make any money. Now I know the SPDC agents and the mine owners fix the jadeite prices at a fraction of their real value. I was so angry but I had no money to leave. I fought with myself for a long time. At first I tried to take only a little heroin as it made me sick. But my friends encouraged me. They are greedy for it. They do it in their thighs and their feet, wherever it cannot be seen. But after a while we all give up trying to hide the scars. There is no one here who can help us.'

It seemed that after all everyone was wise to the jade lie, but by the time they had seen through it, it was far too late. There were no hospitals in Hpakant and the dozens of shops that displayed red crosses sold only penicillin, Tylenol, gauze and teak shavings. We thought there were no doctors until, completely by chance, we came across a middle-aged Burmese medic. We pushed open the door of a hut and found him dribbling liquid into the mouth of an emaciated miner. He dropped the beaker and dashed for the door. Then he recognised our friend. 'I can't talk to them. I am not supposed to be here. I have to go,' he said in English, pushing past. But our friend shouted after him in Burmese and he grudgingly came back into the room. 'Make it quick,' he said. 'What do you want to know? You cannot identify me. The authorities do not allow us to come here.'

In five frantic minutes he laid bare the scale of an epidemic that the doctor in Myitkyina had hinted at. He estimated that more than 60 per cent of the constantly changing residents of Hpakant, more than 500,000 people, were using heroin and 90 per cent of them injected the drug. The heroin that entered Hpakant came straight from the laboratories in the Golden Triangle and was almost 100 per cent pure, far stronger than that which reached America and Australia. Most of the miners he had examined took between 5 and 10 grams a day, compared to the average of 0.5 grams consumed by a user in the US or the UK. Needles, of course, were illegal and the addicts slept with prostitutes (many of them press-ganged into the brothels), without wearing condoms. The cycle of infection was complete. 'How can you expect them to know what AIDS is, when their government claims that it is a foreign disease and denies its presence in Burma?' he asked. 'They call it Jade Disease here, but I examine the bodies, I look at the symptoms displayed by drug users, the sicknesses they develop. It is quite clear that we have a catastrophic HIV problem in the mines, and everyone who injects and has unprotected sex will almost certainly contract it. People don't eat. The mines are malarial. Look at the strength of the heroin and the amount which people take. People here become so weak that they are brought down by everything and anything, from pneumonia to malnutrition. Just look around you. How many miners have you seen over the age of 35? Most of them don't live long enough to develop full-blown AIDS, but they do live long enough to pass on the virus. When they leave the mines and return to the towns and villages, they take with them the scourge of Hpakant.' It was well after midnight, the diesel generators growled and the night shift descended into the cauldron of Hpakant-kyi. We watched the men and women climb down into the pit, lit by ropes of electric bulbs, staves and baskets in their hands. Across the valley of Hpakant-kyi, in the alleys of Seng Tong, through the beggar's bazaar, hundreds of lights shone out like the brilliant specks of phosphorescence that illuminate a dark sea.

⊠

The next morning, Sunday, the Corporal let himself into our room. We were leaving in one hour. So we found our Kachin translator, who had spent his days praying, and walked with him to Hpakant-kyi for the last time. The monsoon was not due for three months but a sudden downpour caught everyone by surprise as it lashed the city of shafts and shacks. Sheltering inside a teashop, we watched a father and son on the far bank of the Uru wrap their Bibles in plastic bags embossed with a photograph of Rambo, before dashing through the rain to church. Above us all loomed a giant cross, tiled with low-grade jadeite that overlooked the deep pits of Hpakant in which the congregation laboured. The Church was barely tolerated by the junta, but the priests and pastors were too frightened to offer succour to the dwindling numbers who turned up for Communion. The father and son crossed the iron bridge over the Uru River and ran towards us, passing under a banner that proclaimed in English: 'AIDS is a national concern'. The boy stopped to point at the strange letters and asked what it said. 'It's in a foreign language,' his father replied. 'I think it's about the A1 disease. Don't worry about A1. You can only catch it if you're bad.' We followed them to a clap-board church and watched as a young minister counselled a couple in the doorway before the service began. The man was bandaged and bloody and the woman stared silently at her muddy feet. When they took a pew we approached and asked the pastor what had happened. The woman had stabbed her husband four times after discovering a diary in which he had recorded his nights spent with prostitutes. Both of them had been sick for some time and the woman now suspected that her illness was caused by his adultery.

'What do I say to them?' the pastor asked us. 'I think they have AIDS. All I can tell them is that this must be God's will. Is that the right thing to say? I don't know what AIDS is, but the banners outside say that it's in Hpakant. I am very afraid that I will become sick. I do not want to even touch these people. Why have you come here? Aren't you afraid of dying too?' He mumbled on: 'God had cursed Hpakant with a plague and the people had to learn to live with death.' With only such a short time left, what could we say to him? Our message was lost in the din of an electric keyboard that struck up a hymn, and he left us as they began to sing 'Onward Christian Soldiers'. He would pray for us, he whispered. All day. The route out of the mines was even more treacherous than the track that had led us in.

Jadeland was unravelling as people sought an explanation as to what was killing them. There were warning signs and posters that only a few could read and no one understood. The disparate community's only leaders were pastors who were prepared to counsel but did not know what to say. Hpakant was Burma's black heart, drawing hundreds of thousands of people in with false hopes and pumping them out again, infected and broken. Thousands never left the mines, but those who made it back to their communities took with them their addiction and a disease that provincial doctors were not equipped to diagnose or treat. As our car slipped out of Hpakant, the bruised sky blackened and rainwater poured into the jadeite pits. We turned to see the Uru burst its artificial banks, spilling thousands of gallons of noxious slurry into Hpakant-kyi. Miners scrambled over each other to get out of the pit as a mud wall gave way, sending a landslide of spoil crashing down on top of them all.

We had seen enough and wanted to get to Rangoon as fast as possible, but the Corporal had another plan. He wanted to visit Indawgyi Lake, a great expanse of water and wildlife that the regime was promoting as a nature reserve. It was the place marked on the Colonel's childish map with the badly drawn knife and fork. But the Corolla eventually pulled up at what seemed to be a lorry park. In front of us were disconnected trailers loaded down with timber and behind, the bald hillside.

'What is it?'

'It's teak, all of it's teak. You're looking at hundreds of thousands of dollars of it, and it's all heading for Thailand.'

'Why?'

'It's our future. The money the government makes from this wood will be used to finance the nature reserve.'

Trees, jadeite, people. Everything in Burma was a commodity. But this was the Corporal's day and he wanted to show us his Great Golden Land. He commandeered a boat and steered us through the storm to a pagoda that appeared to float on the crystal waters of Indawgyi, that Bayfield and Griffith had spied from the crown of a hill. He ordered us to remove our shoes before disembarking and we paddled in its precincts. 'What are the friezes carved around the walls?' we asked.

'These are the vices of man,' the Corporal solemnly intoned. 'All the things we must not do: smoke, drink, steal, be envious, be greedy. You know, like your Seven Deadly Sins.'

'But you smoke and drink,' we gently probed.

'Oh, that's OK,' the Corporal replied. 'These sins have been whitewashed.'

He was right. A thick layer of paint had indeed been applied and now obscured the detail in the runes.

The storm raged for three days but we eventually reached Mingaladon Airport, where this time there was no reception committee waiting. We boarded a Thai Airways flight and would normally have been grateful to receive the freshly pressed copies of the *Bangkok Post* that always seemed filled with news. But this time, as the plane took off, we felt nothing of the cosy anticipation that accompanies the leaving of Burma. When we landed at Don Muang Airport, one hour later, we entered another world.

Back in Thailand, the accusations seemed so damning – the regime's collusion in the mire of Hpakant, its profiteering and promotion of drugs – that we sought out diplomats, aid workers and doctors working on international AIDS programmes. Our evidence, the photographs and testimonies, appalled them all and their advice placed our research in a wider context.

It would have been difficult to believe that the government oversaw and even profited from the poisonous tangle of Hpakant's shooting galleries and brothels if it tried harder to distance itself from the men who run Burma's heroin syndicates. But Thai Intelligence has a video of Lt General Khin Nyunt surveying road- and dam-building projects run by Wei Hsueh-kang, the head of the United Wa State Army (UWSA), named by the US Drug Enforcement Administration (DEA) as 'the dominant trafficking group in Southeast Asia and possibly the world'.[2] The Thai government has recently issued an arrest warrant for Khin Nyunt's associate who, in 1997, was also indicted for drug trafficking, *in absentia,* in New York, a 2 million US dollars bounty placed on his head by the US State Department.

The SPDC's Secretary Number One's ethnic affairs advisor, Luo Xinghan, the man who brokered the deal that isolated the Kachin, also happens to be the leader of a Kokang militia named by the DEA as 'armed and heavily involved in the heroin trade'. Both he and his son, Htun Myint Naing, a.k.a. Steven Law, are on a blacklist preventing them from entering the US. Then, of course, there is Khun Sa, the Shan's former Prince of Death, who within weeks of capture, was seen playing golf with the generals, having moved into a guarded villa adjacent to the lakeside home of the reclusive Ne Win. Now, when strolling down to the water's edge at sunset, Aung San Suu Kyi can look across Inya Lake and see the homes of two of Burma's most notorious recluses.

While our copy of *Myanmar Today* emphasised the regime's determination to eradicate narcotics, US satellite surveillance photographs show that at least 163,100 hectares of Upper Burma are now under poppy cultivation, the majority controlled by Khin Nyunt's gang of three.[3] The DEA estimates that refined opium from these plantations produces 250 metric tonnes of heroin, enough to satisfy the drug market of a country as large as the United States many times over and, of course, engulf forgotten Hpakant.

It is a profitable business. European analysts have calculated that more than 60 per cent of Burma's revenue is derived from unaccountable sources.[4] In 1989 the junta dropped its policy of confiscating assets of dubious origin and replaced it with a 'whitening tax' that allows nationals to deposit money in Burmese banks without having to declare its source. Since then, luxury hotels and shopping malls have mysteriously risen out of the rubble of the Burmese economy.

In 1992 Luo Xinghan's family founded Asia World, an import-export business that runs a supermarket chain and owns the five-star Trader's hotels in Rangoon and Singapore. Asia World, with an estimated turnover of 600 million US dollars, also invests heavily in the mines of Hpakant. In December 1997 Luo completed a highway between Mandalay and the Chinese border town of Ruili that the People's Republic has since complained is the 'main drug highway' out of the Golden Triangle. But Luo, 63, who has recently been enlisted by the junta as a spokesman for its drugs eradication programme, has built a Museum of Narcotics Suppression in Hopang at the heart of Khun Sa's former territory and denies that he has ever been involved in heroin. In a rare interview he told *Asiaweek* that his energies were focused only on legitimate business. 'The older I get, the more there seems to do!'[5]

Another of Luo's Kokang associates, clan chief Yang Maoliang, whose Peace Myanmar Group in Rangoon now runs a Mitsubishi Electric franchise, a distillery producing Myanmar Rum, gin and drinking water, has been accused by the DEA of setting up 23 heroin refineries between 1989 and 1991. In 1994, the year that Peace Myanmar was founded, Yang's brother was executed in China for heroin trafficking and in April 1996, the People's Republic intercepted 598.85 kilograms of Yang family heroin as it entered Guangzhou Province, the largest drugs bust in Chinese history.[6] Yang Maoliang's refineries, that were developed with the money gifted by Khin Nyunt as an incentive to turn against the Kachin in 1989, now produced an estimated 2000 kilograms of heroin every year. Yang himself has publicly boasted that by dealing in heroin he achieved in five years what the junta had been unable to do since independence in 1948: kill off the Kachin insurgency by addling it with drugs.[7]

Wei Hseuh-kang of the UWSA established the Myanmar Kyone Yeom Group in Rangoon, a prolific financial house with interests in construction, real estate, transport and tourism. After its leaders donned pin-stripe suits, the UWSA followed Luo's example and also built a Museum of Narcotics Suppression in the Sino-Burmese border casino town of Mong La, a state-sponsored project opened by Khin Nyunt in 1997. But the museum and the jungle entertainment centre were raised with narco-profits that the UWSA continues to funnel into the Jade Garden Amusement Park in Rangoon and the mines of Hpakant. When we visited the UWSA's museum in 1998, in an isolated region of Shan State that is closed to foreigners, it was surrounded by poppy plantations and inside was a display of photographs depicting addicts injecting heroin, pictures that we had seen before. The museum's curators failed to mention that these photographs had been taken by the government doctors who were sacked after visiting Hpakant. Beside them was an electronic display board with flashing lights and diagrams that explained how to transform a jungle rice kitchen into a heroin laboratory in ten easy stages.

In November 2000 we were smuggled into Shan State again to meet members of Khun Sa's former army, the 'iron-legged soldiers', who had been forced into hiding after their leader's betrayal. They told us how he had prepared for his surrender. In 1990 the Prince of Darkness bought from the KIA what was rumoured to be the largest piece of jadeite rough in the world, a 200-tonne boulder that he concealed in the jungle. After Khun Sa's 'arrest', Chao Cham Huang, his eldest son, struck a deal with a buyer from Taiwan. The jadeite profits were invested in the Good Shan Brothers trading company, a shopping precinct, a five-star hotel in Rangoon, a gems business and a transport company that, according to Western intelligence sources, is now being used to ship heroin. The SPDC also reportedly received a handsome bonus of 500 million US dollars from Khun Sa to guarantee his life-long amnesty. But the regime could do little to influence the Chinese authorities that are currently investigating Khun Sa's daughter for attempting to launder 34 million US dollars in Hong Kong.

While the generals continue to profit from their relations with Burma's drug warlords, the junta has pronounced to the world that the country has been cleared of narcotics and is barely affected by HIV. Major General Ket Sein, Burma's health minister, has stated on several occasions that 'AIDS is a disease caused by foreigners' and that by the end of 1997 there were only 2337 cases in Burma. The junta allocates less than 10 per cent of its annual budget to health, education and social welfare, and its National AIDS Programme receives only 40,000 US dollars annually. Ket Sein argues that the prohibitive costs of HIV testing and treatment limit the country's response, and it is true that one HIV test is equal to two months' salary for a Burmese doctor. But while denying the existence of a crisis and pleading poverty, Burma has, since 1988, invested 1.3 billion US dollars in military hardware, and defence continues to eat up at least 40 per cent of Burma's annual gross domestic product (4.8 billion US dollars).

Before we ventured into the Kachin Hills the World Health Organisation and both the United Nations and European Union AIDS programmes applied for permission to visit the mines of Hpakant. But the junta turned down their requests and offers to set up treatment programmes. One Western doctor, whose application was rejected by a military commander who advised him, 'The answer is no because it isn't yes', recalled, 'The stories coming from the mines were horrific so I asked repeatedly to go there but was told that it was impossible. The WHO had already warned the government that they had a national emergency on their hands. But the SPDC pointed at its banners and placards, the posters in the roadside cafes and said they didn't need any help to sort out the country's health problems. It was an internal problem, not one for the "foreign community".'

International aid agencies have been left scrabbling around the fringes of a crisis. But they have gathered compelling evidence nevertheless. UNAIDS reported that in 1998 an incomplete survey of HIV in Burma found that there were at least 440,000 people infected. Under the junta's current budget provisions for AIDS education, prevention and treatment, that means less than one US cent is allocated for each HIV case. That the mines are at the epicentre of the epidemic is confirmed by a WHO report that found that among drug users in Myitkyina, 91 per cent are HIV positive. One anonymous medical report from 1996 concluded that 99.5 per cent of injecting drug users in the mines of Hpakant were HIV positive. But still the junta has refused to acknowledge that there is a problem.

In the summer of 1998, after an article written by us appeared in the colour supplement of a British Sunday newspaper, letters poured in expressing horror and surprise.[8] Except for one. The writer from 'Sisters Avenue, London SW11' was indignant. Brig. Gen. Maung Win Shu (retired), protesting on behalf of the SPDC, attacked the piece as a 'pot pourri of maliciously selected misrepresentations, misinterpretations, fabrications and rumour-sourced disinformation by two past-masters of malice, journalists Adrian Levy and Cathy Scott-Clark'. The Brig. Gen. harked back to the regime's achievements of 1988:

> There is . . . no necessity for policeman or soldier, since you must be aware our SPDC has made great strides forward in returning Myanmar Maing-ngan to stability and tranquillity, which in 1988 threatened to over-spill into total destabilisation as a result of above ground and underground destructive elements, insane with lust for power, hell-bent on overturning the apple-cart. Such treasonous minions of colonialism, axe handles and puppets under the manipulation of Western governments and acting on the orders of the CIA, Communists and 'that woman' (I'm sure you know who I mean), were soon annihilated in order to safeguard the sovereignty and independence of the Union.

The Brig. Gen. then conjured up a Prozac nation where 'everywhere you travel you will see happy, smiling faces: there are no beggars, the streets are cleaner and the grass is greener'. Burma was the victim in a war against Western imperialism that worked hand in hand with 'the one married to the foreigner with the big nose'. Referring to visible evidence of slavery, photographs published around the world of chains gangs employed by the regime to build roads and tourist sites in Burma, the Brig. Gen. advised that the government would never make the same mistake again. 'Now all such citizens are kept away from the public gaze,' he advised.

And isn't this the story of Hpakant? The city of jade is kept from view while it is stripped and sorted. If you surround the truth with 26 military checkpoints, if you encase it in razor wire and patrol it with orders to shoot on sight, then of course it is impossible to reach the truth that became our story of Hpakant. If you cannot read about it, then there is no debate. If you cannot see the evidence of torture and intimidation because it has disappeared, then maybe it never happened at all. If you ban syringes and condoms, then there is no visible evidence of addiction or infection. If you cannot hear the voices of dissent because they are under house arrest or muddled by narcotics, then it is true to say that there is no repression. And of course it is also then true to say that jadeite is simply an exotic, translucent, beautiful stone, rarer than gold and more precious than diamonds.

The Brigadier's letter was at times forlorn and even wounded, but as with Hpakant, the venom is hard to conceal. Before signing off he lurched into one, last, unprompted diatribe against Aung San Suu Kyi, beginning with a vicious swipe and ending, as many things do in Ptolemy's Great Golden Land, on a note of farce. The truth in Burma still lay undiscovered, he argued, while the lies we had written were not our own. They had been placed in our minds by 'that prostitute who spent all her life abroad, married a mongrel half-breed of mixed race and then returned to Myanmar under the pretext of democracy'. And worst of all, the dilettante of University Avenue had 'spent millions of pounds . . . buying up property in Oxford and in Western fashion and aerobics items'. Apparently reports that Aung San Sun Kyi had tried to keep fit on a Nordic track machine donated by a supporter was too much for the Brigadier to bear.

Thirteen

Romancing the Stone

When a South African jeweller took umbrage with an article in his trade magazine, entitled 'Romancing the Stone', that exhorted dealers to sell gems by wrapping them in fables, he was rounded on. 'You are missing an important point,' wrote Richard Hughes, an American specialist in Burmese stones who penned the article for *Gemkey* magazine. 'We are not selling gemstones, something that has no value to anyone. What we are selling is illusion. The only value a precious stone has is in the illusion in the buyer's mind. People do not buy a stone, they buy a story, a vision of a mine or country, a bit of history, something they can tell their friends about. De Beers knows this, which is why they don't sell diamonds, they sell love.'[1]

Edmond Chin knows this too. 'It's all theatre,' he stage whispers while preparing for the Christie's 1999 autumn sale in the viewing room of the J. W. Marriott Hotel in Hong Kong's pristine Pacific Place. Prepped in a tailored suit, his shirt unbuttoned while those around him are buckled and zipped, his elegant admirers proffer manicured fingers onto which he deftly slips rings. 'All my clients are very different but all are in love with jadeite.' An aside to us in a brief lull, but then he's surrounded once again, flourishing adjectives to seduce another *tai-tai* lady. 'You're only as good as your last show. There are always bitter and disappointed clients who complain the auctioneer put the hammer down too quickly or that the price is ridiculous or that their rival, Mrs so and so, has gone mad by paying so much. There is rivalry between clients, between members of the same family. They are all fighting with one another to get the better jade but it would be very indiscreet for me to say any more.'

A blinding flash of teeth, and then his head whips round even be-

345

fore another circuit-board millionaire enters the room. And Edmond Chin is there, waiting casually, holding up a jadeite ring, its stone cut like a gingko nut, a 77-carat cabochon, estimate on request. 'I certainly feel that jadeite is a matter of fate. Do you and the piece have a certain destiny or not? When jadeite appears to like the owner, it seems more beautiful than on someone else.' And the tycoon has slipped the cabochon onto his finger. 'Jadeite has wonderful characteristics: it reflects your health, absorbs evil influences, offers protection and undoes hexes.' Now he's making a note of the lot number. 'I wear my lucky jadeite ring all the time,' Edmond purrs. The electronics millionaire strolls away contented.

When he entered the market in 1994, lacquering the pages of ever-more lavish catalogues with photographs and fables from the great ages of the Stone of Heaven, Edmond Chin stole 76 per cent of a market dominated by Lisa Hubbard. A contrary gossip-monger, Christie's youthful Director of Jadeite effortlessly mingles Confucian values with Western hedonism and Eastern mysticism with the loot of empire. He sells 'exceptional jewellery', 'a superb necklace', 'an extraordinary cabochon'. He'll show you Qianlong sitting astride his horse and charm you with stories of how he found the Emperor's cinnabar treasure box in a Parisian attic. He'll show you the Dragon Lady posing in her photographic studio and tell how he tracked down the demon-quelling wand to a collector in London. Here's Madame Chiang dazzling the US Congress, and do you know, she still buys jadeite for her birthday? His Imperial catalogue is illustrated with Castiglione's portrait of the Emperor and quotes Lord Macartney: 'Thus I have seen Solomon in all his glory.' There is no mention of the charade to which Macartney was referring, the puppet shows he had watched as a child. But none of this matters, for when Edmond Chin realised 9 million US dollars for Doubly Fortunate he was crowned the new Jade King.[2]

A short totter through the arcades of Pacific Place, past Gucci, Cartier and Tiffany, beside posters of a silver fork twirling gold chains like spaghetti, and you're in the Conrad International Hotel ballroom. Every year, twice a year, the auction houses vie side-by-side and here in the Conrad, Sotheby's is fighting to reclaim the jadeite market. A swirl of wall paintings, blue and pink butterflies borrowed from William Morris, silver-spun hair falls onto linen wraps, bronzed men flex their toes in slip-on suede. Eunice, Angela, Cynthia and Renée parade wearing the lots, and Quek Chin Yeow, Edmond Chin's old school rival from Singapore, now also a jadeite director, dressed in a dinner jacket, a black diamond brooch on his shoulder, casts around for bids. But the room is half empty. Soon there is a flurry of shawls and a vapour trail of Poison that scatters shoppers as the *tai-tai* ladies, laden with catalogues, charge for the J. W. Marriott, where it's standing room only.

François Curiel, Christie's urbane vice chairman, strides up to the podium like the starter at the One Thousand Guineas and with a flourish of the gavel, his stewards corral their clients into position. A bank of telephones to the left is humming. A pen of press, to the back, is straining, trained on the electronic tote board that will flash up the bidding, ready to snap a photo-finish, bound by confidentiality agreements to protect the identities of Christie's clients. Curiel's gavel rises and a skitter of Jimmy Choos paw the shagpile, a line of glossy manes quiver for the off, worsted trousers and crêpe skirts, magnificent bottoms hovering above their important chairs in the style of Louis XIV.

Silver nails, pony-skin handbags, pink bouclé and bespoke wigs, a tissue of gold and a cape of pearls. And the sunglasses finally come off as the hammer goes down and the Stone of Heaven appears. 'And . . . let's start at 50, 50, 50. Who'll give me 50,000?' François Curiel is up but the running is slow. A dumper-faced man to the left picks up the pace. '60, 70, 80, 90,000. To me. To you. Me. You.'

Sammy Chow is here, taking the first furlongs in his stride. Frank and Charlotte Tieh are here, at a discreet distance, pacing themselves for the real running. In front are newlyweds from the Chinese mainland, shopping for honeymoon gifts for each other. Behind is the porcelain Michelle Ong Cheung, the salon set's jewellery designer of choice. Carol Huang, Pierre Chen's personal curator, sits beside Samuel Kung, now Hong Kong's premier dealer in jadeite rough.

'An important gentleman's cabochon. And who will begin?' The anonymous phone bank lights up. 'Edmondo-on-the-phones has 750, 750, 750,000. I have 900, 900, 900,000. The bid is against you, Deb-or-a-on-the-phones, and against you at the back, sir. And it's with me again at one million.' Two. Three. Four – the dollars are flying. 'Anyone for five, five, five? No one for five million? Yes,

I will take 4.5. From you, sir, in the sports jacket, not you, Madam, in the red skirt.' The gavel drops at 4,970,000 Hong Kong dollars (£397,600), and it's the man they call Mr Fuji who's crossed the line first, a Hong Kong Chinese businessman in the photographic film trade, who's here shopping with his daughter Betty.

The action slides for several minutes and a stampede of ostrich feathers rushes for the croissants stuffed with prawns. A woman wielding her catalogue like a mace swats us aside to grab the last free slurp of consommé. And then it's back to the bidding.

'A magnificent jadeite cabochon ring. Seventy-seven carats. And just to let you know, my book is full of bids. Edmondo-on-the-phones again straight in with 5 million Hong Kong dollars.' A gasp from the stalls. The running will be furious. 'Five, six, six, seven, eight, eight million. Not me, with you at the back, sir, in the sports jacket again.' Then Curiel points to the phones. 'The bid is all the way from New York, Geneva, to London, to Paris at 12 million dollars.' Edmondo-on-the-phones is talking furiously, wringing another 2 million from his unseen client. 'One more go, Edmondo-on-the-phones, at 14 million? Yes? No. Too late. It's now with you, Anthony, at 16 million Hong Kong dollars.' And behind Edmond Chin is the slick Anthony Lin, Christie's Hong Kong chairman, dancing with his mobile phone head-set in a silver-tongued ballet. 'Sixteen million Hong Kong dollars.' Excitement gallops around the room. No one can quite believe it, apart from Mr Fuji, who is talking calmly to Betty before his paddle shoots up. 'Seventeen million dollars,' cries Curiel. But Edmondo-on-the-phones is still in the field. 'It's with you for 18 million, Edmondo-on-the-phones.' The gavel hovers and heads swivel. Mr Fuji smiles broadly. A crackle of expectation. Faces flushed with the thrill of the chase. Mr Fuji is silent. Then his paddle goes up. 'Eighteen and a half million Hong Kong dollars.' A brief hush before the gavel falls on £1,480,000. Edmond has replaced the receiver on another bitter and disappointed client. Mr Fuji is swathed in adulation, a steward kneeling before him with a tray of free sandwiches. François Curiel is delighted. The sale has gone exceptionally well. Three world records have been set. But no time for an interview with Edmond Chin. We should call. Talk to his assistant. Not sure when. And as we run behind him like Pekinese puppies, scurrying into the crowded J. W. Marriott lobby, the after-show chatter is of buying back history, of jadeite's fables, of tales to tell absent friends. But there is no one who seems to have heard the story of Hpakant.

A fortnight later Edmond Chin calls. He wants to take us for a stroll down Kowloon's Canton Road and we should come right away. Dressed down in pedal pushers and a fleecy tank top, he steers us into an elevator that takes us to the top of Samuel Kung's empire and, passing through a bullet-proof air-lock, we are ushered into his office. While they talk in Cantonese about a forthcoming sale, we size up a 142.5 kilogram Burmese boulder sliced like a giant potato that Kung bought for 11 million Hong Kong dollars (£880,000). He opens a walk-in safe brimming with the Stone of Heaven, stashed in Tupperware boxes, the familiar swish of the carvers' water-benches in the background.

We are invited to lunch and, passing by private rooms that clink with *mah-jong*, we sit down to a feast of shark's-fin soup, a stew of fish-heads and pigeons dipped in salt and vinegar. 'You only get a boulder like mine once in a lifetime,' Samuel Kung beams like a proud, new father. 'And when a stone like this comes onto the market there is great secrecy and you have to be invited to make a bid. I was born to like jade. I used to sit for hours looking at rough, touching it, feeling it. Deciding how to cut it. But I would never run a mine. I wouldn't go any further than Mandalay. It's far too dangerous.' When he leaves the table Edmond Chin has a pressing question for us, and it's the first and only time that anyone mentions Hpakant.

'Did you see that dreadful piece about the mines, a few months ago? Was it you who wrote it?'

What to say?

'So it was riddled with drugs? It was all rather melodramatic, don't you think? You know, you caused a lot of problems. People told me not to talk to you, but I have nothing to conceal. Tell me, was it really that bad?'

It had been eighteen months since we had visited Hpakant and most of the people we interviewed there were certainly dead. If the epidemiologist's predictions were correct, the situation would have deteriorated drastically and the Burmese government had certainly failed to change. Prophetic love letters written by Aung San Suu Kyi in 1971 had come true. Her husband Michael Aris had succumbed to cancer in Oxford, having been refused a visa to see his wife one last time. A Western doctor who wrote a report highlighting the cycle of destruction in Hpakant, had been promptly deported by the junta. Even the insurgents' librarian, who had helped us to understand the hoodwinking of the KIA, had fallen victim to the war. He had defected to the SPDC, forced into betraying everyone around him, no doubt, by a regime that had held a gun to his family's head.

And yes, we said, it was really that bad, and we recalled an illusion spun by Christie's. 'For the superstitious the identity of the previous collectors is important, many not wishing to own a piece that brings poor fortune or illness,' a catalogue had concluded. 'This is especially the case with jadeite jewellery worn next to the skin and surrounded with mystique, believed by some to be able to absorb the essence of its previous owners.'[3] To us these words had conjured pictures of limbs jumbled like bamboo poles, desperate fingers fumbling over a blade of green. But Edmond Chin's clients read them, enraptured by the lives of the jadeite doyennes. Did anybody ever ask him about the mines of Hpakant? Edmond looked at us pitifully. There was too much ground to cover, too much money that separated our camps, and as Samuel Kung returned, the conversation snapped back to boulders and fate.

We flew to New York to interview the centenarian Madame Chiang Kai-shek, the greatest collector of them all, who still wears the Stone of Heaven next to her skin, Imperial pieces immersed in stories of romance and mystique, jewellery that has come back from the dead, that has survived the voyage from the old world to the new. But despite a half-spoken promise, we only got as far as the security guards that policed Gracie Square. Some friends talked anonymously about the 103-year-old matriarch who had survived war, Chiang Kai-shek and a double mastectomy and now rarely left her apartment. She spent her days in a netherworld, sleeping in a wheelchair, attended to by her white-gloved staff and her niece Rosamond Hwang, Ai-ling Kung's eldest daughter. Madame's forbidden city was filled with souvenirs from her days as China's *fu-jen,* including a Castiglione of a fair-skinned woman in a red dress that hangs on her larder wall.

Waiting for a phone call that never came, we went to the Metropolitan Museum of Art in search of Heber Bishop. His jadeite collection had been bequeathed with a rider that the Met display it in a replica of his Louis XV ballroom. But the salon, with its mirrored doors, crystal chandeliers, rococo gilt walls and Parisian showcases was gone, dismantled in 1937. While Bishop's giant two-volume limited edition catalogue, distributed to the crowned heads of Europe, had eulogised 900 pieces, there were now only a handful on display in a third-floor gallery. James Watt, the Brooke Russell Astor chairman of Asian Art, whose post is sponsored by Barbara Hutton's sprightly society friend and whose office is as cluttered as the Princess's old suite at the Paris Ritz, asked us why we were interested in the Bishop collection. 'It is nothing more than the detritus of the Qing Dynasty funnelled through the Western world by the English and French and then collected by the Americans,' Watt said between phone calls. 'Bishop had high hopes of buying back the Chinese Emperor's jades, and his idea was heroic, but the collection is unpresentable by anyone's standards.'

Bishop had thought he was buying the stones of the Emperors when all he was sold was stories, the illusion of the Summer Palace. Many of Heber Bishop's artefacts are more than likely copies, in the style and of the period but not the possessions of the Qing Emperors, Watt has concluded.

So the Met would be willing to return its worthless Qing art to China, including Count Kleezkowsky's jewels, the first Imperial jadeite pieces to be set in Western jewellery, that now resided unseen in a storeroom protected by a pony-tailed technician called Damien? 'No. Should we ask Qianlong and Pu Yi to give everything back that they stole and they sold? Ninety per cent of China's cultural heritage disappeared from Peking even before the Nationalists took the cream of what was left. If we had to start giving things back, then the Met, the British Museum and the V&A would all close down. Our educational function would cease.' He raced off to another meeting.

We left the Met through Astor Court, a scholar's garden in the style of the Ming, via the Robert H. Ellsworth Collection of Chinese scrolls (dedicated to the memory of La Ferne), out onto Fifth and across the road to what Manhattan society refers to as the 'Met Annexe'. A silver chalice was already brimming in Robert H. Ellsworth's hand.

'What do you think about the great collectors who grace the pages of the auction house catalogues?' we asked.

'There are no great collectors of jadeite, only bitches who wear it around their necks,' he replied.

'What do you mean?'

'Oh, you don't know the description of a bitch? Let me tell you what a bitch is. The last bitch that sleeps in your bed gets everything, including the jadeite jewellery. They all fit into that category. I knew Barbara Hutton very well. The guys who slept in her boudoir – they were bitches, and I knew most of them too. She was a nice lady, very ill-used by bitches of any gender.'

Ellsworth, gimlet-eyed, sipping his way to oblivion, alone in his vast palace despite the court of grinning acquaintances, was in his stride.

'What of the exotic fables that surround the Stone of Heaven?' we asked.

'I don't believe any of that fucking Chinese mythology. It comes from guys in the street who build stories. Nothing will lie like a Chinese bitch,' he snapped.

'How about the 6 million dollars that glitters on your finger?'

He told us: 'There's only one story here. When I die this ring will go back on the market with Lisa Hubbard. It'll be a single-lot sale in a leather-bound volume that says that if you learn anything in life, you learn what the best is. And I got it.'

'Is there a curse surrounding Imperial Green Jade?'

He growled: 'No. It's the curse of being lonely and wealthy.'

✄

Of course the phone call from the greatest collector of all never came, and instead we flew home in search of another legend, and in London we chanced upon a letter from the descendants of the ex-King Thibaw. In the 1950s seven relatives had once again petitioned the British government to return the 'jewelleries entrusted for safe custody to a responsible British colonel', Edward Sladen, the gentleman thief of Mandalay. 'It is only fair and just that those articles be restored or a reasonable compensation be paid to [us] as heirs to King Thibaw.' The memorialists had submitted their claim, having stumbled over a reference to the plunder of Mandalay in the *Ency-*

clopaedia Britannica, '11th edition, Volume 12, page 848'. In 1959, when two Burmese government researchers came to London and identified several items from the Mandalay Regalia in the vaults of the V&A, the museum finally agreed to return them.[4] But five years later, when a delegation flew in for a Foreign Office ceremony to receive a gem-encrusted dagger that had once belonged to King Bodawpaya's father, Thibaw's royal heirs were nowhere to be seen. Instead, on 11 November 1964 General Ne Win, chairman of Burma's revolutionary council, staged another *coup* and personally accepted the symbol of 'goodwill and friendship' from Patrick Gordon Walker, the Labour government Foreign Secretary. One month later, 13 more pieces were sent to Ne Win and a second shipment of 130 pieces arrived in the Great Golden Land the following July. So delighted was the regime that it presented the V&A with a gold-encrusted betel box fashioned into a sacred goose that had once sat before the Lion Throne, 'in recognition of the safe keeping in which the museum had held the Burmese royal regalia for 76 years'.[5] But the V&A held onto its collection of looted Burmese icons, King Mindon's parabaiks, Buddhist altars, *chinthe,* gilded offering vessels and Captain Frederick Marryat's Buddha, stolen by him during the First Anglo-Burmese War. In Rangoon, General Ne Win announced that due to a lack of museum facilities, the ex-King Thibaw's treasures would be locked in a former bank on Pansodan Street that was duly transformed into the National Museum. But where are they today? The National Museum now shows only a replica of the Lion Throne and from a meagre display of items described as the Mandalay Regalia, the vast majority of the Konbaung Dynasty's treasures are missing once again.

What of Thibaw's heirs? For thirteen hours we rumbled along India's Malabar Coast on the Bombay-to-Goa highway, overtaken by camper vans bloated with jubilant travellers heading for the beach. At Kolhapur we turned off towards Ratnagiri into a jam of Tata Sumos, the clumsy four-wheel drives that were ferrying the Indian middle classes to the town's annual mango festival. Sliding through syrupy air caramelised by Alphonso orchards, we asked for directions to Thibaw Palace Road and eventually arrived at a promontory that overlooked the Arabian Sea. Colonel Godfrey's retirement home was still clinging to the rock, its red bricks flaking, its white lattice windows peeling, doors hanging from their hinges, nothing stirring in the paralysing humidity that Thibaw had once complained of. Exam results were now pasted onto the walls and security guards reclining in deckchairs prevented us from entering. 'Mumbai University sub-centre. Not allowed for non-students,' a guard bellowed. So we walked to the back gate that was untended and strolled into the inner courtyard where a fountain spurted a withered tree and every room was abandoned. There was nothing of Thibaw left here, so we drove in search of his tomb.

Everyone pointed in a different direction and for two hours we circled Ratnagiri, weaving between flaming tamarinds and donkey carts, until a postman on a Honda Hero led us to a rubbish tip. And there, mouldering between sacks of discarded rice, was a patch-work bungalow. In front, a gnarled walnut of a woman, glued to a *charpoy,* watched the buses thunder past. Lalit, our genial driver, leapt from the cab into a pack of foaming dogs and shouted across the veranda: 'Burmese tomb, Burmese tomb'. A middle-aged man with sleepy eyes emerged from behind a curtain and spoke to Lalit in Marathi. 'Get out the car,' Lalit bellowed to us and we all made a dash for the bungalow. 'This man says his mother is the grand-daughter of the old Burmese king. She wants to meet you.'

Surely it was not possible that this wispy-haired woman, forgot-ten in her peppermint-green adobe shack, was a relic of the Kon-baung Dynasty. Chandrakhan, her eldest son, a retired bus driver, shouted into his mother's ear. 'Brama, Brama. Listen to me, mother. They have come to talk to you about Brama.' And she cocked her head, her face crinkling like brown tissue paper as she smiled, squeezing bird-claw fingers into a *wai*. 'Mandalay,' she whistled. 'Phayagyi. Thibaw.' Chandrakhan dashed into the lean-to and came back with pictures, a photograph of the ex-King corroded by a century of salt and a painting of the King's eldest daughter, the First Princess, dressed demurely in a silk robe, a peacock at her feet. The wizened old woman was, according to a sheaf of legal docu-ments, none other than the seed of a scandal that had eventually led to the repatriation of Queen Supayalat and her family to Rangoon in 1919. Chandrakhan estimated that his mother was 105 years old, and her legal papers confirmed that she was Tutu, the child born out of wedlock to Phayagyi and the deposed King's chauffeur.

'The world is going backwards,' Tutu whistled through her gums. 'We were once fierce people. But everything is going wrong.'

We shouted at each other for hours, unpicking her knot of history. In 1919 Tutu had been ejected from Colonel Godfrey's retirement home and recalled how the British had auctioned off her family's possessions in the courtyard. Tutu, who had married a local, was housed in a bungalow until 1930 when her husband died, and she was evicted again, given one acre of land on which to build this ramshackle home. 'I remember being driven around in the King's car by Gopal. We used to have servants. We were big people from Burma,' Tutu chuckled to herself. 'We used to eat fresh sea food and chicken soup cooked by the staff. I made paper flowers in the Burmese style and had small purses of pearls. We were happy, but I remember the danger signs, how my grandfather sat on the roof, raging at everyone, in fear of his life. Now our kingdom is finished.'

For 70 years Tutu had lived in her shack, but she had no valid tenancy agreement and was about to be made homeless for the third time in her life by the local magistrate, who had buckled to the demands of property developers. 'No jewellery left – it's all gone now,' she shrugged. 'I don't want the palace back, I want to die here.' Chandrakhan interrupted, stroking his mother's hair: 'Please save the soul of this old lady. Its shameful, a queen living in a hut.'

He took us on a tour of Thibaw's dispersed legacy, to the house of a local official who declined to give his name. Inside we sat on the ex-King's Cleopatra sofa, horse-hair spilling from its silk cover, beside a side-table, its legs carved into elephants, a deer-horn hat-stand in the corner, a Belgian mirror on the wall. 'It all came from the Godfrey house,' the official mumbled, pushing a plate of iced Alphonsos on us before suggesting that we see the district magistrate.

The corpulent Mr Nirmalka, dressed in home-spun cotton, his forehead daubed with rice, vermilion and ash, told us that he would only talk about the past and kept us on the doorstep. 'I remember Tutu's mother before she returned to Burma. I remember when I was a child she used to hand out gems like sweets. All the magistrates took things from the family. How the mighty have fallen,' Mr Nirmalka sighed, pressing a bag of mangoes into our hands and the door into our faces.

And finally we found the ex-King and his minor Queen behind the Kolhapur bus stop, obscured by a new housing estate. Through a broken gate, past burning pyramids of rubbish, lay two moss-covered stone tombs. Thibaw's epitaph in Burmese and English, that no one here could read, had been partially obscured by white-wash:

> In this tomb on the 19th March 1919 were deposited the mortal re-mains of Thibaw the last King of Upper Burma who was deposed on the 1st December 1885 and was moved to Ratnagiri where he died on 5th December 1916 at the age of 58.

Tutu had told us that somewhere inside the stone vault was all that remained of the treasure of Mandalay, jewels that had been buried with her grandfather. 'Also the remains of Teik Su-paya-gai, Thibaw's minor queen, who died at Ratnagiri on 25th June 1912 aged 50', read the epitaph on the adjoining tomb, whose *htee* had been knocked off by a stray football and whose wall had been bored into by a would-be robber. But it was said that the minor Queen's spirit house had always been empty; a souvenir-hunting magistrate had stolen the sandalwood box encased in silver that had contained her ashes, shortly before her funeral in 1919.

We returned to Beijing in search of the ashes of the Qing dynasty, and something unexpected was waiting for us. On a previous trip we had visited the People's Cemetery in the capital but had been un-able to find the remains of the last Emperor. But now our translator had a nugget of information that she had cut from a Chinese news-paper. It was an interview with Li Shuxian, a 75-year-old former nurse who had married the ex-Emperor in 1962, four years after he had been pardoned. Reflecting on her courtship with Citizen Pu Yi, she said: 'Everything happened quickly. We had six dates in six months and then we decided to marry. He was a man who desper-ately needed my love and was ready to give me as much love as he could. Once in a boiling rage at his clumsiness, I threatened to di-vorce him. He got down on his knees and, with tears in his eyes, begged me to forgive him. At last he is back where he belongs.'

Li revealed that in December 1994 she was approached by Zhang Shiyi, a Hong Kong businessman, who had a proposition. He had the political clout, he said, to have Pu Yi's ashes transferred from the People's Cemetery to the Imperial necropolis at Xi Ling and was willing to pay for the ceremony. There was one proviso.

The businessman intended to re-open the necropolis, housing the remains of 4 Qing Emperors, 9 Empresses, 57 concubines and 76 nobles, and auction off burial plots to wealthy expatriate Chinese who desired to be buried in the land of their forebears in Imperial style. 'He told me point-blank that Pu Yi's burial there would be of immense commercial value,' Li said. 'I liked his honesty and I accepted the offer.'

In April 1995, Li Shuxian's friends and relatives had joined her on a hillside 120 kilometres west of Beijing, for a private ceremony to re-inter her husband in a modest grave marked only by a marble tablet that stood 300 metres from Emperor Guangxu's mausoleum. A Son of Heaven was now no more than the shop sign for a Chinese entrepreneur, a Citizen had been resurrected as Imperial bait to lure back to the East that which had fled to the West.

Soon the state media was preoccupied by another auction that was attempting to cash in China's Imperial heritage. The People's Republic was 'affronted and shocked' to learn that Sotheby's and Christie's were planning to sell off in Hong Kong three bronze animal heads commissioned by Qianlong as part of Father Benoist's horological fountain. Now they were prize lots in sales that were brazenly dedicated to the loot of the Yüan-ming Yüan. Sotheby's bronze tiger head was placed on its catalogue cover. Christie's ox and monkey heads were presented in a gatefold display. The catalogue was introduced with an essay by Rosemary Scott, the former curator of London University's Percival David Foundation, that detailed the destruction wreaked by the Allies, her academic credentials lending gravitas to Christie's controversial sale.

Anthony Lin, the Hong Kong chairman, posed with the bronze heads for newspapers while Sotheby's issued a statement: 'We are extremely sensitive to cultural property issues.' Officials from the Chinese State Bureau of Cultural Relics attempted to prevent the sales but they went ahead in May 2000. That which had been taken by the West was auctioned back to the East, the Chinese government paying more than £2 million for the return of its heads.

⌗

What had become of the Qing patrons whose collections had started it all? China's National Highway 102, running east from

Beijing, traces the trail of Imperial yellow sand along which Cixi's catafalque once glided. We sped across broken tarmac, passing factories and dour watchmen who slurped warm Tsing Tao beer from greasy plastic bowls. 'Is this the way to the Qing Dong Ling?' our driver asked a man in a stained flat cap, its crimson star obscured by a smut of soot. 'Qing Dong Ling?' he tried again with the West Country burr of a Beijing accent. Both men splattered each other's shoes with phlegm and stood their distance. 'Qing Dong Ling?' he persevered, pulling up his satin pants. 'Ignorant workers. They never go further than the factory gates.'

Highway 102, running east, also ran back in time. The driver, who said his ancestors had been Manchu bannermen, was known to his friends as Mr Qing and he believed that his road led to the old country. But for now we were lost, he said, somewhere in the suburbs of the Great Leap Forward. So while we waited for direction he talked about history and how his family had worked for the court of Qianlong. He told us how his parents had buried jadeite beneath their *hutong* to conceal it, but he had forgotten the hiding place and his *hutong* had been demolished anyway.

Two more hours, and Highway 102 rolled through freshly tilled fields and into lanes of bicycles that pulled trailers of carrots, beetroot-faced riders balancing their friends on the crossbar. 'Qing Dong Ling. Qing Dong Ling,' they sang, like the chrome bells on their handlebars, mimicking the driver until he forced them off the road. 'Bloody farmers.' His fist pummelled the air. 'Never a care. A country run by lazy farmers and watchmen.'

One more hour on the road running east, and our driver's old China rose up from the Hebei plain where the Qing had built their city of the dead. Down the Avenue of Immortals we drove, scattering the honour guard of silent warriors with gravel, and on into apple orchards that flourished in compost of ash and excrement. Farms had sprung up around the tombs of the Emperors. Shops selling pot noodles, plastic booties and nylon trousers surrounded Qianlong's mausoleum. Young entrepreneurs guarded the Hall of Eminent Favour with bulging baskets of persimmons, pears and paintings of the Fragrant Consort, their trays lined with mottled green glass pendants that might have been peppers.

Chinese day-trippers clutching jam jars of strong jasmine rushed down into Qianlong's marble catacomb, their screams echoing like Sun Dianying's raiding party, leaving behind a trail of pips, pith and spit. Through the enormous stone doors, fractured by KMT explosives, and down into the domed vault, 54 metres below. Under a canopy of Manchurian, Chinese and Sanskrit prayers, sat four coffins: that of the Emperor, Fucha, and two consorts. Qianlong's faded crimson casket, its split wooden slats still dented by the blunt force that had wrenched them apart, drew the crowd forward. A teenager sucked his teeth, his head full of ghosts. A father whispered to his tearful son, wagging a finger at a plaque that explained why nothing was left inside Qianlong's casket. Then back they raced, up to the sunlight and onwards towards Cixi's mausoleum.

We entered the Long'en Hall, its columns of rosewood coiled with gilt dragons, intended as a grand tombstone for the Empress Dowager, and here was Cixi herself. Carved from wax, dressed as the Goddess of Mercy, she eternally bestowed favours on Li Lianying, her grovelling chief eunuch. Beside the tableau was a display case containing all that Sun Dianying's men had left behind: a yellow satin pillow cover, a blue bed-spread, two pairs of platform shoes, one bed-jacket with its pearl buttons missing, three seals and a gilt casket that contained Cixi's hair and nails. Beneath her Precious Citadel, the coach parties were racing down the steep cobbled slope, passing dripping walls that were pockmarked by bullets, and we joined them in the clammy burial chamber. But no one stayed in the musty half-light for long. In life the Dowager Empress had prepared for her death by packing her vault with jadeite, bronze and pearls, her casket inscribed with tens of thousands of demon-repelling prayers that sought to protect her on her journey to 'the place of the nine springs'. But now her lacquered coffin lay bound together with glue and screws, reassembled around her broken corpse. The light from Cixi's burial chamber was now scattered around the world and her glittering dream was nothing more than a spiteful and solitary cave that rang with a dank, black emptiness.

As the tourists charged for their coaches we called in at the Qing Dong Ling Works Department, looking for a necropolis historian who was said to have researched the lives of its residents in Beijing's Imperial archives. Would he be able to lay to rest one of the last myths we had yet to explore, that of the Fragrant Consort? Her story had been retold, embroidered, polished and buffed by so many of the great jadeite collectors that we were beginning to doubt whether Xiang Fei had existed at all. Old Mr Yu puffed on a Hongtashan and said that he had a few minutes to spare. He had inherited the research begun by colleagues twenty years earlier and their work had been meticulous. 'I'll tell the real story of Xiang Fei,' he said.

On 19 June 1758 Yi Boer Han, a 22-year-old Muslim girl, was taken from her village in the far north-west of China, a province recently conquered by Qianlong, and escorted to the Forbidden City by her brother, a fact that was noted in the Regional History of Sinkiang.[6] In February 1760 she was presented to the Emperor, who showered her with 'a Zhou Dynasty necklace, a necklace of gold and a trove of precious earrings, 15 gold coins, 200 white gold coins, silk, cotton and leather', details recorded in the Imperial Gift List for that month and year. On 2 April 1760, Yi Boer Han's brother was also bestowed with gifts. [7] He moved into a 22-room palace in Dongshi 6th Tiao, near the Forbidden City, and was paid for his sister with 500 taels of silver, an annual salary of 240 taels and a monthly bonus of 20 taels, taking his earnings to twice that of a palace administrator.

The Emperor then began to court the abducted girl whose beauty, her pale skin and sapphire eyes, her natural perfume that smelled like the jujube flower, were also noted in the Qing files. The Emperor's intentions are revealed in the court's Honey Melon List that records how in June 1760 Qianlong imported 200 lichee trees and presented them to Yi Boer Han, an opulent gift that was pregnant with suggestion in eighteenth-century China.

The extraordinary attention paid by a Son of Heaven to a captive from a distant war would continue. The Qing meticulously recorded every detail of palace life. Its Court Cooking File for January 1761, abandoned in Peking by Chiang Kai-shek, states that Nu Yi Ma Ge, a chef from Sinkiang, was employed by the palace to prepare Islamic delicacies for Yi Boer Han, using 'special vegetables including peppers, lots of onion and no garlic'.[8] Almost two years later, in December 1762, the country girl was bestowed with the rank of Bing. Now Yi Boer Han was known at court as Xiang Bing, the Fragrant Concubine, the only Muslim in the Emperor's harem, according to the Qing List of Nobles.[9] But the special attention would not stop there. On 4 June 1767 Xiang Bing began to wear Manchu robes instead of her traditional Sinkiang dress, a day that was celebrated with twenty Imperial gifts that included a jade court necklace and a cat's eye head-dress.[10]

In June 1769 Xiang Bing was promoted again, to the rank of Fei, and the girl who smelled of the jujube flower was now the Fragrant Consort.[11] Xiang Fei's name occurs at regular intervals in the Gift List, the Emperor inundating her with jewellery, jade and fruit. Perhaps he was still trying to win her hand or perhaps he had already done so and was rewarding her compliance. But entries in the Qing Royal Family Volumes, from 1785 onwards, refer to Xiang Fei as suffering from a 'strange, slow illness' and on several occasions the Royal Pharmacy is ordered to prepare medicines for the consort.[12] That Qianlong was distraught by her sickness is revealed in the Court Cooking File that records how, despite the demands of office, the attentive Emperor frequently dispatched special gifts to Xiang Fei, persimmons and honeydew melons. One entry, dated 14 April 1788, states that the Lord of 10,000 Years had ten tangerines carried to Xiang Fei's sick-bed, where his doctors Xiang Shau Ji and Zhang Chun administered to her. But five days later Xiang Fei was dead, and the Forbidden City drew up the *Xiang Fei Yi Wu Zhe*, a legacy list for the Fragrant Imperial Consort that reveals how her clothes and jewels, her nephrite and jadeite were divided between the tomb, the palace stores and her family.

Mr Yu silently led us into a walled garden of cypress trees in the shadow of the grand mausoleums of Cixi and Qianlong. Here, like a tented Manchu encampment, were 36 burial mounds that Sun Dianying's men had overlooked in 1928. Yu pulled up an iron grate and down some marble steps we slipped, into a spartan chamber where a single lacquered casket lay in the gloom. 'In October 1979 there was a flood and we opened this tomb. Inside there was much damage. We found a skeleton lying beside a coffin that was inscribed with gilt verses from the Koran,' Mr Yu whispered. 'Behind, in that corner, was a pile of decaying robes and a consort's head-dress decorated with cat's eyes. We also found a greying pigtail over there. The tomb in Kashgar is empty. Xiang Fei died when she was 55 years old and this is where she was buried.'

We emerged into the garden of cypress trees and thought of the Persian Pepper, celebrated over the centuries by Cixi, Elizabeth Wan Jung, Hui-lan Koo and countless others who had all vied to possess one of the most resonant pieces of jadeite in the world. What had become of the token of an Emperor's love?

Poring over the pages of Sotheby's back catalogues, a sale in November 1987 had caught our eye. Lot 337, cautiously marked only as 'the property of a lady', was described as a pendant 'reputed to have been acquired from the Dowager Empress Cixi'. It was a jadeite pepper, with a diamond clasp 'threaded through the tendrilled stem', that bore remarkable similarities to descriptions of Xiang Fei's pendant. It was one of Lisa Hubbard's earliest sales and we asked her what she recalled about the lot. 'It was Hui-lan Koo's pepper. After her death I was approached by a relative who asked me to sell it. Hui-lan had told her that it had been bought from Mr Tieh who had obtained it from the last Emperor of China,' Lisa Hubbard told us. Here at last, slightly forlorn in the catalogue's poorly photographed pages, was the Fragrant Consort's Persian Pepper, eulogised in Hui-lan's memoirs as the stone that broke Sir Victor Sassoon's heart. But the story had a twist that took us completely by surprise. 'You know Madame Koo's pepper didn't sell,' Lisa told us. 'The pendant had a rather obvious flaw. It wasn't the real pepper. Didn't you know?'

How could she be sure? The year before Hui-lan Koo's relatives put the flawed pepper up for sale, Lisa Hubbard had been contacted by a Hong Kong Chinese family that had asked her to value their jadeite, and among the necklaces and bangles was a perfect pepper pendant. 'It was truly magnificent, the greatest piece of jadeite I ever saw. Smaller than Hui-lan's pepper, two inches only, but you almost felt you could squeeze it and juice would gush out. It belonged to an elderly relative who had outbid a Maharajah in Shanghai in 1925. The old man didn't speak much English but he had a story for me. He said that he had bought the pepper from a scrupulous Chinese dealer and that Qianlong had given it to the Fragrant Consort as a keepsake. I tried to persuade him to sell it but he wouldn't be parted from the pendant. It was so perfect, the stone so brilliant that I made a drawing, as though I wouldn't see it again.'

Two years later, the family contacted Lisa Hubbard out of the blue. The old man had died and they wanted to place his pepper on the market as they thought it unfashionable. When news leaked out about the history of the pendant, dozens of collectors converged at the Sotheby's auction in Hong Kong's Mandarin Oriental. And in an old copy of the hotel's in-house magazine we found an account of the sale:

> A murmur along the crowded rows, swelling to a ripple as auctioneer Julian Thompson quietly took steadily rising bids. Then a crescendo of excited whispers, rustling catalogues and frantic telephone calls . . . and at last the gavel fell amid gasps of astonishment and delight.[13]

An anonymous bidder paid three times the reserve price, buying Xiang Fei's Persian Pepper for 1 million US dollars, but Lisa Hubbard would not reveal to whom she had sold it.

It was a slip of a collector's tongue in Taiwan that eventually led us to Johnny Hwang, a Taipei businessman and jadeite collector, who today wears the Fragrant Consort's memento close to his skin. Here at last was the stone that had been brought back from the Yunnanese border in 1785; that had hung heavily around the neck of the forlorn Xiang Fei until Qianlong had locked it away on her death; that had been hurriedly packed by lady Yehenara on her flight from Lord Elgin. It was found in the gloom of the Palace of Established Happiness by Henry Pu Yi, only to be concealed in Elizabeth Wan Jung's belt as a convoy drove the Imperial party into exile where they had cashed in their legacy.

No wonder Hui-lan Koo had felt compelled to slip into the odyssey of the Persian Pepper, to swaddle her pendant in the mystique of someone else's remarkable story. So she boarded the Shanghai Express with the fable and her phoney pendant, dashing with them both to Lord Willingdon's dinner table, where she gave her friends and competitor what they really wanted: an illusion rather than the stone.

⊠

We wanted to go back to the beginning, to the gateway of Qianlong's Jade Road, so we flew as far as we could into southern Yunnan, where we mimed our way into a taxi. Securing the services of a Mr Tang, who nodded vigorously as our arms whirled south-west, we hoped he would head for the Chinese border town of Ruili through which King Bodawpaya's jade-bearing envoys had once passed. But we stopped for doughnuts and condensed milk, we stopped for petrol and a newspaper and we stopped to pick up an unexpected passenger. Finally we were off, through countryside laden down by lush jungle, Mr Tang's girl singing Chinglish love songs as he flung his Nissan around the hair-pins. Dai tribeswomen flailed rice and made hay in the fields while Mr Tang's girl wriggled in her velveteen dress until it rode up over her white pop-socks, revealing a glimpse of creamy thigh. And by the time we careened into Ruili, four hours later, having passed through the territory once ruled by the Dragon Cloud warlord, she had a hand inside Mr Tang's trousers and he was singing along.

Grabbing our 180 RMB (£15), Mr Tang was gone and we plunged into the mysteriously affluent karaoke and neon. Streams of Chinese and Burmese, in Mercedes and Land Cruisers, purred through the border town, men in open silk shirts grazing among teenage girls with their cheongsams ripped to the knee. Flat-capped farmers on motorcycles taking their pot-bellied pigs for a ride, swerving to avoid swarms of Burmese boys buzzing the crowds with envelopes of green stones. And as dusk deepened into night Ruili became a bedraggled old tart, raucous street bars cheering along an old Chinese folk song, the 'Emancipated Serfs Sing', a town brimming with whisky and dubious cabochons of uncertain origin for knock-down prices. Down every side-street, dozens of barbershops, their whirling candy-twist signs strung with fairy lights, their salons blushing a deep shade of pink, their reclining chairs a knot of weary schoolgirls curled up like kittens, tempting passers-by with a blow dry. And as we passed the Happy Hair store someone shrieked and whistled. It was Mr Tang's girl, leaning out of the window, in thigh-length plastic boots, ever so grateful to see us again, chattering away in Mandarin, apparently thankful that we had helped her solicit 180 RMB. And away from the girls and jadeite markets, the steaming woks and slugs of spirits, the sound of an English tea dance led us to a marquee in a car park, guarded by a long, bald man with magnetic eyes of the true cat-green. 'Come in,' he said, fingering his Confucian beard, and it seemed rude to refuse. Inside, jadeite capos were doing the macarena with their molls, and it was time for us to find somewhere to sleep.

Dawn revealed a town heaving with another hang-over and us on our bicycles, wobbling to the outskirts, past a wall postered with the faces of the dead, twenty drug dealers executed that week. We followed trucks laden down with labour heading for the border, lush country slipping into slicks of mud, chrome buildings falling into disrepair, tidy streets sliding into a land of rubble, the smell of caramelised duck swamped by pungent decay. And there before us was an enormous pink gate: 'Welcome to the Golden Land'. Beside it was a hoarding painted with lost valleys brimming with gems, cartoon chunks of a bright green stone that appeared to have been hewn from the ground, and beneath, an arcade of jadeite carvers waiting for their morning supplies. Tense Chinese soldiers armed with automatic weapons guarded the entrance to Luo Xinghan's infamous drug highway. And facing them off, in their aviator shades, the all-too-familiar huddle of MI officers in longyis, mocking China's futile attempts to sieve the traffic that leaks across a delicate frontier.

For us this was the end of the road. The West was banned from going further south into the hills of the Golden Triangle. And as it began to rain we cycled away from the whine of water benches, following the border fence eastwards, passing vast, silent lorry parks and rusting containers, bulging flatbacks with concealed loads, into a grid of lock-up garages, row upon row of dirty cement boxes whose roller-doors sprung open to reveal desperate girls in pink nighties. They soaped their arms and legs in bowls of cold water, smeared *thanaka* across rice-paper cheeks, waiting for the jadeite truckers to roll into China with their pockets full of money. The storm-clouds tumbled in, but teenage boys listed around outdoor snooker tables, shooting balls across waterlogged baize, their limbs a jumble of bamboo poles. 'Smoke?' one of them shouted in English, shuffling over, his face blackened and hollow. 'Want to try?' And his hand shot out, offering an opened sachet of powder. 'Maybe later, alligator,' he grinned as his friends drifted over and asked for money. Had they been to Hpakant, we asked, and all of them nodded. 'Mandalay, Myitkina, Hpakant, Ruili,' they chanted as we cycled away, parallel with the border, past a rusty sign that in English entreated: 'Please do not go any further our foreign friends.'

And barely 50 yards on we spotted a prone figure, lying under the fence, his legs in Burma and his torso in China. He was probably shooting up, and so we rode on, not wanting to watch. But ten minutes later, when we passed again, the man under the fence was still lying there, and this time he cried out in Burmese. He seemed to be stuck in a burrow beneath the border and was covered with a sack, his head resting on a crumpled water bottle, his hands gesturing for food. He was barely more than a teenager, and we had seen those ragged fingernails and his pinched face before. So we guiltily handed him some money, hoping that would be the end of it, but he pushed the notes away and lifted up the sack. His legs had withered into useless sticks covered in running sores and the smell that rose from his infected burrow stung our nostrils. 'Food, water, please. Very sick, please.' He dug deep for some schoolboy English. 'Cannot move,' he said, trying to force his shaking hands into a *wai*. We cycled to a nearby stall, only minutes from where he lay, returning with boxes of curry and bottles of water. He wrapped his arms around the warm polystyrene and began to cry. 'Two weeks. No help,' he sobbed, lying back down on his crumpled water bottle. 'Two weeks. Only you. Very tired.' Pursing his lips, he whispered 'Goodnight.' And his pin-prick eyes flickered as the rain stroked his face.

Notes

One: An Emperor's Obsession

1 *A Jade Miscellany*, Una Pope-Hennessy, Cole & Cole, Westminster, 1946.
2 *Nouvelle Relation de la Chine Contenant la Description des Particularités le plus Considérables de ce Grand Empire*, Gabriel de Magaillans, 1688.
3 Ibid.
4 *The Travels of Marco Polo* quoted in *A Jade Miscellany*.
5 *Jade Lore*, John Goette, Kelly and Walsh, Shanghai, 1936.
6 *A Jade Miscellany*.
7 *Chinese Jade Books in the Chester Beatty Library*, Hodges Figgis & Co, Dublin, 1963.
8 Ibid.
9 Interview with Professor Yang Boda, curator at the Palace Museum, Beijing, November 1999.
10 *An Authentic Account of an Embassy from the King of Great Britain to the Emperor of China*, Sir George Staunton, G. Nicol, London, 1797.
11 Interview with Professor Yang Boda.
12 Ibid.
13 *Arts of Asia*, Yang Boda, Hong Kong, March–April 1992.
14 'Imperial Notations on Ch'ing Official Documents', Beatrice S. Bartlett, *National Palace Museum Bulletin*, Taipei, No. 1, Vol. 7, March–April 1972.
15 *Jade Lore*.
16 Ibid.
17 Ibid.
18 Ibid.
19 Ibid.
20 *Daily Life in the Forbidden City*, Wan Yi, Wang Shuqing and Lu Yanzhen, Harmondsworth, London, 1988.
21 *Castiglione: A Jesuit Painter at the Court of the Chinese Emperors*, Cecile and Michel Beurdeley, Lund Humphries, London, 1972.
22 Ibid. The scroll would later be obtained by Spink & Sons and sold in London to the Cleveland Museum of Art, Ohio, in 1968.
23 *Daily Life*.

24 Quoted in *Castiglione*.
25 *National Palace Museum Bulletin,* Taipei, No. 24, Vol. 4, Sept. 1989.
26 Jesuit Father Jean-Denis Attiret, quoted in *Castiglione*.
27 *Ch'ing Administration,* Ssu-yu Teng, Oxford University Press, Hong Kong, 1968.
28 *From Emperor to Citizen, The Auto-biography of Aisin-Gioro Pu Yi,* Foreign Language Press, Beijing, 1965.
29 Quoted in the catalogue for Christie's *Imperial Sale,* April 1997, Hong Kong, April 1997.
30 Ibid.
31 'Jade and Jade Carving in the Ch'ing', Howard Hansford, *Transactions of the Oriental Ceramic Society,* London, 1963–4.
32 *The Mineral Resources of Burma,* Harbens Chhibber, Macmillan, London, 1934.
33 Ibid.
34 A list of breakfast foods served to Qianlong is quoted in *Daily Life of the Forbidden City.*
35 *The Jade King,* Huo Da, Panda Books, Beijing, 1992.
36 *Orientations,* Jean-Paul Desroches, Hong Kong, November 1998.
37 The letter was written in 1742 and is quoted in *Castiglione*.
38 *Arts of Asia,* Yang Boda, Hong Kong, March 1992.
39 Li Lin-ts'an quoted in National Palace Museum Bulletin, Taipei, No. 5, Vol. 7, Nov.–Dec. 1992.
40 Christie's *Imperial Sale* catalogue, Hong Kong, 27 April 1997.
41 *Jade,* Roger Keverne, Lorenz Books, London, 1995.
42 *Jade Lore.*
43 *The Chinese in Upper Burma before* AD *1700,* Chen Yi-Sein, *Journal of Southeast Asian Researches,* Vol. 2, 1966.
44 *Momein Annals,* translated by William Warry, National Archives of India (NAI), New Delhi.
45 *Tung Hua Lu,* Jing Liang Ji, translated by E. H. Parker, NAI, New Delhi, 1890.
46 *Shêng Wu Chih,* translated by William Warry, NAI, New Delhi, 18 September 1890.
47 Ibid.
48 Ibid.
49 Scholar Chao I, secretary to the final Chinese campaign in Burma, in the *China First Historical Archive,* Beijing, 1769.
50 *History of Burma,* Arthur Phayre, London, 1883.
51 *Tung Hua Lu.*
52 *Shêng Wu Chih.*
53 *Tung Hua Lu.*
54 The poem is translated in Christie's *Imperial Sale* Catalogue, Hong Kong, 27 April 1997.

55 *The Search for Modern China*, Jonathan Spence, W. W. Norton, New York, 1990.
56 *Treasures of the Forbidden City*, Zhu Jiajin, Viking, London, 1983.
57 Quoted in Christie's Imperial Sale catalogue, Hong Kong, April 1997.
58 *The Dragon Empress*, Marina Warner, Vintage, London, 1993.
59 *Xiang Fei*, Yu Shan Pu, Qing Dong Ling Public Works Department, Beijing.

Two: Lord of the Mines

1 *The Burmese Empire 100 years Ago*, Vincente San Germano, Westminster, 1893.
2 Bodawpaya's letters, National Archives of India, New Delhi, 1975.
3 *The Burmese Empire 100 years Ago*.
4 *Tung Hua Lu*.
5 *An Account of an Embassy to the Kingdom of Ava 1795*, Michael Symes, G. Nicol, London, 1800.
6 Ibid.
7 Ibid.
8 Ibid.
9 *The Momein Annals*, translated by William Warry, NAI, New Delhi, 1980.
10 Burney's journals as Resident at Ava, NAI, New Delhi, 1831.
11 Letters from Bodawaya, NAI, New Delhi, 1975.
12 *Shêng Wu Chi*, translated by William Warry, NAI, New Delhi.
13 Ibid.
14 Ibid.
15 *The Chinese in Upper Burma Before AD 1700*, Chen Yi-sein, *The Journal of Southeast Asian Researches*, Vol. 2, 1966.
16 *The Travels of Marco Polo*.
17 *The Chinese in Upper Burma before AD 1700*.
18 Translated by C. A. Winchester, British Consul to Shanghai, NAI, New Delhi, 1867.
19 *Shêng Wu Chih*.
20 Expedition report, Captain S. F. Hannay, NAI, New Delhi, 1835–6.
21 *The Kachin*, Bertil Lintner, Teak House, Chiang Mai, 1997.
22 Ibid.
23 Speech by Col. E. B. Sladen, Royal Geographical Society archives, London, 1869.
24 Telegrams by Sladen to the Resident at Ava, NAI, New Delhi, 1868.
25 Ibid.

26 Ibid.
27 Expedition reports by William Griffith and George Bayfield, NAI, New Delhi, 1837.
28 'Bamboo', Jules Janssen, *Geographical Magazine*, London, June 2000.
29 *Tung-hwa-lu.*
30 Ibid.
31 *An Authentic Account of an Embassy to China*, Sir George Staunton, G. Nicol, London, 1797.
32 *Tung Hua Lu.*
33 Ibid.
34 *Travels and Researches in Western China*, Charles Baber, quoted in *An Australian in China, Being the Narrative of a Quiet Journey Across China to British Burma*, George Morrison, 1895.
35 Ibid.
36 *Jade*, Roger Keverne, Lorenz, New York, 1991.
37 *An Authentic Account.*
38 Ibid.
39 *Shêng Wu Chih.*
40 Ibid.
41 *An Authentic Account.*
42 Ibid.
43 Ibid.
44 *The Search for Modern China*, Jonathan Spence, W. W. Norton, New York, 1990.
45 *An Authentic Account.*
46 Ibid.
47 Ibid.
48 Ibid.
49 *The Story of the British Museum*, Marjorie Caygill, British Museum Press, 1981.
50 *An Authentic Account.*
51 Quoted in *The Search for Modern China.*

Three: A Jungly and Evil Place

1 *The History of Burma*, George Bayfield, National Archives of India, New Delhi, 1835.
2 Henry Burney's letters, NAI, New Delhi, 1831.
3 *The History of Burma.*
4 *The Itinerary of Ludovico di Varthema of Bologna*, translated by John Winter Jones in 1863, Asian Educational Services, New Delhi, 1997.

5 *The Mineral Resources of Burma,* Harbens Chhibber, Macmillan, London, 1934.
6 Ibid.
7 Ibid.
8 *The Kachin,* Bertil Lintner, Teak House, Chiang Mai, 1997.
9 Burney's diary, NAI, New Delhi, 1830.
10 Lord Amherst's letters, NAI, New Delhi, 1824.
11 Bayfield's journals from Ava, NAI, New Delhi, 1834–7.
12 Henry Burney's letters, NAI, New Delhi, 1834–7.
13 Ibid.
14 Letter from Lt. MacLeod to Burney, NAI, New Delhi, 24 Dec. 1833.
15 Letter from Burney to MacNaghton, NAI, New Delhi, 9 May 1836.
16 Letter from Hannay to Burney, NAI, New Delhi, 24 March 1836.
17 Letter from Burney to MacNaghton, NAI, New Delhi, April 1836.
18 Hannay's letter to Burney, NAI, New Delhi, 17 May 1836.
19 Hannay to Burney, NAI, New Delhi, May 1836.
20 Letter from Burney to MacNaghton, NAI, New Delhi, 18 May 1836.
21 Several previous expeditions by Griffith through Assam, Manipur and India were dedicated to the study of tea.
22 Bayfield's letters, NAI, New Delhi.
23 Ibid.
24 Instructions from Burney to Bayfield re mission from Ava to Assam, NAI, New Delhi, 8 Dec. 1836.
25 Suggested equipment for Capt. Grant's proposed expedition through Western Burma, NAI, New Delhi, 1831.
26 Captain Hannay's Kachin report, NAI, New Delhi, 1835.
27 Griffith's log, NAI, New Delhi, 1836–7.
28 Quoted in *A History of Burma,* Arthur Phayre.
29 Quoted in Christie's jadeite catalogue, Hong Kong, April 1996.
30 *Arabian Nights,* Richard Burton, Random House, New York, 1997.

Four: The Palace Plunderers

1 *China Under the Empress Dowager,* J. O. P. Bland and Edmund Backhouse, Heineman, London, 1911.
2 Ibid.
3 *Erotic Colour Prints of the Ming Period,* R. H. Van Gulik, Tokyo, 1951.
4 *China Under the Empress Dowager.*
5 *Two Years in the Forbidden City,* Yu Derling, Dodd Mead & Co., New York, 1924.
6 *Le Figaro,* Pierre Loti, 1900, quoted in *The Forbidden City, Heart of*

Imperial China, Gilles Beguin and Dominique Morel, Thames and Hudson.

7 *John Chinaman*, E. H. Parker, p. 63, 1901, quoted in *The Dragon Empress*, Marina Warner, Vintage, London, 1993.

8 *The Forbidden City*, Frank Dorn, Charles Scribner's Sons, New York, 1970.

9 Quoted in *Erotic Colour Prints* . . .

10 *The Dragon Empress*.

11 *The Forbidden City, Heart of Imperial China*.

12 *Xiang Fei*, Yu Shan Pu, Qing Dong Ling Public Works Department, Beijing.

13 *The Dragon Empress*.

14 *Venerable Ancestor, The Life and Times of Tzu Hsi, Empress of China*, Harry Hussey, Doubleday, 1949.

15 The Song of Solomon refers to 'little foxes which steal grapes', a symbol introduced to China on imported bronze mirrors from Persia.

16 *Venerable Ancestor*.

17 *The Last Days of Peking*, Pierre Loti, 1901, quoted in *The Search for Modern China*, Jonathan Spence, W. W. Norton, New York, 1990.

18 *Décadence Mandchoue*, Edmund Backhouse, British Library.

19 Anti-Manchu propagandist Wen Ching quoted in *The Dragon Lady*, Sterling Seagrave, Vintage, New York, 1993.

20 *Venerable Ancestor*.

21 *Two Years in the Forbidden City*.

22 Ibid.

23 This banner is still displayed in the Western Palaces today.

24 *Jade*, Roger Keverne, Lorenz, New York, 1991.

25 *China Under the Empress Dowager*.

26 *Annals and Memoirs of the Court of Peking*, E. Backhouse and J. O. P. Bland, Houghton Mifflin Co., New York, 1914.

27 All details about Chinese sexual guides come from *Erotic Colour Prints* . . .

28 *Inside Stories of the Forbidden City*, New Word Press, Beijing, 1986.

29 *Daily Life In the Forbidden City*.

30 *Imperial Medicaments*, Professor Chen Keji, Foreign Language Press, Beijing, 1996.

31 Ibid.

32 *With the Empress Dowager*, Katharine Carl, KPI, London, 1986.

33 *Two Years in the Forbidden City*.

34 *Oriental Commerce*, William Millburn, Black, Carry & Co., London, 1813.

35 *The Ever Victorious Army, A History of the Chinese Campaign under Lt-Col C. G. Gordon*, Andrew Wilson, William Blackwood & Sons, London, 1880.

36 *Histoire générale de la Chine*, Henri Cordier, Librarie Paul Geuthner, Paris, 1920.
37 *Illustrated London News (ILN)*, 13 October 1860.
38 Letter quoted in *Castiglione: A Jesuit Painter . . .*
39 The reference to Monsieur Bastard comes from *Earl of Elgin's Second Embassy to China 1760*, Henry Loch, John Murray, London, 1869.
40 *The Loot of the Imperial Summer Palace at Pekin*, Comte de Herrison, Paris, 1864.
41 *Incidents in the China War of 1860*, General Sir Hope Grant, Henry Knolly, London, 1875.
42 Rev. McGhee, quoted in *The Forbidden City, Heart of Imperial China*.
43 *Letters and Journals*, Eighth Earl of Elgin, Theodore Walround, 1873.
44 All details of thefts are recorded in *Investigations and Studies in Jade*, Heber Bishop, De Vine Press, New York, 1906.
45 *ILN*, 22 December 1860.
46 Ibid.
47 Ibid.
48 Ibid.
49 Ibid.
50 Ibid.
51 *Story of Chinese Gordon*, Alfred Egmont Hake, W. H. Allen, London, 1891.
52 Sold at Christie's *Imperial Sale*, Hong Kong, 27 April 1997.
53 Displayed in 1815 at Burlington House.
54 *China Herald*, reprinted in *ILN*, 22 December 1860.
55 Ibid.
56 *Investigations and Studies*.
57 *Story of Chinese Gordon*.
58 *ILN*, 22 December 1860.
59 *Story of Chinese Gordon*.
60 Rev. McGhee quoted in *The Forbidden City, Heart of Imperial China*.
61 *Personal Narrative of Occurrences During Lord Elgin's Second Embassy to China 1860*.
62 *The Forbidden City, Heart of Imperial China*.
63 This story is recounted in *Country Life Magazine*, 'A Famous Pekinese', London, 10 Sept. 1938.
64 Rev. McGhee, quoted in *The Forbidden City, Heart of Imperial China*.
65 *Personal Narrative of Occurrences*.
66 *ILN*, 15 December 1860.

67 *Flashman and the Dragon*, George MacDonald Fraser, HarperCollins, London, 1994.

68 Ibid.

69 *Story of Chinese Gordon.*

70 *Personal Narrative of Occurrences.*

71 Interview with Professor Yang Boda, Beijing, October 1999.

72 *Harper's New Monthly Magazine*, 1875, quoted in *A Grand Design*, Malcolm Baker and Brenda Richardson, V&A, London, 1999.

73 Ibid.

74 Ibid.

75 *Merchants and Masters*, Calvin Tomkins, Henry Holt, New York, 1970.

76 *Investigations and Studies.*

77 The quote, attributed to Henri Vever, appeared in Christie's jadeite catalogue, Hong Kong, November 1996.

78 *Investigations and Studies.*

79 'Notice et analyse sur le jade vert: réunion de cette matière minérale à la famille de wernerites', C. rendus *Academie Science,* Vol. lvi, A. Damour, 1863.

Five: 'The Far Off, the Strange . . .'

1 *The Silken East,* V. C. Scott O'Connor, Kiscadle, Strathclyde, 1993.

2 Ibid.

3 This story is told in an article entitled 'Maha Bandula the Younger', Noel Singer, *Arts of Asia,* Nov.–Dec. 1994.

4 Letters from Thibaw to Queen Victoria, NAI, New Delhi, 1887.

5 Details about life and intrigue at court come from the journals of Robert Shaw, British Resident at Mandalay, National Archives of India, New Delhi, July 1878–June 1879.

6 *Frazier Magazine,* Vol. XXV, NAI, New Delhi, Jan.–June 1882.

7 Telegram from Rawlins to Bernard, NAI, New Delhi, 23 March 1882.

8 *Calcutta Daily News,* NAI, New Delhi, 11 May 1882.

9 Photo caption written on a picture taken by W. W. Hooper, British Library, 1885.

10 Charles Bernard telegrams, NAI, New Delhi.

11 Lord Lytton, Governor General of India, 1876–80, described Afghanistan in 1878 as 'a pipkin to be crushed', NAI, New Delhi.

12 Picture caption on a photograph taken by W. W. Hooper, British Library, 1885.

13 Audit on Loot from Mandalay, NAI, New Delhi, June 1886.

14 Picture caption on photograph taken by W. W. Hooper, British Library, 1885.

15 Ibid.
16 The letter is dated Jan. 1893 and is in the NAI, New Delhi.
17 Telegram from the Viceroy, NAI, New Delhi, 19 February 1886.
18 'The Special Catalogue of Exhibits by the Government of India and Private Exhibitors', Colonial and Indian Exhibition, National Arts Library, London, 1886.
19 Ibid.
20 The throne is still at the V&A. Rudyard Kipling describes Zam Zammah in his novel *Kim*.
21 The Sladen Papers, British Library.
22 *Mandalay*, V. C. Scott O'Connor, White Lotus, Bangkok, 1996.
23 Ibid.
24 *A Short Account of an Expedition to the Jade Mines in Upper Burma*, Major C. H. Adamson, J. Bell & Co., Newcastle-upon-Tyne, 1889.
25 Telegram from William Warry, NAI, New Delhi, 9 June 1891.
26 *The Silken East.*

Six: An Imperial Side-Show

1 All medical details come from *Inside Stories of the Forbidden City*, Rong Shidi, New World Press, Beijing, 1986.
2 *Two Years in the Forbidden City*, Yu Derling, Dod Mead & Co., New York, 1924.
3 Ibid.
4 Robert Hart's journal, quoted in *Dragon Lady*, Sterling Seagrave, Vintage, New York, 1993.
5 These imperial edicts were translated and analysed by Professor Yang Boda, quoted in *Arts of Asia*, Hong Kong, March–April 1992.
6 Burma is described thus in *Geography of China*, Sü Ki-yü, NAI, New Delhi, eighteenth century.
7 *Mandalay Palace Records*, translated by William Warry, NAI, New Delhi, 1886.
8 Ibid.
9 Journal of Captain Crawford Cooke, NAI, New Delhi, March 1874.
10 U Tha Pu's journal, translated by William Warry, NAI, New Delhi, 1886.
11 Ibid.
12 Diary of Weng Tonghe, quoted in *Inside Stories of the Forbidden City*.
13 Ibid.
14 U Tha Pu's journal.
15 Letters to British resident at Bhamo, NAI, New Delhi, 1 March 1875.

16 A bangle made from this boulder, later worn by Barbara Hutton, was sold at Christie's jadeite auction, Hong Kong, 6 Nov. 1997.
17 *Two Years in the Forbidden City.*
18 Ibid.
19 *Annals and Memoirs*, Edmund Backhouse and J. O. P. Bland.
20 *Inside Stories of the Forbidden City.*
21 *Investigations and Studies in Jade*, Heber Bishop.
22 Ibid.
23 *Two Years in the Forbidden City.*
24 Ibid.
25 Ibid.
26 Interview with Professor Yang Boda, October 1999.
27 *China Under the Empress Dowager*, Backhouse and Bland.
28 Kang Yu Wei quoted in *Dragon Lady*, Sterling Seagrave.
29 Ibid.
30 William Warry letters to Rangoon, NAI, New Delhi.
31 *A Narrative of a Quiet Journey*, George Morrison.
32 *Hermit of Peking*, Hugh Trevor-Roper, Alfred Knopf, New York, 1977.
33 Picture is reproduced in *The Forbidden City, Heart of Imperial China*, Gilles Beguin and Dominique Morel, Thames and Hudson.
34 *Art Nouveau*, edited by Paul Greenhalgh, V&A, London, 2000.
35 *Two Years in the Forbidden City.*
36 *Empire Review*, April 1901.
37 *Two Years in the Forbidden City.*
38 *Empire Review*, April 1901.
39 *Letters from Peking*, Sarah Conger, A. C. McClurg & Co., Chicago, 1909.
40 *Palace Museum Magazine*, Collectors and Connoisseurs No. 5, Beijing, 1985.
41 London Missionary Society Archives.
42 *Illustrated London News* (ILN), 21 July 1900.
43 *Two Years in the Forbidden City.*
44 *The Siege at Peking*, Peter Fleming, Rupert Hart-Davis, 1960.
45 *The Guardian*, 27 Sept. 2000.
46 George Morrison's letters to Valentine Chirol, *The Times* archives, London, 13 Oct. 1900.
47 *Hermit of Peking.*
48 *Behind the Scenes in Peking*, Mary Hooker, John Murray, 1910.
49 George Morrison's letters to Valentine Chirol, *The Times* archives, London, 13 Oct. 1900.
50 *Behind the Scenes in Peking.*
51 George Morrison's letters to Valentine Chirol, *The Times* archives, London, 13 Oct. 1900.
52 Ibid.

53 *ILN*, 21 July 1900.
54 *Two Years in the Forbidden City.*
55 Rev. Arthur Smith quoted in *Foreigners Within the Gates*, Michael J. Moser and Yeone Wei-Chih Moser, OUP, Hong Kong, 1993.
56 *ILN*, 8 Sept. 1900.
57 *The International Relations of the Chinese Empire*, Vol. 3, H. B. Morse, Longmans, London, 1910–18.
58 Ibid.
59 *Hermit of Peking.*
60 *The Siege at Peking.*
61 *Jade*, J. P. Palmer, Paul Hamlyn, London, 1967.
62 'Some Important Jades', *Connoisseur*, Arnold Silcock, June 1952.
63 *Ways and Byways in Diplomacy*, William Oudendyk, 1939.
64 *ILN*, 1 Dec. 1900.
65 *Illustrated Catalogue of Chinese Art*, Burlington Fine Arts Club, London, 1915.
66 *Behind the Scenes.*
67 *A Grand Design, The Art of the V&A*, ed. Malcolm Baker and Brenda Richardson, V&A, London, 1999.
68 *'Some Personal Reminiscences from The Journal of the United Services Institution'*, Sir Claude MacDonald, London, August 1914.
69 Henry Savage Landor, the sole correspondent to witness the scene, quoted in *The Siege at Peking.*
70 *Jade*, J. P. Palmer, Paul Hamlyn, London, 1967.
71 *The Siege at Peking.*
72 George Morrison's diary, 28 Aug. 1900.
73 George Morrison's letters to Moberly Bell, *The Times* archives, London, 20 Oct. 1900.
74 *The Memoirs of Count Witte*, ed. A. Yarmolinsky, quoted in *The Siege at Peking.*
75 Quoted in *The Chan's Great Continent*, Jonathan D. Spence, W. W. Norton, New York, 1998.
76 From his personal papers, read by Anthony Du Boulay at the Oriental Ceramics Society, quoted in *Transactions of the OCS*, London, 14 May 1991.
77 Ibid.
78 Ibid.
79 *The Hermit of Peking.*
80 Ibid.
81 *Transactions of the OCS*, 1990–91, Vol. 55, paper read by Anthony Du Boulay.
82 Ibid.
83 *New York Times*, 3 Sept. 1901.
84 Ibid.

85 Paper by George E. Paulsen, Arizona State University, *Transactions of the OCS,* London.
86 *Gump's Treasure Trade,* Carol Green Wilson, Thomas Y. Crowell Co., New York, 1949.
87 *Time,* 6 August 1945.
88 Rev. Arthur Smith quoted in *Foreigners Within the Gates.*
89 Italian eyewitness quoted in *The Siege at Peking.*

Seven: Twilight in the Forbidden City

1 *China Under the Empress Dowager,* Edmund Backhouse and J. O. P. Bland.
2 Imperial record of the funeral ceremony, quoted in *Daily Life in the Forbidden City,* Wan Yi, Wang Shuqing and Lu Yanzhen, Harmondsworth, 1988.
3 *From Emperor to Citizen,* Aisin-Gioro Pu Yi, Foreign Language Press, Beijing, 1989.
4 *Imperial Medicaments,* ed. Prof. Chen Keji, FLP, Beijing, 1996.
5 *From Emperor to Citizen.*
6 Ibid.
7 Ibid.
8 Ibid.
9 *Twilight in the Forbidden City,* Reginald Johnston, Victor Gollancz, London, 1934.
10 *From Emperor to Citizen.*
11 George Morrison's correspondence, *The Times* archives, London.
12 Ibid.
13 *Xiang Fei, Yu Shan Pu,* Qing Dong Ling Public Works Dept, Beijing.
14 Letters to the Bombay government, Denys Bray, NAI, New Delhi.
15 *The Statesman,* 20 May 1919, Calcutta.
16 Rudyard Kipling, *Selected Poetry,* Penguin Poetry Library, London, 1992.
17 *Daily Telegraph,* 6 Feb. 1924.
18 *Twilight in the Forbidden City.*
19 *From Emperor to Citizen.*
20 *Twilight in the Forbidden City.*
21 *From Emperor to Citizen.*
22 Ibid.
23 *The Jade King,* Huo Da, Panda Books, Beijing, 1992.
24 Interview with Frank Tieh, son of Tieh Bao Ting, Taipei, November 1999.
25 Christie's jadeite catalogue, Hong Kong, April 1998.
26 Auction catalogue held at National Arts Library, London.

27 *Gump's Treasure Trade*, Carol Green Wilson, Thomas Y. Crowell, New York, 1949.
28 Ibid.
29 *The Mineral Resources of Upper Burma*, NAI, New Delhi, 1925.
30 Ibid.
31 *From Emperor to Citizen.*
32 Ibid.
33 *Twilight in the Forbidden City.*
34 *From Emperor to Citizen.*
35 *American Biographical Dictionary of The Chinese Republican Movement*, 1940, British Library.
36 *From Emperor to Citizen.*

Eight: Whore of the Orient

1 'Shanghai Express' screenplay quoted in *Shanghai, Electric and Lurid City*, Barbara Baker, OUP, Hong Kong, 1998.
2 Ibid.
3 *Journey to a War*, W. H. Auden and Christopher Isherwood, Faber & Faber, London, 1939.
4 *Shanghai, Electric and Lurid City.*
5 *Shanghai*, Harriet Sergeant, John Murray, London, 1991.
6 *All About Shanghai*, University Press, Shanghai, 1934–5.
7 *The Mystic Flowery Land: A Personal Narrative*, Charles Halcombe, 1888, quoted in *Shanghai, Electric and Lurid City.*
8 *All About Shanghai.*
9 Ibid.
10 Ibid.
11 *Shanghai, Electric and Lurid City.*
12 *The Voyage of the Lord Amherst*, Hugh Murray, 1836, quoted in *Shanghai, Electric and Lurid City.*
13 Ibid.
14 The Treaty of Nanking.
15 *The Sassoons*, Stanley Jackson, E. P. Dutton, New York, 1968.
16 *Shanghai, Electric and Lurid City.*
17 Nayland Smith to Dr Petrie in *The Insidious Dr. Fu Manchu*, Sax Rohmer.
18 Ibid.
19 *Hui Lan Koo*, Mary Van Rensselaer Thayer, Dial Press, New York, 1943.
20 Wesleyan College archive quoted in *The Soong Dynasty*, Sterling Seagrave, Harper and Row, New York, 1985.
21 *American Biographical Dictionary of the Chinese . . .*

22 *Cartier 1900–1939*, Judy Rudoe, British Museum Press, London, 1997.

23 Seagrave coins the name in *The Soong Sisters* and it is also referred to in the National Palace Museum, Taipei, index of republican biographies.

24 The young Chiang Kai-Shek's behaviour is recorded in *Chiang Kai-shek's Secret Past*, Ch'en Chieh-ju, ed. Lloyd E. Eastman, Westview Press, Boulder, 1993.

25 *The Chan's Great Continent.*

26 A description of this train can be found in *Collected Articles on the history of the Ming and Qing Dynasties,* China First National Archive, Beijing.

27 *Soong Sisters,* Emily Hahn, Doubleday, New York, 1943.

28 *Hui Lan Koo.*

29 *Jade Amulets,* Liberty catalogue, London, 1919.

30 *Connoisseur,* Vol. XXI, London, 1908.

31 *ILN,* 2 Dec. 1922.

32 *A Grand Design.*

33 Christie's jadeite catalogue, Hong Kong, April 1994.

34 *Hui Lan Koo.*

35 *Poor Little Rich Girl,* C. David Heymann, Random House, New York, 1983.

36 Ibid.

37 *House and Garden,* May 1918, US Edition.

38 The exhibition was in 1913 and is quoted in *Cartier 1900–1939.*

39 *China Economic Journal,* Vol. 6, June 1930.

40 *Chiang Kai-shek's Secret Past.*

41 Ibid.

42 'The Green Gang Nexus in the Shanghai General Labour Union', Seungjoo Yoon, *Papers on Chinese History,* Vol. 2, Harvard University Press, Spring 1993.

43 *Secret War in Shanghai,* Bernard Wasserstein, Profile Books, London, 1998.

44 *American Biographical Dictionary.*

45 *Sharks Fins and Millet,* Illona Ralf Sues, Little, Brown, Boston, 1944.

46 Ibid.

47 *The Search for Modern China,* Jonathan D. Spence, W. W. Norton, New York, 1990.

48 *Peking,* Juliet Bredon, Kelly and Walsh Ltd, Shanghai, 1922.

49 *Chiang Kai-shek's Secret Past.*

50 Ibid.

51 Ibid.

52 Associated Press, 19 Sept. 1927.

53 *China's Imperial Tombs and Mausoleums,* Luo Zhewen, FLP, Beijing, 1993.

54 *Poor Little Rich Girl.*
55 *Daily Express*, May 1931.
56 *Shanghai, Electric and Lurid City.*
57 Quoted in *The Sassoons* and referred to in *No Feast Lasts Forever*, Isabella Taves, New York Times Book Company, 1975.
58 Royal Opera House programme for Kirov ballet season, Clement Crisp, London, 2000.
59 *Chinese Carvings in Jade*, Spink & Son, London, 1930.
60 *China Economic Journal.*
61 Ibid.
62 *The Curious Lore of Precious Stones*, George Kunz, New York, 1915.
63 *Fortune*, March 1931.
64 *Apollo*, XVIII, 1933.
65 *Shanghai, Electric and Lurid City.*
66 *The Sassoons.*
67 *National Palace Museum Bulletin*, Vol. 1, No. 1, Taipei, 1966.
68 Ibid.
69 Quoted in *Poor Little Rich Girl.*
70 *No Feast Lasts Forever.*
71 *The Duchess of Windsor: the secret life*, Charles Higham, New York, 1988.
72 *All About Shanghai.*
73 'Bowl of Jade' quoted in *Jade Lore.*
74 The Viceroy was appointed in 1931.
75 Quoted in *Liberty or Death*, Patrick French, HarperCollins, London, 1997.
76 *No Feast Lasts Forever.*
77 Ibid.

Nine: As Dead as the Moon

1 *The Sassoons.*
2 *The Soong Sisters*, Emily Hahn.
3 *No Feast Lasts Forever.*
4 Ibid.
5 Ibid.
6 *The Soong Sisters.*
7 Ibid.
8 *Liberty*, Fulton Oursler, 7 August 1937.
9 Francis Richard Burch interviewed by Christopher Cook for the Hong Kong and Shanghai Banking Corporation, quoted in *Shanghai, Electric and Lurid City.*
10 Josef von Sternberg quoted in *Shanghai, Electric and Lurid City.*

11 *Shanghai,* Harriet Sergeant.
12 *Bombs on China,* Livingstone Press, quoted in *Shanghai,* Harriet Sergeant.
13 Ibid.
14 *China To Me,* Emily Hahn, Doubleday, New York, 1944.
15 *Poor Little Rich Girl.*
16 *No Feast Lasts Forever.*
17 Ibid.
18 Ibid.
19 *Secret War in Shanghai,* Bernard Wasserstein.
20 *Shanghai,* Harriet Sergeant.
21 *Journey to a War,* W. H. Auden and Christopher Isherwood, New York, 1939.
22 American diplomat John Paton Davies quoted in Sterling Seagrave's *The Soong Dynasty.*
23 *Lost Chance in China,* Jack Service, New York, 1975, quoted by Seagrave in *The Soong Dynasty.*
24 Ibid.
25 *Country Life,* London, 10 September 1938.
26 Hazel Dews is quoted in *Poor Little Rich Girl.*
27 *The Sassoons.*
28 Ibid.
29 *Journey to a War.*
30 *The Sassoons.*
31 Hugh Collar quoted in *Shanghai, Electric and Lurid City.*
32 *China to Me.*
33 *The Stilwell Papers,* General Joseph W. Stilwell, ed. Theodore H. White, Da Capo Press, New York, 1948.
34 *Lost Chance in China,* Jack Service.
35 *The Soong Dynasty,* Sterling Seagrave.
36 *A History of Burma,* Arthur Phayre.
37 *The Kachin, Lords of Burma's Northern Frontier,* Bertil Lintner.
38 *Inside the Green Berets,* Charles M. Simpson, Berkley Books, New York, 1983.
39 *The Kachin, Lords of Burma's Northern Frontier.*
40 *Amiable Assassins,* Ian Fellowes-Gordon, London, 1957.
41 *Intelligence and the War Against Japan,* Richard J. Aldrich, Cambridge University Press, Cambridge, 2000.
42 *Décadence Mandchoue,* British Library.
43 *Christian Science Monitor,* 16 September 1944.
44 *The Soong Dynasty.*
45 *Poor Little Rich Girl.*
46 Ibid.
47 *Plaque in the National Palace Museum,* Taipei.

48 *The Soong Dynasty.*
49 Interview with Sammy Chow, *The Peninsula,* Hong Kong, November 1999.
50 *Tracing it Home,* Lynn Pan, 1992, quoted in *Shanghai, Electric and Lurid City.*

Ten: The New Lord of the Mines

1 *Poor Little Rich Girl.*
2 *The Kachin, Lords of Burma's Northern Frontier.*
3 Frontier Area Committee of Inquiry, NAI, New Delhi, 24 April 1947, Part II.
4 Letters from Aung San Suu Kyi, *Mainichi Daily News,* Tokyo, 1994.
5 *The Sassoons,* Stanley Jackson, E. P. Dutton & Co., New York, 1968.
6 *The Kachin . . .*
7 Christie's jadeite catalogue, lot 1857, Hong Kong, November 1997.
8 *Chiang Kai-shek's Secret Past,* Ch'en Chieh-ju, ed. Lloyd Eastman, Westview Press Inc, 1993.
9 *No Feast Lasts Forever,* Hui-lan Koo with Isabella Taves, New York Times Book Company, 1975.
10 *Burma in Revolt,* Bertil Lintner, Silkworm Books, Bangkok, 1994.
11 Ibid.
12 *Poor Little Rich Girl.*
13 Ibid.
14 Ibid.
15 *Hermit of Peking,* Hugh Trevor-Roper, Alfred A. Knopf, New York, 1977.
16 Quoted in *Burma in Revolt.*
17 *Freedom From Fear,* Aung San Suu Kyi, Penguin, 1990.
18 Christie's jewellery catalogue, Geneva, 1988.
19 Christie's jadeite catalogue, Hong Kong, Spring 1994.
20 Christie's jadeite catalogue, Hong Kong, April 1996.
21 Christie's jadeite catalogue, Hong Kong, Nov. 1996.
22 Originally from *My Several Worlds,* Pearl Buck.

Eleven: Welcome to Jadeland

1 *South China Morning Post,* Oliver Poole, Hong Kong, November 1997.
2 *Far East Economic Review,* Hong Kong, 7 May 1998.

3 *Union of Myanmar Review of Financial, Economic and Social Conditions 1995–6,* Yangon.
4 Interview with the KIA, October 1999.
5 *Union of Myanmar Review of Financial, Economic and Social Conditions 1996–7,* Yangon.
6 *The Silken East,* V. C. Scott O'Connor, Kiscadale, Strathclyde, 1993.
7 King Bodawpaya's letter to the Viceroy of India, NAI, New Delhi.
8 *The Silken East.*

Twelve: The Valley of Death

1 *All About Shanghai,* University Press, Shanghai, 1934.
2 *International Narcotics Control Strategy Report,* Washington, March 1998.
3 Ibid.
4 Economic Intelligence Unit, *Country Report,* third quarter, London, 1998.
5 *Asiaweek,* Hong Kong, 23 Jan. 1998.
6 Interview with US Drug Enforcement Administration.
7 Interview with David Tegenfeldt, World Concern, Bangkok, Sept. 1999.
8 'Night & Day', *Mail on Sunday,* London, July 1998.

Thirteen: Romancing the Stone

1 *Gemkey,* Bangkok, Nov.–Dec. 1999.
2 The quote is taken out of context in Christie's *Imperial Sale* catalogue, Hong Kong, April 1997.
3 Christie's jadeite catalogue, Hong Kong, Nov. 1996.
4 This story is recounted in *Arts of Asia,* Humphrey Jones, Hong Kong, May–June 1971.
5 'Burmese Art in the V&A Museum', John Lowry, *Arts of Asia,* Hong Kong, March–April 1975.
6 *Sinkiang Chi Lue,* quoted in *Xiang Fei,* Qing Dong Ling Public Works Department, Beijing.
7 Ibid.
8 *Qing Court Cooking File,* Qianlong 30th year and Food File, Qianlong 46th year, China First Historical Archive, Forbidden City, Beijing.
9 *Qing Qao Zhong,* Chapter 651, China First Historical Archive, Beijing. This document also refers to Xiang Bing as Rong Bing.

10 *Palace Gift List,* China, First Historical Archive, Beijing, 4 June 1767.

11 *Qing Nobles List,* Chapter 661, China First Historical Archive, Beijing.

12 *Qing Huan Shi Si Pu,* Vol. 4, China First Historical Archive, Beijing.

13 *Mandarin Oriental,* Vol. 5, no. 2, Hong Kong, 1989.

Bibliography

Aison-gioro, Pu Yi, *From Emperor to Citizen*, Foreign Language Press, Beijing, 1965

Aldrich, Richard J., *Intelligence and the War Against Japan*, Cambridge University Press, Cambridge, 2000

All About Shanghai, The University Press, Shanghai, 1934

Auden, W. H., and Isherwood, Christopher, *Journey to a War*, Faber and Faber, London, 1939

Aung San Suu Kyi, *Freedom from Fear*, Penguin, London, 1990

Aung San Suu Kyi, *Letters from Burma*, Penguin, London, 1997

Aung San Suu Kyi, *The Voice of Hope*, Penguin, London, 1997

Aung, Maung Htin, *Lord Randolph Churchill and the Dancing Peacock*, Manohar, New Delhi, 1990

Backhouse, Edmund, and Bland, J. O. P., *Annals and Memoirs of the Court of Peking*, Houghton Mifflin, New York, 1914

Backhouse, Edmund, *Décadence Mandchoue*, British Library

Baker, Barbara, *Shanghai, Electric and Lurid City*, OUP, Hong Kong, 1998

Baker, Malcolm, and Richardson, Brenda, *A Grand Design*, V&A, London, 1999

Beal, Samuel, *Travels of Fah-hian and Sung Yun*, Trubner, London, 1869

Beguin, Gilles, and Morel, Dominique, *The Forbidden City, Heart of Imperial China*, Thames and Hudson, London, 1997

Bernier, François, *Travels in the Moghul Empire 1656—1668*, Archibald Constable, London, 1891

Beurdeley, Cecile and Michel, *Castiglione: a Jesuit painter at the court of the Chinese emperors*, Lund Humphries, London, 1972

Bishop, Heber, *Investigations and Studies in Jade*, De Vine Press, New York, 1906

Bland, J. O. P., and Backhouse, Edmund, *China Under the Empress Dowager*, Heineman, London, 1911

Bredon, Juliet, *Peking*, Kelly and Walsh, Shanghai, 1922

Burton, Richard, *Arabian Nights*, Random House, New York, 1997

Carl, Katharine, *With the Empress Dowager*, KPI, London, 1986

Caygill, Marjorie, *The Story of the British Museum*, British Museum Press, London, 1981

Ch'en Chieh-ju, *Chiang Kai-shek's Secret Past*, ed., Lloyd E. Eastman, Westview Press, Boulder, 1991

Chhibber, Harbens, *The Mineral Resources of Burma*, Macmillan, London, 1934

Chinese Jade Books in the Chester Beatty Library, Hodges Figgis, Dublin, 1963

Collis, Maurice, *The Land of the Great Image*, Asian Education Service, New Delhi, 1995

Conger, Sarah, *Letters from Peking*, A. C. McClurg, Chicago, 1909

Cordier, Henri, *Histoire Générale de la Chine*, Librarie Paul Geuthner, Paris, 1920

De Herrison, Comte, *The Loot of the Imperial Summer Palace at Pekin*, Paris, 1864

De Magaillans, Gabriel, *Nouvelle Relation de la Chine Contenant la Description des Particularités le plus Considérables de ce Grand Empire*, 1688

Derling, Yu, *Two Years in the Forbidden City*, Dodd Mead, New York, 1924

Dorn, Frank, *The Forbidden City*, Charles Scribner, New York, 1970

Fellowes-Gordon, Ian, *Amiable Assassins*, London, 1957

Fielding-Hall, Harold, *Burmese Palace Tales*, Harper and Brothers, London, 1900

Fitch, Ralph, *England's Pioneer to India*, ed. J. Horton Ryley, Fisher Unwin, London, 1899

Fleming, Peter, *The Siege at Peking*, Rupert Hart-Davis, London, 1960

Fraser, George MacDonald, *Flashman and the Dragon*, HarperCollins, London, 1994

French, Patrick, *Liberty or Death*, HarperCollins, London, 1997

Goette, John, *Jade Lore*, Kelly and Walsh, Shanghai, 1936

Grant, General Sir Hope, *Incident in the China War of 1860*, Henry Knolly, London, 1875

Gray, Jack, *Rebellions and Revolutions*, OUP, New York, 1990

Green Wilson, Carol, *Gump's Treasure Trade*, Thomas Y. Crowell, New York, 1949

Greenhalgh, Paul, *Art Nouveau 1890–1914*, V&A Publications, London, 2000

Greenwood, Nicholas, *Shades of Gold and Green*, Asian Education Services, New Delhi, 1998

Guan Yuehua, Zhong Liangbi, *Behind the Veil of the Forbidden City*, Panda Books, Beijing, 1996

Haggard, H. Rider, *King Solomon's Mines*, Lancer Books, 1968

Hahn, Emily, *China to Me*, Doubleday, New York, 1944

Hahn, Emily, *The Soong Sisters*, Doubleday, New York, 1943

Hake, Alfred Egmont, *The Story of Chinese Gordon*, W. H. Allen, London, 1891

Heymann, David C., *Poor Little Rich Girl*, Random House, New York, 1983

Hooker, Mary, *Behind the Scenes in Peking*, John Murray, London, 1910

Huo Da, *The Jade King*, Panda Books, Beijing, 1992

Hussey, Harry, *Venerable Ancestor, the Life and Times of Tsu Hsi*, Doubleday, New York, 1949

Jackson, Stanley, *The Sassoons*, E. P. Dutton, New York, 1968

Johnston, Reginald, *Twilight in the Forbidden City*, Victor Gollancz, London, 1934

Keeton, Charles L., *King Thebaw and the Ecological Rape of Burma*, Manohar Book Service, New Delhi, 1974

Keji, Chen, *Imperial Medicaments*, Foreign Languages Press, Beijing, 1996

Keverne, Roger, *Jade*, Lorenz Books, New York, 1995

Kipling, Rudyard, *Selected Poetry*, Penguin, London, 1992

Kunz, George, *The Curious Lore of Precious Stones*, New York, 1915

Lattimore, Owen and Eleanor, *Silks, Spices and Empire*, Tandem, London, 1968

Lintner, Bertil, *Burma in Revolt*, Silkworm Books, Bangkok, 1994

Lintner, Bertil, *The Kachin, Lords of Burma's Northern Frontier*, Teak House, Chiangmai, 1997

Loch, Henry, *Personal Narrative of Occurrences During Lord Elgin's Second Embassy to China 1860*, John Murray, London, 1869

Luo Zhewen, *China's Imperial Tombs and Mausoleums*, Foreign Languages Press, Beijing, 1993

MacDonald, Sir Claude, *Some Personal Reminiscences from the Journal of the United Services Institution*, London, August 1914

Millburn, William, *Oriental Commerce*, Black, Carry and Co., London, 1813

Morrison, George, *An Australian in China*, London, 1895

Morse, H. B., *The International Relations of the Chinese Empire*, Vols. 1–3, Longmans, London, 1910–18

Moser, Michael J., and Yeone, Wei-chih, *Foreigners Within the Gates*, OUP, Hong Kong, 1993

Oudendyk, William, *Ways and Byways in Diplomacy*, London, 1939

Palmer, J. P., *Jade*, Paul Hamlyn, London, 1967

Phayre, Sir Arthur, *History of Burma*, London, 1883

Pope-Hennessy, Una, *A Jade Miscellany*, Cole & Cole, London, 1946

Ralf Sues, Illona, *Shark Fins and Millet*, Little, Brown, Boston, 1944

Renaudot, Eusebius, *Ancient Accounts of India and China*, Bible and Anchor, 1733

Rong, Shidi, *Inside Stories of the Forbidden City*, New World Press, Beijing, 1986

Rudoe, Judy, *Cartier 1900–1939*, British Museum Press, London, 1998

San Germano, Vincenzo, *The Burmese Empire a Hundred Years Ago*, Westminster, London, 1893

Scott O'Connor, V. C., *Mandalay and Other Cities of the Past in Burma*, White Lotus, Bangkok, 1996

Scott O'Connor, V. C., *The Silken East*, Kiscadale, Strathclyde, 1993

Seagrave, Sterling, *The Dragon Lady*, Vintage, New York, 1993

Seagrave, Sterling, *The Soong Dynasty*, Harper and Row, New York, 1985

Selection of Papers Regarding the Hill Tracts Between Assam and Burmah and on the Upper Brahmputra, Bengal Secretariat Press, Calcutta, 1873

Sergeant, Harriet, *Shanghai*, John Murray, London, 1991

Simpson, Charles M., *Inside the Green Berets*, Berkley Books, New York, 1983

Spence, Jonathan, *The Chan's Great Continent*, W. W. Norton, New York, 1998

Spence, Jonathan, *The Search for Modern China*, W. W. Norton, New York, 1990

Ssu-yu Teng, *Ch'ing Administration*, OUP, Hong Kong, 1968

Staunton, Sir George, *An Authentic Account of an Embassy from the King of Great Britain to the Emperor of China*, George Nichol, London, 1797

Stilwell, Joseph W., *The Stilwell Papers*, ed. Theodore H. White, Da Capo, New York, 1991

Sun Tzu, *Art of War*, trans. Ralph D. Sawyer, Westview, Boulder, 1994

Symes, Michael, *An Account of an Embassy to the Kingdom of Ava 1795*, George Nichol, London, 1800

Taves, Isabella, *No Feast Lasts Forever*, New York Times Book Co., New York, 1975

Tomkins, Calvin, *Merchants and Masters*, Henry Holt, New York, 1970

Trevor-Roper, Hugh, *Hermit of Peking*, Alfred Knopf, New York, 1977

Van Gulik, R. H., *Erotic Colour Prints of the Ming Period*, Tokyo, 1951

Van Rensselaer Thayer, Mary, *Hui-lan Koo*, Dial Press, New York, 1943

Varthema, Ludovico di, *The Itinerary of Ludovico di Varthema*, trans. John Winter Jones, Asian Education Service, New Delhi, 1997

Walround, Theodore, *Letters and Journals of the Eighth Earl of Elgin*, London, 1873

Wan Yi, Wang Shuqing and Lu Yanzhen, *Daily Life in the Forbidden City*, Harmondsworth, London, 1988

Warner, Marina, *The Dragon Empress*, Vintage, London, 1993

Wasserstein, Bernard, *Secret War in Shanghai*, Profile Books, London, 1998

Wilson, Andrew, *The Ever Victorious Army, a History of the Chinese Campaign under Lt Col C. G. Gordon*, William Blackwood, London, 1880

Younghusband, G. J., *Eighteen Hundreds Miles on a Burmese Tat,*
    W. H. Allen, London, 1888
Yu Shan Pu, *Xiang Fei,* Qing Dong Ling Public Works Dept, Beijing
Zhu Jiajin, *Treasures of the Forbidden City,* Viking, London, 1983
Gump, Richard, *Jade, Stone of Heaven,* Doubleday, New York, 1962
Tsao Hsueh-Chin, Kao Ngo, *A Dream of Red Mansions,* Foreign
    Languages Press, Beijing, 1994

Index